THE M
OF MAN

History is the lie commonly agreed upon

Voltaire

Also by J.P. Robinson

The Alien Enigma

THE MYTH OF MAN

Hidden History and the Ancient Origins of Humankind

JP ROBINSON

EARTHRISE BOOKS

Kingston upon Hull, England

Published by Earthrise Books 2018

A catalogue record for this book is available from the British Library

ISBN 978-1986555470

CONTENTS

PREFACE:
MYTH MATTERS

Perhaps the greatest myth being purveyed is that myths are just myths?

Michael Tsarion

ACCORDING TO A MODERN COMPREHENSION of the term, 'myth' is in no way associated with factual information, but the myths which we shall be investigating throughout this book were not written in modern times. Before delving any further into this book, let us first establish the meaning of the word 'myth' and its context in the past compared with our present understanding of the word.

Definition of *myth* in English:

1 A traditional story, especially one concerning the early history of a people or explaining a natural or social phenomenon, and typically involving supernatural beings or events.

2 A widely held but false belief or idea.

2.1 A misrepresentation of the truth.

2.2 A fictitious or imaginary person or thing.

2.3 An exaggerated or idealized conception of a person or thing.

As self-explanatory as the word appears, what may be considered myth today could well have been the true story of yesteryear; 'References to human experiences prior to the invention of writing around 5,000 years ago have been omitted in their entirety and myth has become a synonym for delusion. Suppose it is not a delusion?'[1]

Many myths from all over the world mention a time when mankind faced some form of cataclysmic event which destroyed everything in its path. Could there be any truth to such stories or will they continue to be considered pure myth by mainstream historians?

The tragic tale of the demise of Atlantis befits the descriptions above but what we are missing is the complexity of such a story and the question of why, if this legend is purely fictitious as is commonly believed, should it have been deemed important enough a story to have survived throughout millennia to reach modern ears.

The truth is that myth meant something different in ancient times; 'myth as it exists in a savage community, that is, in its living primitive form, is not merely a story but a reality lived. It is not of the nature of fiction, such as we read today in a novel, but it is a living reality, believed to have once happened in primeval times, and continuing ever since to influence the world and human destinies.'[2]

In the past, oral traditions were of paramount importance to disseminate knowledge and along with writing and imagery were the only viable means of preserving and sharing historic information over long periods of time. The ancient Greeks in their archaic phase of civilization (600-500 BC) used the word 'muthos' instead of myth which represented a true story, one that unveils the true origin of the world and humankind.

Our present understanding of the meaning of myth is slightly off the mark; 'People often confuse myths with fables, legends and folklore, which may have some mythical elements, but real myths appear to be less about entertainment and more about passing on important religious, spiritual, or natural information.'[3]

Despite the precession of the equinoxes officially having only being discovered in 134 BC by the Greek astronomer Hipparchus, Giorgio de Santillana and Hertha von Dechend's incredibly in-depth work

Hamlet's Mill, suggests that such knowledge may have been widely known much further back in antiquity. *Hamlet's Mill* reveals how all great myths the world over have a common origin in cosmology, and the authors suggest that myth was 'a preliterate form of science – the synapse through which culture, particularly the science of astronomy, was transmitted.'[4]

In this context, according to the authors, the gods and legends which were written into folklore and mythology were never meant as accurate personifications of historical characters but were actually designed as representations of real celestial activity, such as the equinoctial and solstitial movements which occur with such precision over lengthy spans of time. In this way knowledge could spread throughout the ages in the same way that information is shared via the internet in modern times.

"*Hamlet's Mill* shows that precession and astronomical sophistication is written into the mythologies of just about everybody. There's nobody that doesn't have it, no matter how, by our own standards, simple and primitive their society happens to be."[5]

The difference between the factual information we commonly share nowadays and the methods employed to disseminate information in ancient times, is that the data *then* was wrapped up in symbolism and metaphor. Myths were not born out of pure fact alone but rather they were an amalgamation; part fact, part fiction and part metaphor.

'Myths are not absolute truth, but can be described as relative truth to the culture that believes in the myth, in that the myth itself tells of the perception of that culture and of how it brings order to the chaos around it. Myths are the stories we've been told as a species that are embedded with truths, realities, and even historical events such as earthquakes, wars, and meteor strikes. But they are not pure news reporting.'[6]

These days any information expressed through metaphoric means would be immediately dismissed out of hand, as this is no longer a viable means to transmit knowledge. As Egyptologist R.A. Schwaller de Lubicz explained, 'The West inevitably judges antiquity in the light of its own faculties, or more exactly, in the light of what it conjectures to be the case according to the intellective faculties it has cultivated so well, to the point that these faculties seem to be the only ones possible.'[7]

Let us not forget an important discovery made in Hisarlik, Western Turkey in 1870, which brought the ancient city of Troy out of the pages of *The Iliad* and into reality. Until the German pioneer Heinrich Schliemann uncovered the site as an amateur archaeologist, through sheer curiosity and optimism more than anything, Troy had been relegated to the realms of mythology as nothing more than a fictitious citadel cited in Homer's epic poem.

Homer's recounting of the significant events which occurred during the final weeks of the Trojan War and the Greek siege of Troy were always considered to be allegorical, but the revelatory archaeological finds in Turkey have revealed that much of the Greek literature of that period may well have historically founded roots.

Modern scholars are now in agreement that certain aspects of the story told in *The Iliad* may be based in reality as the discovery of Troy certifies, likewise the ancient Babylonian city of Nineveh was also thought to be purely mythical until its rediscovery in the 19th century. Such discoveries bring into question many of the world's myths, and the possibility or even likelihood that such ancient tales may well harbour veracious content between the lines of creative expression, because 'although metaphor, symbol and motif are ever present in all myths, we still see glimpses of hard fact, hard knowledge, and hard science.'[8]

The problem remains however, in proving fact from fiction, and sifting through ancient mythology and writing to discern which stories represent allegory and metaphor, and which were penned to inform future generations of actual historic occurrences worthy of commemoration.

Before arriving at conclusions prematurely we should reassess the evidence at hand, consider the possibility that our ancestors knew infinitely more than we give them credit for, and at least try to understand why the pages of prehistory remain blank and attempt to begin rewriting those pages using the evidence which continues to present itself to us.

Where there are gaps in our current understanding of the world and in particular our hazy distant past before recorded history began; is it not worthwhile reconsidering what the ancients had to say if it aids us in our quest to plug those gaps? Maybe by re-evaluating the way we interpret the various myths around the world, we can gain a greater understanding of prehistory by separating the chaff from the wheat. Mythology can provide us with a framework by which we can glean a resemblance of human prehistory and come to some understanding of who we really are as a species.

INTRODUCTION

What we regard as knowledge today may someday be regarded as error.

Albert Einstein

THE WORLD IS FULL OF MYSTERIES. These unexplained enigmas only remain unsolved due to our current inability to explain their presence in a manner acceptable to present thinking. Many of these mysteries have been passed down to us through myth and legend, and more often than not their mythological status appears as a declaration of their fictitious content, denying us the need for further inquiry. This paradigm of thought, regardless of its' steadfastly appearance, will inevitably shift once again as new discoveries force us to re-evaluate our conceptual boundaries.

Paradigms are constantly changing. Earth is no longer flat, the Sun no longer revolves around *us*, and whales are *not* sea monsters but very intelligent, peaceful mammals.

Yes, we have undoubtedly progressed as a species. Our understanding of most facets of life is vastly and immeasurably improved, our science and technology, our medicine, our knowledge of human history and ancient civilizations, and our geological and astronomical understanding also. Yet still, we are not at the pinnacle of all there is to know, as much as we may consider ourselves to be. We cannot stand still and admire our intellectual prowess just yet.

History is wrong and much of the knowledge we have garnered over the past millennia is in desperate need of an update. Some of the information we are taught from childhood may be closer to myth than reality, whilst some of the stories we have inherited in the form of myths may be closer to the truth than we could ever have conceived.

We are a species suffering with amnesia. History is much older, stranger and more exciting than we could possibly have imagined. We know so very little about our true human history, and not the kind dictated to us by the victors and the royals within society, but the history of our genealogical and cultural development as a species. What do we really know about our human origins? How much do we truly understand about our ancient ancestors and their technological capabilities?

At the present time, we have become so accustomed to the requirement of hard evidence before accepting any information as factual. No doubt that this approach is extremely purposeful and can yield a great deal of knowledge in the process, but some things are not so easy to validate employing such procedures. And what if some of this vital evidence were being discarded, misinterpreted or even worse, deliberately concealed from the common man? Information is, and always has been, power.

Perhaps our current understanding of the world and human origins is outdated? Maybe giants once walked the Earth somewhere in our remote and distant past. And what if there remains to the present day, huge hairy hominids living in the most inaccessible regions of the world, validating the existence of Sasquatch and Yeti?

Maybe the ancient and advanced civilization of Atlantis or some similar kind of antediluvian society did actually exist in a time forgotten to mankind, and the flood myths which have permeated every society on Earth since time immemorial believed to have been responsible for the demise of such a civilization, could actually prove historically accurate.

The Myth of Man was written with these questions firmly in mind. Whilst addressing some of the more popular myths still in circulation today, the information and evidence presented in this book will highlight the many inconsistencies with current theories on human origins and development, and offer a new insight into our mysterious past.

Much of what we have learnt about our past thus far stems from archaeological discoveries which have unearthed previously unknown information, and when put into context by the historians, archaeologists, anthropologists and geologists, finds its way into the bigger puzzle and reveals a bit more of the historical picture. But what we have discovered is only a fraction of what remains below the ground or sea, which undoubtedly suggests that we are clutching at straws and guessing our way through history.

Recent discoveries which are only now coming to light have revealed that vast areas of both Egypt and Mexico are covered with previously undiscovered buildings, pyramids, temples and streets, which remain concealed beneath both sand and dense forestation respectively.

The Myth of Man raises many questions regarding mankind's hidden history and uncovers evidence which extends the realm of human existence way beyond what is considered possible via mainstream evolutionary thinking.

Instead of confirmation of the Darwinist school of thought where humans descended from apelike bipeds, hidden archaeological discoveries have actually revealed the presence of modern human types stretching back millions of years, revealing the extreme antiquity of the anatomically modern human. This evidence indicates that rather than descending from the earlier homo-types which we consider today to be our pre-human ancestors, these ancient humans actually lived contemporaneously with them during certain periods of the distant past.

Our true history may well mirror life's cyclical nature, with great ancient civilizations on more than one occasion reaching astounding heights of advancement both technologically and spiritually before being totally wiped out by some cataclysmic event and erased from both existence and human memory.

'Our notion of progress is an illusion. We are deceiving ourselves if we think we are immune to the forces of nature. Civilization, as the ancients have repeatedly told us, unfolds in cycles.'[9]

Author Brad Steiger also suggested that, 'What once seemed a neat, progressive, evolutionary line has become hopelessly convoluted and chaotic. Civilizations have flourished and have been devastated on this continent many times in an unknown past – perhaps before Egypt was more than a dream and long before Greece constructed her first city-state.'[10]

And the fact remains that there truly exists such a phenomenal amount of unexplained matter in anomalous artefacts and physical traces that with enough time, resources, and most importantly will, we are more than capable of retracing our steps and reconfiguring our extremely questionable present understanding of human history and the multifaceted subject areas which accompany the whole problematic thesis.

This book does not pertain to offer the reader a complete and resolved understanding of prehistory and mankind's rise to dominance through the thick mists of time. What the book does divulge however, is the presence of material which blatantly contradicts the current worldview of our mysterious past and the true origins of humankind as expressed so vehemently by the scientific establishment.

Granted, this author is by no means qualified in any scientific field, neither is he an expert in any of the related disciplines such as archaeology, palaeontology, history or geology, so it must be noted that due respect goes out to all the professionals in these fields of research for their years of dedicated and thorough investigation.

Nevertheless, and it is worthwhile highlighting this fact, that despite this author's lack of expertise in such areas it should not lessen the impact and relevance of the material which shall be brought to light in the chapters ahead for the evidence exists regardless of this author's credentials.

It is the researcher's duty to bring forth information which has hitherto remained concealed and inaccessible for common public consumption. For most people, if something isn't presented to the public via mainstream channels then it will most likely remain in obscurity, destined to gather dust on the fringes of acceptable thought, but 'facts do not cease to exist because they are ignored.'[11]

There will be many readers among you that will contest much of the information offered in this book, just as you should, and others who are more willing to absorb new possibilities and accept already that the history books are wrong or at the very least missing vast amounts of vital information.

Darwin's 'evolution of man' has been force-fed to school children since its conception and the whole notion of evolutionary progression has been explained as linear, an oversimplified version of reality which is not reinforced by hard evidence.

As Professor Charles H. Hapgood noted, 'The idea of the simple linear development of society from the culture of the Old Stone Age through the successive stages of the New Stone Age, Bronze and Iron Ages must be given up. . . We shall now assume that, some 20,000 or more years ago, while Palaeolithic peoples held out in Europe, more advanced cultures existed elsewhere on earth.'[12]

In this world, where the history books have been built on foundations of sand, is it too late to reassess all the data and accommodate new information so we can rewrite our past? With enough care and diligence we may find that some of the world's mysteries shall become a little less mysterious in the process.

Chapter One

THE DEATH OF

DARWINISM

Almost everything we have been taught to believe about the origins and evolution of our species rests on the shaky foundation of academic opinion.

Graham Hancock

ONE MYTH WHICH IS CONSIDERED TODAY by a vast majority of the world's population to be the result of honest, reliable scientific investigation, is the evolution of man. The reasons behind disputing Darwin's widely accepted theory and considering it mythical, as opposed to being well established fact as so many academics contend, will be revealed in due course.

The concept of evolutionary biology did not originate with Charles Darwin. Like most theories and scientific hypotheses, the idea of transmutation, where an entirely new species is born out of an older prototype, arose through hundreds of years of consideration and has its roots in antiquity.

Although the term 'evolution' was not in use in ancient times (even Darwin used the terms 'natural selection' and 'descent with modification'), the philosophers of ancient Greece began expanding on concepts comparable to modern evolutionary theory, the mathematician and astronomer Thales of Miletus, a pre-Socratic Greek philosopher, being one of the first to suggest that all living things originated from water.

Despite not discussing in detail the process of physical beings deriving from less physical matter in a gradual development, the rudimentary concepts were already existent that all creatures must have progressed from a lesser state.

The discovery of skeletal remains and stone tools over the last two centuries has led to our current understanding of a lineal, evolutionary process that was first initiated billions of years ago in a prebiotic soup at the beginning of time. As more evidence is unearthed, it is not only nature that evolves but also scientific paradigms and concepts.

The problem we have today however lies with a scientific establishment that appears to have inadvertently destroyed what it set out to achieve, an honest assessment of raw data and physical evidence which leads the researcher in whatever direction it must go. Instead, some form of 'knowledge filter' seems to have arisen at some point in our recent past, a form of bias that rejects any evidence which doesn't support the already heavily entrenched scientific orthodoxy. We will look more closely at examples of this filtration process in the following chapter.

Needless to say, that certain discoveries which challenge the current scientific paradigm are 'held back' from the public domain, and either through lack of funding or respectable recognition, receive virtually no exposure and remain destined to fall by the wayside alone with their anonymity.

It is also worth considering that private foundations such as the Carnegie Institution and the Rockefeller Foundation played a critical role in financing research in human evolution among other essential fields of interest.

One of the most extensive palaeoanthropological projects undertaken during the twentieth century were the excavations of Peking Man at Zhoukoudian in northeast China during the 1920s and 1930s. The Rockefeller Foundation's funding was pivotal for the success of the excavations which ultimately contributed to the modern perception of human origins. This perception which continues to dominate evolutionary thinking remains theoretical and is not reinforced by physical evidence despite the common consensus to the contrary.

'The origin of fully modern humans denoted by the subspecies name *Homo sapiens sapiens* remains one of the great puzzles of palaeoanthropology.'[13]

Founded in Washington D.C. in 1902, the Carnegie Institution funded the Mount Wilson observatory which led to the first systematic research regarding the idea of an expanding universe, and it was actively involved in both evolutionary thinking and the Big Bang universe that 'lie at the heart of the scientific cosmological vision that has replaced earlier religiously inspired cosmologies.'[14]

THE MARCH OF PROGRESS

As preteen English school children, the idea that man descended from the apes was firmly imprinted in our impressionable young minds. One reason for the longevity of such information was down to the imagery employed in text books to highlight the steady progression from ape to bipedal man. This oversimplified portrayal of a steady, lineal and progressive evolution continues to fulfil modern perceptions of the origins of man today.

The March of Progress (fig. 1) drawn by Rudolph Zallinger was a scientific illustration which presented 25 million years of human evolution depicting fifteen evolutionary forebears. This picture which first appeared in a *Time-Life* book called *Early Man* in 1965 shows the change from the apelike *Dryopithecus* and *Ramapithecus* right through to the more upright *Australopithecus* and *Homo erectus* until finally arriving at modern man.

The *Early Man* volume was authored by anthropologist F. Clark Howell who, to his credit following the meteoric rise in popularity of the image to iconic status remarked, 'the artist didn't intend to reduce the evolution of man to a linear sequence, but it was read that way by viewers. . . The graphic overwhelmed the text. It was so powerful and emotional.'[15]

Fig. 1 *The March of Progress* by Rudolph Zallinger, Time-Life, 1965.

Intentional or not, Zallinger's iconic image is as powerful today as it was the day it was first published and continues to encapsulate that simplified expression of human evolution which still resonates with so many people. The problem being however, that such a simplistic portrayal appears to have done more harm than good, by enforcing a convenient but illusory concept of such significance that is proving difficult to undo.

Now, in so many people's minds, it has become a well established fact that man descended from the apes. They came down from the trees and evolved over time into upright bipedal creatures until eventually becoming what we would consider to be the modern human being. As convenient a package as this ideal may be, it is not backed up by physical proof despite what some 'experts' may insist.

As it stands, there is a clear lack of evidence revealing any evolutionary mechanism which supports the claims that over a relatively short period of time Neanderthals evolved into modern man, let alone proof linking the primates to us.

In 1989, evolutionary biologist Stephen Jay Gould criticized Zallinger's graphic in his book *Wonderful Life*. Condemning the iconology of the image Gould wrote, 'The March of Progress is *the* canonical representation of evolution – the one picture immediately grasped and viscerally understood by all. The straightjacket of linear advance goes beyond iconography to the definition of evolution: the word itself becomes a synonym for progress. . . [but] life is a copiously branching bush, continually pruned by the grim reaper of extinction not a ladder of predictable progress.'[16]

Charles Darwin also advocated the idea of evolution as being more akin to the branches of a tree rather than the predictable progression which the ladder analogy infers. The Catholic scientist Jean-Baptiste Lamarck proposed such a theory in the early 19th century in which he suggested that organisms had a tendency to move 'up' a ladder of progress as they became more complex.

Contrary to Darwin's idea of animals adapting and evolving in order to maximize their physical attributes in accordance with the changing environment, Lamarck believed in the spontaneous generation of simple living organisms from non-related biological matter which he attributed to some material lifeforce.

This concept of spontaneous or anomalous generation means that new organisms are able to form without descending from any previous prototype. For example, maggots could simply manifest themselves into being out of dead rotting flesh, or likewise, fleas could arise from inanimate matter such as dust. This theory has effectively been disproven today, as it was based on the idea that life is continuously created as a result of chance rather than through natural selection as Darwin's research revealed.

Darwin's finches (fig. 2) are the best example of this notion of generational adaptation or transmutation into better and more suitable types of the same species, now referred to as microevolution.

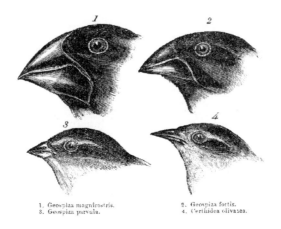

1. Geospiza magnirostris.   2. Geospiza fortis.
3. Geospiza parvula.   4. Certhidea olivasea.

Fig. 2 Modification in the beak design of finches.

This adaptive modification was a breakthrough which was generated by his animal studies on the Galapagos Islands, where Darwin visited four of the sixteen isles there which date back between 3 and 5 million years ago. It was here, 650 miles off the coast of Ecuador, that he studied many different species which all exhibited various physical adaptations that suited the specific environmental niches of the area.

The common finch that we see in our gardens had somehow flown out to the island chain from the South American mainland, and under closer observation Darwin soon noticed a wide range of modifications, the largest and most obvious being the changes in beak design. Different environments required different beaks, whether long, short, thick or thin; these birds were now suited to either seed, insect or fruit eating, the finches had become masters of their surroundings.

Microevolution, which accounts for small changes in species whether at a molecular or DNA level, is clearly visible through such mutations as witnessed with the change in finch beaks over a relatively short period of time, evolutionarily speaking. As each species proliferates, only the superior traits deemed necessary survive, whilst others diminish and are pushed out of the replication process.

The question now however, is can microevolution turn to macroevolution as Darwin and his fellow supporters contested? Going strictly by the available evidence, the answer must be no.

The fossil record has shown us nothing to suggest that species change over time into new species, despite the common consensus declaring such transformational transitions as fact.

As controversial as this argument may sound, looking around us at the world today we still see no signs of it. Maybe it is a case of misunderstanding here, we all know that birds today 'evolved' from dinosaurs, and we have strong enough fossilised proof that land animals originally crawled out from the seas, but does this prove the concept of macroevolution definitively?

Is it not also possible that each species, although anatomically related and similar in design, is not the product of macroevolution but was 'created' or born completely independently from what would be considered its predecessor? Is it not possible that fish remain fish and do not become amphibious; likewise amphibians do not become mammals?

It is one thing accepting that certain animals share a common ancestry like dogs and wolves or domestic cats and tigers, but let us not assume that one came from the other. Wolves may be related to their canine counterparts but this does not mean that they magically transformed into dogs over time. This is an old and consistently refuted argument often touted by Creationists to negate the evolutionary concept, but this is not the purpose of this particular discussion. There is no motive or bias at play here, it is just a thought aimed at provoking alternative thinking.

Recent research has actually revealed that there is no evidence which certifiably proves that dogs came from wolves, instead we find that genome analysis from wolves and dogs shows that dogs are more closely related to each other than they are to the wolves and vice versa.

And despite the physical variations visible in the many different breeds of the same animal, as seen in the canine world which ranges from the tiny Chihuahua to the Great Dane, all plants and animals remain essentially what they are at a molecular level.

As Darwin wrote in *On the Origin of Species*, 'all things have much in common, in their chemical composition, their germinal vesicles, their cellular structure, their laws of growth and reproduction.'

As is well understood today, the size and shape limitations of any given species are guided by the laws of genetics and inherited through the composition of the DNA. The probability of one species evolving out of another has proved to be another issue entirely, one which Darwin himself was careful not to insist upon, 'Analogy would lead me one step further, namely, to believe that all animals and plants have descended from one prototype. But analogy would be a deceitful guide.'[17]

Such an analogy, as Darwin suggested, could prove to be false; 'the fossil evidence clearly indicates that all basic forms of life simply *appear* on Earth, and after arriving and settling in they definitely do not evolve into higher, more complex forms the way Charles Darwin proposed.'[18]

Discussing the mysterious and apparently sudden appearance of new life, renowned biologist Richard Dawkins conceded, 'It is as though they were just planted here, without any evolutionary history.'

This notion of steady and progressive evolution of life also referred to as gradualism, has not been reinforced by physical evidence and continues to be a hot topic of debate.

The term 'Darwinism' actually originated when it was first mentioned in a somewhat derogatory fashion by English biologist Thomas Henry Huxley in 1860, when he wrote, 'What if the orbit of Darwinism should be a little too circular?'

Only one year following the publication of Darwin's *On the Origin of Species*, Huxley was already suggesting that the evolutionary processes advocated by Darwin's 'natural selection' theory could be too good to be true.

Darwin himself was also wary of the implications of premature and inaccurate origin theories and knew full well the difficulties involved in providing evidence to reinforce any hypotheses.

Writing to fellow evolutionist Alfred Russel Wallace regarding human origins he wrote, 'I think I shall avoid the whole subject, as it is so surrounded with prejudices, though I fully admit that it is the highest and most interesting problem for the naturalist.'

In 1859, twelve years after *On the Origin of Species* was published, Darwin became more confident in his ideas of human evolution and with the release of his latest work *The Descent of Man*, he expressed his delay in publishing these theories:

'During many years I collected notes on the origin or descent of man, without any intention of publishing on the subject, but rather with the determination not to publish, as I thought that I should thus only add to the prejudices against my views. It seemed to me insufficient to indicate, in the first edition of my 'Origin of Species', that by this work 'light would be thrown on the origin of man and his history;' and this implies that man must be included with other organic beings in any general conclusion respecting his manner of appearance on this earth.'

Even without the necessary proof required to validate such extravagant claims, such as fossilised remains of species which verify the existence of a transitional link between ancient apes and modern humans, Darwin was quick to establish such a connection, as he wrote in his follow up work *The Descent of Man*, claiming that 'We thus learn that man is descended from a hairy, tailed quadruped, probably arboreal in its habits, and an inhabitant of the Old World.'

Brave contentions indeed given that the only humanoid fossil remains discovered during that time were a couple of inaccurately dated Neanderthal skulls from Germany and Gibraltar and a few other insignificant finds of modern morphology. No wonder then that so many people were revolted at the suggestion of the highly evolved human sharing a common ancestry with the lowly ape, and calls of 'prove it' were soon reverberating around the halls wherever Darwin frequented.

Over time as Darwin's theories became more recognised and accepted, his influence on society began to be felt and a sea change took place. Religion had fresh opposition in the form of science, and the repercussions have been felt ever since.

As author Lloyd Pye explains, 'Darwin's theory of natural selection was an intellectual asteroid that in one brilliant stroke unseated the religious hierarchy that had ruled society until then. It gave science and scientists the upper hand, and they have clung to their newfound power as fanatically as the ecclesiastics ever did. In fact, Darwinism itself has become a kind of religion to them, to be taken on faith no matter how the evidence stacks up against it.'[19]

While Creationists insist on God creating the world and all of its inhabitants during a very small window of time as recently as six thousand years ago, Darwinists prefer to cling to the more 'logical' explanation which gradualism offers.

However, like most unexplained mysteries in this world, personal opinion and preference have no bearing on the facts and whether or not we understand our unusual back-story, a full explanation to human origins *does* exist despite remaining just beyond our grasp. Maybe the truth lies somewhere in the middle between Creationist and Darwinist schools of thought?

The sudden appearance of all lifeforms over the last four billion years raises many questions. How can life just begin with no precedent? Could there be intelligence behind the creation of life? Where did the seeds of life originate if time reveals that they did not simply come into being on our planet by pure chance?

PANSPERMIA

Today it is accepted by modern palaeoanthropologists almost without exception that Darwin's postulations have been realised thanks to more recent evolution-affirming discoveries of fossilised remains of our human ancestors in Asia and Africa among other places.

We shall examine the evidence against these popular misconceptions more closely in the following chapter, but for now let us go back in time to the beginning of Earth's history and try to understand how life seems to have just appeared out of the blue as the fossil record reveals.

In the beginning, Earth first became a protoplanet by coalescing from a primordial mixture of dust and gas which had the thickness of a heavy soup. Geologists have set the date of this inaugural occurrence at 4.5 billion years ago by dating remnants of Earth's original crust referred to as cratonal rocks.

Gradually, over the next 500 million years as the entire ball cooled, the crust thickened and over time rock was scattered throughout the thick soup like the chunks of meat and vegetables in a stew. At this point there was more liquid than rock, but as the cooling process continued, more rocks were formed which in turn began venting gases, being mostly steam at this point which after condensation became water, and at around 2.5 billion years ago enough rock had hardened and water formed, that what we consider land and sea had finally emerged.

Only now could the earliest precursors to life get a foothold, and ultimately kick-start the necessary actions required to begin the process of some form of material existence which would gradually evolve into the higher forms of life we recognise today.

Life first appeared suddenly around 4 billion years ago, arriving in two very complex forms which shared both genetic similarities and differences simultaneously.

The fact that they appeared with some recognisably similar genes meant that they must share a common and simpler ancestry or predecessor, but if these were reportedly the 'first' living organisms to appear on our planet then how could they have evolved from earlier organisms?

As there would not have been enough time for any simpler predecessor to have formed during the Earth's initial 500 million years, this would suggest that these earliest signs of life did not originate on this planet but must have 'arrived' here from somewhere in the vastness of space.

The theory of panspermia supports this idea by proposing that dormant microscopic life throughout the universe can become trapped in space debris such as comets or meteorites, inadvertently being hurled into planetary orbits such as our own where they can become active again upon meeting the ideal conditions for their renewal. Although such a hypothesis cannot answer *how* life actually begins, it does offer a solution to the problem of *where* life begins, by suggesting that this could well be the method of distributing life either via interstellar or interplanetary means.

French diplomat Benoit de Maillet wrote a book in 1715 called *Telliamed* (de Maillet backwards) in which he suggested that life originated in outer space before gradually developing into marine organisms in the oceans. Not only was he a pioneering advocate for panspermia but he was also ahead of his time with regards the theory of evolution as he was of the opinion that fish crawled onto the land, becoming reptilians, birds and animals over millions of years (an idea shared by Charles Darwin's grandfather Erasmus Darwin in his 1803 long poem *The Temple of Nature*).

De Maillet published his ideas on evolution eleven years after his death as he feared the repercussions and had no intention of jeopardising his standing as a government official. Despite his apparent anonymity in scientific circles, De Maillet should in truth be heralded as the creator of the theory of evolution and also an early proponent of the panspermia theory.

It was the bacteriologist Carl Woese in the late 1970's who discovered that there was actually more than one type of prokaryote (pro-carry-oat), the name given to the first single-cell bacteria which left traces of its existence in the oldest rocks on the planet. Much to his and his fellow scientists' amazement, there were two distinctly separate types of prokaryotic cells, the first being the more predominant ones which he named 'eubacteria' which are known today simply as bacteria, and the other group he called 'archaebacteria' (now referred to as archaea) due to the fact that they seem more primitive and therefore more ancient than their more adaptive counterparts.

As Lloyd Pye explains, 'Woese's discovery was the bacteriological equivalent of finding two distinct types of human beings, each with roughly half the same genetic sequences and half completely different.'[20]

What proved that these prokaryotes were clearly related weren't just the shared genetic sequences, but the absence of a cell nucleus which left their genes floating in a kind of limbo within their body membranes.

Nothing changed for another two billion years when the next form of life, a more sophisticated bacteria named eukaryotes, finally appears in the fossil record. Although also unicellular, the eukaryotes were the first organisms that enclosed their genes inside a nucleus surrounded by an inner membrane.

So could this evidence alone prove or condemn Darwinian schools of thought? In essence, the concept of life evolving from one basic life-form into another more advanced type looks on the surface, to match the notion of evolution or progressive growth as Darwin asserted over 150 years ago. The problem however, and this is one which continues to hinder any advocates of gradualism, is the sudden appearance of the eukaryotes, with no intermediaries linking them to their more basic cousins the prokaryotes. Of course we are talking about the one term which still proves problematic to any evolutionist today, and that is 'missing links'.

Whilst biologists have been unsuccessful in their search for evidence of at least one bacteria linking one form to another, when an archaebacteria called *Methanococcus jannaschii* (which is found in the harshest environments on Earth similar to those which must have been present when the planet was still in its infancy) had its entire genome of 1.7 million genetic letters completely sequenced, scientists found that over half (56%) of the genes were completely different from any known gene already sequenced in other known unicellular organisms.

This discovery only reinforces the panspermia hypothesis which states that because there was not enough time for these early life forms to evolve despite their common ancestry, it is indicative that such organisms must have evolved somewhere out in the universe before landing on our earthly shores.

The vast difference and increase in complexity between the humble prokaryote and the eukaryote is equivalent to comparing a rustic village to New York City.

Despite various theories suggesting alternate ways in which the prokaryote invaded the eukaryote sometime during the two billion year gap that separates them – which subsequently either began a symbiotic relationship with its new host leading to it evolving into a eukaryote itself, or the idea of smaller prokaryotes being eaten by larger ones which in turn led to the formation of a nucleus – no proof has come to light which can adequately explain how something can transform or jump from one form to another, especially a jump that is comparable to inanimate molecules becoming animated life.

And besides, any explanation offered, as plausible or implausible as they may sound, still does not explain how both prokaryotes and eukaryotes gained life to begin with.

Even today with all the high technology available in the science sectors, biochemists are unable to assemble even the internal components of the complex prokaryote yet alone the entire organism. This situation is problematic for gradualist thinkers because despite previous experiments which suggested that since the beginning of our planet's formation, Earth provided all the necessary elements required to create life, scientists still cannot replicate the first vital stages which led to the creation of life.

THE MILLER-UREY EXPERIMENT

At the University of Chicago in 1952, Harold Urey and one of his graduate students Stanley Miller carried out an experiment that would further the 'primordial soup' theory and generate great excitement among the Darwinists of that time.

Urey suggested that Miller make an experiment that would replicate what they believed could have been similar atmospheric conditions to those of prehistoric Earth, based on calculations that the early atmosphere's main constituents were methane, ammonia, hydrogen and water. The purpose of trying to imitate these ancient conditions was to attempt to synthesise organic compounds from this seemingly sterile environment, thus proving that life could arise from nothing under the right conditions.

By sealing the mixture of water, hydrogen, ammonia and methane in a sterile flask and heating it sufficiently enough to evaporate the water and produce water vapour, Miller passed a continuous spark discharge at 60,000 volts though the flask and its' contents in an attempt to simulate lightning and hopefully ignite a chemical reaction which could trigger life.

When the results were analysed after a week, they discovered the presence of tiny amounts of two amino acids, the essential ingredients of proteins, considered to be 'the building blocks of life'. With most of the ammonia and methane having been consumed, aside from an accumulation of dark material in the water which included a range of organic polymers, the remaining products were nitrogen and carbon monoxide. Alongside several fatty acids, hydroxy acids and amide products (used in nature to link amino acids to form proteins), analysis of the aqueous solution also revealed that 25 amino acids such as glycerine, alanine and aspartic acid had been synthesised during the experiment.

The scientists were lauded and the experiment was hailed a success and recognised as an important breakthrough in origin studies, mostly because it proved that several of the key molecules required in the process of creating life which were likely to have been present on the primitive Earth, would be able to synthesise into the necessary components under such conditions.

However, certain problematic issues have arisen since the 1950s which question the validity of the Miller-Urey experiment as the answer to how life started on our planet in the remotest past. Our current understanding of the early atmosphere has changed, and it is no longer the consensus view that it was highly reducing as was initially thought. Instead of a reducing atmosphere which prevents oxidation by removing oxygen and other similar oxidizing gases due to the presence of reducing gases such as carbon monoxide and hydrogen, the ancient atmosphere is believed to have had no oxygen available to actually be removed, instead the main constituent is considered by most atmospheric chemists to have been carbon dioxide.

Although no-one can be certain of such facts considering the age in question, if today's scientists are correct in their hypotheses then the entire range of molecules required to construct even one living organism would have been almost impossible to synthesise, thus putting the Miller-Urey experiment in its place, as a speculative attempt to imitate an atmosphere in which the precise ingredients remain completely unknown.

Despite the significant influence which the experiment has exerted over the development of life origin theories and prebiotic chemistry as a scientific discipline, we should remain grounded knowing that the most any experiment has ever produced before or since, is a handful of amino acids, life's most primitive 'building blocks' which were not even organic in their makeup.

Despite later experiments by other researchers producing all but one of the twenty biological amino acids, some fatty acids and nucleotides, another essential element of DNA and RNA, the sugars ribose and deoxyribose, have never been reproduced.

Besides missing the key ingredients necessary to create life, the ancient atmosphere on Earth would have succumbed to the extremely volatile nature of the newly formed planet with intense temperatures rapidly reducing any organic compounds back to their constituent elements. Such a scenario, which must be considered highly likely, puts into doubt the potential existence of any prebiotic soup to begin with.

Even if the prebiotic soup theory is correct, despite all of the arguments above, and time proves that this ancient liquid actually contained all of the necessary building blocks required to facilitate life, how could they possibly be assembled correctly so that they become an actual living prokaryote?

As Pye questioned, 'How were those disparate components brought together to create functioning units when, even today, with all the high technology available to our best biochemists, they cannot approach the first stages of actually creating life? Its simplest form – the multigened prokaryote bacteria – is so mind-bogglingly complex that none of its internal components can be assembled, much less the entire organism.'[21]

The astronomer Fred Hoyle, a proponent of the panspermia theory, recognised the implausible, bordering on impossible likelihood of any living organism (in the context of this debate, a prokaryotic ancestor, should one have ever existed) naturally emerging from a prebiotic soup. Hoyle analogised the probability of life appearing from out of this soup and adequately forming as equal to 'a tornado sweeping through a junkyard and assembling a Boeing 747 from the materials within.'

Hoyle was highlighting how something as complex as a modern aircraft, which he commented upon having the same level of complexity as a yeast cell regarding the number of parts (the Boeing 747-400 has six million parts), could never have formed by natural means alone hence Hoyle's idea that life originated outside of the Earth and not from the terrestrial prehistoric waters.

To this day Darwinists believe that the humble eukaryote must be the seed from which all subsequent life on Earth evolved, despite the fact that most bacteria and archaea have stayed virtually unchanged since they first burst onto the scene around four billion years ago. If they weren't still around today then Carl Woese would never have had the opportunity to analyse them and the eukaryotes as he did.

Much of Darwinist thinking is based on assumptions. As there is no fossil evidence of intermediate forms of eukaryote predecessor, there is no legitimate proof that such organisms are truly capable of evolving gradually into higher forms of life. Darwinists have to assume that all eukaryotes have nuclei in their cells and that all plants and animals also have nuclei in their cells, and despite the lack of physical proof of links between plants, animals and eukaryotes to reinforce these assumptions, they insist that such links must exist.

As Ghandi wrote, 'A seeker after truth cannot afford to indulge in generalization. Yes I have criticized even Darwin's generalization as being unwarranted. Science tells us that a proposition may hold good in nine hundred ninety-nine cases and yet fail in the thousandth case and thus be rendered untenable as a universal statement.'[22]

Here lies some of the fundamental flaws in Darwinist thinking, right at the foundation of a very complex theory of evolution which arose long before any evidence was unearthed to backup such concepts. Now it would appear that the search is on for something substantial enough to fill the gaps in a seemingly hole-riddled evolutionary theory.

THE CAMBRIAN EXPLOSION

Another severe problem facing gradualists is the occurrence of what has come to be known as 'the Cambrian explosion' which took place around 530 million years ago. In 1992, evolutionary biologist Jeffrey Levington described the period as 'evolutionary biology's deepest paradox,'[23] and if one delves further into the facts regarding this incredible geological epoch it is easy to see why.

Thanks to 3.5 billion years of microscopic creatures permeating the land, water and atmosphere of prehistoric Earth with oxygen, a literal explosion of animal forms in the oceans, seas and rivers appears throughout the fossil record. Evolutionary biologist Rudolf Raff wrote, 'All of the known animal plans seem to have appeared in the Cambrian radiation.'

In late August 1909, high upon a mountainside in the Canadian Rockies in British Columbia, an expedition led by long-standing Secretary of the Smithsonian Institute, Charles D. Walcott, accidentally unearthed one of the most important fossil finds of all time. Legend has it that here, in an area now referred to as the Burgess Shale, the horse which Walcott's wife Helena was riding, slipped on the shale and inadvertently overturned a slab of rock that revealed an extraordinary fossil imprint of an unknown creature we now know as the lace crab.

Returning the following year Walcott discovered a trove of new animal forms, the likes of which the world had never seen before. As a result of the Burgess Shale discoveries, a plethora of new species came to light which had only appeared for the first time during the Cambrian period. The assemblage of fossilised finds has accumulated into a vast collection numbering around 65,000 specimens which represent about

127 species. And even though today there are more sites around the world where evidence of other Cambrian fossils have been found, the Burgess Shale, by some fortuitous accident of geology, preserved these ancient organisms in their entirety allowing the soft parts, delicate tissue, antennae and eyes, to remain clearly visible.

Considering that the previous 3.47 billion years preceding the Cambrian brought only bacterial forms of life into our world, it is even more remarkable that all twenty-six animal phyla (a scientific way of grouping together related organisms of similar body design) which includes all types of invertebrate life, appeared in large numbers within 5–10 million years. It should be noted however, that the timeline offered here is a speculative guesstimate at best, and some biologists have suggested that it is also possible that it could have happened overnight. Whatever the timeline proves to have been, one thing we know for certain is that everything changed in a geological instant.

If we imagine the entire history of our planet being condensed into a single day, one 24-hour period, starting the clock at the moment the first single cell organisms appeared in the oceans four billion years ago. After six hours we would see no change, just the same single cell organisms we found in the beginning – twelve hours would reveal the same thing – eighteen hours, the same thing still. So after three quarters of the day have passed, all that we would have are the same single cell bacteria. Only after 21 hours of the day had gone, and in the space of about two minutes, would most of the major animal forms present today materialise. All that creativity occurred in the equivalent of two minutes out of an entire day. That's how comparatively quick the Cambrian explosion actually was.

In a sudden and explosive burst of creativity, Cambrian strata the world over reveals the presence of the basic blueprints for the majority of the animal kingdom which formed out of the blue. For the first time in Earth's long and convoluted history, biologically complex structures like skeletons, spinal cords, compound eyes and articulated limbs unexpectedly appeared.

The Cambrian era remains the greatest obstacle in the fossil record holding back Darwin's theory from reaching fruition, a situation that the man himself was fully aware of. As Darwin himself acknowledged, 'several of the main divisions of the animal kingdom suddenly appear in the lowest known fossiliferous rocks', a 'serious' problem which he commented 'at present must remain inexplicable; and may be truly urged as a valid argument against the views here entertained.'[24]

The sudden appearance of sponges, arthropods (trilobites, crustaceans and chelicerates) and molluscs among countless other species, contradicts the very notion that before these phyla were formed there must have been immense periods of time during which life must have thrived with a multitude of living things. Darwin's theory relied upon such evidence existing within the fossil records but unfortunately for him and his ardent followers this does not seem to be the case. Palaeontologist Stephen Jay Gould commented that 'nothing distressed Darwin more than the Cambrian explosion'.

Vertebrate palaeontologist Dr. Robert L. Carroll wrote, 'The extreme speed of anatomical change and adaptive radiation during this brief time requires explanations that go beyond those proposed for the evolution of species within the modern biota'.

And just like the prokaryotes and eukaryotes discussed earlier, the original twenty-six phyla which appeared during the Cambrian explosion remain the only phyla on the planet today, no improvements, no ancestors, just the same phyla that appeared over half a billion years ago. So much for 'descent with modification' as Darwin advocated so vociferously. Even after 140 years of intense and diligent searching by every renowned Darwinist there is, none have discovered any organism fit to be considered a legitimate precursor to even one creature that appeared during the Cambrian explosion.

The sheer lack of Cambrian predecessors continues to be a thorn in Darwinist sides and despite some flawed attempts to explain away such problematic concerns, it remains a seriously contentious issue invalidating the theory of evolutionary biology altogether.

Darwin wrote, 'If my theory be true it is indisputable that before the lowest Cambrian strata was deposited, long periods elapsed, and during these periods of time the world swarmed with living creatures. To the question of why we do not find fossiliferous deposits belonging to these assumed earlier periods prior to the Cambrian, I can give no satisfactory answer'.[25]

This 'inexplicable mystery' as Darwin referred to this particular geological epoch, continues to cause great controversy amongst evolutionary biologists everywhere.

Those who believe in the neo-Darwinian mechanism will insist that there are perfectly logical reasons which explain the absence of fossilised creatures in pre-Cambrian strata, mainly that the Cambrian predecessors were unable to be preserved and fossilise successfully due to their soft body structure which would simply erode before fossilisation could take hold. This theory simply doesn't wash. Soft bodied creatures including microscopic sponge-like embryos have been discovered in pre-Cambrian rock in China, and if *they* can survive the fossilisation process, then so can any soft-bodied creature.

Darwin's preferred Latin phrase 'natura non facit saltus' or 'nature takes no sudden leaps' would appear to prove inaccurate according to the scientific data available to both Darwin during his lifetime and to us now in ours. As Darwin declared quite vehemently, if evidence of saltation, or abrupt evolutionary changes were to be found in the fossil record and definitively proven, it could mean only one thing – that it would be evidence of special creation or intelligent design, thus putting to rest his lifelong work on the gradual natural evolution of all living beings.

INTELLIGENT DESIGN

The concept of intelligent design brings forth thoughts of Creationism and God, and although this idea of being created by a higher order may ultimately prove legitimate, that is not what we are discussing here.

The existence of the biologically diverse fossils discovered during the Cambrian explosion have caused such a stir within the broad scientific community with its varied disciplines, that many scholars are having to totally revise previous understandings of the origins of life on this planet.

There are those devout Darwinists out there who continue to seek the missing links required to validate the gradualist argument, despite the common consensus insisting that there is nothing to be found beneath the Cambrian strata, whilst other more proactive scientists are pushing the boundaries further than they have ever gone before.

Even Darwin's close associate and fellow evolutionist Alfred Russel Wallace believed in the idea of intelligent design, which seems unusual considering his scientific orientation. As Wallace wrote in 1870, 'A superior intelligence has guided the development of man in a definite direction, and for a special purpose, just as man guides the development of many animal and vegetable forms.'[26]

Continuing, Wallace suggested that 'if we are not the highest intelligence in the universe, some higher intelligence may have directed the process by which the human race was developed, by means of more subtle agencies than we are acquainted with.'

The 'anthropic principle', as named by astronomer Brandon Carter, states that in order for humans to exist as observers we have to find ourselves in a certain position within a universe with specific characteristics, meaning that our universe has been created in such a way as to allow life capable of observing the universe it was born into.

As physicist John Wheeler wrote, 'It is not that man is adapted to the universe. The universe is adapted to him. Imagine a universe in which one or another of the fundamental constants of physics is altered by a few percent one way or the other. Man could never come into being in such a universe. . .'[27]

Musing on the creation of stars, English astronomer Fred Hoyle came to the conclusion that intelligent design must come into play, when one considers the perfect complexity of the finely tuned resonances that enabled the production of heavy elements in the stellar interior such as hydrogen, helium and carbon.

Hoyle said, 'I do not believe that any scientist who examines the evidence would fail to draw the inference that the laws of physics have been deliberately designed with regard to the consequences they produce inside stars.'[28]

But today 'intelligent design' is no longer just a term used to suggest that all life must have been guided in accordance with some sort of plan or blueprint by unknown hands; it also refers to a scientific research program and community of like-minded scientists, philosophers and scholars on the forefront of modern thinking, all of whom seek evidence of design in nature.

This recent theory maintains that certain aspects within all living things, including specific features of the universe also, cannot be explained employing the natural selection hypothesis which states that life exists as a result of natural processes, undirected and random. Thorough scientific analysis of a system's components is undertaken by design theorists to determine the way in which natural structures are produced – by chance, natural law, intelligent design or possibly a combination of these methods.

By reviewing modern kinds of information which we know come as a result of intelligent planning, for example, by understanding how computers require the whole preconception of its designers in order to be manufactured for the given purpose, we recognise how certain products only exist as the result of a set blueprint with the required specifications purposely met prior to construction.

'Intelligent design has applied these scientific methods to detect design in irreducibly complex biological structures, the complex and specified information content in DNA, the life-sustaining physical architecture of the universe, and the geologically rapid origin of biological diversity in the fossil record during the Cambrian explosion approximately 530 million years ago.'[29]

The central mystery of the Cambrian explosion is the inexplicable leap in complexity from single pre-Cambrian organisms with four or five cell types, into trilobites with at least ten times the amount of different cell types. In order to make such a vast leap in complexity, an enormous amount of new genetic information is needed, and the question of where that information comes from is vital to understanding life's origins. Evolutionary biologist Richard Dawkins stated that 'without gradualness . . . we are back to a miracle'.

Without the discovery of Cambrian predecessors the whole gradualist theory disintegrates whilst reinforcing the idea of the involvement of some kind of intelligence. Stephen C. Meyer, author of *Signature in the Cell* and *Darwin's Doubt* and proponent of the intelligent design (ID) theory explained how such a notion could solve one of life's biggest mysteries:

'The absence of those forms [pre-Cambrian links] is profoundly mysterious, but from the standpoint of intelligent design it's not mysterious at all because we know that intelligent agents can bring things into existence that didn't exist before because they had an idea. They had a blueprint in their minds that they realised in their creative activity.'

Continuing Meyer said, 'There's no need to tinker through millions of years of evolutionary history if you can actualise a plan at a discreet moment in time and that's what appears to have occurred in the Cambrian explosion.'[30]

Meyer contends that researching the available evidence reveals that the origin of complex life was not undirected but was planned, designed and intended. Despite his work clearly contradicting the present theory of evolution, Meyer concedes that Darwin essentially pioneered a kind of forensic science which utilises found clues to reconstruct events that took place in our ancient past. By employing methods of reasoning, science attempts to explain past and distant events by invoking causes in operation today that are known to produce the effects in question.

The phrase 'survival of the fittest' was originally coined by English biologist and philosopher Herbert Spencer in the 1864 publication *Principles of Biology* after having read Darwin's *On the Origins of Species*. But as Meyer asserts, natural selection explains the survival but not the arrival of the fittest.

'An experience-based analysis of the causal powers of various explanatory hypotheses suggest purposive or intelligent design as a causally adaptive – and perhaps the most causally adaptive – explanation for the origin of the complex specified information required to build the Cambrian animals and the novel forms they represent', wrote Meyer in *Darwin's Doubt*.

In the 1950s the complexity of the structure of proteins was discovered which highlighted the specificity of the protein's form. The importance of proteins cannot be overstated as they are the molecules responsible for all the important jobs inside each individual cell. Proteins catalyse reactions, build structural parts and process information attached to DNA; basically proteins are the key molecules which perform all the jobs that keep living systems alive.

Each protein has a highly intricate shape which is critical to their function, for example, the active site of an enzyme is shaped in such a specific way that it only enables certain substrate molecules to fit onto it in a snug hand-in-glove kind of perfect fit. Only once the substrates, such as sugars like fructose and glucose, have nestled perfectly into position in the enzyme can the enzyme function properly and break down the sugars as it is required to do.

Proteins all consist of twenty smaller amino acids which must line up in a specific sequence before becoming a functioning active protein. This sequence or arrangement is critical, as an incorrect alignment leads to a non-functioning purposeless protein. This is known as sequence specificity, and it is mirrored also in the DNA molecule as Watson and Crick discovered in 1953, one year after the importance of the protein sequence was fully recognised.

Sequence specificity can also be seen as the key component of written languages and computer code alike. In fact, in 1957 Francis Crick came up with possibly the most important insight in the history of biology – the sequence hypothesis. Crick proposed that the four chemicals known as bases which attach themselves along the spine of the DNA molecule actually function like alphabetic characters in a written language or the zeros and ones used in machine coding.

The chemistry of the constituents does not determine their function however, it is the precise arrangement of those characters that is critical. Much like Scrabble letters, it isn't important what they are made of, it could be plastic, wood or metal, until they are arranged coherently in an appropriate linear sequence then their true functionality is not met.

Likewise, genes may specify the formation of molecular raw materials but lack the capacity to organise those materials into functioning parts. Just as the raw materials at a factory, whether in the form of steel, glass or plastic, cannot arrange themselves into an automobile or any other product, but instead rely on factory workers to shape and place the materials accordingly.

Comparably, the A's, C's, T's and G's found in the DNA molecule are also sequentially arranged in order to direct the construction of the proteins, and it is the DNA molecule which encodes information in a digital form, much like computer code as mentioned earlier. If one wished to improve a computer's performance then software would be added which upgrades the previously programmed data found therein. Living organisms work in a similar way as they initially require information first, encoded in the DNA, which in turn builds the proteins to measure, and ultimately produces the required functionality. Such a sequence of events is necessary in even the simplest single cell organism.

Richard Dawkins also utilised the computer analogy, 'The machine code of the genes is uncannily computer-like. Apart from differences in jargon, the pages of a molecular biology journal might be interchanged with those of a computer engineering journal.'

THE DNA ENIGMA

Our current understanding of DNA is vastly improved but the mystery today is not what DNA looks like, neither is the question of *how* and *why* the DNA functions in the manner it does, as such concerns are now understood. The DNA enigma revolves around the question of *where* did the information already encoded in the DNA actually originate?

As German theoretical biologist Bernd-Olaf Kuppers remarked, 'The problem of the origin of life is clearly basically equivalent to the problem of the origin of biological information.' So, if we can explain the origin of the information, maybe we can explain the origin of life itself.

Proposed naturalistic explanations for the origin of information are very limited in their approach and do not present a convincing argument. One such explanation given by those with Darwinist sensibilities suggests that chance alone could explain the mysterious presence of information within DNA and also the remarkably intricate sequential requirements necessary for the creation of working proteins.

Some scientists believe that given enough time, the correct sequences may inadvertently stumble upon a functioning sequence by default. It is akin to pulling out Scrabble letters from the bag at random and waiting to see which letters manage to complete a legible word by chance alone. If one was to experiment with this method it would soon become apparent that only a fraction of the letters selected succeed in lining up in a coherent fashion, whilst the majority of letters produced make no sense whatsoever when placed alongside each other.

Chance is not within the realms of impossibility if only small amounts of information were required but the facts show us that is not the case. One gene is considered to need between 1200 and 2000 bases to be properly sequenced, and each gene has one protein. A single cell requires between 250 and 500 proteins along with their corresponding genes, so based on those figures one cell must have between 300,000 and one million genetic characters in order to function properly. Such large figures suggest that chance is not a plausible theory in the process of information acquisition.

Another reason that chance does not seem to be a viable explanation for the chemical origin of life is that the odds of the right 100 amino acid subunits required to form a functional protein, which must arrange itself in the correct order, is about 1 in 10^{65} (10 followed by 65 zeros) which equates to the number of atoms in our galaxy.

Biochemist Michael Behe compared the probability of a sequence of 100 amino acids lining up correctly in order to function as a protein, being as likely as finding one marked grain of sand in the Sahara desert – three times in a row![31] Not the greatest odds in the world.

Another theory being bandied around scientific circles in direct opposition with the intelligent design hypothesis is that of natural law, which is referred to as the self-organisational theory. The idea is that the information-carrying constituents, the bases, manage to form a coherent sequence by means of chemical processes or natural forces of attraction, just as magnetic opposites naturally pull together or the way water forms into a natural vortex before disappearing down the plughole.

ID theorists question the validity of the self-organisational theory by suggesting that despite the plausibility that some form of magnetic attraction could possibly pull specific characters of genetic code into functional positions, physically adhering them to the proteins and keeping them locked in place, no natural chemical process has the capacity to arrange the bases in the necessary sequence needed to transmit the information.

The Hungarian-British polymath and colleague of Albert Einstein, Michael Polanyi wrote in 1967, 'As the arrangement of a printed page is extraneous to the chemistry of the printed page, so is the base sequence in a DNA molecule extraneous to the chemical forces at work in the DNA molecule.'[32]

In layman's terms Polanyi was telling us that the physical properties of both the page and the ink have no bearing on the order in which the letters are written down and play no part in the transmittal of the transcribed information. Magnetic powers may keep magnetic letters stuck to the fridge but they have no influence on the decision-making which takes place prior to the letter order selection.

Darwin himself would have tried to explain away the complex nature of information at cellular level in natural terms as being another product of natural selection, suggesting that some inherent inner-force guides our biological mechanisms as nature dictates, with only the most important information progressing further and impacting the rest of the body's functions. But no theory put forward to date gets to the heart of the problem, which remains *where* does the information come from?

ID theorists seem to be closest to solving the DNA enigma and the whole question of the origins of life and therefore the origins of man. As we continue to progress ever further onwards, science seems to be going full circle and realising that some form of intelligence must be responsible for the evolution of living beings on this planet and most likely elsewhere throughout the universe.

Meyer concluded that, 'When we find information in the DNA molecule . . . we can infer with confidence that we are seeing evidence of a prior designing intelligence.'[33] Austrian physician Henry Quastler echoed Meyer's sentiments when he wrote, 'The creation of new information is habitually associated with conscious activity'.

To add even more controversy to the debate, William Brown, a biophysicist and research scientist at the Resonance Project Foundation and Hawai'i Institute for Unified Physics, posits some astounding information concerning human genetics. Brown's research has led him to the conclusion that humans have been tampered with in the distant past by advanced intelligent beings that have intervened in our genetics via retro viral engineering.

During a 2014 interview with David Whitehead, Brown claimed, 'From an evolutionary perspective, what you have is a series of insertions of genetic material by retrovirus elements into the primate genome. Hundreds of thousands of regulatory elements have been introduced into the human genome through retroviruses.'

But what is a retrovirus? HIV is a retrovirus, a virus that is composed of RNA not DNA, which has an enzyme called reverse transcriptase which allows the RNA to be transcribed into the DNA once it has entered the cell. This genetic transcription is reversed from the usual DNA to RNA, instead transcribing the RNA to DNA. The retroviral DNA is then capable of integrating into the chromosomal DNA of the host cell for the production of new RNA retroviruses.

Brown declared that 'the human species, it's not even controversial to say, is the result of retroviral genetic engineering. That's just a fact that can be seen from the structure and architecture of our genome.'

Considering our gene pool is believed to contain over 4,000 defects, one wonders what may have caused such a massive deficiency and why 98% of our DNA is junk. Why are only 2% of our DNA working prosaic segments and who is responsible for these 'series of insertions of genetic material' as Brown contends? Could it be the same intelligence responsible for creating and directing the informational code we have inside of us?

Lloyd Pye received an email from an anonymous geneticist which also concurs with the information offered by Brown. Part of the email read, '. . . by certain methods of DNA dating one can tell that numerous genes have been recently added to the human genome.' Explaining the reasons for anonymity the scientist wrote, 'If geneticists were to speak out openly on this, they would be ostracised, and their work rejected without any form of appeal.'

This discussion opens up another contentious aspect of human origins and also reiterates the notion of intelligent design despite taking it deeper into a more conspiratorial direction. I shall not delve any further into this debate at this particular juncture but it is definitely worthwhile contemplating such possibilities in the context of this research. Pye often referred to the work of biblical scholar and controversial figure Zecharia Sitchin, and regarding this notion of genetic interference related it to the influence of the Annunaki, 'the men who from heaven came', a group of space travellers which Sitchin claims are responsible for creating mankind. His information is derived from ancient Sumerian cuneiform tablets which Sitchin translated into print for his *Earth Chronicles* book series. Despite being a highly controversial figure, Sitchin's ideas, as fanciful as they may prove to be, are not in isolation. The 'ancient aliens' theory is one shared by many different researchers all over the world, but proving such extreme hypotheses continues to be problematic.

IRREDUCIBLE BIOLOGICAL COMPLEXITY

DNA is not the only part of biology which defies evolutionary explanation because of the sheer complexity and precision required to structure the molecules in an effectively sequenced order. The human body is replete with complex organs and parts, most of which baffle Darwinists since they are unable to explain in any detailed manner how such complicated structures may have evolved from simpler forms, when in most cases a simpler functioning organ would prove impractical.

Michael Cremo wrote, 'The great complexity of the organs found in the human body defies evolutionary explanation. Darwinists have not explained in any detailed way how these organs could have arisen by random genetic variations and natural selection.'[34]

The human eye for example, requires every complex detail in order to function properly as an eye, any minor deviation or simpler version simply would have no purpose. Cremo highlights this conundrum in his book *Human Devolution*, 'It is hard to see how the eye could function without all of its parts being present.'

Even Darwin was aware of the problematic issues which the complexity of the human eye raises as he wrote in 1872, 'To suppose that the eye . . . could have been formed by natural selection, seems, I freely confess, absurd in the highest possible degree.'

It would seem that Darwin had more than one concern which contradicted his theories on the natural evolution of life, but it didn't deter him from pushing forward his ideas. One wonders how he might feel were he alive today and whether he may change his mind on a few issues considering the vastly improved knowledge presently available to us.

Concerning the complex nature of the human eye, Darwin suggested that it could have developed gradually from the simpler light sensitive spots seen in some creatures to simple depressions with simple lenses, before eventually evolving into the vastly improved and complex camera-like human eye. By comparing and contrasting the various eye types present in the natural world, Darwin ultimately offered a superficially plausible argument without actually producing a scientific explanation for the origin of the eye. He ignored the real question of how the first light sensitive spot came into being in the first place.

Let us familiarise ourselves with the long and complex biochemical processes which take place in order to create human vision, as summarised by Michael Behe:

'When light first strikes the retina a photon interacts with a molecule called 11-cis-retinal, which rearranges within picoseconds to trans-retinal. . . The change in the shape of the retinal molecule forces a change in the shape of the protein, rhodopsin, to which the retinal is tightly bound. . . Now called metarhodopsin II, the protein sticks to another protein, called transducin.

Before bumping into metarhodopsin II, transducin had tightly bound a small molecule called GDP. But when transducin interacts with metarhodopsin II, the GDP falls off, and a molecule called GTP binds to transducin. . . GTP-transducin-metarhodopsin II now binds to a protein called phosphodiesterase, located in the inner membrane of the cell.

When attached to metarhodopsin II and its entourage, the phosphodiesterase acquires the chemical ability to 'cut' a molecule called cGMP. . .Initially there are a lot of cGMP molecules in the cell, but the phosphodiesterase lowers its concentration, just as a pulled plug lowers the water level in a bathtub. Another membrane protein that binds cGMP is called an ion channel. It acts as a gateway that regulates the number of sodium ions in the cell, while a separate protein actively pumps them out again.

The dual action of the ion channel and pump keeps the level of sodium ions in the cell within a narrow range. When the amount of cGMP is reduced because of cleavage by the phosphodiesterase, the ion channel closes, causing the cellular concentration of positively charged sodium ions to be reduced. This causes an imbalance of charge across the cell membrane that, finally, causes a current to be transmitted down the optic nerve to the brain. The result, when interpreted by the brain, is vision.'

Now, if you are as perplexed as this author was when reading such a detailed and comprehensive analysis of the process which precedes vision, fear not, as the purpose of the above paragraph's inclusion was indeed to induce a sense of the sheer complexity of design inherent in the genetic makeup of the human eye.

Behe stated, 'Ultimately . . . this is the level of explanation for which biological science must aim. In order to truly understand a function, one must understand in detail every relevant step in the process. The relevant steps in biological processes occur ultimately at the molecular level, so a satisfactory explanation of a biological phenomenon – such as sight, digestion, or immunity – must include its molecular explanation.'[35] Evolutionists are yet to produce such an explanation.

It really makes one wonder how such a convoluted and intricate process could have emerged by natural means without the interaction of some form of intelligence in the formation of the blueprints. Is it even possible for such complexity to suddenly appear, as the Cambrian fossils reveal, without the existence of a predecessor?

The human eye is not the only complex mechanism to baffle those advocating Darwinist thinking. Equally as contradictory to the whole concept of gradual evolution we have the blood clotting mechanism, the DNA replication system, the neural connections in the brain, the placenta and the vesicular transport system.

Speaking of the latter, Behe explained, 'Vesicular transport is a mind-boggling process, no less complex than the automated delivery of vaccine from a storage clinic a thousand miles away. Defects in vesicular transport can have the same deadly consequences as the failure to deliver a needed vaccine to a disease-racked city. An analysis shows that vesicular transport is irreducibly complex, and so its development staunchly resists gradualistic explanations, as Darwinian evolution would have it. A search of the professional biochemical literature shows that no one has ever proposed a detailed route by which such a system could have come to be. In the face of the enormous complexity of vesicular transport, Darwinian theory is mute.'

Each of the aforementioned biological systems raises the same problematic concerns for the evolutionist, namely that any intermediate forms for such complex mechanisms simply could not function. It is these processes in their entirety which allows the almost miraculous systems to function as they do, and if Darwin was correct in saying that all complex living things evolved from simpler living organisms then some form of intermediate should be present in the fossil record (which it is not) and should have the means to function also, albeit in a more primitive fashion.

If any one element is removed from these biological systems then that system will cease to function, and a non-functioning eye defies its very existence and purpose.

Behe wrote, 'In the past ten years, *Journal of Molecular Evolution* has published more than a thousand papers . . . There were zero papers discussing detailed models for intermediates in the development of complex biomolecular structures. This is not a peculiarity of JME. No papers are to be found that discuss complex biomolecular structures, whether in the Proceedings of the National Academy of Science, Nature, Science, the *Journal of Molecular Biology* or, to my knowledge, any science journal.'

So it would seem that the absence of these intermediates is another contentious issue which is currently being swept beneath an ever-expanding carpet, along with a plethora of authentically problematic matters which some mainstream scientists appear unwilling to confront.

Next we shall uncover the presence of some form of knowledge filter that only allows concurrent information to penetrate the scientific community before reaching the public domain.

We shall delve into the world of hidden archaeology and rediscover evidence of the presence of human activity so far back into antiquity that it seriously questions our current understanding of human origins by pushing the dates for the existence of mankind further then has ever been conceived possible.

The incredible discoveries of modern human skeletal remains along with the presence of manmade tools shall serve as confirmation of how wrong ancient history truly is, condemning the story of man to no more than a mythical status when in fact the reality could prove to be infinitely more fascinating than anyone could ever have imagined.

Chapter Two

BONES AND STONES

Practically speaking, archaeologists have buried as much as they've dug up.

Michael Cremo

THE THEORY POPULARISED BY THE SCIENTIFIC musings of Charles Darwin has progressed greatly since his death, with much more physical evidence coming to the surface to reinforce certain aspects of the modern concept of mankind's lineal growth from tree-dweller to king-of-the-castle in a moderately short period of time. But one of the problems with our current understanding of human development derives from the apparent denial of the existence of some key evidence.

If, as most anthropologists contend, *Homo sapiens* evolved into modern humans in Africa around 195,000 years ago (a date which continually shifts as more evidence comes to light), then *any* modern human skeletal remains or manufactured stone tools found earlier than this period would suggest that this hypothesis is need of an update. Just one piece of proof alone is all that is required to force us to re-evaluate the current ideas on human evolution.

By turning our attention to the meticulous research of Michael Cremo, who amassed a wealth of evidence regarding the greater antiquity of anatomically modern humans in our ancient past, we shall witness the fallibility of evolutionary thinking.

Most of the information he offers derives from science journals and publications during the nineteenth and early twentieth centuries, but despite the age of some of the data revealed here, it should not detract from the legitimacy of the content as 'this controversial evidence is no better or worse than the supposedly noncontroversial evidence cited in favour of current views about human evolution.'[36]

The model of human prehistory which has been meticulously built-up over the past two hundred years by scientists and scholars alike is completely devoid of physical proof, and contrarily, evidence disputing such claims has surfaced, literally having been dug up.

Further research reveals anatomically modern human skeletal remains along with anomalously old artefacts which point to the fact that intelligent tool-making beings existed as far back into antiquity as the Eocene, 55 million years ago.

THE LAETOLI FOOTPRINTS

Ancient human footprints were discovered in volcanic ash deposits at the Laetoli site in Tanzania, East Africa in 1979. The 27-metre long trail of around seventy early human footprints found by palaeontologist Mary Leakey and her team are believed to have been made by *Australopithecus afarensis* 3.6 million years ago because other fossils of this ancient hominin were discovered in the same layer of sediment.

As the two ancient humans walked through the wet volcanic ash it is understood that subsequent layers of ash from a later eruption covered their tracks, thus preserving them for millions of years. Leakey and her colleagues said 'the Laetoli footprints' as they have come to be known were 'indistinguishable from those of modern humans'.

In an article for *National Geographic* magazine titled '*Footprints in the Ashes of Time*', Mary Leakey cited Louise Robbins, a footprint expert from the University of North Carolina, who following her analysis of the prints said 'they looked so human, so modern, to be found in tuffs so old.'

Robbins also stated that the remarkable prints 'share many features that are characteristic of the human foot structure', concluding that 'the four functional regions – heel, arch, ball, and toes – of the hominoids' feet imprinted in the ash in a typically human manner', and that 'the hominoids walked across the ash surface in characteristic human bipedal fashion'.

These descriptions given by the experts left scientists having to explain that our human ancestors of 3.6 million years ago must have had remarkably modern feet. But such a self-explanatory statement actually contradicts the physical evidence, as other scientists such as physical anthropologist R. H. Tuttle of the University of Chicago, were quick to contend.

Tuttle revealed that fossil foot-bones from known australopithecines of that period show that they actually had distinctly apelike feet contrary to the description offered by Mary Leakey and her team.

Whoever left these prints were most definitely bipedal, with their big toes lining up with the rest of the foot, a sign which is more indicative of a human presence than some ancient apelike creature. The big toes found on apes are highly divergent, allowing climbing and grasping much like the way thumbs are employed. But it is not only the big toe that gives the Laetoli footprints their human appearance; the ancient imprints also reveal the gait of these early humans as a heel-strike, where the heel hits the ground first, followed by a push off from the toes – just as modern humans do when they walk.

Tuttle stated that, 'The shapes of the prints are indistinguishable from those of striding, habitually barefoot humans' just like 'small barefoot *Homo sapiens*'.

But this contradicting information causes a conundrum for science. How can modern human footprints exist during a time when anthropologists insist that apelike australopithecines walked the Earth? In a 1990 article published in *Natural History*, Tuttle himself confessed 'we are left with somewhat of a mystery'.

Is it possible that the footprints left in the African ash millions of years ago during the Pliocene (Table 1) could have been made by modern human types as the raw data would suggest? Putting our preconceptions aside for a second and purely assessing the evidence at hand, the Laetoli prints which have been created by feet 'indistinguishable' from our own, show the presence of modern humans much further back in time than evolutionists will allow.

(Table 1)

Geological Eras and Periods

Era	Period	Start in Millions of Years Ago
Cenozoic	Holocene	0.1
	Pleistocene	2
	Pliocene	5
	Miocene	25
	Oligocene	38
	Eocene	55
	Paleocene	65
Mesozoic	Cretaceous	144
	Jurassic	213
	Triassic	248
Paleozoic	Permian	286
	Carboniferous	360
	Devonian	408
	Silurian	438
	Ordovician	505
	Cambrian	590

The constant drive to prove man's animal ancestry is so strong that the most basic principles of science appear to have been tainted, and many

Creationists have shown (despite their own sense of purpose and intent) that *they* are able to recognise that a human footprint regardless of age must have been made by a human foot and not that of an ape.

The age of the prints has never been in question, as Leakey's methodology and reputation as an expert in the field has already been firmly established, but what remains as contentious an issue today as the day the prints were discovered, is what kind of creature was responsible for their presence.

After years of extensive research Tuttle concluded that the real problem for scientists and anthropologists alike is not the prints themselves but their extreme age. As he explained in *Natural History* in 1990, the footprints 'resemble those of habitually unshod modern humans . . . [If the] footprints were not known to be so old, we would readily conclude that they were made by a member of our genus.'

Evolutionists (Mary Leakey included) have been forced to assign the prints to *Australopithecus afarensis* because of the dates involved, but this appears to be an inaccurate assumption given that these hominids have already been considered as chimp-like that could only walk marginally more upright than modern chimps.

Yet, because science has deemed the evolutionary theory of man's ascension from ancient apes as postulated by Darwin to be the correct one, all subsequent archaeological discoveries must adhere to that particular framework despite its flaws and problematic rigidity.

THE CONVENTIONAL ORIGINS OF MAN

Before we endeavour to untangle the inconsistencies which mar the intricate story of human evolution, let us first familiarise ourselves with the conventional script which modern science continues to adhere to.

It is believed that around twelve million years ago during the Miocene, the last lush forests began to fall as precipitation lessened, and by the Pliocene, seven million years later, grasslands had formed where forests once thrived. It was then that our most ancient ancestors, a type of ape called *Ramapithecus*, chose to come down from the trees and inhabit the recently formed savannahs instead.

Three million years down the line and the ape had evolved into *Australopithecus afarensis*, the same type as the hominin 'Lucy' (originally referred to as AL 288-1), a forty percent complete skeleton discovered in 1974 by palaeoanthropologist Donald Johanson. Lucy is considered to be 3.2 million years old and is commonly referred to as 'the first human' as she appears very 'human-like' according to Johanson.

Many other anthropologists are less convinced however, as Richard Milton explains, 'These bones have been restored to resemble a missing link, part-human/part-ape and Lucy is now thought of as being our long lost ancestor.'

'But this is merely an interpretation of one group. Those same bones can be, and they have been taken by scientists and identified as simply an extinct ape, nothing to do with us at all',[37] he commented.

Later, the more evolved *Australopithecus africanus* which followed the 'Lucy type' is believed to have existed until around 2.1 million years ago.

Then, as the Pleistocene era began around two million years ago, an Ice Age took a hold of the planet which would last for 65,000 years, with the interglacial periods producing deserts, and it was during this timeframe that *Australopithecus* began his inaugural ascent towards becoming what would later be recognised as the same genus as man – *Homo habilis* then *Homo erectus*, whose brain was twice the size of *Australopithecus*.

500,000 years ago, a mysterious event occurred when the 'brain explosion' – an inexplicable expansion of the brain which led the human brain to increase one third in size – took place. Scientists have been unable to account for this bizarre and relatively swift biological improvement, but author Robert Ardrey came up with a theory which he believes may explain the anomalous event.

A gigantic meteorite, or perhaps a small asteroid, exploded over the Indian Ocean 700,000 years ago, which scattered tektites (tiny fragments) over a twenty square mile radius. Simultaneously, the poles reversed with North becoming South and vice-versa, the reasons for which are still unknown despite this occurring on more than one occasion.

Ardrey hypothesised that during this period when the Earth would have been without a magnetic field, a bombardment of high-speed particles and cosmic rays could have caused genetic mutations. Whatever the cause, man evolved more in half a million years than in the previous three million.

This genetic change ultimately led to the rise of the Neanderthals between 300 and 150,000 years ago, a human-type which were subsequently destroyed by the emergence of Cro-Magnon man around 30,000 years ago. Until recently, the oldest 'official' *Homo sapiens* skeletal remains on record dated back to 195,000 years ago, and were found near Kibish, Ethiopia in 1967. However, palaeoanthropologists digging at a site in Morocco called Jebel Irhoud discovered fossilised early human remains that were initially considered to be Neanderthal when they were first discovered in the sixties, but they have recently been reassigned as *Homo sapiens* and dated at around 315,000 years old.

The fascinating aspect of this conventional history of human origins and evolution must be that the whole theory has been solely based on a very small amount of fossil evidence. One would imagine that by now we have amassed such an incredible amount of bones to prove the human lineage thesis that there should no longer be any doubt over the age and order of our ancient ancestry, but the reality is very different. Of the millions of hominids that walked the earth in prehistory, we merely have fragments of what should be a vast haul of remains.

As renowned palaeoanthropologist Richard Leakey commented in his book on human origins *People of the Lake*, 'If someone went to the trouble of collecting together in one room all of the fossil remains of our ancestors (and their biological relatives). . . he would need only a couple of large trestle tables on which to spread them out.'

Dr. Lyall Watson concurred when he stated in 1982 that 'the fossils that decorate our family tree are so scarce that there are still more scientists than specimens. The remarkable fact is that all of the physical evidence we have for human evolution can still be placed, with room to spare, inside a single coffin!'

Similarly, a 1994 article in *Time Magazine* explained that 'despite more than a century of digging, the fossil record remains maddeningly sparse. With so few clues, even a single bone that doesn't fit into the picture can upset everything. Virtually every major discovery has put deep cracks in the conventional wisdom and forced scientists to concoct new theories, amid furious debate.'

The 'Out Of Africa' theory of human evolution is currently coming under a great deal of scrutiny by researchers and scholars, some of whom contend that the empirical data actually points to the Australian continent as the birthplace of humankind. More evidence continues to come to light which supports this fledgling hypothesis, and it may simply be a matter of time before such theories take hold and force us to re-evaluate man's murky origin story.

CONTROVERSY AT HUEYATLACO

As a researcher of life's mysteries and the unexplained, this author is only too familiar with the concept of hidden knowledge and in many cases, conspiratorial acts intent on concealing the facts from the general public.

It is not unusual for those in the higher echelons of society to have access to information which they may not deem suitable for public consumption, either for the purpose of political or hierarchical power or possibly considered too important for reasons concerning national security. Either way, there exists today, and has always existed, a great amount of hidden knowledge, accessible to only a select elite group who consider themselves (by means of their select bloodlines) to be above mainstream society.

The discipline of science however, in its many different guises is one of those institutions which just like the medical profession have a reputation for respectability and trustworthiness. Our current understanding of human origins is based upon the information given to us from this scientific establishment, so why should we doubt these experts in scientific development as their very existence is based on certain principles being met.

Using methodical processes, scientists of all disciplines are taught to prove their hypotheses by devising experiments which could prove their theory – then analysing, recording and explaining the results.

A scientist should not endeavour to constantly prove his hypothesis should results fail to reinforce his ideas, as it is his responsibility to reveal the outcome regardless of the scientific implications. Science deals in facts. Speculation should always be reported as such, and all data should be included even if it disproves any given theory. For example, when dating a particular bone sample employing more than one dating method like carbon-14 testing or potassium-argon testing, it is common for each method to offer different age outcomes. The scientists should publish this data in its entirety and not be drawn towards the result which best suits his hypothesis.

Michael Cremo explained this unprofessional approach during a television interview, 'Scientists may run several tests on the same piece of bone. Some of the ages will be very great, some very small, and they will tend to pick the date to publish in their scientific literature that most fits the idea that they start out with about how old the fossil should be.'[38]

This seemingly conspiratorial view is not an isolated one as Dr. Richard Thompson concurs, 'In science you find that evidence that doesn't fit the accepted paradigm tends to be eliminated.'[39]

There exists an old guard mentality at work in most scientific fields which seeks to preserve the status quo as there are people with egos and reputations based on a lifetime's work of orthodoxy. Information that conforms to the accepted theories will pass through the knowledge filter unhindered, but any material that challenges the existing paradigm is rejected even if facts and data support their radical theses.

As author Graham Hancock believes, 'archaeology is too much constrained by a rigid reference frame of what is possible and what is not, and tends to ignore, sidestep, or ridicule evidence that challenges that reference frame.'[40]

In 1962, at an archaeological site at Hueyatlaco, near Valsequillo, 75 miles southeast of Mexico City, evidence of human activity and manmade artefacts of quartz, flaked flint and bone were unearthed amid the bones of mastodons, camels and mammoths. Animal bones were excavated with spearheads embedded in them whilst others showed signs of deliberate butchering, leading the investigation team from the U.S. Geological Survey to conclude that Hueyatlaco must have been a kill site where animals were hunted and later butchered.

Juan Armento Camacho and Cynthia Irwin-Williams discovered human artefacts in several layers of sediment, starting with the simpler tools in the lower levels, showing more complexity in the upper levels. The sheer diversity of tools found which were made from non-local materials indicated that the entire region had been in use by many different groups of people over a considerable period of time.

Unable to carbon-date the site at that time due to the absence of carbon in and around the artefacts, the team theorised that the site could date back to 22,000 years old, a controversial age which contradicted the popularised version of the history of human habitation in the Americas.

The long-standing theory claims that the Americas were first populated by peoples from Asia who travelled across the Bering land-bridge to North America between 13 and 16,000 years ago before finally migrating south. The Clovis people were big game hunters who existed around 13,000 years ago in the Americas and left behind very distinctive stone tools of which none of the found artefacts at Hueyatlaco resembled. So if the tools that were unearthed did not belong to the only recognised group of people commonly accepted as occupying Mexico at that time, then the history books would have to be rewritten should the site prove to be 10,000 years older as the archaeologists were suggesting.

In 1966, a young PhD student from Harvard called Virginia Steen-McIntyre joined the team at Hueyatlaco looking for a new and interesting site for her doctoral dissertation. She was invited to join the team in order to date the dig site which she intended to do before writing up the results as part of her dissertation. But things didn't go according to plan.

In mid-1969, a team of geologists which included Steen-McIntyre and Irwin-Williams managed to carbon-date the animal remains at around 35,000 years old, and the stone implements were dated using the uranium series dating method which yielded even more astounding results; the tools found at Hueyatlaco were 250,000 years old. This controversial age was not accepted and reasons for the anomalous results were forthcoming, possibly the tool-bearing strata had been eroded by an ancient streambed and mixed up older and newer strata together thus confusing the dating process?

Virginia Steen-McIntyre returned to the site in 1973, and along with her colleagues set out to accurately determine an age for the tool-bearing strata once and for all. The geologists used four different dating methods which all independently yielded significantly old ages for the found objects. The dating methods employed were (1) uranium series dating, (2) fission track dating, (3) tephra hydration dating and (4) study of mineral weathering.

Once the stratigraphic location of the stones was agreed upon as being around 250,000 years old – the Pleistocene period conventionally understood to have been the time of the Neanderthals – the controversy which arose at Hueyatlaco came about because of the apparent age of the stone tools which rivalled the best work of Cro-Magnon man in Europe 30,000 years ago.

This anomalous new data, if accepted, would not only have revolutionised New World anthropology but would put into question our present understanding of human origins. Human beings capable of making such sophisticated tools using the current view of evolution did not exist until 100,000 years ago, and that was thousands of miles away on the African continent.

Well, as Steen-McIntyre was soon to discover, the outlandish dates were not accepted, despite other sites across Mexico also yielding conflicting evidence of human activity way beyond the constrained parameters set by scientific orthodoxy which insists upon the earliest arrival of humans in the Americas being as recent as 13,000 years ago.

In the same valley as Hueyatlaco, ancient footprints were found fossilised in volcanic ash like those discovered in Tanzania. The imprints were dismissed as indentations made from pickaxes during an old mining operation but one scientist dated the ash strata as far back as 1.3 million years ago, again, reminiscent of the Laetoli prints.

Elsewhere in Mexico, carved bones and hearths have been excavated and dated to around 30,000 years old. At the Babisuri site on the island of Espiritu Santo off the coast of Baja California, shell samples found *in situ* at a cave shelter were carbon-dated to between 36,000 and 42,000 years old, suggesting the presence of human activity in Mexico during the Pleistocene.

Advanced stone implements called Folsom points were discovered beneath a layer of stalagmite also considered to be a quarter of a million years old, this time in Sandia Cave, New Mexico in North America. Some of these ancient artefacts were found actually embedded in the lower surface of a travertine crust (a form of limestone deposited by mineral springs). Steen-McIntyre was shocked to learn about these archaeological finds that agreed with the Hueyatlaco dates, which she said 'disagreed violently with the commonly held hypothesis for the date of entry into the New World'.

When author Michael Cremo contacted her regarding reports and photos of the Sandia artefacts, Steen-McIntyre wrote in an accompanying note, 'The geochemists are sure of their date, but archaeologists have convinced them the artefacts and charcoal lenses beneath the travertine are the result of rodent activity. . . But what about the artefacts *cemented in* the crust?'

Steen-McIntyre and her colleagues wrote a paper on their anomalous findings at Hueyatlaco and presented them for the first time at an anthropological conference in 1975 which was set to appear in a symposium volume shortly after. Inexplicably, the publication of her paper was held up for years, and four years later with still no sign of the Hueyatlaco finds being published, Steen-McIntyre wrote to one of the editors of the allegedly forthcoming book, H.J. Fullbright of the Los Alamos Scientific Laboratory:

'Our joint article on the Hueyatlaco site is a real bombshell. It would place man in the New World 10x earlier than many archaeologists would like to believe. Worse, the bifacial tools that were found *in situ* are thought by most to be a sign of *H. Sapiens*. According to present theory, *H.s.* had not even evolved at that time, and certainly not in the New World.'

Explaining the unexpected reactions from within the archaeological community following the extreme dating of the Mexican Stone Age tools, Steen-McIntyre told Fullbright, 'Archaeologists are in a considerable uproar over Hueyatlaco – they refuse even to consider it. I've learnt from second-hand sources that I'm considered by various members of the profession to be 1) incompetent, 2) a news monger, 3) an opportunist, 4) dishonest, 5) a fool. Obviously none of these opinions is helping my professional reputation! My only hope to clear my name is to get the Hueyatlaco article into print so that folks can judge for themselves.'

On February 8, 1980, Steen-McIntyre contacted the editor of *Quaternary Research*, Steve Porter, with regards to finally having her article printed. She wrote, 'The ms [manuscript] I'd like to submit gives the geologic evidence. It's pretty clear-cut, and if it weren't for the fact a lot of anthropology textbooks will have to be rewritten, I don't think we would have had any problems getting the archaeologists to accept it. As it is, no anthro journal will touch it with a ten foot pole.'

Porter replied stating that he would consider the controversial article for publication but agreed that certain archaeologists may struggle to offer her objective reviews to endorse the article. It is a standard procedure in scientific publishing to submit an article for potential publication to several other scientists for anonymous peer review. One can imagine how easily specific and unwanted information which does not conform to the entrenched scientific orthodoxy could be manipulated through this process so that the data never reaches publication.

Eventually in 1981, *Quaternary Research* published an article by Virginia Steen-McIntyre, Roald Fryxell and Harold E. Malde which upheld an age of 250,000 years for the Hueyatlaco site. Despite these remarkable findings finally reaching the print room, the American archaeological community, including Cynthia Irwin-Williams, the woman responsible for originally discovering the artefacts, have continued to reject the controversial dating of Hueyatlaco by Steen-McIntyre and her team.

Cremo explained how Hueyatlaco offers the unique opportunity to witness the 'knowledge filter' at work: 'The anomalous findings at Hueyatlaco resulted in personal abuse and professional penalties, including withholding of funds and loss of job, facilities, and reputation for Virginia Steen-McIntyre. Her case opens a rare window into the actual processes of data suppression in paleoanthropology, processes that involve a great deal of conflict and hurt.'

Both Cremo and co-author Thompson tried to secure permission to reproduce photographs of the Hueyatlaco artefacts for their work but were subsequently informed that permission would be denied should they mention the 'lunatic fringe' date of 250,000 years.

The controversial date given for the stone tools at the Mexican site came about through vigorous testing using accepted scientific methods. Why would any discerning scientist resist acknowledging such results simply because they contradict current theories of human evolution? Isn't the purpose of science to further our current understanding rather than hinder it with our own rigid preconceptions of what we *should* find as opposed to what we actually *do* find?

The Hueyatlaco case exposes the existence of a scientific prejudice which seems hell-bent on proving conventional evolutionary theories at any cost whilst simultaneously putting the entire institution into disrepute. Steen-McIntyre became all too aware of the implications of such a flawed system and wrote to Estella Leopold, the associate editor of *Quaternary Research* to express her thoughts on the matter:

'The problem as I see it is much bigger than Hueyatlaco. It concerns the manipulation of scientific thought through the suppression of 'Enigmatic Data,' data that challenges the prevailing mode of thinking. Hueyatlaco certainly does that! Not being an anthropologist, I didn't realize the full significance of our dates back in 1973, nor how deeply woven into our thought the current theory of evolution had become. Our work at Hueyatlaco has been rejected by most archaeologists because it contradicts that theory, period. Their reasoning is circular. *H. sapiens sapiens* evolved *ca.* 30,000-50,000 years ago in Eurasia.

Therefore any *H.s.s* tools 250,000 years old found in Mexico are impossible because *H.s.s.* evolved *ca.* 30,000. . . etc. Such thinking makes for self-satisfied archaeologists but *lousy* science.'

CONTENTIOUS EOLITHS

The stone tools unearthed at Hueyatlaco show signs of sophistication and are regarded as advanced paleoliths and neoliths which were deliberately manufactured by humans. Stone tool industries from ancient man fall into three basic divisions: 1) eoliths, 2) crude paleoliths, 3) advanced paleoliths and neoliths.

Eoliths, being the crudest and least worked on, are considered to be the oldest implements, followed by the paleoliths and neoliths as they become slightly more advanced. Eoliths or 'dawn stones', as is the Greek origin of the name, are believed today to be nothing more than flakes of flint or stone which are 'naturally produced by geological processes such as glaciation' due to their crude and seemingly untouched appearance. For decades, a debate ensued questioning whether or not eoliths were products of minor alteration by human hand or simply the result of natural erosion.

The discovery of stone tools at Olduvai Gorge in Tanzania during the 1930s by the renowned archaeologists Louis and Mary Leakey seemingly put an end to the debate on the origin of eoliths, instead the Oldowan tools (as they became known) were soon believed to have been the earliest stone tool industry in prehistory.

Dated from the Lower Paleolithic period between 2.6 million and 1.7 million years ago, Oldowan tools are understood to have been manufactured by a primitive hominoid species *Homo habilis*, and represent the earliest evidence of cultural behaviour, the oldest known site where they have been found being at Gona in Ethiopia. Oldowan technology is typified by 'chopper' type tools created by removing flakes from the surface of a stone core to make a sharpened edge for cutting, chopping and scraping.

Despite the common consensus relegating the primitive eolith to a completely natural origin, 19th century scientists discovered many stone tools and weapons in Pleistocene, Pliocene, Miocene and even older strata. These discoveries were reported in scientific journals of the period and discussed at scientific congresses, but today the anomalous stone finds have largely been ignored and much of the data concerning the artefacts has disappeared from view.

Eolithic stone implements were selected for their apparent use even prior to modification, as stones with natural edges had obvious uses. But despite often appearing indistinguishable from ordinary broken stones to the untrained eye, special criteria were developed to identify signs of human usage and modification.

Many Eolithic implements reveal one edge that has been retouched to create a sharper edge, the rest remaining untouched and in its natural state. Such methods continue to be employed today among people in primitive tribes across the globe that pick up stone flakes and chip away at one side to use as a cutting or scraping tool.

As we will see shortly, the reason for eoliths being so contentious is because of the age of the strata and the location of which so many of these most basic of tools were discovered. If any stone is to be considered a human artefact then it cannot appear in layers predating the world's earliest known stone tools, namely the Oldowan stones, as this would contradict popular theories on early human activity.

But if simple and crude stone tools are still in use today then surely they shouldn't be ruled out as evidence if found in anomalously old strata simply because they look too natural to have been used by primitive people. Of course, one cannot just pick up any old stone and claim that it is a prehistoric tool because it potentially looks like one, but following the criteria set out by scientists over a century ago we should surely include artefacts discovered in *any* strata if we are to remain scientifically open-minded.

About twenty-seven miles southeast of London sits the small town of Ightham in Kent, where Benjamin Harrison kept a grocery shop during the Victorian era. Working closely with the famous English geologist Sir John Prestwich, Harrison liked to search the nearby hills and valleys for flint implements, once the centre of scientific controversy for a matter of decades.

Through regular correspondence with scientists within the paleoanthropological community he learned to catalogue his finds according to standard procedure. Harrison initially found many stone artefacts from the Neolithic period, which are considered to have belonged to cultures dating back only 10,000 years, but as he began to dig in the ancient river gravels of the area, Harrison found tools cruder than their Neolithic counterparts, but which were still easily recognised as objects of human manufacture.

The Palaeolithic tools were considered by Harrison and Prestwich and other 20th century geologists, such as Francis H. Edmunds of the Geological Survey of Great Britain, were in agreement that the gravels in which many of the stones were discovered were in fact Pliocene in age. A leading palaeoanthropologist of his time, Hugo Obermaier, also stated that the implements found by Harrison on the Kent Plateau did indeed belong to the Middle Pliocene.

A Late or Middle Pliocene date for Harrison's Kent Plateau stones would give them an age of around 2-4 million years, a date which is not in keeping with modern thinking on the subject. The oldest currently recognised stone implements of this nature in England are about 400,000 years old. Among the Palaeolithic implements found by Benjamin Harrison on the Kent Plateau (Fig. 3), appeared to belong to an even older, more primitive culture. The eoliths that he unearthed were natural flint flakes which displayed only slight retouching along the edges. Despite their crude appearance, the eoliths exhibited definite signs of being worked on, as some clearly resembled spear-heads and other tools.

Harrison had his critics though; those who believed his finds to be just broken pieces of flint, but many other professionals backed him and were happy to comment on the authenticity of the ancient artefacts. Leland W. Patterson for example, an authority on stone tools, claimed that it is easy to distinguish even the crudest tools from naturally eroded stones; 'It would be difficult to visualize how random applications of force could create uniform, unidirectional retouch along a significant length of flake edge.'

Many of Harrison's eoliths were unifacial in appearance, where the chipped edge was usually confined to one side of the surface; meeting one of Patterson's criteria for evidence of human manufacture. And as Sir John Prestwich highlighted in a published article from 1892, 'Even modern savage work, such as exhibited for example by the stone implements of the Australian natives, show, when divested of their mounting, an amount of work no greater or distinct, than do these early Palaeolithic specimens.'[41]

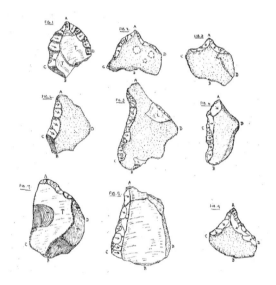

Fig. 3 Eoliths found in ancient upland gravels on the Kent Plateau reveal the presence of ancient humans in England between 2 and 4 million years ago.

It is exactly because such simple artefacts are still in use among tribes today that we needn't attribute the plateau eoliths to some primitive race of ape-men, since *Homo sapiens sapiens* use practically the same technique to fashion appropriate natural stones to suit their intended purpose. It becomes a real possibility that modern human types could have been responsible for making the eoliths at a time which geologists insist the stones surfaced from, during the Middle or Late Pliocene, 2 to 4 million years ago in England.

Similar tools exactly resembling Harrison's eoliths have been confirmed by modern experts as being genuine human artefacts, a status which has not been challenged by scientists. The Oldowan cobble and flake tools excavated from the lower levels of Olduvai Gorge in Tanzania have been accepted as manufactured objects because the timeframe which they fit into does not contradict modern theories of human evolution.

Unconvinced by Harrison's eoliths, some critics claimed that were they actually produced by humans that it was most likely they had been dropped into the Pliocene gravels during more recent times. A prestigious scientific society called the British Association set out to settle the debate once and for all by financing excavations in the Kent Plateau gravels and surrounding areas, in an attempt to show that the eoliths were to be found *in situ*, deep within the preglacial gravels as Harrison had asserted, and not just strewn along the surface.

Harrison was selected to supervise the excavations under the direction of a committee of scientists, and it wasn't long before they found many examples of *in situ* eoliths which included 'thirty convincers' as Harrison revealed. In 1895, Harrison attended a Royal Society meeting where he had been invited to exhibit some of his eoliths. As was to be expected, some scientists remained sceptical, but others were suitably impressed by the tools, among them was a Fellow of the Royal Society and member of the Geological Survey of Britain, E.T. Newton.

Newton wrote to Harrison on December 24 of the same year to express his enthusiasm for the implements, 'Some of them, to say the least, show human work. . . they have been done intentionally, and therefore, by the only intellectual being we know of, *Man.*'

Today, evidence of this kind would in all likelihood be marginalised and disregarded, but anomalous artefacts such as Harrison's eoliths were often the centre of serious scientific discourse and debate within elite scientific circles, with prestigious members of the scientific community both advocating and condemning such evidence.

When Harrison died in 1921, a memorial tablet was set in the north wall of St. Peter's church in Ightham with the inscription:

'IN MEMORIAM – Benjamin Harrison of Ightham, 1837-1921, the village grocer and archaeologist whose discoveries of eolithic flint implements opened a fruitful field of scientific investigation into the greater antiquity of man.'

The discovery of the Java ape-man in the 1890s by Eugene Dubois, which was found in Middle Pleistocene strata, dating the skeletal remains of *Homo erectus* at between one million and 700,000 years old, soon put the Kent Plateau finds out of serious contention as genuinely ancient human artefacts. It was now considered impossible for tool-making hominids to have existed millions of years before their alleged ape-like ancestors; so Harrison's discoveries, and many other discoveries like them which fell outside the normal constraints of theoretical expectation, fell by the wayside, ignored and left to gather dust.

Among the artefacts relegated to the back shelves were yet more stone tools proving the existence of modern toolmakers in ancient England, back in a time when humans are not believed to have been capable of such intelligence, 2 to 3 million years ago.

In 1909, flint specimens were discovered in East Anglia by J. Reid Moir, a fellow of the Royal Anthropological Institute, which show that the stones found in Kent were not isolated examples of human activity in ancient times.

Found in a former seabed known as the Red Crag formation, the manufactured tools discovered by Moir raise yet more questions about the age of human existence, as Moir stated 'it becomes necessary to recognize a much higher antiquity for the human race than has hitherto been supposed.'

Henry Fairfield Osborn, an American geologist and palaeontologist, who was also the president of the American Museum of Natural History for 25 years, was impressed by the flints discovered in England by Moir.

'The discoveries of J. Reid Moir of evidence of the existence of Pliocene Man in East Anglia open a new epoch in archaeology . . . They bring indisputable evidence of man in southeast Britain, man of sufficient intelligence to fashion flints, and to build fire before the close of the Pliocene.'[42]

As Osborn himself maintains, such discoveries were accepted a century ago and were considered by the experts to act as 'indisputable evidence' of a greater antiquity of man. Clearly, times have changed, and discoveries like Moir's are barely disputed these days, rather they appear to have been discarded and ignored entirely.

EARLY MIOCENE FLINTS

Flint implements have been found in much older strata than even the Red Crag specimens, strata which geologists claim was formed during the Early Miocene period, 15-20 million years ago. At Thenay in north central France, L. Bourgeois discovered scrapers, blades and borers which exhibited clear indications of human manufacture such as unifacial flaking, symmetrical chipping, and signs of usage.

Bourgeois presented his remarkable finds to the International Congress for Prehistoric Anthropology and Archaeology in Paris on August 19, 1867, but as one might expect, not all the scientists were suitably impressed or convinced of either their true age or even if they were actual artefacts or not.

One of the first to be convinced that the flint tools were as Bourgeois had insisted was Gabriel de Mortillet, and due to the common consensus at the time being one of doubt concerning the true location of the anomalous finds, in 1869 Bourgeois was forced to disprove the objections by digging out a new pit into the top of the plateau.

As his objectors expressed alternative explanations as to how the flints could have slipped down through fissures starting in the top of the plateau heading down to the Miocene beds, Bourgeois excavated specifically to highlight his assertion that the objects were truly found *in situ* as he had originally contended. During this dig he soon reached a limestone layer about one foot thick through which no Pleistocene tools could possibly have penetrated due to the absence of fissures, as so many had postulated was the cause of the flints presence in the lower levels of strata. Digging deeper still, at a depth of around 14 feet in

Early Miocene sediment, Bourgeois discovered many more flint tools, much to the surprise of his doubters.

In *Le Prehistorique*, De Mortillet wrote, 'There was no further doubt about their antiquity or their geological position.' Others were still far from convinced despite the clarity of his demonstration, and in 1872 a meeting of the International Congress of Prehistoric Anthropology and Archaeology was held in Brussels to finally put the matter to bed.

Here Bourgeois was able to present many specimens to the Congress which would be included in the published proceedings for future generations of scientists. Describing one of the implements which Bourgeois suggested resembled a knife or cutting tool, he stated 'The edges have regular retouching, and the opposite side presents a bulb of percussion.'

The presence of a bulb of percussion helps distinguish between human workmanship and natural breakage, as a bulb or swelling are rarely present if the stone flake (which makes up the tool) has simply broken off by natural means. The bulb is left directly below the point of impact where the stone has been struck to separate the flake from the rest of the rock.

Fig. 4 A Miocene pointed artefact retouched near the front, Thenay, France

While bulbs of percussion were rare on the Thenay flints, most of them showed clear signs of retouching, sometimes along both edges, but mainly concentrated on just one edge, a technique referred to as unifacial flaking. Explaining why he considered another of his specimens (Fig. 4) to be a projectile point or awl – a small pointed tool used primarily to pierce holes, often in leather – Bourgeois highlighted the presence of retouching along the edges which led the flake to taper off to a sharp point: 'The most prominent edge has been chipped down by a series of artificial blows, probably to prevent discomfort to the hand grasping the implement. The other edges remain sharp, which shows this flaking is not due to rolling action.'

A fifteen-member commission was nominated by the Congress of Prehistoric Anthropology and Archaeology to judge Bourgeois' Miocene discoveries in an attempt to finally resolve the controversy. One member expressed no opinion, another had reservations but still supported Bourgeois, five believed there to be no evidence of human workmanship in the Thenay flints; leaving a majority of eight members voting in his favour and convinced that the implements truly were the product of human manufacture.

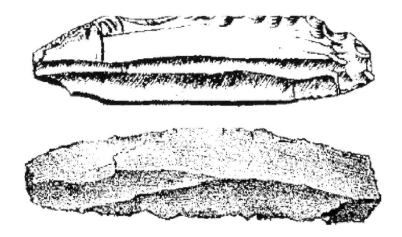

Fig. 5 Top: An Early Miocene implement found in Thenay, France. Bottom: A Late Pliocene flint implement created nearly 20 million years later.

One of his critics was quick to comment that there were only a few 'very good' specimens on offer from the Thenay dig, which he counted at around thirty. But as de Mortillet rightly stated, 'Even one incontestable specimen would be enough, and they have thirty!'

Many of the flint tools which Bourgeois unearthed revealed that fire was used in order to fracture large pieces of flint to make flakes of flint more manageable for tool-making. Exposure to fire produced finely cracked surfaces, another sign of human interaction which was evident on the Thenay flints.

If the artefacts discovered in France prove to be as old as the strata in which they were found, then we have a very interesting situation which points to the existence of intelligent tool-making beings as far back as 15-20 million years ago. Such a proposition would cause havoc among evolutionists and anthropologists everywhere should such evidence prove authentic as it appears.

The flints exhibited by Bourgeois should in all honesty be considered in exactly the same light as artefacts found in Late Pleistocene strata, implements which have officially been recognised and confirmed as true human artefacts by the scientific community. The problem being that the difference in age between the two stratas is so immense; the Early Miocene being close to 20 million years ago in comparison with the Late Pleistocene set between 126,000 and 119,000 years ago. By comparing two different flint tools (fig. 5) discovered in strata from vastly different points in time, it is evident that whoever was responsible for making them existed during both eras.

Samuel Laing, a Scottish writer who was well known during the Victorian era, shared his knowledge of the Thenay finds with his readers, and in his 1894 book *Human Origins* he wrote:

'The human origin of these implements has been greatly confirmed by the discovery that the Mincopics of the Andaman Islands manufactured whet-stones or scrapers almost identical with those of Thenay, and by the same process of using fire to split the stones into the requisite size and shape. . . On the whole, the evidence for these Miocene implements seems to be very conclusive, and the objections to have hardly any other ground than the reluctance to admit the great antiquity of man.'

Some scientists believed that the Miocene tools found in France must have been fashioned by our primitive, apelike ancestors, according to evolutionary theory, but as Laing vehemently expressed, similar tools continue to be made today; 'Their type continues, with no change except that of slight successive improvements, through the Pleistocene, Quaternary, and even down to the present day. The scraper of the Esquimaux and the Andaman islanders is but an enlarged and improved edition of the Miocene scraper.'

Is it possible, as the evidence suggests, that anatomically modern humans could have been present as far back as the Miocene despite the common consensus arguing against such a thesis? As we shall see shortly, scientists did in fact discover human skeletal remains in the Tertiary (a term which denotes the geologic period from 66 million to 2.58 million years ago), bones indistinguishable from *Homo sapiens*.

The Thenay fossils were once considered by scientists with a belief in evolution to have belonged to an apeman-like precursor of the human type, whose bones they expected to find someday as physical proof of their existence. The ancient bones discovered by Eugene Dubois in Java in 1871 in a Middle Pleistocene formation of less than one million years old, put an end to any speculation regarding the possibility of the aforementioned precursor existing as far back as 20 million years ago.

The Java remains became the latest benchmark in the evolutionary line which proved (in the minds of the scientific community at least) that tool-making creatures that can be considered to be the transitional type between the more apelike beings and modern humans, were inhabiting the planet much later than the Miocene artefacts suggested. Once the finds of Dubois became firmly established as scientific fact and an integral piece of the evolutionary puzzle, the Thenay flints along with all other evidence of Tertiary humans, was effectively removed from consideration so thoroughly that such evidence has been all but forgotten, filtered out and discarded like so many other reports which oppose orthodox scientific opinion.

Cremo wrote, 'The extensive evidence for the presence of toolmaking hominids in the Tertiary was in fact buried, and the stability of the entire edifice of modern paleoanthropology depends upon it remaining buried.' Continuing he added, 'If even one single piece of evidence for the existence of toolmakers in the Miocene or

Early Pliocene were to be accepted, the whole picture of human evolution, built up so carefully in this century, would disintegrate.'

OLIGOCENE STONE TOOLS

The flints discovered in France were not the only examples of Miocene tools to be reported during the 19th century. Geologist Charles Tardy discovered a flint knife from the exposed surface of a Late Miocene conglomerate ay Aurillac in Southern France around 1870. Similarly, one of Tardy's doubters, another French geologist named J.B. Rames, unearthed more flint tools seven years later, from sediments which lay between layers of volcanic materials dated at about 7-9 million years ago.

Max Verworn of the University of Gottingen in Germany, was not convinced by either of the geologists' finds and took it upon himself to conduct a number of excavations at sites near Aurillac, employing a vigorous method of analysis to assist in his quest to prove whether or not the stone implements being dug up from the Miocene strata were truly manufactured by humans.

Verworn concluded, 'With my own hands, I have personally extracted from the undisturbed strata at Puy de Boudieu many such unquestionable artefacts. That is unshakable proof for the existence of a flintworking being at the end of the Miocene.'

The 'unshakable proof' of which Verworn so adamantly claimed appears to have been shaken out of the scientific journals and no longer constitutes valid evidence for no other reason than it no longer fits the modern concept of human evolution. More proof of a knowledge filter being firmly set in place.

The size of the implements discovered by Max Verworn pointed towards 'a being with a hand of the same size and shape as our own, and therefore a similar body' which would suggest that a being of similar design to ourselves was responsible for the alteration of the stone tools to suit their designated purpose.

Verworn wrote about whom he considered to be the makers of the tools, 'While it is possible that this Tertiary form might possibly have stood closer to the animal ancestors of modern humans than do modern humans themselves, who can say to us that they were not already of the same basic physical character as modern humans, that the development of specifically human features did not extend back into the Late Miocene?' The truth is that evidence exists which extends even further back in antiquity than even the Miocene discoveries on French soil.

A. Rutot was the conservator of the Royal Museum of Natural History in Brussels, and at the beginning of the 20th century he made a number of prominent discoveries regarding anomalous stone tool industries. The majority of his finds were dated to the Early Pleistocene, but in 1907, in sandpits near Boncelles in the Ardennes region of Belgium, Rutot dug up ancient tools from Oligocene layers dating back from 25 to 38 million years ago.

In the *Zeitschrift fur Ethnologie*, Georg Schweinfurth described the tools which Rutot discovered, 'Among them were choppers, anvil stones, knives, scrapers, borers, and throwing stones, all displaying clear signs of intentional work that produced forms exquisitely adapted for use by the human hand . . . the fortunate discoverer had the pleasure to show the sites to 34 Belgian geologists and students of prehistory. They all agreed that there could be no doubt about the position of the finds.'

Boncelles wasn't the only site to have revealed remarkable implements of great antiquity such as the kind unearthed by A. Rutot; other Oligocene human artefacts were also found at Baraque Michel and the cavern at Bay Bonnet. Rutot wrote, 'Now it appears that the notion of the existence of humanity in the Oligocene . . . has been affirmed with such force and precision that one cannot detect the slightest fault.'

To highlight the relatively modern style, Rutot noted that the Boncelles tools around 25 million years ago shared a striking resemblance with Tasmanian workmanship made within the last few centuries (fig. 6).

Among the various types of implement discovered by Rutot (fig. 7) were plain choppers, sharpened choppers, pointed choppers and re-touchers; a tool specifically used on re-sharpening the working edges of the other tools. All of the objects displayed evidence of chipping which made them both sharper for their designated purpose, and easier to hold in the hand. Also part of his collection were scrapers, borers and what appeared to be sling stones which showed traces of repeated impacts, most likely for the purpose of making fire.

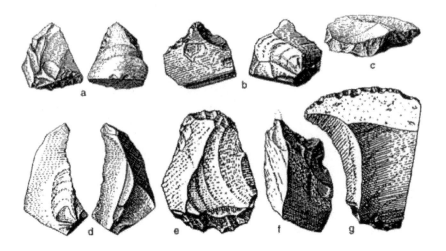

Fig. 6 Implements manufactured in recent historical times by native Tasmanians which Rutot said resemble almost exactly those discovered from the Oligocene period at Boncelles, Belgium (Fig. 7 below).

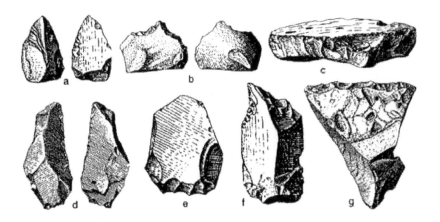

Fig. 7 Stone tools from below the Late Oligocene sands at Boncelles, Belgium which could date back 25 million years. (a) Side scraper, (b) Pointed implement, (c) Anvil, (d) Stone knife, (e) Double end scraper, (f) Awl, (g) End scraper.

On discussing his remarkably ancient finds Rutot concluded, 'We find ourselves confronted with a grave problem – the existence in the Oligocene of beings intelligent enough to manufacture and use definite and variegated types of implements.'[43]

So, why do scientists today ignore the discovery of Oligocene stone tools which prove the existence of intelligent human 'types' possibly as far back as 38 million years? Michael Cremo believes there are two main reasons, 'unfamiliarity with evidence such as Rutot's and unquestioning faith in currently held views on human origin and antiquity.'[44]

BENEATH TABLE MOUNTAIN

On the slopes of the Sierra Nevada Mountains in central California in 1849, hordes of adventurers arrived in their droves once the discovery of gold from within the gravels of the ancient river beds was publicized.

What started out with solitary miners panning for flakes and nuggets of gold soon progressed with the involvement of gold-mining companies, who used more effective large-scale methods to get to the precious metal, some sinking shafts deep into the mountainside, following the gold-bearing gravel deposits whichever direction they led. It was during this process that the miners began uncovering hundreds of stone artefacts and on rare occasions, even human fossils. The state geologist of California, J.D. Whitney, reported the most significant finds to the scientific community.

Whitney believed that the tunnels and deep mine shafts created by the gold hunting companies led down into the auriferous gravels of the Pliocene but modern geologists contend that the strata is much older, dating as far back as the Eocene up to 55 million years ago. Table Mountain in Tuolumne County was one of the sites used for mining gold, and the shafts here had to be sunk beneath thick layers of latite, a basaltic volcanic material, before the gold-bearing gravels could be reached.

Speaking of a remarkable Tuolumne Table Mountain artefact which belonged to Dr. Perez Snell, of Sonoro, California, Whitney wrote,

'This was a stone muller, or some kind of utensil which had apparently been used for grinding.' Dr. Snell had informed Whitney 'that he took it with his own hands from a car-load of 'dirt' coming out from under Table Mountain.' He also presented Whitney with a human jaw that some miners had discovered from gravels beneath the latite layer.

Another piece of a fossil human skull was recovered from the Valentine mine shaft in the same location as a fifteen-inch wide stone mortar found by one of the owners of the mine, Mr. Albert G. Walton. The mortar was found situated in a horizontal passageway leading out from the bottom of a vertical shaft which would suggest that it would be almost impossible for it to have simply fallen from above, despite such claims being bandied around as a viable explanation for the presence of such an anomalous human artefact.

One such person suggesting the mortar must have fallen into the shaft, William J. Sinclair, believed that perhaps the object had entered that particular shaft via connecting tunnels from other mines, but on closer inspection Sinclair had to admit that during his personal visit to the mine in 1902, he was unable to even locate the Valentine shaft. This didn't deter him from dismissing Walton's report however. Regarding Sinclair's unsupported brush-off, Michael Cremo wrote, 'Operating in this manner, one could find good reason to dismiss any paleoanthropological discovery ever made.'

'One could simply refuse to believe the evidence as reported, and put forwards all kinds of vague alternative explanations, without answering legitimate questions about them,' insists Cremo.

One must wonder what fossilised human skulls and stone human artefacts are doing in the gold-bearing gravels of California, in strata dating back between 9 and 55 million years ago. Historians are already struggling to explain who is responsible for the oldest known human tools ever to be found (disregarding the many examples cited in this book) which are considered to be the Oldowan tools dating back 3.3 million years. But these tools, as we covered earlier, are the simplest kind of tool found on Earth, namely the eoliths and Neolithic implements, or stones with minor alteration. Stone mortars are much more refined tools used for grinding and pounding various ingredients into powder, either for pharmaceutical applications or as a food additive.

The most ancient mortars on record stretch back only as far as 37,000 years ago in Late Pleistocene Southeast Asia, which reveals how anomalous the Californian gold mine finds truly are. As is commonly assumed, the earliest occupation of the Americas is still considered to have begun at the end of the last ice age across the Bering land-bridge from Siberia into Alaska approximately 13,000 years ago. New evidence is continually emerging to contradict this theory regarding the Clovis people having been the original human migrants to occupy North America.

Older and older artefacts are being discovered every year which reveal the presence of man much earlier than what has previously been understood to have been the time of arrival for the first human migration into the Americas from the opposite continents, but no ancient artefacts as old as those reviewed here have been accepted as evidence of human existence all the way back to the Eocene.

Science can deal with rewriting timelines to fit the present human evolutionary theory if it is only a matter of stretching them back a few thousand years, tens of thousands at an absolute push, but millions? No wonder then that the data concerning the tools discussed in this chapter has slipped under the radar; it would take a complete rewrite to explain the presence of human bones and stones in Eocene gravels, and I expect that such a revision may not be on the immediate horizon. Another unusual find beneath Table Mountain was made by J.H. Neale who signed the following statement on August 2, 1890, regarding discoveries he had made three years earlier:

'In 1877 Mr. J.H. Neale was superintendent of the Montezuma Tunnel Company, and ran the Montezuma tunnel into the gravel underlying the lava of Table Mountain, Tuolumne County. . . At a distance of between 1400 and 1500 feet from the mouth of the tunnel, or of between 200 and 300 feet beyond the edge of the solid lava, Mr. Neale saw several spear-heads, of some dark rock and nearly one foot in length. On exploring further, he himself found a small mortar three or four inches in diameter and of irregular shape. This was discovered within a foot or two of the spear-heads. He then found a large well-formed pestle, now the property of Dr. R.I. Bromley, and nearby a large and very regular mortar, also at present the property of Dr. Bromley.

Continuing, Neale's affidavit read, 'All of these relics were found . . . close to the bed-rock, perhaps within a foot of it. Mr. Neale declares that it is utterly impossible that these relics can have reached the position in which they were found excepting at the time the gravel was deposited, and before the lava cap formed. There was not the slightest trace of any disturbance of the mass or of any natural fissure into it by which access could have been obtained either there or in the neighborhood.'

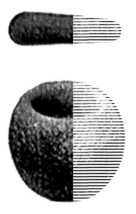

Fig. 8 Mortar and pestle found beneath Table Mountain in strata dating as far back as 55 million years ago.

If the items (Fig. 8) were located where Neale so adamantly declares, in gravel close to the rock, this would place them at an age of between 33-55 million years old, a quite astounding possibility to say the very least. As is always the case with incredible information, one feels inclined to question the integrity of the individuals involved in the discoveries, but despite the items thus far been found by men in the mining trade, it must be noted that any authoritative figure willing to sign an affidavit must at least be totally convinced themselves that what they are saying is legitimate.

Geologist George F. Becker read a paper before the American Geological Society in 1891, in which he was happy to accept the authenticity of Neale's findings; 'Someone may possibly suggest that Mr. Neale's workmen 'planted' the implements, but no one familiar with mining will entertain such a suggestion for a moment. . . The auriferous gravel is hard picking, in large part it requires blasting, and even a very incompetent supervisor could not possibly be deceived in this way. . . In short, there is, in my opinion, no escape from the conclusion that the implements mentioned in Mr. Neale's statement actually occurred near the bottom of the gravels, and that they were deposited where they were found at the same time with the adjoining pebbles and matrix.'

Besides, miners were not the only folk to have unearthed unusual objects beneath Table Mountain; a scientist by the name of Clarence King, a director of the Survey of the Fortieth Parallel who was conducting research at Tuolumne Table Mountain, also discovered a stone pestle at the site. This time it was firmly embedded in a deposit of gold-bearing gravel lying beneath the cap of basalt or latite, and had been exposed by erosion. Again, the location of the implement indicates that it must be over 9 million years old.

Becker commented on this find also by stating, 'Mr. King is perfectly sure this implement was in place and that it formed an original part of the gravels in which he found it. It is difficult to imagine more satisfactory evidence than this of the occurrence of implements in the auriferous, pre-glacial, sub-basaltic gravels.'

The pestle found by King was placed in the collection of the Smithsonian Institution and even the hardest to impress sceptic William H. Holmes was forced to admit that the King pestle 'may not be challenged with impunity.'

As we shall see in later chapters, human artefacts have been discovered that go even further back into antiquity which raise many questions concerning human history on this planet. If the items discussed thus far were the only significant and anomalous finds to have surfaced over the years then one could be forgiven for seeking alternative and more rational explanations for their apparent extreme age, but when there are countless anomalies being unearthed all over the globe then any rational mind must surely consider the possibility that these amazing discoveries may actually be authentic and open up a completely new perspective of man's evolutionary status.

JAVA MAN

This idea of a knowledge filter or scientific bias has revealed its mechanism on plenty of occasions in the field of palaeoanthropology. Granted, science must contain a healthy amount of inherent scepticism to remain objective enough to evaluate data without bias or preconceived notions of what results should be expected, but stray too far and the sceptic destroys the science as much as the overly zealous individuals intent on proving their own theories.

When anomalously ancient human artefacts or skeletons have been unearthed from improbable locations, more often than not the sceptics appear in their droves to dismiss in any way feasible the authenticity of such finds. As we have already seen, any tools or bones found in strata predating the conventional origins of mankind are quickly dismissed by the claims that either the data is wrong, or the objects in question have somehow managed to slip down into the ancient beds from a much more recent sedimentary layer.

One would expect such scepticism surrounding the more anomalous archaeological discoveries which question already firmly entrenched scientific paradigms concerning human evolution and the rise of civilized man. The problem remains however, that the same scepticism does not apply to finds which *do* fit the evolutionary model already set so firmly in place. Consistency in these scientific fields is surely paramount if we are to further our knowledge of human history and put our preconceptions aside in favour of following the evidence.

James B. Griffin, an anthropologist at the University of Michigan, believes that any archaeological site must adhere to certain rules in order to withhold the validity of the area in question. He explained that a proper site must possess 'a clearly identifiable geologic context . . . with no possibility of intrusion or secondary deposition.'

Along with this seemingly obvious necessity, Griffin insisted that any successful location must have been satisfactorily studied by several geologists in order to properly ascertain the age of the site, and of course by also employing the required dating methods on all artefacts found *in situ*.

As a layperson, Griffin's expert advice seems to be what one would hope or even expect, is already the minimal required set protocol for digs of such importance to the whole of humanity. But as Michael Cremo explains, the opposite is often the case.

Concerning Griffin's advisory regulations Cremo wrote, 'By this standard, practically none of the locations where major paleoanthropological discoveries have been made would qualify as genuine sites. For example, most of the African discoveries of *Australopithecus*, *Homo habilis* and *Homo erectus* have occurred not in clearly identifiable geological contexts, but on the surface or in cave deposits, which are notoriously difficult to interpret geologically. Most of the Java *Homo erectus* finds also occurred on the surface, in poorly specified locations.'[45]

With this in mind, Dutchman Eugene Dubois' discovery of *Pithecanthropus erectus* near the Javanese village of Trinlil in 1891 raises many questions. Dubois was fascinated by Darwin's theory of evolution and was only too aware of the lack of fossil evidence that was constantly pointing out by Darwin's retractors. He knew a significant skeletal find was necessary to further his theory of transitional human progress.

Influenced by a painting of a creature commissioned by the German scientist Ernst Haeckel, which showed how a missing link might appear (Haeckel called it *Pithecanthropus* – *pitheko* means ape in Greek and *anthropus* means man), Dubois was intent on someday finding the bones of this ape-man which he adamantly believed must exist somewhere, buried beneath the surface. Haeckel's influence on the Dutch anatomist didn't end there as we shall soon discover.

Whilst excavating on the bank of the Solo River in central Java during the dry season of 1891, a primate tooth was discovered along with many other animal fossil bones. On first inspection, Dubois believed the tooth to have belonged to some extinct giant chimpanzee but ordered his labourers to continue to dig in the same area. And sure enough, just before the onset of the rainy season they uncovered what at first glance appeared to be a turtle shell, which on closer inspection was recognised as a skull cap, most likely from an ape of some kind. At no point did Dubois suspect the fossil to have belonged to a transitional human ancestor, and no mention of such a possibility was inscribed in the published mining bulletin report.

The following season, in August 1892, a fossilised human femur was discovered 45 feet from the site of the skullcap, among a plethora of animal bones belonging to deer, rhinos, hyenas, crocodiles, tigers and extinct elephants. Later another molar was dug up about 10 feet from the skullcap. Assessing the finds, Dubois was convinced that the teeth, skullcap and femur belonged to the same creature, in all likelihood some extinct type of giant chimpanzee. Here is where Ernst Haeckel's influence over Dubois becomes all too apparent.

As Richard Carrington wrote in his 1963 book *A Million Years of Man*, 'Dubois was at first inclined to regard his skull cap and teeth as belonging to a chimpanzee, in spite of the fact that there is no known evidence that this ape or any of its ancestors ever lived in Asia. But on reflection, and after corresponding with the great Ernst Haeckel, Professor of Zoology at the University of Jena, he declared them to belong to a creature which seemed admirably suited to the role of the 'missing link'.'

On hearing from Dubois of his discovery, Haeckel telegraphed this message, 'From the inventor of Pithecanthropus to his happy discoverer!' *Pithecanthropus erectus* became popularised as Java Man, and today he is more commonly referred to as *Homo erectus*.

With so many scientists from all the varying disciplines eager to further Darwin's theory, it seems that they were more than happy to welcome Java Man onboard the evolutionary train, so to speak, with little solid proof of whom the ambiguous relics derived from. It is perfectly clear that both men were resolved to prove the existence of an intermediary human type, so much so that Haeckel actually thought up a suitable name for the being before the search had actually begun!

According to Cremo, 'Haeckel had a history of overstating physiological evidence to support the doctrine of evolution', as an academic court at the University of Jena where he worked once found him 'guilty of falsifying drawings of embryos of various animals in order to demonstrate his particular view of the origin of species.' Not the behaviour one would expect from a respected professor.

In 1894, Dubois published his complete report in which he wrote, '*Pithecanthropus* is the transitional form which, in accordance with the doctrine of evolution, must have existed between man and the anthropoids.'

It is particularly interesting to note the wording here, where he insists that it 'must have existed' as if declaring his whole discovery to be essentially what it is, guesswork . . . and speculative guesswork at that. Today, if a scientist has reached the stage where he or she is writing up the final report, one would expect a better explanation to be 'existed' rather than 'must have existed'. Maybe one is being rather pedantic here, but in the light of certain 'scientific' attitudes on show, one can surely understand the heightening frustrations of the researcher.

To be fair, despite Haeckel's obvious influence, Dubois found that the volume of the skull was in the range of 800-1000 cubic centimetres, which in comparison with modern apes that average 500 and modern human skulls averaging 1400 cubic centimetres, does put the Trinlil skullcap somewhere between the two.

But as Cremo highlights, 'To Dubois, this indicated an evolutionary relationship. But logically speaking, one could have creatures with different sizes of brains without having to posit an evolutionary progression from smaller to larger.' As has been proven already, many mammals from the Pleistocene were much larger in form than their modern ancestors, which could explain the presence of a fossilised primate skullcap from a period of history when those primates were much larger than today.

Let us not forget also that the femur Dubois found was a whole 45 feet away from the skullcap amidst stratum containing an enormous array of other animal bones. It was the presence of this humanlike femur which he associated with the apelike skull, and by putting two and two together, he assumed that the owner of the skull fragment must have been able to walk upright, hence the species designation *erectus*. Again, 'assumptions' are by no means adequate methodologies to employ scientifically.

In the documentary *Mysterious Origins of Man*, Dr. Richard Thompson remarked on the assumptive manner in which Dubois assimilated the two findings into one upright creature by stating, 'The important point to make about the Java man discovery is that it's based on a speculative leap in which two pieces of evidence are put together in a way that's not really warranted.'

On his return to Europe, Java Man received mixed reviews from Dubois' contemporaries, and in December of 1895 experts gathered from around the world to pass judgement on his *Pithecanthropus* remains, at the Berlin Society for Anthropology, Ethnology and Prehistory. Among his dissenters were the president of the Society, Dr. Virchow, (who vehemently refused to chair the meeting) and the Swiss anatomist J. Kollmann. Both were convinced that the skullcap belonged to a primate and not a human ancestor.

Virchow claimed that in his opinion the femur was fully human and went on to assert, 'The skull has a deep suture between the low vault and the upper edge of the orbits. Such a suture is found only in apes, not in man. Thus the skull must belong to an ape. In my opinion this creature was an animal, a giant gibbon, in fact. The thigh-bone has not the slightest connection with the skull.'

So, even during the period when the discovery was still new it was surrounded in controversy, and it is apparent that despite the many evolutionist advocates lauding Java Man as the find of the century – evidence of a missing link which could now put Darwin's hypothesis beyond doubt – there were many who felt that Dubois had jumped the gun somewhat, and arrived at a preconceived conclusion which best befitted the Darwinist concept.

Kollmann, like Virchow, was so adamant that what Dubois had unearthed was nothing more than an ape skull alongside a non-related modern human bone that he pushed *Pithecanthropus* to a side branch, excluding him from the human ancestry line altogether, believing that the creature must have died out long before human evolution even began.

Dr. Franz Weidenrich wrote, 'This is a striking example of the extent to which palaeontological facts were disregarded and replaced with purely speculative constructions when evolution of man was the topic and when facts did not agree with preconceived ideas.'[46]

This is a sentiment shared by Michael Cremo, who also stated that 'It is the unquestioned belief that humans did in fact evolve from apelike ancestors that has determined what evidence shall be included and how it should be determined'. Should Cremo and Weidenrich's evaluations prove legitimate then it is certainly a very sad state of affairs indeed. If science can be so easily swayed towards a conclusion which meets hopes and expectations, then what value does science hold if true objectivity is denied?

In a eulogy following the death of Dubois in 1940, Arthur Keith described him as 'an idealist, his ideas being so firmly held that his mind tended to bend facts rather than alter his ideas to fit them.' And despite the fact that more and more people eventually came to the conclusion that the Trinlil skullcap was from a large ape and the thighbone from a man, Java Man was prominently displayed at the Museum of Natural History in New York until 1984.

Another fascinating aspect of the Java finds is that later discoveries in China and Africa show *Homo erectus* femurs to be very different from the femurs discovered in Trinlil. Further analysis of the Java femurs reveals that they are in fact 'indistinguishable from those of modern humans and distinct from those of *Homo erectus*.'[47] This information leads us to the distinct possibility that anatomically modern humans co-existed *alongside* more ape-man-like creatures during the early Middle Pleistocene in Java.

If one considers that Louis Leakey discovered the skeletal remains and tools of anatomically modern humans in Western Kenya in 1932, which were dated to at least two million years old, it suggests that modern human types existed contemporaneously with Java Man and

Beijing Man (also classified *Homo erectus*) meaning that neither could be direct human ancestors.

It is interesting to note how many double standards are in play when it comes to dating human fossils; how anomalously old bones are subjected to much stricter and rigorous examination than scientifically accepted finds. Dubois didn't find any of the *Homo erectus* fossils himself, it was the labourers he had employed who dug them out and brought them to him. No protocols were set in place to establish the exact location of the bones so dating them accurately was nigh on impossible.

As M. H. Day and T. I. Molleson reported in 1973, 'If the rigorous criteria that are demanded in modern excavations were applied to all the Trinlil material subsequent to the calotte and Femur I, it would all be rejected as of doubtful provenance and unknown stratigraphy.'

Relating to other archaeological finds in Java, Cremo concurred with Day and Molleson stating that, 'It is obvious that if one were to apply Boman's extreme scepticism across the board one could raise suspicions of fraud about almost every paleoanthropological discovery ever made.'

And as we shall see in the following section, one particular scientist was so intent on furthering his career and adding to the already dubious pile of bones responsible for the modern understanding of human evolution from simian ancestors, that he faked his results.

PILTDOWN MAN HOAX

Following the discovery of Java Man in the 1890s, scientists were chomping at the bit to discover the next missing link to fill the void in the evolutionary line between ancient apelike hominids and modern *Homo sapiens*. It was during this period of enthusiasm and anticipation that Charles Dawson discovered a humanlike skull besides an apelike jaw which became known as Piltdown Man.

We have already seen how Eugene Dubois' hunt for a missing evolutionary piece led to the unlikely discovery of Java Man, albeit a dubious find, but nevertheless, that clamour for such a find led to a notable scientific discovery through sheer will more than skill. In

Dawson's case his enthusiasm and fervour led him to a discovery which would later be proved as fraudulent, though the man responsible for attempting to deceive science is still to be held culpable.

Britain had to sit and watch as incredible fossil remains of our human ancestors were being discovered in Germany and France, leaving British scientists with a desperate urge to unearth evidence of ancient human activity on home soil. The discovery of Piltdown Man answered their prayers, at least for a while, as finally England could lay claim to having been the birthplace of mankind.

It was sometime around 1908, near Piltdown, Sussex in England, where lawyer and amateur anthropologist Dawson was informed by some local workman of a pit being dug on a nearby estate which had been yielding flints. On subsequent visits to the Piltdown pit, Dawson was handed a small portion of 'an unusually thick parietal bone' by a worker but further investigation revealed nothing. It wasn't until 1911 when Dawson noticed 'another and larger piece belonging to the frontal region of the same skull', as he wrote in 1913.

On Valentine's Day of 1912, Dawson contacted Sir Arthur Smith Woodward who worked at what is now the Natural History Museum, London. That summer, Woodward joined Dawson in excavating further at the Piltdown site where they found more fragments of human skull amongst the fossilised remains of extinct British animals that included rhinos and elephants. Alongside these bones they also discovered primitive stone tools, some comparable to eoliths, others more advanced, and also the most controversial fossil which they discovered – an apelike mandible (jawbone).

Dawson and Woodward believed the Piltdown fossils were from the Early Pleistocene, placing them somewhere near to one million years old, whilst the Eolithic stone implements were likely from an earlier Pliocene formation. It was from the skull fragments, which were always deemed morphologically humanlike, and the more apelike jaw, that Woodward constructed a skull which seemed to fit the evolutionary model and represent how the 'missing link' was expected to appear; with a brain the same size as ours but with a more robust and apelike jaw-line, hence Piltdown Man was born.

Charles Dawson reached celebrity status as the find was officially named *Eoanthropus dawsoni* meaning 'Dawson's dawn man', but his unexpected death in 1916 meant that his enjoyment of fame was very short-lived.

On the day of a Geological Society meeting in London, on December 18, 1912, sensational headlines ran around the world, of news that the amazing new member of our human lineage having being discovered in England. The discovery was heralded as a breakthrough of scientific discovery as *The New York Times* wrote later in 1931, 'Piltdown Man Marks Dawn of Human Race'.

Other headlines highlighted the fact that finally Darwin's theory had been realised, and 'the oldest Englishman' in history revealed that human types existed as far back as one million years ago in Britain, discounting the previous claims that mankind only migrated to Europe around 30,000 years ago.

However, on 21 November 1953, Piltdown Man was dramatically exposed as a deliberate hoax by a team of British scientists; the skull fragments were revealed to have been much older than the mandible and the teeth, thus proving that they could not have possibly have belonged to the same creature. Also, the jaw was proved to have belonged to an orangutan and not some ancient species of ape-man.

Employing new dating techniques, the results of nitrogen and fluorine tests showed that despite the difference in age between the

DARWIN THEORY IS PROVED TRUE

English Scientists Say the Skull Found in Sussex Establishes Human Descent from Apes.

THOUGHT TO BE A WOMAN'S

Bones Illustrate a Stage of Evolution Which Has Only Been Imagined Before.

CREATURE COULD NOT TALK

Probably Lived at a Time When Other Species of Humans Had Developed Further Elsewhere.

jaw and skull fragments, the skull at least seemed native to the Piltdown Pleistocene gravels in which they were discovered *in situ*. However, further analysis revealed that the pieces of skull appeared to have been deliberately stained to match the colour of the gravels in which they were found.

Frank Spencer, a professor of anthropology at Queens College of the City University of New York, said that the evidence 'had been tailored to withstand scientific scrutiny and thereby promote a particular interpretation of the human fossil record.'

Kenneth P. Oakley of the British Museum, the man who played a prominent role in the Piltdown exposé wrote, 'The Trinlil [Java man] material was tantalizingly incomplete, and for many scientists it was inadequate as confirmation of Darwin's view of human evolution. I have sometimes wondered whether it was a misguided impatience for the discovery of a more acceptable 'missing link' that formed one of the tangled skein of motives behind the Piltdown Forgery.'

Bearing in mind that the Piltdown fossils had already been accepted by scientists as evidence of human ancestry only forty years previously, and now they were being subjected to much more rigorous testing then before in order to prove their fraudulence; it becomes apparent that the dating methods were employed in such a way until a satisfactory conclusion was reached.

As Cremo explains, 'Regarding the two fluorine tests by Oakley, we see that the first indicated both the skull and jaw were of the same age whereas the second indicated they were different ages. It was stated that the second set of tests made use of new techniques – that happened to give a desired result. This sort of thing occurs quite often in paleoanthropology – researchers run and rerun tests, or refine their methods, until an acceptable result is achieved. Then they stop. In such cases, it seems the test is calibrated against a theoretical expectation.'

Theories concerning the identity of the Piltdown culprit continue to this day, ranging from the amateur Dawson to the famous author of Sherlock Holmes, Sir Arthur Conan Doyle who was a member of the same archaeological society as Dawson, but was on a mission to further the cause of spiritualism of which he was becoming more involved.

Others believe the hoax was instigated by Woodward, as he was much more capable of fooling the scientists than the amateur Dawson, whilst some have suggested that it could have been the handiwork of Martin Hinton, a volunteer at the Museum when Piltdown was discovered, as he was known to have had a disagreement with Woodward over payment for his work.

Due to the complexities of the hoax however, it has proven somewhat problematic proving which single suspect is responsible for one of the greatest scientific hoaxes of all time, and maybe it isn't important who decided to try and fool the scientific authorities but more about why they felt compelled to even attempt such a trick. The sheer importance given to the search for our human ancestors is so great that acts such as the fraud exposed in the Piltdown case show what depths some men will go to in their pursuit of fame and notoriety.

Despite the fact that it was exposed as a hoax, hundreds of people obtained their PhD's by writing their theses on the Piltdown Man. Needless to say that after it was exposed nobody took back their PhDs, and who knows how many people learnt information from those particular essays?

'And it may seem harmless to you now that it's been exposed. But, did you know that over 500 people obtained their PhDs by writing their thesis on "the Piltdown Man"? I dare say no one took back those PhDs after it was exposed, and those people taught hundreds of thousands of people.'[48]

This being a seemingly isolated case doesn't exactly set alarm bells ringing, but the real mystery in the Piltdown hoax lies in the details. It doesn't appear to have been a simple case of one man faking the age of some bones for fame and fortune but a much more elaborate and schematic undertaking seems to have occurred. And as Cremo highlights, whilst attempting to discredit the legitimacy of the fossilised bones, some form of bias could possibly have been responsible for reaching the appropriate conclusions.

The skull for example was found in the Pleistocene layers of the pit, which under any normal circumstances would have put the human skull fragments at an already anomalously old age of up to a million years old. This simple fact seems to have been sidestepped somehow, and history tells us that the skull was as recent as 500 years old, and the ape mandible even younger.

In proving the relics to have been faked, they also seem to have gone a step further and completely discredited them altogether. If one delves a little deeper into this story, a process which we do not have the time to cover in this book, one will see that there are many inconsistencies involved in the Piltdown case which suggest that the human artefacts discovered in Sussex back in 1908 may well prove to have been much older than they have been catalogued as – another mystery which will fade away with the passing of time, one which could well have changed the way we understand human history, and improved our knowledge of our true human lineage.

'The impact of Piltdown remains, therefore, damaging. But incidents of this sort appear to be rare, given our present knowledge. There is, however, another more insidious and pervasive kind of cheating – the routine editing and reclassifying of data according to rigid theoretical preconceptions.'[49]

ANOMALOUS HUMAN SKELETONS

If one researches in greater depth, there are many reported human skeletal finds which are in discordance with current evolutionary beliefs. One intriguing report surfaced in an American journal called *The Geologist* dated December, 1862.

'In Macoupin County, Illinois, the bones of a man were recently found on a coal-bed capped with two feet of slate rock, ninety feet below the surface of the earth. . . The bones, when found, were covered with a crust or coating of hard glossy matter, as black as coal itself, but when scraped away left the bones white and natural.'

The coal in which the remains were found have been dated at between 320 and 286 million years old, which despite a lack of supporting evidence and little information on the discovery is certainly worthy of inclusion here.

A better documented account of an anomalous find is of a human jaw discovered at Foxhall, England, in 1855 which was dug out of a quarry at a level of sixteen foot under ground level, dating the specimen to at least 2.5 million years old. American physician Robert H. Collyer described the Foxhall jaw as 'the oldest relic of human existence'. The problem with this particular fossil was its modern appearance. A more apelike looking mandible would have been more acceptable despite its great antiquity, but many dissenters disbelieved the authenticity of the bone 'probably because the shape of the jaw was not primitive', according to palaeontologist Henry Fairfield Osborn.

Fig. 9 This modern human skull found in Buenos Aires could be 1.5 million years old.

A fully modern human skull (Fig. 9) was found in Buenos Aires, Argentina, in an Early Pliocene formation, revealing the presence of modern humans in South America between 1 and 1.5 million years ago. But once more, the modern appearance of the skull doesn't fit with conventional thinking on human origins so was discounted on these grounds alone. Here we see a clear example of dating by morphology, and a distinct disregard of all other data, no matter how credible. The thinking is simple; if it looks modern – it must be modern. No modern humans could possibly have existed that far back in time so it must be ruled out.

This approach employs illogical thinking if one considers that the skull was found in a Pre-Ensenadean stratum, which according to present geological calculations dates back up to 1.5 million years. The scientific data, as with a plethora of cases worldwide, does not match the final analogy, and instead of pursuing the matter further until a satisfactory scientific conclusion is arrived upon, the discovery has slipped unsurprisingly into anonymity.

In a quarry on the Avenue de Clichy, Paris, parts of a human skull were discovered along with a femur, tibia and some foot bones by Eugene Bertrand in 1868. The layer in which the Clichy skeleton was dug out from would make the fossils approximately 330,000 years old.

It wasn't until Neanderthals became accepted as the Pleistocene ancestors of modern humans that French anthropologists were forced to drop the Clichy skeleton from the human evolutionary line, as a modern type of human could not predate their allegedly older Neanderthal relatives. Neanderthals are conventionally understood to have existed from 30,000 to 150,000 years ago, and the Clichy skeleton which dated at over 300,000 years ago was simply not an acceptable find despite the evidence to support its authenticity.

In 1911, another anatomically modern human skeleton was discovered beneath a layer of glacial boulder clay near the town of Ipswich, in England, by J. Reid Moir. Found at a depth of about 4.5 feet between a layer of clay and glacial sands, the skeleton could be as much as 400,000 years old.

Naturally, the modern appearance of the skeleton was the cause of great opposition, but if the find had of been Neanderthal-like, there would have been no questions raised over its position in the glacial sediments. As Scottish anatomist and anthropologist, Sir Arthur Keith explained, 'Under the presumption that the modern type of man is also modern in origin, a degree of high antiquity is denied to such specimens.'[50]

The deposits in which the Ipswich skeleton was excavated from were recorded by the British Geological Survey as an intact layer of glacial boulder clay which had been laid down between the onset of the Anglian glaciation and the Hoxnian glaciations, a period that stretched between 330,000 and 400,000 years ago. Some authorities have even put the beginning of the Mindel glaciation (which is equivalent to that of the Anglian) at around 600,000 years ago, which could potentially allow the Ipswich skeleton to also date back that far.

So why does its modern appearance override the other factors? It doesn't seem to be a very scientific approach to disregard an archaeological find simply because it does not conform to contemporary evolutionary theses. The examples cited in this book are only a small selection which has been rescued from obscurity by vigilant researchers, but how many more cases have suffered similar dismissal due to their anomalistic circumstances?

If science continues to sweep unusual discoveries under the carpet, how are we supposed to progress as a species if we are intent on denying data which contradicts our rigid paradigms? It would appear that the knowledge filter has been in place for some time, much to the detriment of humankind and our quest to illuminate our foggy, mysterious ancient past.

Situated in the southern slopes of the Alps, at Castenedolo, six miles southeast of Brescia, lay a low hill called the Colle de Vento, where millions of years ago during the Pliocene period, layers of molluscs and coral were deposited by a warm sea washing in.

In 1860, Professor Giuseppe Ragazzoni travelled to Castenedolo to gather fossil shells in the Pliocene strata exposed in a pit at the base of the Colle de Vento. Reporting on his finds there Ragazzoni wrote, 'Searching along the bank of coral for shells, there came into my hand the top portion of a cranium, completely filled with pieces of coral cemented with blue-green clay characteristics of that formation. Astonished, I continued the search, and in addition to the top portion of the cranium I found other bones of the thorax and limbs, which quite apparently belonged to an individual of the human species.'[51]

Once more, negative reactions ensued by both geologists and scientists who were unwilling to accept the Pliocene age offered by Ragazzoni for the skeletal remains. It was explained away by an insistence that the bones, due to their clearly modern characteristics, must have come from a recent burial and somehow or other found themselves among the Pliocene strata. If in doubt, simply explain it away with logical thinking, even if you ignore the facts within plain sight and filter out the parts which do not fit.

Ragazzoni was understandably not pleased with the reception he received and the disregard given to his legitimate discovery of an anomalously ancient human skeleton, so he kept his eye on the site where he had found the relics once the land was sold to Carlo Germani in 1875, (on the advice of Ragazzoni, who had advised that the phosphate-rich clay could be sold to farmers as fertiliser).

Many more discoveries followed from 1879, as Germani kept his word and informed the professor immediately upon finding more bones in the pit. Jaw fragments, teeth, backbone, ribs, arms, legs and feet were all dug out of the Pliocene formation which modern geologists have placed at around 3-4 million years old.

'All of them were completely covered with and penetrated by the clay and small fragments of coral and shells, which removed any suspicion that the bones were those of persons buried in graves, and on the contrary confirmed the fact of their transport by the waves of the sea', said Ragazzoni.

And on February 16, 1880, Germani informed Ragazzoni that a complete skeleton had been discovered, enveloped in a mass of blue-green clay, remains which turned out to be that of an anatomically modern human female.

'The complete skeleton was found in the middle of the layer of blue clay. . . The stratum of the blue clay, which is over 1 metre thick, has preserved its uniform stratification, and does not show any sign of disturbance' wrote Ragazzoni, adding, 'The skeleton was very likely deposited in a kind of marine mud and not buried at a later time.'

After personally examining the Castenedolo skeletons at the Technical Institute of Brescia in 1883, Professor Giuseppe Sergi, an anatomist from the University of Rome, was convinced that they represented the remains of humans who had lived during the Pliocene period of the Tertiary.

Writing of his disdain towards the naysayers within the scientific community Sergi commented, 'The tendency to reject, by reason of theoretical preconceptions, any discoveries that can demonstrate a human presence in the Tertiary is, I believe, a kind of scientific prejudice. Natural science should be stripped of this prejudice.'[52]

Unfortunately, this prejudice which continues to this day, shows no signs of abating, as Professor Sergi recognised back in the 19th century, 'By means of a despotic scientific prejudice, call it what you will, every discovery of human remains in the Pliocene has been discredited.'

Regarding the Laetoli footprints which are commonly regarded as having belonged to *Australopithecus afarensis*, Mary Leakey wrote, 'At least 3,600,000 years ago, in Pliocene times, what I believe to be man's direct ancestor walked fully upright with a bipedal, free-striding gait. . . the form of his foot was exactly the same as ours.'

Again, as we discussed at the onset of this chapter, why is it that if we find modern skeletons and modern footprints, despite the common consensus insisting that australopithecines had apelike feet, can we not accept the possibility at least, that modern humans are much older than we currently understand? Is it not possible that what we regard as our apelike ancestors could in fact belong to another type of creature altogether since evidence reveals that we lived contemporaneously and not after these beings walked the earth?

'An abundance of facts suggests that beings quite like ourselves have been around as far back as we care to look – in the Pliocene, Miocene, Oligocene, Eocene, and beyond. Remains of apes and apelike men are also found throughout the same expanse of time. So perhaps all kinds of hominids have coexisted throughout history. If one considers all the available evidence, that is the clearest picture that emerges.'[53]

What appears to have occurred is the humanisation of some of the key skeletal finds which have contributed greatly towards cementing the notion of man's lineal progression from apelike ancestors. *Australopithecus afarensis*, discovered in Hadar, Ethiopia in 1974 by Donald Johanson and Tom Gray became humanised the day she was named 'Lucy'.

With a skull which 'looked very much like a small female gorilla', according to Johanson himself, Lucy is much more apelike than she has been portrayed to the public, and just like *Homo habilis* she has been misrepresented to fit the evolutionary model.

'Even if one believes Lucy could have evolved into a human being, one still has to admit that her anatomical features appear to have been misrepresented for propaganda purposes', stated Cremo.

The status of *Australopithecus*, *Homo habilis* and *Homo erectus* as human ancestors is also extremely questionable despite being widely accepted as integral pieces of human history. *Australopithecus africanus* – the southern ape of Africa, whose skeletal remains were discovered in 1924 in a limestone quarry at Buxton near a town called Taung, in South Africa, was estimated to be around one million years old by Dr. Raymond Dart who was responsible for naming it.

What Dart described as being 'of importance because it exhibits an extinct race of apes intermediate between living anthropoids and man' has been accepted into the human lineage in conventional text books, but not everyone is in agreement that the specimen belongs there.

Speaking of the Taung skull which brought Dart much fame, Grafton Elliot Smith declared, 'the posture and poise of the head, the shape of the jaws, and many details of the nose, face and cranium upon which he relied for proof of his contention that *Australopithecus* was nearly akin to man, were essentially identical with the conditions met in the infant gorilla and chimpanzee.'

Regarding the lack of human characteristics inherent in the australopithecines, Charles E. Oxnard came to the conclusion that 'it is rather unlikely that any of the Australopithecines . . . can have any direct phylogenetic link with the genus *Homo*.'

And Pat Shipman stated, 'We could assert that we have no evidence whatsoever of where *Homo* arises from and remove all members of the genus *Australopithecus* from the hominid family.'

But despite evidence positing the need to attribute a more anthropoid genealogy to our alleged ancestors, 'The voices of authority in paleoanthropology and the scientific community in general have managed to keep the humanlike view of *Australopithecus* intact', explains Cremo. 'The extensive and well-documented evidence contradicting this favoured view remains confined to the pages of professional journals, where it has little or no influence on the public in general, even the educated public.'

In 1960, Jonathan Leakey, the son of Louis and Mary, discovered *Homo habilis* or type specimen OH 7, at Olduvai Gorge in Tanzania. Nicknamed 'Jonny's child', *Homo habilis* (meaning 'handy man') was believed to be the first true human because of his larger skull capacity denoting a larger brain, and was therefore considered to have been the most likely candidate responsible for the thousands of tools found at Olduvai Gorge according to Louis Leakey and his team.

With a skull larger than even the biggest australopithecine, but smaller than the smallest *Homo erectus*, Leakey theorised that as *Homo habilis* was contemporary with the early australopithecines, living between 2.4 and 1.4 million years ago, that *Australopithecus* could not have belonged in the direct line of human ancestry. And as *Homo erectus* was believed to be a descendant of *Australopithecus*, then *Homo erectus* would also have to be removed from the human lineage.

This idea led Louis Leakey to speculate that the Neanderthals were probably the result of crossbreeding between *Homo erectus* and *Homo sapiens*, but most palaeoanthropologists still favour a progression from australopithecines to *Homo habilis*, *Homo erectus*, and early *Homo sapiens*, before the eventual appearance of both Neanderthals and modern humans.

Homo habilis has always been portrayed as very humanlike, with clear ancestral lineage; however, contradictory fossil evidence reveals that related discoveries could well have been derived from a mixture of skeletal remains belonging to *Australopithecus* and *Homo erectus*, and anatomically modern humans. It is the culmination of bones found over a number of years at different sites which have been reconstructed to create the concept which is *Homo habilis*.

This amalgamation of parts has confused matters to such a degree that what was once described as very human-like was later characterised as quite apelike. This seems to be a constant theme, the battle between different scientists on whether certain skeletal remains or footprints belonged to creatures closer to apes or beings more like us.

Cremo explains, 'This demonstrates once more an important characteristic of paleoanthropological evidence – it is often subject to multiple, contradictory interpretations. Partisan considerations often determine which view prevails at any given point in time.'

Oxnard summarised his research by stating, 'The various australopithecine fossils are usually quite different from both man and the African apes. . . Viewed as a genus, they are a mosaic of features unique to themselves and features bearing some resemblance to those of the orangutan. If these estimates are true then the possibility that any of the australopithecines is a direct part of human ancestry recedes.'

So, there is plenty of food for thought here concerning the standard views of human evolution; enough to suggest that should *all* of the anomalous finds have been properly considered and included alongside the popular and accepted discoveries of what have been deemed our ancient ancestors, we may well be rewriting human history to accommodate them all.

We have also seen how easy it is to manipulate data to fit an already well established paradigm and likewise how some information is simply quietly denied or ignored.

Graham Hancock expressed his thoughts on this negative aspect of the profession by stating that 'the dead hand of orthodox archaeology may once again have prevailed, in what appears to be a deliberate strategy to prevent us from learning the truth about our past.'

The following chapter focuses on the myth surrounding Bigfoot and the other hominids which some claim to have witnessed in the remote areas of our planet.

If, as we have discussed, anatomically modern humans existed much further back in time than the current theorem allows, and the representatives portrayed as belonging to the human family prove to be nonrelated but were contemporaries of our true ancestors, then who, if anyone *has* descended from those apelike beings?

Is it possible that a correlation can be made between the mysterious sightings of hairy hominids still reported to the present day, and the creatures from the past which science has insisted so vehemently as being part of our genealogical heritage?

As Cremo suggests, 'wildmen may represent surviving representatives of the Neanderthals or *Homo erectus*. If there is uncertainty about what kinds of hominids may be around today, how can we be so sure about what kinds of hominids may or may not have been around in the distant past?'

Chapter Three

LIVING HOMINIDS

For those who believe, no proof is necessary. For those who don't believe, no proof is possible.

Stuart Chase

EARLY WRITTEN REFERENCES OF A CREATURE called Bei-Shung existed in many ancient Chinese manuscripts. This bamboo-shoot-eating "white-bear" was described as being black-*and*-white and lived high up in the rugged mountain ranges of the Sichuan Province in China.

Bei-Shung was considered to be nothing more than an Oriental myth by Western authorities, a fanciful creation invented by the Chinese which belonged firmly within the realms of folklore. It was a well established fact that bears were carnivores not vegetarians, and as for the black-and-white colouring, this was clearly an amusing result of imaginative expression on the native's behalf.

Following 2,000 years of unaccepted reports, on 11 March 1869, French missionary and naturalist, Father Armand David travelled to Baoxing County in west-central Sichuan Province and witnessed for the very first time, the actual full skin of the legendary Bei-Shung, hanging on a wall in a village elder's home.

This incredible discovery led Father David to the reported habitat of this amazing creature in search of a living specimen, and after twelve days the locals he had employed to hunt the bear returned successfully from the mountains with a captive Bei-Shung.

The captured bear was so extremely confused and agitated that it started beating itself to death during its transportation to France and had to be euthanized on humanitarian grounds. As devastated as David was, he knew that he still had physical proof of Bei-Shung's existence, which would eventually lead to more successful live captures in the future, so he forwarded the preserved remains of his astounding find to the Paris Museum. Naturally, Bei-Shung was a worldwide sensation, a legendary myth come to life.

Thirty-one years after Father David's original discovery, all of the museums which had financed expeditions to find and capture the allusive creature in the mountainous regions of the province roughly the size of Italy, finally decided to call it a day due to their lack of success.

It wasn't until 1910 that Bei-Shung was renamed 'giant panda' by the Western media and as the only physical evidence of its existence was David's stuffed specimen, the absence of any follow-up sighting was enough to convince the majority of experts that the giant panda had in all likelihood become extinct.

In 1929, the scientist's assertions were eventually corrected sixty years after the West first caught their first glimpse of the legend, when Theodore Roosevelt's two sons, Kermit and Theodore Jr. spotted a panda during a hunt in Sichuan and killed the helpless creature, resurrecting the giant panda once more from mythological obscurity.

Finally, in 1937, a remarkable lady named Ruth Harkness led an expedition which captured a live panda and successfully returned it to Brookfield Zoo in Chicago, USA. She named it Su Lin. Following this success, five more giant pandas were brought to London in 1938, but with the onset of WWII, the fifty years following the London arrivals brought no more attention to the animals and the West continued to know very little about the once mythical Bei-Shung.

The story of the panda's rise from Chinese folklore to popular tourist attraction illustrates perfectly how easily such large and allusive creatures can remain undiscovered for so long. Only after sixty-nine years of searching and wondering did somebody from the West finally succeed in bringing a living panda onto western shores.

The discovery of the once mythical panda acts as a reminder that a lack of physical evidence alone is not always enough to discount the existence of something that has proved difficult to authenticate, and the giant panda is not the only mythical beast to jump from the pages of folklore tradition into modern encyclopaedias, this scenario also befits the gorilla, giraffe and giant squid to name but a few.

The gorilla, also once considered nothing but a myth, at a time when it was still unknown to science, was described by British explorer Andrew Battel in 1625 as a 'monster' which fed on fruit and slept in trees.

Batell described the beast, known locally as a Pongo, claiming that it was 'in all proportions like a man, except for the legs, which have no calves, but are of gigantic size. Their faces, hands and ears are without hair; their bodies are covered, but not very thick, with hair of a dunnish colour. When they walk on the ground it is upright, with their hands on the nape of the neck . . . they cannot speak, nor have they any understanding beyond instinct.'

It wasn't until 1847 that physician Thomas Savage managed to obtain a gorilla skull and several other bones whilst in Liberia, publishing the first formal description of the great ape.

Regarding the beast's larger cousin, the mountain gorilla; he remained a myth until 1902. As anthropologist and author Myra Shackley contends, 'It can be said, with some truth, that yesterday's myths are today's scientific discoveries, and this has certainly been the case with the mountain gorilla, whose existence was dismissed in the 19th century as improbable.'[54]

As for the giant squid, most likely the inspiration behind the classic monstrous Kraken myth, it was only photographed for the first time in its natural habitat as recently as 2004. All these creatures which were once considered to be fictitious highlight the fact that not all myths are nonsense whilst raising the possibility that many other unknown animals may well exist in the numerous scarcely populated regions of the planet.

As this book aims to authenticate some of the world's myths and legends to reveal the truth behind these mysteries, it wouldn't be complete without a proper study of one of the only ongoing mysteries which continues to confound people to this day, the legend of Bigfoot.

This section deals not only with the North American creature also referred to as Sasquatch, but also his Asian counterpart living in the Himalayas – the Yeti, as well as two other species of hairy hominids reportedly co-habiting our planet, the Almas or Kaptars of eastern Europe and the smaller African Agogwes. But let us first familiarise ourselves with the most famous of them all, the beast they call Bigfoot.

THE LEGEND OF BIGFOOT

As is always the case with fringe subjects such as the many covered throughout this book, the research commonly leads you into a minefield of misinformation, hearsay and oftentimes just pure fantasy. It is always sensible to step with caution before contributing more nonsense into the already overflowing ether, encapsulated by the very presence of the internet.

Thousands of eyewitness reports of giant bipedal hominids, commonly emanating from the montane forests of the western United States and Canada, have been reported throughout the twentieth century. Hundreds of large humanoid footprints have been discovered, many also photographed and preserved as plaster casts for evidence. The legitimacy of the eyewitness accounts will always be impossible to verify but physical proof alone in the form of footprints surely warrants further scientific analysis. We shall take an overview of some of the more prominent cases throughout this chapter.

When looking for the earliest recorded accounts of Bigfoot or Sasquatch, one will no doubt stumble upon the tale of Norseman Leif Ericson landing in the New World in 986 AD. His tale of witnessing "huge hairy men" which they allegedly referred to as 'Skellring', would make a fitting introduction to the allusive creature, but closer inspection exposes this story as a completely misinterpreted version of events which appears to have its roots in Peter Byrne's *The Search for Bigfoot: Monster, Myth or Man?*

The earliest authentic references to Bigfoot are most likely Native American Indian in origin. Amongst many of the northern tribes, the existence of this huge hairy hominoid is accepted as reality not rejected as a mythical creation. As Henry James Franzoni III wrote, 'I have never heard anyone from a North-western tribe suggest that Bigfoot is anything other than a physical being, living in the same physical conditions as humans and other animals. He eats, he sleeps, he cares for his family members.'[55]

The western Sioux or Lakota tribe, call Bigfoot 'Chiye-tanka', 'chiye' meaning 'elder brother' and 'tanka' means 'great' or 'big'. In English however, the Sioux usually refer to him as 'the big man'. As far back as 1784, the *London Times* newspaper reported that a 'huge, manlike, hair-covered' creature had been captured by Indians at a place called Lake of the Woods in Manitoba.

On Saturday May 25, 1957, John W. Burns, a onetime Chehalis Indian Reserve schoolteacher-Government Indian Agent, told *The Vancouver Sun* newspaper that he 'regrets that these harmless people of the wilderness are to be hunted with dogs as if they were criminals and, if captured, exposed to the gaping and gaze of the curious.' Continuing he said, 'they have been referred to as monsters. But they have committed no monstrous acts.' Burns claims that he borrowed the word 'Sasquatch' meaning "hairy giant", from the Chehalis Indians which would later become the popularised term alongside 'Bigfoot'.

THE JERRY CREW CASTS

One year later in 1958, American newspapers printed what is generally accepted as the first nationwide news report of a Sasquatch-related incident. The story tells how tractor driver Gerald Crew found a series of human looking footprints in the mud that formed a continuous track to, around, then away from his machine. The prints measured sixteen inches in length, and the weight of the creature responsible for making the indentations was later confirmed by engineers to have weighed around 750 pounds.

It was the morning of August 27, and he was working with the rest of the crew pushing a new lumber-access road into the uninhabited and barely surveyed territory near the borders of Humboldt and Del Norte counties in Northwest California. Crew's initial instincts were that this was just a hoax, but as he followed the tracks straight down a very steep incline and into the forest, he observed that the consistent length of the stride was enormous and ranged from 46 to 60 inches, averaging almost twice that of his own.

His experience was shared with his co-workers, some of whom admitted having also found similar footprints during their time there, but nothing more was said until the following month when a lady called Mrs. Jesse Bemis, the wife of one of the most sceptical and outspoken members of the road crew wrote a letter to the *Humboldt Times* of Eureka.

The letter said, 'A rumour started among the men about the existence of a wild man. We regarded it as a joke. It was only yesterday that my husband became convinced that the existence of such a person (?) is a fact. Have you heard of this wild man?'

After somewhat reluctantly deciding to print the unusual letter, the newspaper editor Andrew Genzoli, honestly expecting an onslaught of derision, began receiving reports from the Willow Creek area confirming the creature's existence. It was during this period that the name 'Bigfoot' originated.

On the second of October, footprints were made once again in precisely the same region as before, and this time Jerry Crew was ready and armed with a supply of plaster-of-Paris. Crew made a series of casts of both left and right feet, and before long he was able to show them in person to editor Genzoli. The next day, photographs of Crew and his casts (fig. 10) filled the front pages of the *Humboldt Times*, attracting the attention of every paper in America, before interest from abroad began flooding in.

Despite many unconvinced locals who hadn't seen any tracks for themselves, Genzoli's fascination with Crew's findings and the affirming correspondences he had personally dealt with, led him and senior staff photographer Neil Hulbert out into Bluff Creek where they found fresh tracks along with a pile of human-looking faeces which Genzoli described as being 'of absolutely monumental proportions'. As more Bigfoot reports continued to reach the *Humboldt Times* office, reporter Betty Allen managed to speak with the Hoopa and Yurok Indians about their experiences regarding this anomalous beast.

Fig. 10 Jerry Crew with one of his Sasquatch footprint casts in 1958.

Upon being informed about the increasing national interest in the Bigfoot mystery, one Hoopa native simply remarked "Good Lord, have the white men finally got around to that?" Oscar Mack, an elder of the Yurok clan of the Klamaths, told Mrs. Allen that "The Bigfoot were run out of this country by the miners in the 1848-49 gold rush. Before that there were quite a number of them."[56]

JACKO

On July 4, 1884 *The Daily British Colonist*, a Canadian newspaper from Victoria, British Columbia published an extraordinary story recounting the capture of an unusual animal, under the headline: 'What is it? A strange creature captured above Yale. A British Colombian Gorilla.'

The article explained how employees of the British Columbia Express Company on a regular train from Lytton, spotted what is now considered by researchers to have been a juvenile Sasquatch, laying at the bottom of a 30-foot rock ledge from where he must have fallen, knocking himself unconscious.

The report was as follows: 'the workers 'succeeded in capturing a creature which may truly be called half man and half beast. 'Jacko', as the creature has been called by his capturers, is something of the gorilla type standing about four feet seven inches in height and weighing 127 pounds. He has long, black, strong hair and resembles a human being with one exception, his entire body, excepting his hands (or paws) and feet is covered with glossy hair about one inch long. His forearm is much longer than a man's forearm, and he possesses extraordinary strength, as he will take hold of a stick and break it by wrenching it or twisting it, which no man living could break in the same way.

Since his capture he is very reticent, only occasionally uttering a noise which is half bark and half growl. He is, however, becoming daily more attached to his keeper, Mr. George Tilbury, of this place, who proposes shortly starting for London, England, to exhibit him.'

Despite the story happening over a century ago, it remains a clearly documented and undeniable capture by sensible down-to earth westerners and reported with no sense of sensationalism. The journal itself was a respectable publication with a wide readership and a reputation for non-speculative journalism. With a tradition of accurate reportage, the paper's inclusion of names and details which will have been checked as standard procedure before their inclusion in the article shows the integrity of the publishers and only highlights the authenticity of the story.

THE PATTERSON/GIMLIN FILM

Probably the most controversial and compelling video footage of an alleged Sasquatch is the 1967 film shot up in the Bluff Creek Valley area of Northern California by Roger Patterson. Now it is no secret that Patterson already held a deep fascination with the legend of Bigfoot, ever since reading Ivan T. Sanderson's 1959 article on the subject printed in *True* magazine - *Abominable Snowmen: Legend Come to Life*: an encyclopedic collection of evidence for Bigfoot and similar creatures discovered worldwide, including recent findings in the Bluff Creek area.

Patterson's curiosity turned to fieldwork when he began visiting reported hotspots in search of any clues that might shed some light on the mystery of the beast's existence, and in 1964 he discovered some fresh Sasquatch footprints at Laird Meadows with local worker Pat Graves. Becoming a steadfast Bigfoot enthusiast, Roger Patterson invested many hours and dollars into searching Bigfoot territories for more solid evidence, eventually leading to the founding of The Northwest Research Foundation which enabled him to raise enough funds and interest to lead a number of expeditions.

In 1966, less than a year before his famous film was shot, he self-published a paperback book *Do Abominable Snowmen of America Really Exist?* In fact, as recently as one month before his incredible Sasquatch encounter fellow researchers John Green and Rene Dahinden had already extensively photographed anomalous Bigfoot tracks along the Blue Creek Mountain Road.

In the early afternoon of Friday October 20, whilst trekking on horseback with his partner Bob Gimlin in the very same region where Gerald Crew made his Bigfoot print casts nine years previous, the two men turned a sharp bend in a creek when their horses reared unexpectedly at the sight of a very large animal walking across the creek about 90 feet away.

As Gimlin tried to control the horses, which could have been frightened by either the creature's unusual appearance or the foul smell which both men had remarked upon at the time, (a common feature of both Bigfoot and Yeti encounters), Patterson grabbed his loaded movie camera and filmed en route as he ran nearer towards the animal, causing the film to appear jerky and blurred. The resulting footage reveals a continuous sequence of colour film 23.85 feet long which runs for 59.5 seconds. Although only short and a little shaky, the film caught what appears to be a female Sasquatch, about 7 ft 4 inches tall and weighing an estimated 600-700 lbs.

Her footprint casts which are still available along with accompanying photographs, show that she left detailed tracks one inch deep in the hard pact sands of the creek bed, a 200 lb man walking alongside the tracks sank about a ¼ of an inch, proving that whatever the creature proves to have been, it was an extremely heavy and robust unit.

Taxidermist and Sasquatch researcher Bob Titmus visited the site the following day and took plaster casts of ten consecutive prints, each showing subtle differences in foot pressure that one would expect to see in authentic tracks. They exhibited clear differences in weight shifts, depth and distribution, along with appropriate toe placements and grip forces, pressure ridges and breaks, all of which would easily expose a hoaxer employing one or two foot-shaped cut-outs to forge the impressions in the hard mud. How would anyone fake realistic prints of this kind anyway? Primitive cut-out foot shapes would surely be recognisable instantly to even the totally inexperienced.

Author Dr. John Napier, a former Professor of Primate Biology at the University of London, wrote in 1972, 'One might pose the question: who other than God or natural selection is sufficiently conversant with the subtleties of the human foot and the human walking style to 'design' an artificial foot which is so perfectly harmonious in terms of structure and function?'[57]

Nicknamed "Patty", the creature seen in the film (fig. 11) walks upright, swinging her long arms which reach just above the knees, and turns to look at Patterson who must've been making some noise as he scrambled across the terrain attempting to keep up with her. This turning of the head allowed for a quick head-and-shoulders profile of Patty, and as she turned her breasts moved pendulously, before she finally disappeared into the forest.

Once the footage hit the news it became known worldwide and still holds its place at the top in the Bigfoot archives so far caught on film. Other films do exist of course, what with the increased availability and advances in camera technology, but none hold the same intrigue and fascination as the Patterson/Gimlin footage.

Fig. 11 "Patty", taken from the Patterson/Gimlin film shot in 1967.

It is so easy to manipulate imagery these days through video and photo editing software that any modern films or photographs are easier to discredit than something taken at the back end of the sixties when such software was only really accessible to those within the professional arena. In fact, the 1967 clip is so compelling and controversial that its authenticity continues to be heavily debated to this day.

Sceptics hold onto the one obvious question in order to disprove Patty as just a hoax, is the figure in the film just a man in a costume? Surely it shouldn't be that difficult to conclusively prove once and for all that Patty is only somebody dressed up in some sort of gorilla outfit? Well, apparently it is not as easy as it may seem, even with all the computer technology available today.

Bob Gimlin himself was aware that proving Patty wasn't just a costume was *the* key factor in the whole mystery and showed the film to the technicians responsible for the special effects used to create King Kong, and asked whether or not they could reproduce the figure seen in the creek.

They replied, 'We could try, but we would have to create a completely new system of artificial muscles and find an actor who could be trained to walk like that. It might be done, but we would have to say that it would be almost impossible.'[58]

Don Grieve, Reader in Biomechanics at the Royal Free Hospital in London, also believed that the most difficult thing to fake would be the muscle masses which he could see were in precisely the right places. The sheer size of breadth of the shoulders also would prove extremely difficult to imitate, as the effect could only be successfully achieved with the right amount of padding that would in turn effect how the arms swing, causing an unnatural sway when faked.

'The skin *could* be faked by a fur suit over a polystyrene foam 'musculature', but this would surely be detectable,' claims author Myra Shackley.

Hollywood costume designer Bill Munns studied the Patterson/Gimlin film (PGF) in detail, looking from the perspective of an expert on the materials required to realistically imitate a creature of Patty's stature and gait. Munns insists that there was no stretch fur technology back in 1967 as it only became available during the early eighties. The standard of none-stretch furs was very low and basically behaved in the same way as ordinary cloth, folding, bending and creasing as one would expect a low budget costume to.

"If we look at the Patterson film, there's a lot of subtle curvatures in the body that are apparent by the highlights and shadows that suggest either it was masterfully tailored or it's simply not fur cloth at all,"[59] explains Munns.

After analysing the footage closely, he was not convinced that a man in a costume could actually pull off the desired effect to move as naturally as Patty does in the film. Using computer software, Munns superimposed the frame of a human being over the creature in the footage, revealing that a human figure is unable to fit within Patty's proportions.

None of the joints of the body – shoulders, hips, pelvis, knees and elbows have been shifted in any way in the film, leading Munns to comment, "We can say with confidence that a human of this proportion absolutely could not wear a suit and look like what we see in the film. There may not be a human on the face of the earth who has the proportions and the height necessary to be this creature."

As an expert in costume design which requires a realistic appearance on camera, Bill Munns' opinion regarding this contentious issue is noteworthy and his conclusion is that it was not a simple hoax. "That is not a human being in a fur costume. What it truthfully is, I am mystified by, but it is not a human being in a costume."

Bigfoot researcher M.K. Davis controversially believes that he found evidence of another, larger Bigfoot in the same film footage. He claims that Patty eventually caught up with her larger counterpart who had already reached the safety of the forest moments before her.

When investigating cases such as the PGF discussed here, what is just as important as the actual footage itself is the intent and integrity of the individuals involved in producing the film. Whilst researching the life of Roger Patterson for his autobiography David Murphy said, "I've interviewed over 70 people that either had some acquaintance, whether they were friends or associates, with Roger Patterson and Bob Gimlin, and I've yet to find one person who didn't think highly of both individuals."

In fact, Patterson's integrity was tested further when *National Wildlife* editor Kirk Patrick ordered a polygraph test to attempt to expose the prank, but Patterson passed with flying colours. He died in 1972, but continued to adamantly swear that his film was authentic, right until the end. Likewise, Bob Gimlin, despite falling out with Patterson over monetary and copyright issues shortly after the film was made, remained loyal to the story and not once took it upon himself to discredit the man responsible for the most compelling piece of Bigfoot footage ever caught on camera.

THE BOSSBURG CRIPPLE

In Bossburg, Stevens County, Washington on November 24 1969, local butcher Joe Rhodes discovered unusual Sasquatch footprints embedded in the snow close to the Bossburg community garbage dump, where a local woman had reported a Bigfoot sighting to the Police earlier in the year. The sighting was reported to Ivan Marx who passed on the details to Rene Dahinden and John Green. Numbering 1,089 in total, what makes these particular prints unique and worthy of closer inspection is the way in which the right foot appears to exhibit some sort of deformity.

Some experts claim that the right foot shows signs of Liz Frank injury – a dislocation or fracture between forefoot and mid-foot joints commonly caused by trauma – whilst Bigfoot expert Dr. Grover S. Krantz believed the Bossburg Cripple's deformity was due to the congenital condition known as metatarsus adductus or skew-foot. The left footprint measured 17.5 inches long, 6.5 across the ball of the foot and 5.5 inches across the heel, whilst the right was 16.5 inches long, 7 inches across the ball and the right heel measurements matched the right.

Dr. John Napier examined the Bossburg casts thoroughly for his own research and concluded: 'Apart from satisfying the criteria established for modern-type walking, the Bossburg prints have, to my way of thinking, an even greater claim to authenticity. The right foot of the Bossburg Sasquatch is a club-foot, a not uncommon abnormality. . .

The forepart of the foot is twisted inwards, the third toe has been squeezed out of normal alignment, and possibly there has been a dislocation of the bones on the outer border (but this last feature may be due to an imperfection in the casting technique). To me the deformity strongly suggests that injury during life was responsible.

A true, untreated, congenital usually results in a fixed flexion deformity of the ankle in which case only the forepart of the foot and toes would touch the ground in normal standing. In these circumstances the heel impression would be absent or poorly defined; but in fact the heel indentation of the Sasquatch is strongly defined. I conclude that the deformity was the result of a crushing injury to the foot during early childhood.'[60]

Dr. Jeff Meldrum, Professor of Anatomy and Anthropology at Idaho State University, also examined the Bossburg footprint casts looking for evidence of a midtarsal break, a flexible area of the foot found in great apes but not in humans. The break which acts like a hinge in the middle part of the foot allowing the heel to move somewhat independently from the forepart of the foot is what separates our human prints from that of apes, and if found in alleged Sasquatch or Yeti prints acts as strong evidence in favour of their existence.

Meldrum laser-scanned the casts to create detailed animated models which he could then examine to determine the presence of the midtarsal break. The three dimensional model allowed Meldrum to see how the creature walks to find whether the tracks were made by a large non-human primate as this is of the upmost importance according to Meldrum, "The recognition of the midtarsal break in Sasquatch footprints is very, very significant. I mean, it's huge. Personally, I think this is all but short of proof of the existence of Sasquatch."

Below, Dr. Meldrum explains in more detail the differences between the walk of a human and that of the Sasquatch:

'Human walking is characterized by an extended stiff-legged striding gait with distinct heel-strike and toe-off phases. Bending stresses in the digits are held low by selection for relatively short toes that participate in propulsion at the sacrifice of prehension. Efficiency and economy of muscle action during distance walking and running are maximized by reduced mobility in the tarsal joints, a fixed longitudinal arch, and elastic storage in the well developed calcaneal tendon, plantar aponeurosis and deep plantar ligaments of the foot.

In contrast, the Sasquatch appear to have adapted to bipedal locomotion by employing a compliant gait on a flat flexible foot. A degree of prehensile capability has been retained in the digits by maintaining the uncoupling of the propulsive function of the hindfoot from the forefoot via the midtarsal break. Digits are spared the peak forces of toe-off due to the compliant gait with its extended period of double support. This would be an efficient strategy for negotiating the steep, broken terrain of the dense montane forests of the Pacific and Intermountain West, especially for a bipedal hominoid of considerable body mass. The dynamic signatures of this adaptive pattern of gait are generally evident in the footprints examined in this study.'

Regarding the evidence left in the Bossburg snow (fig. 12), Dr. Grover Krantz wrote a letter on February 2, 2001, a full year before his death, stating that he had 'deduced the major aspects of the foot anatomy to be consistent only with an 8-foot tall, powerfully built bipedal primate.' Convinced of the authenticity of the Bossburg tracks he wrote 'the problems involved in producing such tracks were such that any human manufacture could be ruled out.'

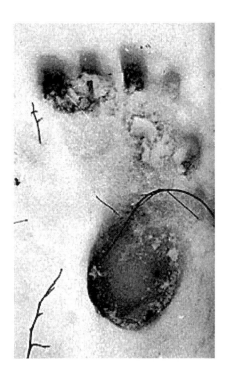

Fig. 12 Sasquatch footprint in the snow, found in Bossburg, 1969.

Discovering anomalous footprints of this nature makes a hoax all the less likely due to the complexity of the tracks. Photogrammetric analysis of hominoid tracks reveals how differently they walk compared to humans, without the heel-strike, toe-off pattern. Some differences may not be spotted by the untrained eye but any anthropologist or tracker would easily recognise the difficulties involved in faking tracks such as those left in the snow that day in 1969. Napier wrote, 'It is very difficult to conceive of a hoaxer so subtle, so knowledgeable - and so sick – who would deliberately fake a footprint of this nature. I suppose it is possible, but it is so unlikely that I am prepared to discount it.'

Orthopaedic surgeon Dr. David Howe echoed Napier's sentiments saying, "I think it would be very difficult to come up with the knowledge and the ability to hoax this type of footprint. There is quite a bit of evidence out there that points favourably towards the real thing." Dr. Meldrum agreed by stating, "The probability of this being a hoax is almost non-existent".

Because of the anatomical accuracy of the Bossburg prints, with the metatarsal dislocations appearing in different areas than where they would be found on an elongated human foot, Lloyd Pye wrote, 'Only an expert in foot anatomy would know how to create such a malformation in exactly the right places, in exactly the right manner. Combined with their dermal ridges, their unusual anatomy gives the Bossburg cripple's prints unassailable credibility.'[61]

THE FREEMAN FOOTAGE

Whilst working as a watershed patroller for the U.S. Forest Service, Paul Freeman was very sceptical of the whole Bigfoot myth. He was based in a 177,000-acre stretch of prime Sasquatch territory near Walla Walla, where the flatlands of south-eastern Washington ascend into the Blue Mountains of the Umatilla National Forest.

It was here on June 10, 1982, where Freeman's scepticism would be tested as he had his first encounter with a shaggy, reddish-brown Bigfoot nearly eight feet tall. "He was 60 yards away," recalled Freeman. "I watched him walk the length of two football fields. He'd take a few steps, look back at me, and take a few more steps. Then he went up over a hill and disappeared."[62]

Once Freeman's dramatic tale gained the attention of the media, newspaper reporters hounded him and he had threats at home from anonymous callers. Ridicule from co-workers and supervisors caused him to quit his job and relocate, but his fascination with the Bigfoot phenomenon had only just begun. "I'm going to find one of them. . . I'm going to rub their noses in this", he was quoted as saying following his decision to leave the Forest Service.

In 1994, Sasquatch tracks were reported near Deduck Springs in the Blue Mountains, which sit on the border of Oregon and Washington State. Freeman went to document the tracks by taking measurements and making plaster casts, which he had learnt from Dr. Grover Krantz, a professor at Washington State. As Freeman was filming the muddy track where the footprints were located, he looked up with his camera when out of nowhere a Sasquatch came out of the forest and into the clearing where he was stood, camcorder in hand.

He recorded the Bigfoot moving cautiously from left to right, but just as suddenly lost sight of it, "Damn, where did the doggone thing go?" he retorted and began to pan the camera to the right in an attempt to get the creature back in frame. What he didn't realise at the time is that it was actually stood very still, looking directly at him, almost camouflaged amidst the forest foliage where it eluded his detection whilst waiting for an opportunity to escape from the clearing and back into the density of the forest.

The Freeman footage has become as important as the Patterson film as it clearly shows a large hairy biped of unknown origin passing through the forest, despite having been shot on low quality 8mm tape which had reportedly been reused many times. By freeze-framing the video, closer inspection reveals that the creature stood by a cedar tree was a female with a grey skinned face and a cranial keel or sloped head, and she wasn't alone, there was a juvenile accompanying her as Freeman himself noted despite the difficulty in seeing this in real-time in the actual footage.

Once again, Freeman reported his sighting to the Forest Service who were so impressed by the prints that they brought in a forest tracker to examine them, which some of his former co-workers had already acknowledged the presence of prior to Freeman's arrival at the site. Before his death in 2003, Dr. Meldrum met up with Paul Freeman and was impressed with the man's honesty and integrity.

In Meldrum's opinion, "this video clip on its own merits depicts something that looks very spontaneous and natural in its appearance and behaviour, and is quite consistent with descriptions of Sasquatch."[63]

IDENTIKIT SASQUATCH

So, how would one best describe a Sasquatch? Which features appear often enough in eyewitness accounts to warrant inclusion in such a description? In *Manlike Monsters on Trial*, author John Green provides a summary collated from the thousand or so reports he analysed, along with the many footprints which are consistently similar in shape and size, by summarising all of his knowledge of the creature and assimilating the descriptions into an atypical Sasquatch. Green's study along with other researchers' collaborative input produced the following information about the average Bigfoot:

Appearance - All Sasquatch are consistently taller than humans of comparable age and sex, with the average height calculated at 7 ft 6 in. except in Oregon, where the average exceeds 8 ft. Males are in the 8-10 foot range; females within 6-8 feet and juveniles between 4-5 feet. They are also of a much wider and heavier build than the average human, with large, thick limbs and enormous torsos allowing them incredible strength. Bigfoot feet are 23% longer and 33% wider than human feet, meaning that their feet have roughly twice the surface area of ours.

Conical or bullet-shaped heads with sloping foreheads and protruding brow ridges, flat faces, large flat noses, short necks and broad shoulders combined with great height and heavy build giving an overall 'primitive' appearance.

Thin lips, not much of a chin and virtually no neck at all; their heads appear to sit flush on their highly-set shoulders obscuring what little neck they do have. Due to this head/shoulder connection, all hominoids, just like all primates, have upside down funnel-shaped rib cages instead of the human type oblong rib cage.

Sasquatch arms are longer and bulkier than ours, often described as "hanging down around the knees". The extreme width of the shoulders was in all likelihood adapted to deal with this added length. The legs are heavily muscled and stout in comparison with their long arms, built to withstand the enormous weight of the entire body, allowing them to walk with splendid efficiency.

Eyewitness accounts consistently describe all hominoid eyes as small, beady and close set in large round eye-sockets. They are said to "shine" intensely in daylight and have a "reddish glow" when it is dark. Like most primates, Bigfoot and the hominoids can be nocturnal and it is these enlarged retinas which allow the use of dim lighting that gives the illusion of glowing at night and shining during the daytime.

Only 8% of observers stated that the hair was longer on the head than the body, most described the hair being the same length all over, and it is hair *not* fur which covers Bigfoot's body. The same applies to all four hominoid types. Horses for example, have fur covered bodies with hair for the tail and mane; fur being packed tightly with hundreds of follicles per square inch compared to hair which is spread out over the skin, growing longer than fur to compensate for the loss of insulating capacity.

The Bigfoot pelts are typically primate in colour; black, light/dark/reddish brown and russet, and although there appear to be variations of hair length reported it is most often described as short-to-medium; between 2 and 4 inches long. The palms, soles of the feet, cheeks below the eyes and the bridge of the nose are all hairless and grow darker in colour with maturation.

Hominoid body odour has being described during close range human encounters as thoroughly repugnant. This stench which some claim smells like "garbage" or "sewage" could be used, like many other animals, to claim and mark territories and/or to advertise sexual availability over a wide area.

Habitat - Of the four hominoid types, the Sasquatch has the widest habitat diversity. Primarily dwelling within the lower montane forest belts which grow at the bottom of mountain ranges and valleys, Sasquatch can also adapt to living in the upper montane forests, as well as jungles and swamps if that is where their hunt for food takes them. One reason for Sasquatch being so suited to the lower montanes is due to the growth density of these areas making them so inaccessible to human activity. Despite over-logging threatening to decimate this type of region, huge swaths of lower montane forests still cover the Earth. Within these forested zones, common places of habitation for Sasquatch are caves, rock overhangs and other natural formations suitable for shelter from the weather.

Usually observed as solitary creatures - often spotted during one of their extended walkabouts - occasional reports have identified females with one or two offspring, and on rare occasions small groups of between 10 to 20 have been seen gathered together. Sasquatch are believed to be largely nocturnal, which leads one to wonder how many more sightings would be reported if they were out more during daylight. 50% of all sightings are reported at night, and it has been estimated that up to 90% of all tracks so far discovered were also made at night.

Behaviour - Seemingly omnivorous, Sasquatch will eat whatever they can get their hands on. They subsist on the natural foodstuffs available in their particular ecological niches in a wandering food-gathering lifestyle which one associates with our primate predecessors. Attracted to the seasonal offerings of both tree and ground nuts, vegetables, fruits, roots and tubers, Sasquatch will supplement these types of food with insects, fish and small (slow and easy to catch) animals.

Observations suggest a clear seasonal variation; spring sightings are rare, and there are twice as many sightings in summer compared to winter (possibly due to increased human activity during summer months). They seem to travel north and south with the seasons in search of food, and eat whatever is around them and within their reach. When they are ready to sleep, they simply make a bed from foliage or dry vegetation and lie down wherever they happen to be.

Strong connection with water; tracks ending in lakes or rivers have been reported on six occasions. Five sightings report Sasquatch swimming whilst another twelve reports witnessed them walking or standing in water. No accounts of tool-making or fire-using exist, nor have the creatures been seen carrying food in their hands.

Although sounds are rarely reported, distinct vocalisations in the form of a high-pitched kind of scream or whistle seems the most consistent sound associated with their presence. These high-pitched blood-curdling frequencies echo for miles across open country and have contributed to the 'Bigfoot is a monster' conception.

In 1974, the US Army Corps of Engineers spent $200,000 on a Washington state project designed to assist government and private planners. *The Washington Environmental Atlas* which was prepared over a three year period includes sections on geologic features of the area, archaeological sites, historical points of interest and also lakes and rivers of environmental interest. Included in the atlas is a detailed description of Sasquatch and provides a map of actual Bigfoot sightings in the state. Despite the Corps acknowledging that the existence of the creature is 'hotly disputed' it quite clearly recognizes the mythical Sasquatch as a real living species in the state of Washington inhabiting the montane regions of the Pacific Northwest Mountains.

The atlas describes the beast as being strong and agile but shy enough to leave 'minimal evidence of its presence' or as Shackley maintains, 'The Sasquatch population must number at least in the thousands, and possibly many thousands. Since all efforts to hunt one have failed, it is clear that the Sasquatch has a strong sense of self-preservation and, indeed, may even be adept at hiding its tracks or evading dogs.'

The atlas goes on to explain how the creature is 'reported to feed on vegetation and some meat and is covered with long hair, except for the face and hands, and has a distinctly humanlike form'. Also included in the text of *The Washington Environmental Atlas* was a reference to the analysis of physical evidence, 'Alleged Sasquatch hair samples inspected by F.B.I. laboratories resulted in the conclusion that no such hair exists on any human or presently known animal for which such data are available.'

THE MINNESOTA ICEMAN

During the summer of 1967, several months prior to the capture of the Patterson/Gimlin film, a man from Minnesota named Frank Hansen first revealed to the public an incredible exhibit in the form of a sideshow attraction which he labelled 'The Minnesota Iceman' (figs. 13 and 14).

The unusual exhibit consisted of an extraordinary primitive-looking, hair-covered humanoid which had been shot dead and laid in water in a refrigerated coffin and subsequently frozen until the creature became fully encased in a large block of ice.

Following a controversial and most dubious origin story which Hansen concocted no doubt to add some mystery to the exhibit, in which he claimed that the Iceman belonged to an anonymous Californian who had acquired it in Hong Kong where it had been sold to him by fishermen who had found it frozen in an iceberg floating in the Bering Sea, Hansen reluctantly was forced to change his story. As the corpse had obvious bullet holes in it, witnesses were quick to point out to Hansen how incredulous the whole iceberg story was, leading him to confess to killing it himself somewhere in the woods of northern Minnesota.

The initial lie was enough to taint the whole affair with an overall feeling of gamesmanship and hoaxing, a feeling which stuck like mud and became increasingly difficult to discard. Hansen's somewhat amateurish approach put off any prospective scientists from looking any closer and indeed put a stop to any serious research from taken place, with the exception of cryptozoologists Ivan T. Sanderson and Bernard Heuvelmans. As Lloyd Pye remarked 'Had Frank Hansen been a different kind of man, the issue of hominoid reality might be far behind us today'.[64]

Fig. 13 Photo of the original exhibit in ice, taken by American cryptozoologist Loren Coleman at the Illinois State Fair.

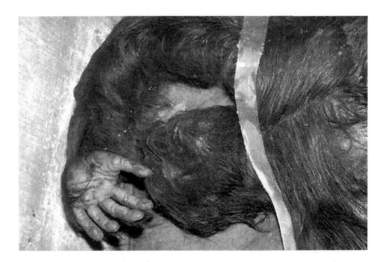

Fig. 14 Some believe this to be the original Minnesota Iceman, but the absence of ice to preserve the creature suggests this could be the replica Hansen made to exhibit on tour.

The FBI became aware of his claims to having murdered this primitive human-type creature, which led Hansen to retract his story once again by announcing that he was just trying to make money and the "monster" had in truth been manufactured by professionals in Hollywood. This may have been the case once Hansen was beginning to attract the attention of the law, and also the Smithsonian museum, which sent out Sanderson and Heuvelmans to Frank Hansen's farm to inspect and take photographs of the iceman through the ice in December 1968 (fig. 15).

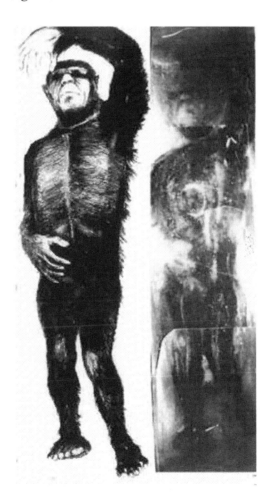

Fig. 15 Left: Drawing of the Iceman by Heuvelmans. Right: Original photograph taken by Heuvelmans.

By May 1969, Hansen had switched the bodies, and was now exhibiting in St Paul, Minnesota and Grand Rapids, Michigan, a dummy version of the original Iceman which he was now billing as a deliberate hoax. *Time-Life* magazine's photographs of the new exhibit revealed many differences between the original and the replacement now on show.

As the widely-renowned Ivan Sanderson soon discovered during his examination of the body, the anatomical technical accuracy on show revealed that whatever originally lay frozen in that opaque block of ice was no latex creation constructed by human hand, but a very real, fresh corpse of unknown origin. Because of 'the switch' the whole story became very clouded, and with the original now stored away out of sight it became increasingly difficult to prove the existence of the Bigfoot type creature which had already been seen by so many.

In a letter to Dr. John Napier, who had recently informed zoologist Bernard Heuvelmans that the Smithsonian were backing out of further investigations due to the possibility of a hoax, which was looking more likely due to Hansen's involvement with Hollywood model makers in creating a replacement for the original Iceman, Heuvelmans expressed his disappointment:

'I have examined the specimen very carefully for 11 hours (eleven!) over three days and am absolutely positive about it being genuine. In my scientific notice I had to consider the possibility of a fake because it was theoretically one of the possibilities, but practically I can assure you that I cannot have been fooled.'

Sanderson wrote an analysis of the frozen anomaly after having studied the creature alongside Heuvelmans, of which he titled *Preliminary Description of the External Morphology of What Appeared to be the fresh corpse of a Hitherto Unknown Form of Living Hominid.* Peter Byrne's 1975 book, *The Search for Bigfoot*, reprinted all 36 pages of Sanderson's analysis in which he noted that the dimensions of the frozen beast – about 6 ft. tall and 250 lbs in weight – would suggest that this particular specimen was most likely to be in the 10 to 12 year old range, meaning that Ice*child* would be a more accurate description.

Viewed from no closer than one foot, Sanderson's first impressions were of the immense bulk of the body, with the hands seeming out of proportion, a trait shared by most primates during adolescence, where the extremities are enlarged as they continue to 'grow into' their adult bodies. His second dominant impression was the uniformity of the hair coverage over the majority of its body, with the hairs averaging 2-3 inches long in most places, which due to the frozen water led the hairs to be suspended upwards allowing great views right down to the skin.

He had an extremely wide face and jaw with prominent cheekbones and thin lips. The bullet through the left eye socket had blown away the crown, but still the eye sockets on show were of extreme size and very round like that of a fossil hominid. The left eyeball was missing and the right was dislodged due to the impact of the bullet, with tendrils of blood streaming up from both sockets.

The face was hairless except for the brow ridges which had short bristles growing out, and the light yellowish to pinkish colour of the face was consistent with the Bigfoot's immature age. The nasal structure was like that of a gorilla; large, round, heavy with fleshy nostrils which jutted up rather than appearing flattened.

Another bullet hole, this time in the middle of the chest, revealed more bloody tendrils flowing upwards into the ice. The upper arms appeared more slender than the hair covered massive forearms with extremely wide wrists. A compound fracture which was caused by another bullet lay three inches from the left wrist.

Dr. Bernard Heuvelmans was convinced of the authenticity of the Iceman and was more than happy to say so on record; "we examined this creature for three days very carefully, and we were very suspicious I can tell you, at the start. But after a while that was quite ruled out. There is absolutely no doubt for me that I have been examining a Neanderthal man – a surviving Neanderthal man."[65]

Both men noted that the Iceman was neither human nor primate but somewhere in-between, and was not modelled on any known existing living creature. Sanderson wrote, 'This body is not that of any known hominid or pongid and, what is much more significant, it does not conform to any reconstruction or artist's conception of any fossil man or ape or other anthropoid. Its general features and particular characters as detailed above display an extraordinary mixture of what have until now been assigned either to men or apes, but it also shows others that have never been assigned or attributed to any of either.'

He believed that the specimen he had studied was 'a survivor of a line divergent from, and possibly lying between, the hominid and the pongid branches, but derived from a common ancestor to all three.' Both Sanderson and Heuvelmans left convinced of the creature's authenticity but still none the wiser as to its origin or type, despite the close proximity of their examination.

'It is Heuvelmans' opinion, which he states categorically in his paper, that this body represents the fresh remains of a neanderthaloid human. Such hominids are currently classed as a sub-species of *Homo sapiens*, yet Heuvelmans has named this item *Homo pongoides*, and thus of full specific rank', wrote Sanderson.

He concluded his analysis by stating, 'the specimen we inspected was that of a genuine corpse as opposed to a composite or a construction — and that it is some form of primate. We would categorize it, as of now, as an anthropoid, but whether it is a hominid, a pongid, or a representative of some other previously unsuspected branch of that super-family we are not prepared either to say or even to speculate.'

They both advised cautiously against confirming any definite answers to the Iceman riddle, recommending that the ideas they were putting forward should 'serve only as a pointer to the possible continued existence of at least one kind of fully-haired, ultra-primitive, anthropoid-like primate, and be used only as a lever to pry open the hitherto hidebound notion that any such thing is impossible.'

In 2013, Steve Busti, the owner of The Museum of the Weird, in Austin, Texas, paid $20,000 on eBay for what was advertised as the original Minnesota Iceman. The exhibit is now on show at Busti's museum, but one would be naive to accept that the creature he bought to be the original and authentic specimen which was so diligently examined by Bernard Heuvelmans. It would appear most likely that the exhibit which Busti purchased was the original rubber replica which Frank Hansen used to replace the original specimen.

Of course, one has to be open to the possibility that the frozen mystery was always just a clever creation used to make a few dollars during a time of innocent public gullibility of which Hansen, just like P.T. Barnum before him, milked for everything he could get. However, anything capable of convincing zoologists of its genuineness must be worth consideration in the context of this research.

It is the accumulation of evidence, the Minnesota Iceman being just one element, which serves as proof of the existence of the legendary Bigfoot of North America. The sightings are not isolated incidents either, more and more witnesses come forward every year which suggests that the allusive Sasquatch may be more common than one might assume. Author Myra Shackley agrees, 'the popular idea of Bigfoot as a rare hominid is incorrect; it seems to be an inoffensive large bipedal ape with a secure population and widespread distribution.'

The Sasquatch isn't the only living hominid roaming the Earth however; equally notorious is the beast of Himalayan folklore whose name has become synonymous with the desolate snowy landscapes of the largest mountain range on the planet, the Abominable Snowman.

YETI OF THE HIMALAYAS

Between 20,000 and 21,000 feet up on the Llapka-La pass during the very first reconnaissance Everest expedition in 1921, Lieutenant-Colonel C.K. Howard-Bury, along with a large party of people which included Sherpas, porters and fellow explorers, saw through binoculars a number of 'dark forms' moving about far above them on a snowfield. After some time and a lot of effort they finally reached the area where they had spotted the unusual shapes and discovered lots of huge anomalous footprints which Howard-Bury described as being about 'three times those of normal humans'.[66]

His Sherpas were quick to declare that they belonged to *meteh kang-mi* (meaning 'filthy or disgusting man-of-the-snows'); the more commonly known name *Yeti* derives from the Nepalese *yeh-teh*.

Such was the Colonel's respect for the Sherpas, that despite regarding their stories as local folklore, he chose to include the incident in a report that he sent to Kathmandu in Nepal which would be telegraphed to his representatives in India. It was then that mistakes occurred during the translation of the name *meteh kang-mi*. The Sherpas had apparently used a generic term for the sake of clarity and chose to use *kang-mi*, a Tibetan colloquialism, with *kang* being of Chinese origin and *mi*, a form of the Nepalese *meh*.

The Indian recipients of the telegram passed on the information to a remarkable gentleman and fountain of knowledge Henry Newman of *The Calcutta Statesman*, who had written a column for years on many different and fascinating subjects. It was Newman who in 1921 quickly mistranslated *meteh kang-mi* by categorically declaring that it was Tibetan for an 'abominable snowman'. In a letter to *The Times*, Newman wrote that 'the whole story seemed such a joyous creation I sent it to one or two newspapers'.

Daily Mail journalist Ralph Izzard later explained in his 1955 book, *The Abominable Snowman Adventure*, 'whatever effect Mr. Newman intended, from 1921 onwards the Yeti – or whatever various native populations chose to call it – became saddled with the description "Abominable Snowman", an appellation which can only appeal more to the music-hall mind than to mammalogists, a fact which has seriously handicapped earnest seekers of the truth.'

Without Newman's creative embellishment the whole legend of the Abominable Snowman would almost certainly have remained in obscurity, despite the incredible evidence which would surface in later years, and the concept of a man-like snow monster prowling the frozen wastelands of the Himalayas would in all likelihood have become relegated to the pages of comic books occupying the same space as 'sea-monsters' and other fictitious ramblings.

Along with an article on Howard-Bury's Everest story, on Thursday, 3 November 1921, *The Times* also printed a letter to the editor written by H.J. Elwes concerning other sightings of the Abominable Snowman. The letter is printed in full below:

"ABOMINABLE SNOWMEN"
A TRAVELLER'S EXPERIENCE

TO THE EDITOR OF THE TIMES

'Sir, Dr. Douglas Freshfield has had better opportunities than most men of confirming or explaining the belief current in Sikkim, among the people of the higher valleys, that "wild men" exist.

I can hardly believe that the tracks in the snow seen by some members of the Everest Expedition would have been mentioned in a telegram if there were any question that the tracks were those of a human being.

When I was travelling in the forests on the Nepal frontier of British Sikkim in March 1914, with Mr. Gent, then Forest Officer of the Darjeeling district, he told me that the coolies employed by him in cutting jungle at an elevation of 8,000-9,000 ft. had been on more than one occasion driven from their work by what they believed to be wild men. I was unable to cross-examine the men who reported this, but I asked Mr. Gent to make further enquiries, and he, being a good shikari, would have known the tracks of a bear from those of a human being. I thought it possible that the tracks of a large langur monkey, which goes up to 9,000-10,000 ft. in Sikkim, might have been mistaken for human tracks.

But the war put an end to this, as to many other scientific enquiries, and we must await the return of the expedition for more definite information as to what they actually saw.

The Athenaeum, Nov.2.   - H.J. ELWES'[67]

During this century, Western mountaineers who have publicised the creature's existence greatly contributed to the worldwide fame of the Yeti, but records of Yeti sightings stretch back to the 19th century when the British military and Indian Civil Service had already included tales of encounters with the mysterious man-beast in their reports.

The first mention of the Yeti, in Western literature at least, is generally credited to B.H. Hodgson, British Resident at the Nepalese court from 1820 to 1843. He wrote about an incident where a hairy, tailless wildman had frightened some of his porters in Northern Nepal. The first large footprints were found at 17,000 ft in Sikkim by Major

L.A. Waddell in 1889 who was promptly informed by *his* porters that the tracks belonged to the Yeti. Sceptical of the tales of such a beast, Waddell dismissed the tracks as belonging to the snow bear, *Ursus isabellinus*.

THE RAWICZ ENCOUNTER

More often than not, evidence for the existence of the Yeti has derived indirectly from either tracks in the snow or unusual hairs found on the ground. Actual sightings are few and far between, which is either confirmation of their allusive nature or suggests that there is nothing to such tales. The validity of any personal experience involving a sighting or close encounter with a Yeti is very much dependent on the integrity of the individual telling the story. An alleged encounter told by someone with high credentials and nothing to gain financially from such an incident surely holds more weight than that told by a man who has set out solely to prove the Yeti's existence for his own profit.

One story worthy of legitimate interest is recounted in a fascinating non-fiction book which tells of the incredible and harrowing experience of a Polish prisoner-of-war escaping with six friends from a Soviet labour camp based in Siberia during World War II in 1941.

In *The Long Walk*, Slavomir Rawicz shares his account of the escape as he journeys through China, the Gobi Desert, Tibet, then finally over the Himalayas and into British India. It was whilst trekking across the Himalayan terrain that he encountered a creature baring a close resemblance to the infamous Yeti, in fact his book holds the most detailed descriptions of the creature to date.

Throughout the whole journey crossing the Himalayan region, Rawicz and his companions encountered nothing but men, dogs and sheep. As they began their descent of the final mountain they noticed 'two moving black specks' against the whiteness of the snow about a quarter of a mile below them. Thinking that they must be animals and a possible source of food, they set off to investigate further half expecting whatever they were to have wandered off before they arrived, however, as they approached nearer they saw that they were still there and only about a hundred yards away and roughly twelve feet below them.

Rawicz was struck immediately by their enormous size and by the fact that they were walking on their hind legs. Amazed by what they were seeing, they decided to stay and observe the 'unknown creatures' for a solid two hours. Whatever they were, they certainly were not afraid of the men's close proximity and remained steadfast.

Rawicz described the anomalous figures in more detail, 'They could not have been much less than eight feet tall. One was a few inches taller than the other, in the relation of the average man to the average woman. . . Their faces I could not see in detail, but the heads were squarish and the ears must lie close to the skull because there was no projection from the silhouette against the snow. The shoulders sloped sharply down to a powerful chest. The arms were long and the wrists reached the level of the knees. Seen in profile, the back of the head was a straight line from the crown into the shoulders.'

He explained that they were 'shuffling quietly' around on a flat area which formed part of the route that the men were due to pass as they continued their descent and they were expecting the creatures to move away at some point if they waited long enough, allowing them to be on their way, but the Pole noted that it was 'obvious they had seen us, and it was equally apparent they had no fear of us.'

He wrote that they appeared not to be engaged in anything in particular, but rather they just moved around slowly and stopped occasionally as if to admire the view. Despite turning their heads and their attention towards the escaped soldiers now and again, they appeared to hold little interest in the men. The opposite could be said of the men's interest towards them. What they had stumbled upon defied explanation and has become part of the Yeti legend which continues to confound those with a penchant for the mysterious.

'We decided unanimously that we were examining a type of creature of which we had no previous experience in the wild, in zoos or literature. It would have been easy to have seen them waddle off at a distance and dismiss them as either bear or big ape of the orangutan species. At close range they defied description. There was something both of the bear and the ape about their general shape but they could not be mistaken for either. The colour was a rusty kind of brown. They appeared to be covered by two distinct kinds of hair - the reddish hair which gave them their characteristic colour forming a tight, close fur against the body, mingling with which were long, loose, straight hairs, hanging downwards, which had a slight greyish tinge as the light caught them', cites Rawicz in more detail.

Could this encounter be proof of the Yeti's existence? What else could fit descriptions of a long-haired, tall and robust biped capable of roaming the extremities of the Himalayan mountain range?

Slavomir Rawicz has his own opinion on what he saw back in 1941, 'For years they remained a mystery to me, but since recently I have read of scientific expeditions to discover the Abominable Snowman of the Himalayas and studied descriptions of the creature given by native hill-men, I believe that the five of us that day may have met two of the animals.'

The sheer sincerity of the author's entire account lends great credibility to the whole affair, with the almost incidental manner in which he shares his experience this particular incident continues to emanate an air of authenticity, but of course one can never discount the possibility of exaggeration or creative expression.

FOOTPRINTS IN THE SNOW

As mentioned previously, footprints in the snow account for the majority of Yeti related incidents recorded by Europeans, most having been witnessed by expedition personnel which includes such notables as Lord John Hunt (leader of the British Expedition to Mt. Everest in 1953), H.W. Tilman and Sir Edmund Hillary who conquered Everest with Sherpa Tensing in May 1953.

British mountain climber Eric Shipton found and photographed the most famous Yeti footprints on record, and such was his reputation that even today sceptics struggle to completely discount the Shipton tracks as proof that something unusual and unexplained does actually occupy at least some parts of the Himalayas.

While on his fifth visit to Mount Everest, on November 8, 1951 at 4pm, Shipton discovered some large and bizarre footprints as he was returning from an Everest reconnaissance expedition with their doctor Michael Ward. The tracks set in deep snow appeared as they were exploring the saddle at the head of the Menlung Glacier at close to 19,000 ft. near the Nepal/Tibet border.

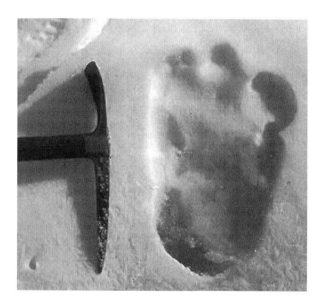

Fig. 16 Yeti footprint in the snow alongside ice pick for size comparison, taken by Eric Shipton, Himalayas, 1951.

The most popular and often reproduced Shipton photo of a single footprint next to his ice-axe for size comparison (fig. 16) was not actually part of the trail of tracks which he found and followed for about a mile along the edge of the glacier but was taken in roughly the same area earlier in the day.

This one single image has succeeded in bringing much attention to the Yeti mystery and as author Myra Shackley noted, it 'mysteriously endowed the whole Yeti business with respectability as being something discovered by people with no hope of commercial gain or need for sensational publicity.' Along with Ward and Shipton, the expedition party consisted of Tom Bourdillon, Edmund Hillary, Earle Riddiford, W.H. Murray, Sen Tensing and six other Sherpas.

In an extract taken from *The Six Mountains-Travel Books*, Eric Shipton recalls the day's events in 1951:

'. . . late one afternoon, we came across those curious footprints in the snow, the report of which has caused a certain amount of public interest in Britain. We did not follow them further than was convenient, a mile or so, for we were carrying heavy loads at the time, and besides we had reached a particularly interesting stage in the exploration of the basin. I have in the past found many sets of these curious footprints and have tried to follow them, but have always lost them on the moraine or rocks at the side of the glacier.

These particular ones seemed to be very fresh, probably not more than 24 hours old. When Murray and Bourdillon followed us a few days later the tracks had been almost obliterated by melting. Sen Tensing, who had no doubt whatsoever that the creatures (for there had been at least two) that had made the tracks were 'Yetis' or wild men, told me that two years before, he and a number of other Sherpas had seen one of them at a distance of about 25 yards at Thyangboche. He described it as half man and half beast, standing about five feet six inches, with a tall pointed head, its body covered with reddish brown hair, but with a hairless face. . . Whatever it was he had seen, he was convinced that it was neither a bear nor a monkey, with both of which animals he was, of course, very familiar.'

Shipton discussed his findings in a report written for *The Times* newspaper, 'The tracks were mostly distorted by melting into oval impressions, slightly longer and a good deal broader than those made by our mountain boots. But here and there, where the snow covering the ice was thin, we came upon preserved impressions of the creature's foot. It showed three 'toes' [further analysis reveals there were actually four] and a broad 'thumb' to the side. What was particularly interesting was that where the tracks crossed a crevasse one could see quite clearly where the creature had jumped and used its toes to secure purchase on the other side.'

Yeti is considered to be more primitive than Sasquatch and the other hominoids yet to be discussed in this chapter, in that it appears to be more closely connected to the great apes (gorillas) than the others. Yeti feet share distinct similarities with pongid (ape) feet and eyewitnesses have described its walk as lumbering and shambling compared to the smoother glide of its counterparts. It has also been noted that in order to move faster, the Yeti prefers to scramble down-on-all-fours as opposed to its usual upright walking posture. Its broad feet appear ideal for trekking through deep snow whilst the two big toes allow for a solid purchase on narrow rock ledges as Shipton's observations suggest. Such highly specialised feet, whilst biomechanically perfect for the Himalayan terrain, will in all likelihood stop the creature responsible for the tracks from expanding their range beyond the mountains of which they are accustomed.

Shipton's photos have taken on great importance due to the clarity of the images, the integrity of the photographer along with the remoteness of the discovery. As Ivan Sanderson noted, a 'sort of revolution began within the ranks of science' because of his photos. The subject has been taken much more seriously since those images were made public because, as John Napier remarked, the Shipton Yeti print photo 'is unique, for it is the only item of evidence of the Yeti saga that offers the opportunity for critical analysis.'

In an issue of the *New Scientist* magazine from May 12, 1960 the editor wrote that 'the idea of a sort of land-based coelacanth, a living fossil skulking in the mountains of Tibet, takes the whole concept of the Snowman out of the science fiction category.'[68]

Ex British army officer Lord John Hunt, who led the successful British expedition to Everest in 1953 alongside Shipton, Hillary and the others, originally applied to lead the 1936 expedition but failed on medical grounds with a minor heart problem. Despite the setback, Hunt made a trip to the Himalayas the following year, in which he summited the south-western Nepal Peak and also the Zemu Gap between Kangchenjunga and Simvo. It was here where he first encountered tracks in the snow which the Sherpas insisted belonged to the Yeti.

On two occasions, in 1953 and again in 1978, he heard the creature's high-pitched call, accompanied by more footprints in the snow at high altitude (15,000-20,000 ft), which is far beyond the habitat of the

Himalayan black and red bears. The tracks found in 1978 were so fresh that Hunt was able to see a clear impression of the toes, convincing him that the prints accurately represented the actual shape and size of the Yeti foot, about 13 ¾ inches long and 6 ¾ inches broad (compare this to a man with size 44 shoes having a print length of 11 ½ inches).

Following his initial Everest expedition in 1953, Lord Hunt is on record in Charles Stonor's 1955 book, *The Sherpa and the Snowman*, as saying 'And I believe in the Yeti. I have seen his tracks, heard his yelping call, listened to first-hand experiences of reputable local people. . . That evidence will be produced sooner or later, sufficient to convince the doubters, is beyond doubt.'

After a trip to Peking with a Parliamentary delegation, Hunt expanded on his views that the Yeti exists in an article printed in *The Sunday Express* (June 28, 1981): 'I talked to experts in Peking and discovered that the Chinese are doing a lot of research into this mystery. They showed me photographs of footprints found in China and Russia and they are remarkably similar to ones I have seen in the Himalayas. Now I'm even more convinced there is a very strong case in favour of the animal's existence. It is definitely not a bear. It looks more like an ape and the Chinese believe it could be a primitive form of man.'

This is a theory that some researchers believe explains what happened to the Neanderthals which lived alongside our *Homo sapiens* ancestors before disappearing into thin air and out of human history once and for all. As Shackley wrote, 'The idea that Neanderthal man *must* be extinct because modern man can be the only surviving hominid is outmoded biological arrogance.'[69]

If, as we have discussed in earlier chapters, man hasn't evolved from the so called pre-humans whose fossil skeletons led to the concept of natural evolution, what *did* happen to those hominids? What did they evolve into? Or did they simply die out, unable to adjust to constantly changing environmental conditions?

Author and Professor of human genetics at Oxford University Bryan Sykes wrote, 'It now seems as though our Homo sapiens ancestors shared the planet with several other human species and even interbred with them. The notion that there could be parts of the earth where these other humans survive to this day, either as a completely separate species or as a type of genetic hybrid, does not seem anywhere as ridiculous as once it did.'[70]

Michael Cremo believes that if one studies the relevant fossil data, evidence reveals the presence of contemporaneous living between human and ape-types; 'when all the evidence, including that for very ancient humans and living ape-men, is objectively evaluated, the pattern that emerges is one of a continuing coexistence rather than a sequential evolution.'[71]

So is it possible that the hominoids are the native indigenous bipeds of planet Earth? The split from quadruped primates to bipedal primates certainly took place as modern science decrees, but the descendants may not be us but the hominoids.

We have already seen how anatomically modern human remains have been discovered much further back into antiquity than is presently considered feasible, and such incredible finds force us to question not only who the true descendants of the pre-humans may be, but more importantly, who were the real human ancestors if it proves to not be the Neanderthals and those preceding them. Could Sasquatch, Yeti and their counterparts actually be their living descendants instead of us? They certainly fit the model physically much more than modern humans, as the reported descriptions of these mysterious creatures confirm.

'Having to accept hominoids as real will require having to acknowledge that the pre-human fossil record is comprised entirely of their bones, rather than ours. That admission will then force each of us – including, however reluctantly, all Darwinists and Creationists – to confront a truly awesome question: Where *did* humans come from?'[72]

But before science will even begin to ask these questions, they first need to recognise the existence of these mysterious large bipeds which have been spotted inhabiting the remotest parts of our planet. They will also need to admit to having ignored vital evidence which reveals the greater antiquity of man, which the research of Michael Cremo has brought out of the shadows, and reconsider the true origins of humankind.

As Pye stated, 'Right now science and religion stand united against hominoids, with scientists carrying the brunt of responsibility for keeping them ridiculed out of existence. However, as soon as one is brought in, those same scientists will be forced to publicly take their lumps and accommodate the new reality.'

ALMAS AND AGOGWES

If Sasquatch and Yeti continue to be mysterious creatures hidden amongst the most inhospitable regions of this planet, then the other two groups of reported hominids are verging on the practically invisible. So little is truly known of their existence that they firmly belong in the mythological category, products of legend and folklore which are rarely reported, yet I feel compelled to include them here despite their inherent anonymity.

Despite the sheer lack of evidence one might associate with their larger cousins Bigfoot and Yeti, their apparent existence must at least be acknowledged in the context of this research. Almas accounts differ from Yeti and Sasquatch accounts as there is a general lack of mythological overtones. Only in the northwest of Mongolia does there exist some mythological perception of the wild creatures. To the locals 'they are regarded as different, more primitive, forms of man whose presence in an area is hardly a cause for remark.'[73]

Mongolian for "wild man", the 'Almas' is another albeit lesser known type of hominid which is believed to inhabit areas of Central Asia, Russia, Pakistan and the Altai Mountains of Southern Mongolia. The female of the species is often referred to as an 'Almasty' and alternatively in Kazakhstan, the term 'Kaptar' is used. Typically described as between 5 and 6 feet and covered in hair ¾ to 3 inches in length, with Neanderthal-like prominent brow ridges and flat noses, Almas recorded sightings go back as far as the 15th century.

Along with one of the first recorded European sightings of Przewalski or Dzungarian horses, a rare subspecies of endangered wild horse native to Central Asia, Bavarian nobleman Hans Schiltberger recorded his personal observations of Almas in a journal of his trip of

Mongolia back in 1420. He was taken prisoner by the Turks, and was destined to be sent to a Mongol prince named Egidi. Schiltberger managed to return to his home around 1427 and his journal which was completed three years later is now housed in the Munich Municipal Library. The following excerpt is taken from his journal which he completed in 1430:

'In the mountains themselves live wild people, who have nothing in common with other human beings. A pelt covers the entire body of these creatures. Only the hands and face are free of hair. They run around in the hills like animals and eat foliage and grass and whatever else they can find.'

Nicholai Przewalski, who only rediscovered the rare horses that would later be named after him in 1881 also claimed to have seen 'wildmen' in Mongolia ten years earlier in 1871. The presence of these wildmen in Central Asia were commonplace in folklore since the Middle Ages, in fact so much so that descriptions of the Almas were included in a book considered to be a standard work on Mongolian natural history written by a Mongol savant called Dondubjalstan (1792-1855).

The book which now resides in the central library of the Scientific Committee in Mongolia might be considered a standard work on natural history, with applications for Buddhist medicine it translates as the *'Anatomical Dictionary for Recognising Various Diseases'*. It contains thousands of illustrations of various classes of animals including reptiles, mammals and amphibians. Not one of these classified creatures had a mythological status when it was classified, in fact quite the opposite, each and every specimen he recorded are living and observable to the present day, and in order to have been included in such a book, the Almas may have been quite commonplace and sufficiently well known to travellers between Tibet and Mongolia.

The following description of an Almas which was included in the book was written in Tibetan alongside a 'wildman' picture, 'The wild man lives in the mountains, his origins close to that of a bear; his body resembles that of a man, and he has enormous strength. His meat may be eaten to treat mental diseases and his gall cures jaundice.'

On 13 February 1974, a shepherd called Musai recalled seeing an Almas in the Asgat Mountains and gave the following detailed description of the allusive creature:

'. . . half men and half beasts with reddish-black hair. Their face is hairless and their abdomen is sparsely covered with hair. The back of the head has a conical shape as it were; the forehead is flattened, prominent brow ridges and a protruding jaw. The size of a medium-height man, an Almas walks with his knees bent, stoops as is in-toed. He has broad shoulders and long arms; his big toe sticks out. Almases are easily frightened, suspicious, though not aggressive, and lead a nocturnal life. No one has ever heard them speak. They were usually seen at dawn and in the dusk and are believed to live on roots, leaves, grass and other vegetation. They prefer to stay in places far away from man, in mountains for instance. For some reason they keep close to wild rams and goats. In summer, when the cattle are moved from their winter mountain pastures to distant ones their place is taken by the wild rams and goats, and then, as a rule, Almases make their appearance. Cattle breeders once met a couple and once a baby Almas.'[74]

The shepherd's descriptions above mirror those of the locals, many of which were collected during studies conducted in the northern Azerbaijan and Kabardino-Balkaria area by French doctor, anatomist and mountaineer, Dr. Zh. I. Kofman. Her early investigative work of the Almas applied modern polling techniques to the local inhabitants in order to build 'identikit' Almas. The results led her to publicly state her understanding that these unusual 'wildmen' were in fact relict Neanderthals.

The decline of the species has been reported as the result of both an increase in human activity in Almas territory, coinciding with the emergence of the trans-Mongolian railway connecting Peking with Irkutsk in Russia. This significant increase in human disturbance also affected the wild horse and camel populations which are said to have retreated into the more remote western regions.

Finally, let us briefly familiarise ourselves with the fourth group of hominid known to inhabit this Earth, albeit even more scarcely than the other three. Very little is known of this minority group but the simple fact that sightings have been made and reported is enough to warrant further enquiry into their existence.

The Agogwe have been described as little furry men who frequent the remote Ussure and Simbiti forests on the western side of the Wembare Plains in Tanzania, East Africa. Often described as small human-like bipeds between 2-5 feet in height, and covered in brownish woolly hair with a yellow/reddish skin, rounded forehead, small canines and small feet with an opposable big toe. The December edition of the London magazine *Discovery* in 1937 published the first recorded sighting of an African Agogwe by a non-African native named Captain William Hichens.

In the article *African Mystery Beasts*, Capt. Hichens described his encounter which took place in 1900, 'Some years ago I was sent on an official lion-hunt to this area and, while waiting in a forest glade for a man-eater, I saw two small, brown furry creatures come from the dense forest on one side of the glade and disappear into the thickets on the other. They were like little men, about four feet high, walking upright, but clad in russet hair. The native hunter with me gaped in mingled fear and amazement. They were, he said, *agogwe*, the little furry men whom one does not see once in a lifetime. I made desperate efforts to find them, but without avail in that well-nigh impenetrable forest.'

In 1938, a British Officer Cuthbert Burgoyne wrote to *Discovery* magazine after having read the Hichens article which had gone into print the previous year. Burgoyne recounted his own personal experiences whilst travelling through East Africa aboard a Japanese cargo boat.

His story speaks of a sighting in 1927 as their boat neared the shoreline, where they saw a troop of baboons hunting for shellfish and crabs along a sloping beach. Amongst the many baboons he recalled seeing two pure white baboons for the first time, which although quite rare, were known to inhabit those regions. But then from out of nowhere, Burgoyne recalled the following:

'As we watched, two little brown men walked out of the bush and down among the baboons. They were certainly not any known monkey and they must have been akin or they would have disturbed the baboons. They were too far away to see in detail, but these small human-like animals were probably between 4 and 5 feet tall, quite upright and graceful in figure.'

Known by many other names in various other regions such as Zimbabwe, Congo, Zaire, the Ivory Coast and Northern Mozambique, cryptozoologist Bernard Heuvelmans postulated that the Agogwe could possibly be a surviving ancestor of australopithecine which existed 2.5 million years ago. Apart from the opposable big toe which could be the product of millions of years of evolution, the Agogwe descriptions do appear to fit what we know of australopithecine features.

HABITATION

One major argument against hominid existence today comes from dogmatic claims that because humans already occupy most ecological niches on the planet, it would be impossible for a population of hominoids to inhabit large areas without them being regularly seen. But if they live in the most heavily dense forested pockets of the Earth or in the remotest wilderness of the Himalayas, then surely they could survive in isolation and only risk being spotted or disturbed once they reach the boundaries of these areas.

The vast majority of sightings occur in such boundaries where the creatures are forced to cross open terrain in search of food or water. Both the Freeman footage and the Patterson film caught their subjects unawares in open areas which led both creatures to instantly head back into the undergrowth once spotted as they attempted to conceal themselves once more.

'Most human encounters with humanoids occur by accidental approaches from downwind. When they realize they are in a human's presence, they tend to hustle themselves out of sight. No signs of panic, though, like prey animals exhibit when taken by surprise, just the make-yourself-scarce reaction of a creature used to being alone or exclusively in the company of its own kind.'[75]

Exactly how much of the Earth's surface, including polar caps and deserts, have actually been physically surveyed on foot? A conservative estimate is less than 30 or 40 per cent, which leaves between 60 and 70 per cent as unchartered territory. Since the advent of flight, most of the densely forested regions have had to be surveyed from the air, which would allow for vast amounts of land to have never been properly accounted for.

If one looks at the figures it is very interesting to note precisely how much territory remains uninhabited by humans. Earth's land surface is around 55 million square miles. One third is icy wastelands and deserts, essentially unfit for human habitation. Another 30 per cent is covered by temperate forests. So, excluding the ice caps, deserts, tundras and dense forests, the remaining 36 per cent, around 20 million sq. miles, is the arable land suitable for comfortable human habitation. So if one third of Earth's total land surface is easily suitable for human living and one third is either too parched or too frozen, could the final third belong to the hominids?

According to research, 17 per cent of the entire United States or 383 million square miles of Federal land has never even been surveyed. It was a century ago when 2.2 per cent (around 50 million sq. miles) were last surveyed. In fact, a 1990 census counted 572,000 people in an area covering 950,000 sq. miles – a quarter of the entire country – which equates to around two or less people per square mile over 143 counties in 15 western states. This suggests that 25 per cent of the western states are practically uninhabited as they are so sparsely populated. These regions which include upper and lower montane forests suit Sasquatch, who out of all the types probably have the widest habitat diversity. Although preferring the lower regions they can adapt to the upper forested areas and even jungles and swamps when necessary.

In comparison, the Himalayas which consists of five immense and sprawling mountain ranges joined together across central Asia which combined are nearly the same size as the entire U.S., allows plenty of room for Yeti inhabitation and roaming where they can exploit the upper montane forests that grow there. Every creature on this planet lives in ecological niches best suited for its needs and survival.

Humans live on the margins of every environment thanks mainly to our ability to overcome our natural state of being, for example, clothing, vast range of food availability, transport etc. Without these resources, naked humans would not be even remotely successful in most of these living zones; instead we would see a population increase in the tropical and subtropical regions of our planet.

As things stand, our niches adjoin but do not overlap the niches best suited to hominid habitation. As Pye highlights, 'hominoids "own" the equatorial forests and temperate woodlands, leaving the prime open-country niches to humans and other animals that share them with us. And wouldn't you know? – where our niches adjoin theirs is where the majority of hominoid encounters occur.'

In comparison with the North American Bigfoot, Yeti are said to have extra-long body hair in the 6 to 10 inch range in order to conserve heat in the colder Asian climate, and the limited amount of vegetation has forced them to succumb to a more carnivorous diet with the added high-energy protein that meat offers being a necessity. Many Sherpas in Nepal and Tibet have described finding the ravaged carcasses of sheep, goat, cattle and yaks, torn savagely but efficiently limb from limb by some unknown predator. Often the spine appears to have suffered a severe blow as if killed by force before the rest of the animal is consumed.

Sasquatch need never go hungry as their environment provides a feast of both plant and animal foods for them to live off. Just as humans would in the same situation, Bigfoot individuals migrate north and south with the seasons in search of nourishment and shelter. Their sheer stature and body musculature is testament to the harsh, physically demanding environment they find themselves surviving in.

Another concern of the sceptics regarding hominid existence is the absence of their physical remains. So where are the hominoid corpses? Why are hominoid remains never discovered once they have died? Just as other non-prey species know when they are dying, perhaps the hominoids must seek out secluded and secure areas for their final resting place before nature takes over and slowly discards of the body over time.

First the scavengers do their bit and strip all the flesh from the bones, leaving the worms and insects to finish off the bone marrow and any leftovers. The bones are then attacked by moulds and fungus, as the acidic soils of the forest floor dissolve whatever remains. After all, it is forested areas like this which have neatly discarded *all* fossilised chimpanzee remains, none have ever been found. The absence of such animal remains in wooded areas however, does not discount the possibility that large numbers lived and died there.

So, plenty of food for thought regarding the possible existence of living hominids and the plausible theory that they could actually be the true ancestors of the pre-humans whose ancient lineage is usually exclusively reserved for us modern humans. Such a thesis will remain inconclusive at this juncture but who knows what future scientific discoveries will reveal.

What can be spoken with supreme confidence is that something very real does appear to inhabit the remotest regions of the Earth, and the subsequent sightings, video footage and footprints attest to this reality despite the mythological status which these creatures have been assigned. Surely, further investigation of Sasquatch and Yeti in particular, could yield unexpected scientific results should the authorities deem such a venture worthwhile.

In the words of Dr. John Napier, 'Either some of the footprints are real, or all are fakes. If they are all fakes, then an explanation invoking legend and folk memory is adequate to explain the mystery. But if any of them are real then as scientists we have a lot to explain. Among other things we shall have to rewrite the story of human evolution. We shall have to explain that *Homo sapiens* is not the one and only living product of the hominid line, and we shall have to admit that there are still major mysteries to be solved in a world we thought we knew so well.'[76]

If time reveals the existence of Sasquatch and Yeti to be authentic, and future DNA testing connects them to that ancient hominid line which is presently accepted as the path of human ancestry, then what other mythical beasts could eventually prove to be based in reality?

Next we shall turn our attention towards one of the world's most popular legends which appears in texts from every corner of the globe, from the Bible, to Norse and Greek mythology, to ancient Britain, that unknown yet fearsome race we call giants.

Chapter Four

THE FORGOTTEN RACE

The eyes of that species of extinct giants, whose bones fill the mounds of America, have gazed on Niagara, as ours do now.

Abraham Lincoln

COULD ANCIENT GIANT HUMAN BEINGS have walked the Earth in prehistory as the many myths and legends contend, or are all the stories of old which have been told around the world for millennia simply fanciful metaphoric expressions employed as literary devices?

In 400 BC, the Greek poet Homer wrote 'on the Earth there once were giants,' but evidence to prove such a claim is few and far between, and in order to establish some kind of truth behind the many extravagant myths which have perforated the human psyche since time immemorial, one first has to wade through the thick mire of fictive content blocking the avid researcher's path.

Although this book highlights some unexplained and unsolved mysteries of the world, it is not this author's intent to deal in pure speculation but rather to search for the truth behind such tales in a hope of further understanding our forgotten history. The purpose of this book is to attempt to ascertain some elements of truth, by searching for suitable evidence which can raise our awareness of previously unaccepted data commonly considered fictitious.

It is with this in mind that no mention of biblical references shall be included in this book, as is commonly the case when speaking of giants. Not that the passages written in *The Holy Bible* and *The Book of Enoch* have no value or truth behind them, just that in the context of this research such material cannot offer the proof that this author seeks. After all, the 'Nephilim', often considered the antediluvian giants mentioned in the *Book of Genesis*, actually have no literal reference to height in Hebrew, and only translates to 'giants' in Greek and English mistranslations.

So aside from referring to such ancient texts, if one endeavours to investigate the information currently available on giants one will no doubt encounter many stories or 'discoveries' from overzealous researchers which only serve to muddy the waters of information for the true fact-finders among us. 'Fake news' has unfortunately become an integral aspect of the internet, so researchers must be vigilant and veer away from websites offering fantastic tales of giant 'facts' and instead resort to good old fashioned reading of well-researched books or accurately sourced articles.

World mythology is replete with legends of giants, many of which are portrayed as gargantuan beasts capable of destroying villages with their cumbersome stride. Could these stories, some of them at least, have derived from actual events or are they just tall tales? Are we looking at metaphoric musings, exaggerated history, or maybe a combination of both?

We are all aware of the concept of giant folk, whether from some children's story like Jack and the Beanstalk or the biblical Goliath who was slain by the sword of David before becoming the King of the Israelites. Often giants have been considered godlike or born of the gods, like the titans of Greek mythology, whilst others have been presented as cannibalistic ogre-like figures that eat children and fight amongst themselves, causing havoc wherever they go.

Nobody is certain of the origins of the word 'giant' but it could possibly have derived from the Greek 'gigantes', a term which actually referred to men of normal stature, albeit heavily-armed Greek soldiers in Archaic and Classical representations.

If we discount the many mythical accounts of monumental giants of unrealistic proportions, the size of mountains, whose heads scrape the clouds, and instead focus our attention on the more plausible cases, then it is increasingly more likely that genuine information can be attained. It is for this reason that we shall be focusing our attention on archival documentation further in the chapter, examining the alleged reported discoveries and exhumations of real giant human skeletons.

Many ancient texts attribute the megalithic structures which stand on every continent to be the handiwork of giant beings, and should you choose to visit one of these colossal monuments; whether at Stonehenge in England or at Baalbek in Lebanon, it would be easy to understand why. This assumption appears most natural when one considers the sheer immensity of some of these mysterious constructions, but assumptions alone will not shed any light on the validity of such connections.

Some ancient Arab writings profess that the first and oldest stages of Baalbek, which includes the three 800-ton trilithon blocks, were built by a race of giants at the command of King Nimrod following the Great Flood. This may prove to be a legitimate claim, it certainly is not an isolated idea, giants building the megaliths, but for now it remains just an idea until their giant ancient bones can reinforce their existence.

Surely though, in order to manually shift stone blocks of up to a thousand tons, we are talking of giants of such stature as to be well beyond the realms of reality. There must be a limit to what height a man is capable of walking and holding his own weight, and the size implications required to be able to construct the dolmens, cyclopean walls and megalithic standing stones which lay strewn across the globe as reminders of high civilizations that evade living memory, must in all likelihood exceed all physical restrictions on a planet with such a strong gravitational pull as Earth's.

That said, some would counter-argue that the atmosphere and gravity of this planet was very different in the distant past, maybe allowing for such extremities of growth to become feasible. One need only consider the Jurassic period which played host to creatures of immense size, epitomised by the existence of the dinosaurs. But men of such extreme size would require an enormous amount of both oxygen and food in order to survive and one must question the plausibility of such a proposition.

Determining whether or not a forgotten race of giant beings once roamed the Earth has proved problematic to say the very least, considering that physical evidence appears to be very scant indeed. But if we are to open our minds in order to shed more light on our murky and mysterious past, then we should allow ourselves the opportunity to revisit the archives and see what we can reveal.

TALLEST MEN ON RECORD

Before we continue it may be worth considering what qualifies as giant and not just really, really tall. There are many people over seven foot, just take a look at the American basketball league to find some prime examples (in fact only twenty players in NBA history have exceeded a listed height of 7 ft 3 inches) but these men aren't what one would consider to be giants. A giant should be *extraordinarily* tall, abnormal compared to the majority of the human population, with giant hands and feet, a ferocious appetite, and unable to wear normal clothes or sit in normal chairs.

Robert Pershing Wadlow (fig. 17) was a true giant who reached 8 ft. 11.1 inches tall on 27 June 1940, just over two weeks before his death. This remarkable height remains the tallest reached by any human in medical history, and photo and video footage of Wadlow shows us how incredible it must have been to be in the presence of a living giant. Born in Alton, Illinois, in the USA on February 22, 1918, Wadlow has firmly imprinted his name into the history books as the tallest man on Earth.

In order to maintain the energy required to move his gigantic body, Wadlow's peak daily calorie consumption reached 8000, which is more than three times the average amount recommended for most men. This huge amount of food consumption led to his greatest weight which was recorded on his 21st birthday at 35 stone 11 pounds or 222.71 kg.

Fig. 17 Robert Wadlow stood next to his father, Harold Franklin Wadlow who was 5 ft. 11.5 in.

As a result of a septic blister on his right ankle which was caused by a poorly fitted brace only a week earlier, Wadlow died on July 15, 1940 in a hotel in Manistee, Michigan aged only 22 years old. He was buried in his home town of Alton in a coffin which measured an immense 10 ft. 9 inches which took twelve men to carry, at the funeral where around

5,000 people came to pay their respects to the gentle giant whose name had become known all over the western world.

Robert Wadlow or the 'Alton Giant' as he was commonly known, suffered from hyperplasia of his pituitary gland which involves the over production of human growth hormones to abnormally high levels. His unusual growth was still continuing but as he died so young, one can only wonder at what height he would have peaked if his life hadn't have been cut so tragically short. It is very possible, considering he was less than an inch away from reaching 9 ft. at the time of death that he could have grown 10 ft. tall and beyond.

His case is actually quite unique, even by giant's standards, as he didn't suffer from the normal causes of gigantism, a condition which has afflicted so many of the world's tallest people. Gigantism is caused by a tumour pushing against the pituitary gland which forces the gland to effectively squeeze out more height growth hormone. But in Wadlow's case, it was the gland itself that was abnormally large and not a tumour pushing against it which was responsible for his incredible growth.

An article stated that his hypertrophic pituitary gland had actually prevented Wadlow from experiencing puberty, as his bones were denied the usual information which hinders abnormal growth and sends signals for the growth plates to close, thus controlling the height and weight of the individual. And despite his decision to never use a wheelchair, his height took an inevitable toll on him, as his bones lacked the density of normal bones simply because they were too busy growing upwards, thus forcing him to wear leg braces that could support his ever-increasing weight. With numbing sensations in his legs and incredibly large feet, he struggled to walk normally, and it was the infection caused by the introduction of the new leg brace which ultimately led to his death.

John Rogen, the tallest man in the world before Wadlow was born, reached an astounding height of 8 ft. 9, but was unable to even stand due to a condition called ankylosis, which has even been found in dinosaur fossil specimens which includes the Tyrannosaurus Rex. Ankylosis is stiffness in the joints following rigidity and the abnormal adhesion of the bones of the joint, which in Rogen's case disabled his ability to stand or walk.

The world's tallest living man today (as of 2018) is farmer Sultan Kösen, whose height has reached a phenomenal 8 ft. 2.82 in. Interestingly, he also holds the world record for the largest hands, at 28 cm (11.02 in). Kösen's abnormal growth stems from a tumour affecting his pituitary gland as we have just discussed as being the basis of gigantism, although Kösen's height also derives from a similar condition called acromegaly. According to the University of Virginia, on August 25th 2010, doctors confirmed an increased height of 8 ft. 4 in. which they stated was possibly Kösen's actual height that had been artificially lowered by both his scoliosis and bad posture.[77]

Despite developing from the same region in the body, the pituitary gland, gigantism and acromegaly are not the same disease although both are treatable. Gigantism occurs only in children, and it is the excessive amount of growth hormone that is produced which triggers bones to grow in length at the growth plates. Acromegaly on the other hand, is a rare condition found only in adults, which is not associated with increases in height because the growth plates fuse after puberty, but both conditions overproduce growth hormones due to a benign tumour on the pituitary gland.

As of the time of writing (2018), Kösen is alive and well at the age of 35 years old, but this may be down to the advancements in science rather than fortune alone. His life may well have been extended thanks to doctors at the University of Virginia Medical Center, who successfully treated Kösen's acromegaly by using a novel form of radiation therapy known as gamma knife radio-surgery which uses hundreds of highly focused radiation beams to target tumours and lesions within the brain.

Oddly enough, despite Kösen being the tallest man alive with the largest hands, he cannot lay claim to owning the largest feet in the world. This record belongs to the Moroccan Brahim Takioullah, with his left foot measured by officials from Guinness World Records at 38.1 cm (1 ft. 3 in.) and his right, 37.5 (1 ft. 2.76 in). He remains the tallest man in Morocco at 8 ft. 1, only two inches shorter than Kösen.

Although many of the tallest men on record owe their incredible size to some physical abnormality, not all giants share this unfortunate commonality. Some are just tall people who live to a reasonable age despite the obvious difficulties they have had to face because of the stresses of such tremendous physical stature.

THE GIANTS OF SEVILLE

The title of 'tallest married couple' in history goes to Captain Martin Bates and his wife Anna Swan, who married on 17 June, 1871. This remarkable pair (fig. 18) both grew close to 8 feet tall, with Anna measuring 7 ft. 11 compared to her husband of 7 ft. 9, giving them a combined height of 15 ft. 8.

Fig. 18 Captain Martin Bates and Anna Swan with friend Lei McFarland.

Anna Haining Swan weighed 18 lbs when she was born in Nova Scotia on August 6th 1846. She was almost five feet tall by the time she was four years old, and once she reached her maximum height, half an inch short of eight feet, she began an exhibition career working with P.T. Barnum in his New York Museum, shortly before her seventeenth birthday.

Swan travelled Europe with Barnum at the age of nineteen where she was introduced to Queen Victoria, and also visited the homes of her Scottish ancestors, but despite earning a lot of money working with the famous promoter her life was rife with disaster. She barely survived a fire at the original Barnum Museum, as she was trapped on the third floor, and due to her immense size firemen were unable to rescue her, which very nearly cost her her life. It took the aid of a crane from a nearby construction site to demolish the outside wall before the servicemen were able to get her out safely.

Once rebuilt, the museum experienced another fire in which the giantess lost all of her possessions, leading her to quit for a while and return home. Barnum managed to persuade her to embark on a tour of the United States in 1869, and it was here where she met her future husband, a Kentucky gentleman named Martin van Buren Bates.

Bates, a former Confederate Captain during the Civil War also happened to be close to eight foot tall, and the couple fell in love and married shortly after. Billed as the 'World's Tallest Couple', the pair received many wedding gifts, and Queen Victoria herself actually gave them the wedding gown and diamond ring.

Once settled in Seville, Ohio, the giant couple put their vast career earnings to good use and built themselves a colossal home fit for their specific purposes. Every door was over 8 feet high, the ceilings reached 14 feet, and all the furniture was custom built to suit their immense frames. In 1872, Swan gave birth to a baby girl weighing 18 lbs, coincidentally the same weight she herself had been at birth, but tragically the child did not survive long. Seven years later she gave birth to a boy who weighed even more than the girl, a huge 22 lbs, but once again he didn't survive long.

The size of her babies implied that her children would have grown up to be giants also, just like their parents, but sadly it was not to be. Anna Swan died unexpectedly the day before her 42nd birthday in 1888, and left a distraught husband behind who erected a monument to his late wife which included a 15 ft. statue of a Greek goddess atop the grave. Bates remarried a woman of regular stature 11 years later, and died in 1919 of nephritis, an inflammation of the kidneys, at the age of 85.

The reason for the inclusion of these modern giants is to highlight the fact that despite its rarity, the human body is very capable of growing to eight feet and beyond, and not necessarily because of some growth disorder such as gigantism. As the previous case of Martin Bates reveals, a man close to 8 ft. tall can live a normal and even successful life, dying at a more than reasonable age of a non size-related disease.

One wonders if the more recent cases link back to a past where giants were more common than they are today. Maybe, as we shall soon discover, races of giant men and women walked this earth, whose presence and sheer existence has been commemorated in the world's myths and legends. So let us now review the available literature on the subject, in particular, news articles which have surfaced over the years which report apparently authentic giant archaeological finds.

GIANTS OF ALBION

Living in England, this author was curious to uncover any reports of giants in Great Britain. There are a number of interesting documents pertaining to their existence on these shores but they appear to be few and far between. Of course there are a number of extremely tall British folk, some which have been recorded, others will have lived and died without even a mention, and there are those whose name exists only in legend and folklore.

Great Britain once was known as Albion, a name derived from the Atlantis titan of the same name. Legend claims that giants either founded Albion or were the original inhabitants of the land. In the 12th

century, Geoffrey of Monmouth wrote in *Historia Regum Brittanniae* (*The History of the Kings of Britain*) about the legends of giants living in Britain. His accounts are clearly not literal representations of factual events but seem to have originated from numerous sources and historical accounts and could possibly have at least their roots in reality.

He tells of the time Brutus of Troy escaped from Gaul with his fellow Trojans and 'set sail with a fair wind towards the promised island'. 'The island was then called Albion, and inhabited by none but a few giants. Notwithstanding this, the pleasant situation of the places, the plenty of rivers abounding with fish, and the engaging prospect of its woods, made Brutus and his company very desirous to fix their habitation in it.'

He then explains the origins of the island's current name, 'at last Brutus called the island after his own name Britain and his companions Britons; for by these means he desired to perpetuate the memory of his name.' Whether there is any truth behind these stories remains to be seen but it is certainly interesting to discover such an early connection with giants in Britain.

In reality, presently the tallest British-born man and tallest in Europe is the English actor and former basketball player, Neil Fingleton, who stands at 7 ft. 7.56 inches tall. He is among the twenty-five tallest men in the world. Historically speaking there are a number of giant folk from the British Isles worthy of mention, some lived for sure whilst others are only reputed to have occupied these shores.

Giant Porters

In the Royal Collection at Hampton Court in England hangs a portrait of Queen Elizabeth's giant porter, a picture which is said to be life-sized. Painted by Frederic Zucchero in 1580, the huge porter was mentioned in both Shakespeare's *Macbeth* and the 1842 *Handbook to the Public Galleries of Art in and Near London: with Catalogues*. The handbook states: 'Full-length. Dated 1580. This personage was seven feet six inches in height. Walter Scott has introduced him into "Kenilworth" with great effect.'

There is no reason to doubt the true stature of this man as it would serve no real purpose to exaggerate his height, but what it does highlight is that very tall people have been around throughout the ages and have often been recognised for their extraordinarily tall demeanour, even by royalty, who must have been glad to have had such an imposing figure on their side.

The Queen was not the only one to have had the services of a giant porter, as Oliver Cromwell's porter Daniel also reached a height of seven feet six inches. Not just a giant of a man, Daniel was a renowned clairvoyant in his day, and despite some failed predictions he successfully prophesized some famously historic moments. He predicted the crowning of Charles II which would be followed by the presence of a great comet which he said would light up the night sky so brightly that a newspaper could be read by its light.

In 1660, Charles took the throne two years after Cromwell had died in 1658, and in 1665 the great comet appeared just as the giant porter had foreseen. Samuel Pepys described the event in a letter writing that the light was so brilliant 'that night was day'.

Daniel also predicted that a great plague would hit England during Charles' reign that would be followed by a devastating fire which would leave London decimated. Sure enough, the year 1666 witnessed a plague hitting London and the surrounding areas, and of course the Great Fire of London started in Pudding Lane, which destroyed over 13,000 homes and 90 churches.

Glastonbury Giant

One story which has survived the ages is the apparent discovery of the 'Glastonbury Giant' which was allegedly unearthed in 1190, on orders of King Henry II, following rumours that the legendary King Arthur was in fact buried at that specific location. Here, between two ancient pyramid-shaped pillars at Glastonbury in Somerset, England, workers dug down to a depth of seven feet where they found a leaden cross with the inscription:

HIC JACET SEPULTUS INCLYTUS REX ARTURUS IN
INSULA AVALLONI

This translates as 'Here lies buried the renowned King Arthur in the Isle of Avalon.'

This discovery inspired the excavators to dig even further in the hope of finding solid proof of the legend's existence, and at sixteen feet deep they finally struck a large coffin hollowed out from the trunk of an old oak tree. Inside they discovered the skeletal remains of a man who had once measured close to nine feet tall, laid next to the skeleton of an average-sized woman, assumed at that time to be Arthur's Queen, Guinevere.

It is said that their bones were reinterred in the church there about a century later, right before the altar and in the presence of King Edward I. It is from that time that Glastonbury's long association with the Arthurian legends was cemented in history, despite the opposing arguments claiming that the inscribed leaden cross must have been placed there much later than the original grave, as it was buried nine feet above the actual coffin.

Many believed that the cross must be a fraud, possibly left there by the monks at the nearby Benedictine Abbey, in an attempt to reap fame upon the abbey and the area by encouraging the nobility to offer donations supporting such a hallowed spot where the body of one of England's greatest ever legends was laid to rest.

The *Encyclopaedia Britannica* supports this theory, 'The identification of Avalon with Glastonbury is equally likely to have been an attempt by Glastonbury monks to exploit the prestige of the Arthurian legends for the benefit of their own community, just as later the popularity of the Grail legend led them to claim that Joseph of Arimathea had established himself at Glastonbury.' Others have suggested that the bodies were likely Celtic in origin, as hollowed-out oak trunk coffins had been a method used by the Celts in the past.

Despite the conspicuous discovery of Arthur's alleged gravestone, the actual find of a giant figure is not really up for dispute, as the respected historian Giraldus Cambrensis personally examined the massive bones in 1194, just four days after the initial discovery, and he pronounced them genuine. Then hundreds of years later, in 1962-63, archaeologist Dr. Ralegh Radford studied the ancient giant remains following additional excavations of the site and 'confirmed that a prominent personage had indeed been buried there at the period in question.'

The Childe of Hale

In 1578 in the chapelry of Hale just southwest of Manchester, John Middleton was born, and he 'grew almost tall enough to look Goliath straight in the eye.' Said to have been endowed with extraordinary strength, Sir Gilbert Ireland, the sheriff of Lancashire, dressed Middleton up and took him to London to meet King James I in 1620. Once they had returned home, Middleton had his portrait painted whilst still 'dressed-up', and this painting has been preserved in the library of Brasenose College at Oxford.

Dr. Robert Plot, the British naturalist, later made measurements of the portrait, and gave this description in his report:

'John Middleton, commonly called 'The Childe of Hale', whose hand from the carpus to the end of the middle finger was seventeen inches long, his palm eight inches and a half broad, and his whole height nine foot three inches, wanting but six inches of the height of Goliath, if that in Brasenose College Library (drawn at length, as 'tis said, in his just proportions) be a true piece of him.'

Middleton was buried in the Hale churchyard at the age of 45. This epitaph was inscribed on the twelve-foot-long stone covering his grave:

HERE LYETH
THE BODIE OF JOHN MIDDLETON THE CHILDE.
NINE FEET THREE. BORNE 1578.
DYEDE 1623

His presence acts as another reminder of an unknown part of our past, a time where men and women of great stature walked the earth, maybe as commonly as the average person does today. And whatever the truth turns out to be, the existence of men over nine feet tall in Britain is so relatively unknown that it is worthy of a brief mention in the context of this study.

The Norfolk Giant

Robert Hales was born on 2nd May 1820, in the village of West Somerton near Great Yarmouth, Norfolk, England. The son of a farmer, he reached the remarkable height of 7 ft. 8 inches tall (fig. 19). One of nine children, with a mother and father both over 6 feet tall, his entire family were all exceedingly tall.

Fig. 19 Robert Hales – The Norfolk Giant.

His five sisters averaged about 6 ft. 3 inches and his brothers averaged 6 ft. 5 inches. Mary Hales, one of his sisters, measured 7 ft. 2 inches, only a few inches taller than their sister Anne. Hales weighed an astounding 32 stone (208 kg), had 36 inch wide shoulders and measured 62 inches around his chest, and 64 around his waist.

Robert Hales first started to 'exhibit' himself at the Tombland Fair in Norwich and the Brittannia Fair in Great Yarmouth. Later he joined his sister Mary and her manager/husband Joe Laskey before sailing to New York in December, 1848. Here he met P.T. Barnum who signed him for his American Museum where he was billed as the 'Norfolk Giant'. It was whilst working for Barnum during a two-year American tour that he met and married the giantess Eliza Simpson. The following newspaper clipping, albeit with slightly exaggerated proportions, reported the wedding:

THE STAR & BANNER,
FRIDAY EVENING, FEBRUARY 23, 1884
GETTYSBURG

A TALL WEDDING – The English giant and Scotch giantess, exhibiting at Barnum's Museum, N. York, were married on Saturday evening last. The fair one is a delicate Quakeress, 21 years of age, nearly 8 feet high, and weighs 337 pounds! The bridegroom is 27 years of age, stands plump 8 feet in his stockings, and weighs 508 pounds!

Quite bizarrely, another report in the press announcing Hale's death made a most unusual claim concerning his wife:

BROOKLYN NY DAILY EAGLE, 1863

ONE OF BARNUM'S GIANTS DEAD – Robert Hales, the Norfolk Giant, who was exhibited in Barnum's Museum some years ago, died at Yarmouth, England, November 22nd last, at the age of 48. . . It will be remembered that he went through a marriage ceremony with a giantess when under Barnum's control, at the Broadway Tabernacle, but it afterwards turned out that this giantess was a giant dressed up in feminine attire. Whether Barnum knew the truth of the case at the time we cannot say, but it would not have been a remarkable fact if he did.

If the newspaper description was accurate then it would appear the marriage was a hoax, most likely orchestrated by Barnum to gain publicity by promoting them as the 'World's Tallest Couple', a title which would eventually go to the Giants of Seville later in the century. Hale actually wrote a short book with a long title called *Memoirs of Mr. Robert Hales, The English Quaker Giant, And His Wife, The Giantess, The Tallest Couple In The World*. This looks like an attempt at financial gain on Hale's part, which would be quite a news story today should the same situation be exposed in the present day media.

Once back on English soil after the American tour ended, Hale was invited to Buckingham Palace to appear before Queen Victoria, Prince Albert and six of the royal children. He went on to become the landlord of the Craven Head Tavern in Drury Lane and died in Great Yarmouth in 1863 before being buried back home in West Somerton.

Despite the scarcity of giant figures in Britain, as we shall discover, large skeletal human remains have been unearthed across the world, bringing into question why such anomalous finds are not included in the history of mankind if they were such a common feature of our distant past.

Chris L. Lesley noted that, 'Seven foot skeletons are a global phenomenon, people were larger in the past as the animals were larger in the past. It was also said that the funerary urns that were found were well fired, meaning that there was examples of technology, ingenuity and knowledge. This covers all of Greater Ancestry and paints a different historical picture than what is currently politicized.'[78]

Documented reports of giant skeleton discoveries in Britain are relatively scarce but they do exist, as the reports which follow demonstrate. Naturally, the validity of the reports remains questionable but they needn't be dismissed out of hand simply because they do not fit the prevailing model of evolution.

The following newspaper article was covered by the American media in Utah, despite the story coming from a small English village in central Bedfordshire. The report whih dates back over a century ago, claims that the giants could have originated sometime during the Neolithic period between 10,200 BC and 2,000 BC.

DESERET EVENING NEWS, NOVEMBER 19, 1910
PERFECT SKELETONS OF THE STONE AGE
Prehistoric Human Remains of Man and Woman, of Priceless Value, Found in Bedfordshire
(Special Dispatch) LONDON, Saturday.

A remarkable discovery of the skeletons of a man and woman belonging to the stone age, which antiquarians consider of priceless value, has just been made at Astwick, in Bedfordshire. Some workmen were laying a conduit near the line of the bed of the river Ivel when they came across the skeletons. They were examined by Dr. Waddell, a well known antiquary, who at once gave it as his opinion that they belonged to the Neolithic period and were of great importance to the world of science. The male is believed to have been a chieftain, and he must have been a man of magnificent physique, as the skeleton measures six feet six inches, while the head is massive. The woman was laid at right angles to the man, with her feet resting against the side of his body. Apparently when her lord died she had been slain and buried with him, according to prehistoric custom. Both skeletons are complete and in a good state of preservation, due to the nature of the soil. Their ultimate resting place will in all probability be the British Museum.

An article in the *Cambridge Chronicle* from May 27th, 1854 mentions the discovery of nine skeletons which were found embedded in the chalk on the very top of Lime Kiln Hill where men were excavating the reservoir for the Cambridge Waterworks. The skeletons were lying in various positions 'nearly together' and several of them were described as being 'remains of men who reached to a greater height than ordinary men in the present day.'[79]

Written in an 1825 document, this next quote mentions the discovery of a seven foot skeleton that was dug up at Stonehenge in

Wiltshire, England; 'A farm plough strikes something and six large flagstones are removed in what appears to be a cistern, and a seven foot skeleton is uncovered.'[80] The following article relates a quite bizarre story of a giant man named O'Brien in Ireland, whose remains were fished out of the sea following his death, and preserved at a local museum.

PUBLIC LEDGER, APRIL 15, 1868
An Irish Giant's Skeleton

The London Examiner, in the course of a literary review, tells this story: Some five and thirty years ago or more, we recollect hearing from the lips of the then curator of Hunter's noble museum, in Lincoln's Inn Fields, the interesting particular of the war in which John Hunter, not his brother William, became possessed of the body of the celebrated giant, whose skeleton, if our memory does not play us false, was said to be eight feet three inches high. We recollect being strongly impressed with the idea that the skeleton we were approaching to examine was that of a tall man between those of two children, such being the relative proportion between O'Brien and the skeletons right and left of him. Upon taking a nearer view we found those which had appeared to be children, were in fact skeletons of men at least six feet high. But to our story, which Mr. Clift, as distinguished for his love and care of the splendid museum of which he was the honoured curator, narrated to us. He was also, we should add, a man full of anecdote, and only too happy when pouring out the stories of an exceedingly retentive memory. He told us that John Hunter had long determined that O'Brien's skeleton should grace and enrich his museum. The giant became aware, before his death, of Hunter's design upon his anatomical frame, and with a view to defeat these, left by his will a distinct command that his body should be weighed and cast into the sea. His commands were faithfully fulfilled by his executors, and his body launched into the deep, somewhere about the Nore.

Another report of a giant being discovered in Ireland, on this occasion the man found in Dysart, County Louth measured ten feet in height.

EVENING STAR, APRIL 3, 1914
GIANT SKELETON FOUND
Two Others Credited to Prehistoric Times Unearthed in Ireland

LONDON, April 3 – According to dispatch published here today, the skeleton of a person who had been apparently ten feet in height has been found at Dysart, County Louth, Ireland. The skeleton was unearthed together with that of two others supposed to have been buried in prehistoric times. The three bodies had been interred in separate graves, all encased with stones. The skull of the giant measured eighteen inches from the crown of the head to the chin.

A report made by the *London Telegraph* in 1903 claims that a seven foot skeleton was discovered in a small town in Lincolnshire:

LONDON TELEGRAPH, 1903
GIANT SKELETON UNEARTHED
Lifted Intact, But Relic Hunters Break It Into Fragments.

The complete skeleton of a human giant has been found at Holbeach, a little Lincolnshire fen town between Lynn and Spalding, during excavations for the foundations of two new houses. Every bone was in perfect condition and not a tooth was missing, but it was soon broken into fragments, and several townspeople seized sections as mementos. The skeleton measured seven feet two inches.

A curious key, five inches long, with triangular handle, was found near the bones. Stukeley, the famous antiquary, who was born at Holbeach, records that at the spot where the discovery has just been made a Roman Catholic chapel, dedicated to St. Peter, formerly stood.

Leaving the British Isles, we shall now cross the Atlantic and examine the connection between giant bones and the mysterious ancient mounds which lay strewn across America, as we attempt to fathom some elements of truth from the many historical accounts that remain archived to this day.

MOUND BUILDERS OF NORTH AMERICA

Physical evidence of a forgotten pre-Columbian civilization can be found throughout the United States of America where a significant number of large ancient mounds still remain.

The earthen mounds have been constructed by various ancient cultures indigenous to North America, stretching as far back as 250 BC with the formation of the Criel Mound in South Charleston, West Virginia which has been attributed to the Adena culture that is believed to have existed during an era known as the Early Woodland period from 1000-200 BC. The Adena societies covered a large area including parts of present day New York, Pennsylvania, Wisconsin, Indiana, Maryland, Kentucky and Ohio.

Mounds were still being constructed, albeit over much older ones, as recently as the early 1700's by the Natchez People of Mississippi at the Grand Village of Natchez – also known as the Fatherland Site – which encompasses earthwork mounds and a prehistoric indigenous village built over 128.1 acres of land. The original village complex was constructed by the prehistoric Plaquemine culture starting at around the year 1200.

Despite the various cultures being given names, rough estimates concerning their existence and the true age of the mounds, little is really known about the pre-Columbian cultures that built these structures.

The largest pre-Columbian earthwork in the Americas and also the largest pyramid north of Mesoamerica is Monks Mound near Collinsville, Illinois which covers 13 acres at its base, roughly the same size as the Great Pyramid at Giza which spans 13.1 acres. The earthen mound is approximately 1,000 ft. (300 m) long, 700 ft. (200 m) wide and 100 ft. or 30 metres high.

It is understood that the Mississippian culture began work on the mound between 900-950 CE, and completed the monumental task around 1100 CE. The Mississippians were the last major prehistoric cultural development in North America and lasted from about 700 AD to the time of the arrival of the first European explorers at the onset of the 16th century. This influential culture spread over a vast area of Middle America and the Southeast, reaching the river valleys of what are now the states of Mississippi, Ohio, Georgia, Alabama, Missouri, Arkansas, Indiana, Kentucky and Illinois, with some tribes extending into Wisconsin and Minnesota in the north, and also into the Great Plains of the west.

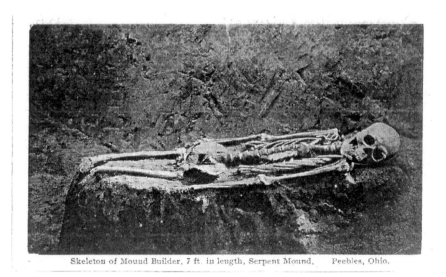

Skeleton of Mound Builder, 7 ft. in length, Serpent Mound,   Peebles, Ohio.

Fig. 20 A 7 ft. skeleton of a Mound Builder cut-off at the knees, Serpent Mound, Ohio.

The reason for discussing the presence of the American mounds here is due to the one commonality which they all share, they have all allegedly housed giant skeletons ranging from 7 to 10 feet tall (fig. 20).

The following newspaper reports were written over a two hundred year period when over 1000 accounts of giant human skeletons seven-foot and taller discovered in ancient burial sites in North America were reported. Such reports appeared in a variety of different sources including newspaper accounts, scientific journals, town and county histories, and were also carefully documented in Smithsonian ethnology reports.

These remarkable findings have been unearthed from beneath the ancient mounds, caves, burial chambers, stone crypts and even sites reported to have been ancient battlefields, all stretching coast to coast across the United States.

As quoted in *Fate Magazine*, 'The Iroquois, the Osage, the Tuscaroras, the Hurons, the Omahas, and many other North American Indians all speak of giant men who once lived and roamed in the territories of their forefathers. All over what is now the U.S. are traditions of these ancient giants.'[81]

THE SMITHSONIAN CONNECTION

The involvement of the world renowned Smithsonian Institution in Washington D.C. cannot be ignored, as dozens of the reports mention them as the recipients of many of the skeletons discovered from the various sites nationwide. It is worth considering that the Smithsonian Institution holds a vast amount of archives which rival those of the Vatican in quantity, and quite possibly in variety of depth and scope also.

Originally established using funds from British scientist James Smithson (1765-1829), the Smithsonian Institution which was signed into law by President James K. Polk on August 10, 1846 was founded as 'an establishment for the increase and diffusion of knowledge'.[82]

Describing the ethnological work of the Smithsonian Institution's Division of Eastern Mounds, the Director of the Bureau of Ethnology, John Wesley Powell claimed that:

'It is officially recorded that agents of the Bureau of Ethnology have explored more than 2,000 of these mounds. Among the objects found in them were pearls in great numbers and some of very large size. . . It is a matter of official record that in digging through a mound in Iowa the scientists found the skeleton of a giant, who, judging from actual measurement, must have stood seven feet six inches tall when alive. The bones crumbled to dust when exposed to the air. Around the neck was a collar of bear's teeth and across the thighs were dozens of small copper beads, which may have once adorned a hunting skirt.'[83]

According to their annual reports, Smithsonian scientists reportedly identified at least 17 skeletons that each reached over 7 ft. tall, including one example that was 8 ft. tall with a skull which had a 36-inch circumference (compared to an average human skull with a circumference of about 20 inches). Many of the skeletal remains documented from nearly every American state included such anomalies as elongated skulls, double rows of teeth and jawbones bigger than a human face.

With dozens of reports ending with something along the lines of, 'The bones were shipped to the Smithsonian Institution for further study', it remains a mystery as to why the museum today adamantly denies ever having received even *one* giant skeleton.

Jim Vieira and Hugh Newman cover this controversial aspect of the giant's mystery in their book *Giants on Record*, in which they conclude that 'a cover-up may have been instigated in the late 1800s because it did not fit in with their new ideologies of 'Manifest Destiny' and 'Evolution.'[84]

It would seem somewhat ironic then to consider that the Smithsonian was originally conceived 'for the increase and diffusion of knowledge' as dictated by Smithson himself, if it is indeed true that they chose to conceal archaeological discoveries which contradicted the scientific paradigms of the age. Of course, such a proposition is not in isolation, if we think back to the second chapter of this book and consider how a knowledge filter seems to have been installed into certain areas of learning in an attempt to protect long held beliefs or theorems.

One interesting incident highlights the fact that artefacts entering the Smithsonian often vanish into obscurity. In 1892, a number of ancient carved wooden coffins were discovered in the Crump Burial Cave near Birmingham, Alabama. Despite eight of these coffins having being reportedly taken to the Smithsonian, in the 1950s they claimed that they had "not been able to find the specimens in our collection, though records show that they were received."

It wasn't until 1992 that David Barron, the President of the Gungywamp Society, was informed by the Smithsonian that the reason the coffins could not be viewed was because they were 'housed in an asbestos-contaminated warehouse that would be closed for the next ten years, and which no one was allowed into except Smithsonian personnel.'[85]

Workmen apparently discovered giant human skulls measuring an extreme 22 to 24 inches from base to crown, whilst bulldozing a group of hills to make way for an airstrip on the island of Shemya, in the Aleutian Islands south of the Bering Strait during World War II. The average size of a human skull is about eight inches meaning that these anomalous skulls must have belonged to a race of massive giants. Furthermore, every skull had also been neatly trepanned, an ancient surgical procedure which used a cylindrical instrument called a trephine which would cut a precise hole in the skull.

An engineer stationed there wrote a letter to zoologist Ivan T. Sanderson regarding the enigmatic finds and the story was later confirmed by another worker at the unit. Sanderson was informed that once again, the Smithsonian had taken possession of the ancient bones which were never seen or heard of again, and was quoted as saying ". . . is it that these people cannot face rewriting all the textbooks?"

It is also interesting to note that in many of the reports of that era, the same name is mentioned in association with the giant finds, and that is Dr. Aleš Hrdlicka, curator of the National Museum of Physical Anthropology and an employee of the Smithsonian. If the

Smithsonian's present day pleas of ignorance regarding these anomalous discoveries are to be believed, then one can only wonder as to why one of their specialists in this field of research continues to be linked to them in the media reports.

Some researchers are under the impression that these 'missing skeletons' which many reports claim were sent to the Smithsonian and have never been heard of since, constitutes a conspiracy which is upheld for the sake of continuing with current thinking on human evolution and the history of mankind.

Author Dr. Greg Little perceives the matter slightly differently; 'I don't see the Smithsonian as being in a conspiracy in the true definition of the word. I see it as a sort of stupidity in the sense that they have ignored an aspect of their own findings that the public sees as intriguing. Instead of engaging the public, they alienate it. I also see that American archaeology resents all outsiders, resists all beliefs that go against their beliefs, and they utilize sceptics as a sort of police force to silence critics and others.'[86]

Richard Dewhurst, author of *The Ancient Giants Who Ruled America*, agrees with this sentiment which suggests that maybe the lack of public awareness on the topic of ancient giant discoveries is most likely due to the covert intentions of institutions like the Smithsonian.

'The fact that almost no one is aware of these giants today is a telling comment on the role played by the Smithsonian Institution and other institutions of higher learning, on which we rely to explore, preserve, and offer insights into our heritage, perhaps most especially those aspects that hint at broader horizons.'[87]

INTO THE ARCHIVES

The reader may be aware of the sensationalistic reporting which unquestionably circulated in the media during the 19th and 20th centuries, but one would be naive to presume *all* reports which appear controversial in nature to have been fabricated for increased sales and readership. The size of the giant skeletons mentioned in the examples you are about to read are all within the realms of reality, with no overly exaggerated reports of men fifteen to twenty feet tall.

In fact, there is a consistency to the reports which this author finds intriguing, with many of the discoveries offering a legitimate tone, some of which are also reinforced with photographic evidence which must have been difficult to fake at the time of print. The location of each discovery is always precisely reported along with any artefacts that were unearthed at the time, and despite the lack of evidence to confirm the authenticity of the reports there is nothing but our innate predisposition to the existence of giants in which to prove the fallacy of the content.

The majority of cases published here reveals the intrinsic link between the giants of America and the mound builders, an association which does not necessarily equate to the mounds having being built by the giants themselves. It could well be the case that the mound builders arrived later and built on top of what was already considered sacred ground where their giant ancestors were laid to rest.

Either way, what is clear in many of the reports is that the buried skeletons were revered within their tribes as they were most likely very important leaders judging by the array of ornamental jewellery, tools, weapons and personal artefacts found alongside the bodies, many of which were made of copper. The ritualistic positioning of many of the skeletons also gives credence to such a hypothesis.

With all this in mind, let us now take a look at some of the reports in question in chronological order, taking note of the details allocated to each account and consider the possibility at least, that some of the discoveries making the headlines back then may have originated through genuine reportage.

In an 1871 newspaper report from Cayuga County, New York State, it was claimed that 200 skeletons were removed from a collapsed mound on the banks of the Grand River. Said to be in a perfect state of preservation, the report detailed that the skeletons of the men 'were of gigantic stature, some of them measuring nine feet, very few of them being less than seven feet.'

The report also mentions the discovery of a 'lost city' on a farm in Dunville, where 'axes, tomahawks, beads and several smoking pipes, some engraved with dogs heads' were also discovered, along with 'two tons of charcoal and various implements' believed to indicate that the site was an ancient forge. Some of the giant skeletons which were unearthed had skulls that were described as being 'an enormous size and all manner of shape, some being twice the size of a normal human.'[88]

The following two reports, one which was picked up by the *New York Times*, documents the discovery of giants between 7 and 9 ft. in height, all of whom were found in the state of Ohio where many ancient Native American Indian tribes were known to have lived.

NEW YORK TIMES, MAY 5, 1885

Centerburg, Ohio: Licking County has been for years a favorite field for students of Indian history. Last week a small mound near Homer was opened by some school boys. Today a further search was made and several feet below the surface of the earth, in a large vault with stone floor and bark covering, were found four huge skeletons, three being over seven feet in length, and the other a full eight feet. The skeletons lay with their feet to the east on a bed of charcoal in which were numerous burned bones. About the neck of the largest skeleton were a lot of stone beads. The grave contained about 30 stone vessels and implements, the most striking being a curiously-wrought pipe. It is said to be the only engraved stone pipe ever found. A stone kettle, holding about a gallon in which was a residue of saline matter, bears evidence of much skill. Their bows, a number of arrows, stone hatchets, and a stone knife are among the implements that were found at the site.

STEVENS POINT DAILY JOURNAL, MAY 1, 1886

It is very evident that an early day in the history of this country, this section of Ohio was an important camping ground for the American Indian. And, indeed, discoveries are frequently made, which lead people interested in the matter of prehistoric America to believe that a race of mankind, superior in size, strength, and intelligence to the common red man of the forest, flourished not only along the coasts East and South, but right here in southern Ohio. There are in this county several burying grounds, and two of them are located five miles of this city, near Jasper, one on the farm of Mr. William Bush and one on Mr. Matthew Mark's farm. In a conversation with a gentleman who has seen [skeletons] unearthed at the Mark bank, we were told that many dozens of human skeletons have been exhumed since the bank was first opened. Some of these skeletons have been measured, and the largest have been found to be nine feet long and over.

At one time ten skeletons were exhumed. They had been buried in a circle, standing in an erect position, and were in a comparatively well-preserved condition.

DAILY NORTHWESTERN, OSHKOSH, WISCONSIN, JULY 8, 1886

At Petersburg, Kentucky, twenty-five miles below here, an excavation for a new building has brought to light a peculiar find; it being a strange-looking Indian grave, the receptacle of which has been made of stone and clay, formed into a kind of cement, about three feet in height, and fully nine feet in length. Within the rude vault lay a giant human skeleton that measured seven feet, two inches, in length. The bones were all of large proportions, and the monstrous skull, with teeth perfect and intact, was more than half an inch thick at the base.

A number of copper pieces, evidently worn for ornaments, a stone pipe, and a quantity of arrowheads were found with the decaying bones.

CINCINNATI COMMERCIAL GAZETTE, SEPTEMBER 26, 1889

Soon after the 1st of March relics were collected to be placed on loan to the Smithsonian Institution at Washington D.C.

During the last two months eleven mounds have been opened and their contents taken to the museum and placed on exhibition. These mounds vary in height from eight to thirty feet, are generally conical in shape, and contain all the way from 300 to 10,000 square yards of dirt. They were built by the aborigines of this country hundreds of years ago to serve as burial places for the distinguished dead. They are generally placed near some stream in a valley and not infrequently on high points of land, which command a good view of the country, but the larger ones are in the valleys. These mounds are usually composed of clay, sometimes of sand, and often have layers of charcoal or burnt clay in them. These layers are often brightly colored as if they had been painted.

About five feet above this layer, or nine feet from the summit of the mound, was a skeleton of a very large individual who had buried by the side of it the bones of a panther. Whether the person had killed the panther and it was buried with him as an honor, or whether the panther had killed the individual, one cannot say.

CHICAGO TRIBUNE, 1892

Near Carthage, Illinois, about one year ago, a mound was plowed up and the bones, principally the skulls of human beings, were found at sufficient quantities to warrant the conclusion that hundreds of people had been buried there. From measurements taken of some of the skulls and principal bones, it was decided that the persons buried were of a race of giants. Some of the femur bones measured 19¼ inches, and the measurements of the skulls and other bones indicated that these people must have attained an average of seven to eight feet in height. The entire country lying between the Illinois and Mississippi Rivers, between Galena and Cairo, is honeycombed with Indian mounds that are believed to be the handiwork of a pre-historic race. Nansook County, especially in localities bordering the Mississippi River, is covered with evidences of Indian burials.

In 1895, historian George Sheldon wrote in *The Town History of Deerfield*:

'At the foot of Bars Long Hill, just where the meadow fence crossed the road, and the bars were placed that gave the village its name, many skeletons were exposed while plowing down a bank, and weapons and implements were found in abundance. One of these skeletons was described to me by Henry Mather who saw it, as being of monstrous size—'the head as big as a peck basket, with double teeth all round.' The skeleton was examined by Dr. Stephen W. Williams who said the owner must have been nearly eight feet high.'

BALTIMORE AMERICAN, NOVEMBER 15, 1897

There has just been received at the Maryland Academy of Sciences, the skeleton of an Indian seven feet tall. It was discovered near Antietam. There are now skeletons of three Indians at the Academy who at one time in their wilderness roamed over the state of Maryland armed with such instruments as nature gave them or that their limited skill taught them to make.

Two of these skeletons belonged to individuals evidently of gigantic size. The vertebrae and bones of the legs are nearly as thick as those of a horse and the length of the long bones exceptional. The skulls are of a fine proportion, ample and with walls of moderate and of great strength and stiffened beyond with a powerful occipital ridge. The curves of the forehead are moderate and not retreating, suggesting intelligence and connected with jaws of moderate development.

The locality from which these skeletons came is in Frederick County, near Antietam Creek. It was formerly supposed to have been the battleground of two tribes of Indians: the Catawbas and the Delawares. Before the coming of the white man, this site was occupied as a village by Indians of great stature, some of them six-and-a-half to seven feet in height.

THE NEW YORK TIMES, DECEMBER 20, 1897
WISCONSIN MOUND OPENED

Skeleton Found of a Man Over Nine Feet High with an Enormous Skull. MAPLE CREEK, Wis., Dec. 19. – One of three recently discovered mounds in this town has been opened. In it was found the skeleton of a man of gigantic size. The bones measured from head to foot over nine feet and were in a fair state of preservation. The skull was as large as a half bushel measure. Some finely tempered rode of copper and other relics were lying near the bones.

The mound from which these relics were taken is ten feet high and thirty feet long, and varies from six to eight feet in width. The two mounds of lesser size will be excavated soon.

OHIO SCIENCE ANNUAL, 1898

A rare archaeological discovery has been made near Reinersville in Morgan County, Ohio. A small knoll, which has always been supposed to be the result of an uprooted tree, was opened recently and discovered to be the work of mound builders.

Just below the surrounding surface, a layer of boulders and pebbles was found. Directly underneath this was found a skeleton of a giant 8 feet, 7 inches in height. Surrounding the skeleton were bone and stone implements, stone hatchets, and other characteristics of the mound builders.

The discovery is considered by the scientists as one of the most important ever made in Ohio. The skeleton is now in the possession of a Reinersville collector.

FOND DU LAC BANNER, JUNE 6, 1899

An Indian skeleton was dug on the farm of Matt and Joseph Leon, one mile south of St. Cloud on Saturday. There is nothing strange in finding an Indian skeleton, but this one was a giant in size, his frame measuring seven feet. He must have been a man of note among his people, for he was buried in a large mound, sixteen handsome arrows surrounding his body. The skull was brought to this city and is on exhibition in one of the Main Street windows.

PORTSMOUTH HERALD, AUGUST 17, 1899

Relics of a prehistoric age have been brought to light in Noble County. The find is in York Township where workmen excavating for a public highway found the skeleton of an inhabitant of early days. The bones indicate that the person was fully nine feet tall. The bones are unusually large and the position of the skeleton when found indicated that the person had been buried in a sitting position. The belief is advanced that the remains are those of a mound builder.

THE TANEY COUNTY REPUBLICAN, FEBRUARY 25, 1904
GIANT SKELETON FOUND

Workman engaged in digging gravel at Winnemucca, Nev., the other day uncovered at a depth of about 12 feet a lot of bones, part of the skeleton of a gigantic human being. Dr. Samuels examined them and pronounced them to be bones of a man who must have been nearly 11 feet in height. The metacarpal bones measure four and a half inches in length and are large in proportion. A part of the ulna was found and in its complete form would have been between 17 and 18 inches in length. The remainder of the skeleton is being searched for.

OHIO MORNING SUN NEWS HERALD, APRIL 14, 1904

A giant skeleton of a man has been unearthed at the Woolverton farm, a short distance from Tippecanoe City, Ohio. It measures eight feet from the top of the head to the ankles, the feet being missing, says this newspaper reporter. The skull is large enough to fit as a helmet over the average man's head. This skeleton was one of seven, buried in a circle, the feet of all being towards the center. Rude implements were near. The skeletons ate thought to be those   of the mound builders.

Thomas Weston reported in the *History of the Town of Middleboro, Massachusetts*, in 1906:

'A few years ago when the highway was straightened and repaired, remains were found. When his skeleton was measured by Dr. Morrill Robinson and others, it was found that the thigh bone was four inches longer than that bone in an ordinary man, and that he had a double row of teeth in each jaw. His height must have been at least seven feet and eight inches.'

A year later in 1907, Lyman Simpson Hayes wrote this account in the *History of the Town of Rockingham, Vermont*:

'When the earth was removed from the top of the ledges east of the falls, a remarkable human skeleton, unmistakably that of an Indian, was found. Those who saw it tell the writer the jaw bone was of such size that a large man could easily slip it over his face and the teeth, which were all double, were perfect.'

The following account taken from the most widely distributed newspaper in Montana, recounts the bizarre discovery of four-foot-tall pygmy skeletons which included the remains of one giant over eight feet in length buried amongst them.

THE BILLINGS GAZETTE, AUGUST 30, 1907
PYGMY SKELETON DUG UP
Prehistoric Cemetery Discovered by South Dakota R.R. Graders

Oacoma, S. D., Aug. 29 – A remarkable prehistoric burying ground has been cut into by railroad graders near here, and the remains of what appears to be a pygmy race have been discovered. The old burying ground is now a great deposit of gravel, and it is in this that the bones are found. Some 50 skeletons have so far been unearthed. These are all of a race of dwarfs about four feet high, and physicians have pronounced them the remains of adults, not children. The bodies were buried standing or sitting. One of the skeletons, however, is that of a giant more than eight feet high. Near the giant's skeleton was found a number of copper implements, as well as several of bone. In one of the graves were two copper idols about eight inches tall.

THE MIDDLETON DAILY NEWS-SIGNAL, MARCH 21, 1908
SKELETONS OF GIANT INDIANS
Found in Gravel Bank on Warren County Farm

Lebanon, O. – Yesterday when digging into a gravel bank on his farm near Stubbtown, in Warren County, John Watkins discovered the burial ground of Miami Indians. The skeleton of a huge woman was unearthed. It measured seven feet and five inches in length. About her neck were ropes of pearls and in her tomb other articles of value.

Much excitement was aroused among the farmers in the vicinity, and further excavations brought to light many other skeletons of the extinct race. Some were found in sitting positions and some on their faces. Watkins will try to interest the Ohio Archaeological society in his find.

Interestingly, the account above was covered in a number of different publications of the day, suggesting that the story may have authentic roots. As shown below, the same incident was reported in Washington two months later where the story remained the same, except for a slight variation in the spelling of the town name and some rather speculative suggestions connecting the site to the Garden of Eden.

THE WASHINGTON TIMES, MAY 5, 1908
THE STUBTOWN SKELETON

The finding of the skeleton of a giantess, seven feet two inches in stature, on a farm near Stubtown, Ohio, reopens the question as to the site of the Garden of Eden. John Watkins, on whose farm the bones were unearthed, the mayor and some of the "prominent citizens" of Stubtown, are contending that the Watkins farm is the place, and that the relics are none other than those of Eve herself; and they point to the opinions of certain more or less famous archaeologists to bear them out.

And another account appeared in 1908 in *The Story of Martha's Vineyard* by Charles Gilbert, 'Some 15 years ago the skeleton of an Indian Giant in almost perfect preservation was dug up in the same locality (Cedar Tree Neck), the bones indicated a man easily six feet and a half possibly seven feet high. An unusual feature was a complete double row of teeth on both the upper and lower jaws.'

THE DAILY GATE CITY, MAY 16, 1910
GIANT'S SKELETON FOUND OUT WEST

Bones Discovered by Bursting Water Pipe, Which Dug Hole in the Ground ENCAMPMENT, Wyo., May 16. – That Carbon County, Wyo., was inhabited by a race of men, or at least one man in the prehistoric age, has been proved by the discovery of a human skeleton which indicates that the man in life was nine feet, three inches in height. The bones were disclosed by means of preservation, being in a fossiliferous condition.

ARIZONA JOURNAL-MINER, OCTOBER 13, 1911

Peter Marx of Walnut Creek, discoverer of a prehistoric human giant on his farm several years ago, while in the city yesterday, stated that the curiosity is attracting such deep interest in scientific circles that he is almost delayed with his letters and during the past two weeks he has been visited by Mr. And Mrs.

Shoup, the former an attaché of the Smithsonian Institution at Washington, who made the long journey for the express purpose of viewing the frame of the giant of other days. Mr. Shoup was provided with photographic instruments and took several pictures.

Mr. Shoup, of the Smithsonian, also desired to take it (the giant skeleton) back to Washington, but this request was held up by Mr. Marx stating that as the subject was found in the territory it should be kept there.

Mr. Shoup was very much interested in those proportions of the human frame that were unusually large, particularly the skull , which indicated that the giant was of such abnormal size as to be beyond comprehension as that of a human being. Mr. Marx has uncovered another burying ground near the point where the skeleton was found.

This next article includes so much detail that one would naturally tend to lean towards accepting such a story as being the result of honest factual reporting. It is interesting to note that the giant skeletons, which most journalists considered to belong to an ancient tribe of Indians, were superior both 'physically and mentally' to the present day tribes, with a greater intellectual capacity also. The fact that this particular discovery was made by a museum curator and not the average man on the street, helps to reinforce the legitimacy of the content.

THE SAN JUAN ISLANDER, AUGUST 23, 1912
SKELETON OF GIANT INDIAN IS FOUND
Seven Foot Four Inches Was the Height of Member of Extinct Race Whose Bones Were Dug Up by California Scientist

San Francisco, Cal – Up to about 300 years ago a giant race of Indians inhabited the coast regions of California. Remains of these have been discovered in the islands of the Santa Barbara channel. To William Altmann, assistant curator of the Golden Gate Park Memorial museum, belongs the honor of discovering one of the best preserved skeletons of this extinct tribe.

Altmann utilized his vacation in excavating an old Indian burial mound in the nursery of Thomas S. Dunne, two miles from Concord, in Contra Costa County. The giant skeleton was found ten feet from the surface, and around it were large a number of mortars and pestles, charm stones and obsidian arrow heads.

The skeleton has not yet been mounted, but the bones were assembled on a table in the curator's office and placed on private exhibition. The bones have in good state of preservation, being hard and firm, although brown with age. Two or three of the vertebrae are missing, and the skull is broken in three parts. The skeleton measures seven feet four inches. The tibia is seventeen inches length.

The skull is in great contrast with that of the Digger Indian of the present day, being of a much more intellectual type. The under jaw is square and massive, being remarkably thick and strong. Either the dead Indian was of great age or he subsisted on hard food, as shown by his molars, which were worn perfectly flat and close to the gums.

The find is of the greatest importance to anthropologists the world over, confirming as it does, the theory advanced when the giant skeletons were unearthed in the Santa Barbara islands, that a superior race of Indians, physically and mentally, preceded the Digger and other native races of the present day. This is evidenced also in the pestles and charm stones found near the body.

GRAND FORKS DAILY HERALD, JUNE 29, 1915
GIANT'S SKELETON AT FERGUS FALLS

Fergus Falls, Minn., June 29 – A giant skeleton has been unearthed on the farm of County Commissioner Thore Glende, in the town of Everts. The jaw bones and some of the teeth were in a fair state of preservation, and the teeth were nearly twice the size of an ordinary man's teeth. Other bones indicated that the man must have been eight feet tall. Tourists from St. Louis secured the bones and sent them to scientists in that city. It is supposed the remains are those of prehistoric man.

CHARLESTON DAILY MAIL, SEPTEMBER 20, 1916

On July 13, Professor Skinner of the American Indian Museum, excavating the mound at Tioga Point, near Sayre, Pennsylvania, uncovered the bones of 68 men, which he estimates had been buried at least seven or eight hundred years. The average height indicated by the skeletons was seven feet, but many were taller. Evidence of the gigantic size of these men was seen in huge axes found beside the bones.

THE BUTTE DAILY POST, FEBRUARY 27, 1917

Oakland, Cal. – A skeleton believed to be that of an Indian chief was discovered by working men engaged in digging gravel on the Frank Wallace ranch, a mile and a half west of San Leandro. The bones have been taken in charge by Deputy Coroner Morgan, who declares that from the size of the thigh bones it is evident that the skeleton is that of man of at least eight feet tall. The skeleton is to be sent to the anthropological department of the University of California.

OAKLAND TRIBUNE, DECEMBER 20, 1925

Out of a mound in Iowa was dug the skeleton of a giant who, judging from the measurement of his bones, must have stood six inches over seven feet high when he was alive. In another there was a central chamber containing eleven skeletons arranged in a circle with their backs against the walls. In the midst was a huge sea shell which had been converted into a drinking cup.

Two individual giant reports were printed in the *Oakland Tribune* on the same day, despite one of the accounts originating nearly forty years in the past. This would suggest that there may well have been a common public interest in such discoveries if they were willing to recount such an old incident as can be seen in the second of these stories. Interestingly, the 1888 report comments on the identical dimensions of the 'secret cave' where this particular skeleton was found, with another cave discovered in Tennessee, roughly 400 miles away from the Indiana site.

OAKLAND TRIBUNE, JANUARY 3, 1926

Within the last few weeks it has been reported from Missouri the discovery of the skeleton of a man who was a trifle more than seven feet, two inches tall. Frank Plumb, a student of archaeology who made the find, reported discovering inside the skull a pear-shaped stone such as the Mayas placed in the mouths of their dead.

OAKLAND TRIBUNE, JANUARY 3, 1926

Another discovery was made of eight skeletons, one clad in copper armor, buried in a perfect circle, made when the Logan Grays, a military group led by A. M. Jones, were conducting military exercises in 1888 on a small island on Eagle Lake near Warsaw, Indiana. Under a flat stone, they discovered a hole that led to the entrance to a secret cave with the skeleton of a 6'9" giant buried next to a stream that led to what was called a sacred pool. It is interesting to note that the dimensions of this secret room are identical to one described in Tennessee, i.e. 25 feet long by 15 feet wide by 8 feet deep.

THE NEW SENTINEL, APRIL 19, 1926
ANCIENT BURYING GROUND UNCOVERED
Skeletons Found Indicate That Race of Giants
Once Lived on Banks of Sycamore Creek.

A prehistoric graveyard on Sycamore Creek, where the grade of the Verde railway passes through, has been uncovered by a crew of laborers under the direction of Conductor C.W. Corbin, in performing certain excavations to improve the roadway. There has thus been revealed a very interesting situation that prevailed at some time or another, in the physical make-up of a race as is reflected in the massive remains that have been recovered, and which are indisputable of a giant type of humanity that is bewildering to those of this generation. The skull of a human is in the possession of Mr. Corbin together with a portion of the frame that would indicate one who in life must have attained a height of at least 8 feet. The sides of the face have been severed, but when placed in their natural position, on the head of the living they were so massive as to shield the features like unto a perfect mask. The bones of the legs likewise are of a greater length and are heavier than any today.

The following news article from a 1931 report in the *San Antonio Express* (fig. 21) revealed that in association with the University of Texas, the Works Progress Administration (WPA) archaeological team discovered a giant skull in a Victoria County mound which they claimed was 'believed to be the largest human skull ever found in the United States and possibly the world.'

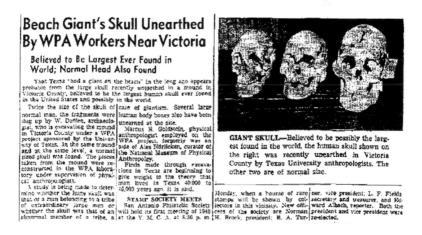

Fig. 21 The giant human skull found in Texas (far right) was described as being twice the size of a normal man's.

The photograph accompanying the piece shows what the journalist described as being 'twice the size of the skull of normal man' found at a site where 'several large human body bones' were also unearthed.

American researchers Jim Vieira and James Clary investigated the following account written for *The Steelville Ledger* on June 11, 1933, as part of television documentary *Search for the Lost Giants*:

'An Ancient Ozark Giant Dug Up Near Steelville:
Strange discovery made by a boy looking for arrowheads, gives this
Missouri Town an absorbing mystery to ponder'

The article claimed that '...he turned up the complete skeleton of an 8 foot giant. The grisly find was brought to Dr. R. C. Parker here and stretched out to its enormous length in a hallway of his office where it has since remained the most startling exhibit Steelville has ever had on public view. . . An appeal to Dr. Aleš Hrdlicka, anthropologist of the National Museum in Washington and celebrated authority on primitive races is expected to help. Dr. Parker has written to him, offering to forward the skull or the whole skeleton, if necessary for scientific study.'

Fig. 22 Les Eaton (6 ft.) lying on the floor beside an 8 ft. skeleton.

Upon further investigation Vieira and Clary found the precise location where the 8-foot skeleton had been removed, which was along the north wall of a cave in Missouri. In order to legitimise the discovery they later met with several relatives of Billy Harmon, who all confirmed the find to have been authentic. They also met with one of Dr. Parker's former patients once they had located Dr. R. C. Parker's office.

They also uncovered three more reports of the find whilst reading through the microfilm at the Steelville library, one of which included a photograph (fig. 22) that shows a 6 ft. tall man by the name of Les Eaton, laid in Dr. Parker's office next to the 8 ft. skeleton for size comparison. Like many other reports on the subject, *The Steelville Ledger* also claimed that the giant skeleton was packed up and sent to the Smithsonian and was never heard of again.

CAT. NO.	NAME .... Skull (No lower Jaw or face)
....377,860....	People .... Aleut
....	Locality .... Kagamil Island, Alaska (Mummy caves)
ACC. NO.	....
....138,127....	Collector .... A. Hrdlicka
....	How acquired Coll. for Museum Date acc'd Feb. 4, 1937
ORIG. NO.	Where placed *P.374 5- A :*
....	Remarks .... Male Adult. Very large - capacity about 2,000 cc

B I - 1/3

Skeletal parts present:

	Rt. Lt.		Rt. Lt.		
Hum..		Fem. .		Sternum. . .	
Rad. .		Tibia . .		Ribs	
Ulna .		Fib. . .		Sacrum . . .	
Scap..		Innom..		Vert. ...C ....T	
Clav..		Foot . .		L	
Hand..					

U. S. NAT. MUSEUM   GPO 16—28000-1   DIVISION OF PHYSICAL ANTHROPOLOGY

Fig. 23 A. Hrdlicka's 1937 report card of a giant skull discovery from Alaska.

A report card (fig. 23) in the name of the collector A. Hrdlicka, the man so consistently linked to the Smithsonian Institution, reveals the find of a large human skull in Alaska, dated to 1937. Cards such as these were used as part of standard procedure, and this particular example appears legitimate as it collaborates with the following news article from the *Rochester Journal* in 1936:

ROCHESTER JOURNAL, OCTOBER 5, 1936
SMITHSONIAN GETS HUGE INDIAN SKULL

After a summer spent nosing around the Aleutian Islands, Dr. Alex Hrdlicka is home with a big head. In fact, the skull, which the Smithsonian Institution anthropologist picked up, once contained the largest human brain on record in the Western Hemisphere, Institution scientists say. The skull believed to have belonged to an Aleut who lived hundreds of years ago, had a brain capacity of 2,005 cubic centimetres. The average man has about 1,450 cubic centimetres and the average woman 1,300.

That was not the only documented report of giant remains being found in Alaska, the following newspaper article from a Vancouver report also reveals the presence of giants in the northern state:

SKELETONS OF GIANTS IN ALASKA

Ancient Cemetery Uncovered in VANCOUVER, Nov. 17 — James L. Perkinson, an American miner of Atlin, arrived here to-day with news of the finding of a number of skeletons in an ancient Indian cemetery in the north, which is of startling scientific interest. Perkinson is one of the owners of the Yellow Jacket, a rich claim, which is supposed to be the fountain head of Pine, the principal creek in Atlin district. Two weeks ago the first excavations were being made for a new tunnel and what appears to have been an old Indian burying ground was opened up. Five skeletons, nearly complete, were exhumed and each is the set of bone that belonged to a giant of prehistoric times. One of the skeletons measures over seven feet in length, so that the man must have been considerably over that height. Then there were two others of within an inch of seven feet and the remaining two "were more than six feet in length and the men were of gigantic frame." The altitude is high and the ground was half frozen, so that the bones were preserved almost intact Perkinson says that he expects if they had kept on digging they would have found many more, as these were lying comparatively close together. The bones of the fingers and toes had crumbled away, but the finger of one skeleton hand was sufficiently strong to hold a ring of what appears to be lead or some similar base metal. The skeletons were unusually well formed, but one unique feature was that the arms were several inches shorter than ordinarily appears, while the size of the bones of the forearm was enormous in comparison to the usual models. Beside two of the skeletons were spears, rudely shaped with a soft metal and pointed with sharp stones. The spears were only about three feet long and five' inches thick at the top tapering at the lower end. The top contained a socket into which a wooden shaft was probably placed, in order to wield the big piece of metal. Other pieces of stone and carved metal were found. This is what the 5 skeletons would look like, the tallest being 7 feet.

The general physical appearance of the skeletons, according to the cursory examination of the miners, was similar to that of the Indians of the present day. They were certainly of the flathead type of tribes. That the burying place is of ancient origin is evidenced by the fact that the Indians say none of their tribesmen have lived within fifty miles of this place as far back as stories have been handed down. There are several mounds, presumably made by the Indian's in the vicinity of the new mine tunnel now being extended.

This next report speaks of excavation work undertaken in Georgia which was sponsored by the Smithsonian, revealing yet more evidence linking the discovery of giant human skeletons to the Washington anthropological museum. Photographic evidence of this archaeological dig from 1936 was included in another newspaper report of the same discovery of giants in coastal Georgia (fig 24).

Fig. 24 Georgia newspaper article from 1936 covering the discovery of giant human skeletons.

SALT LAKE TRIBUNE, AUGUST 2, 1936

Perhaps the discovery of the first dinosaur bones on the North American continent created no more sensation in scientific circles than the recent revelations of prehistoric man lately developed off the coast of Georgia. Excavating in the sand dunes of the sun-sprayed Golden Isles, Georgia, archaeologists have gouged out the strange record of an amazing prehistoric race of giants.

With pick ax and spade, these searchers into the past have burrowed their way beneath the surface of the palm-clad dunes of Georgia's semi-tropical islands, to delve into the mysteries of a previously unsuspected race of mankind. The question uppermost in their mind today is: What manner of men were these, the members of whose tribe all averaged between six and one half and seven feet tall?

Preston Holder, archaeologist, is directing the excavation work, which has been sponsored by the Smithsonian Institution. Slowly, painstakingly, Holder is endeavoring to piece together the slender threads that will lead him into the past. He has expressed the opinion that the Smithsonian will throw important light upon a thus far unrecorded tribe, and perhaps establish a new link in the history of mankind in North America.

HAMMOND TIMES, FRIDAY, JUNE 30, 1939

Discovery of ancient skeletons and priceless relics in an Indian mound in North Benton, northwest of Salem, by two Alliance, Ohio mail carriers, has brought hundreds of visitors to the scene and attracted the attention of expert archaeologists. The two amateur archaeologists Roy Saltsman and Willis Magrath, made the excavation on the farm of John Malmsberry. After examining the mound, Richard G. Morgan, state archaeologist, declared that the work of the two Alliance men was the most important archaeological discovery in this section of the state in recent years. He estimated the age of the findings at more than 2,000 years old. One skeleton uncovered was that of a man, apparently a chief, estimated to have been seven feet tall, whose skull was 25 inches in circumference. Other findings included flint arrows, the stones of three sacrificial altars, spear heads, flake knives and beautifully wrought objects of copper.

CHARLEROI MAIL, MAY 7, 1953

Along the Susquehanna River in Indiana County, Pennsylvania a major Indian burial site was uncovered. All together, forty-nine skeletons were exhumed, the tallest being eight feet tall. These skeletons were reportedly taken to the Harrisburg Museum for reassembly and then shipped to the Smithsonian for further study. However, the Smithsonian denies any knowledge of them. On the site of the William H. Rhea farm (circa 1871-1880) in Conemaugh Township just west of the mouth Black Legs Creek, skeletons of men, probably Indians, were found. Noted local historian Clarence Stephenson says "One of the skeletons is of a giant nearly eight feet tall. The giant's skeleton measured 89 inches from the top of the skull to the phalanges of the feet. It was covered with small stones, lay on the back, and measured 26 inches across the chest."

So, as can be seen by the many examples of giant reports we have just covered it is evident that there may well be some factual basis to the many recorded accounts of archaeological discoveries if the consistent nature of the content is anything to go by. If one is looking for hard physical evidence of the existence of a forgotten race of giants then one will no doubt be sorely disappointed, as there is no such proof which is accessible to even the most ardent researcher. However, were we given uninterrupted access to the Smithsonian Institution's hidden archives of stored anthropological artefacts, perhaps we may all come out of there with more physical evidence in which to reinforce the notion of a former unknown race of super humans.

But what we do have here is the appearance at least, of plausible material which suggests there could have been men and women of great stature roaming the vast plains of North America, who quite possibly had a global presence in times gone by. It would be very easy albeit somewhat premature to simply dismiss such ideas as nonsense, yet to consider the possibility that a forgotten giant race were once part of the tapestry of human evolution requires an open mind and lateral thinking.

As giant enthusiasts Newman and Vieira explain, 'Most people do not believe in giants, however, but rather scoff at the idea, regarding it as folklore that has been mixed up and sensationalized by newspaper journalists. We disagree, as there is ample evidence within Native American mythology, genetic data, ethnological studies, scientific reports, early excavation records, first-hand accounts, and discoveries featured in newspapers and Town History books. Now is the time for academia to take a look at this data and to expose what really happened at the Smithsonian; for an important chapter in human history is on the verge of being lost forever.'[89]

The physical disorder gigantism is often cited by sceptics as the cause of many of the anomalously large skeletons which have surfaced over the years. This is often the first port of call for those vying for a simple explanation to this extraordinary situation which confronts us all, an explanation which Dr. Greg Little claims to be a 'weak attempt to explain away and dismiss the issue'. But how likely is it that all the giant remains printed in the reports we have just revisited could have been the result of gigantism?

Little believes it is extremely unlikely, 'Gigantism is exceedingly rare, so rare that there is no actual incidence statistic for it. America has less than 100 cases of gigantism recoded in its history. In fact, the overwhelmingly vast majority of tall people today, those reaching or approaching 7 feet, do not have the disorder of gigantism. The actual percentage of modern humans who reach 7 feet in height is 0.000007%. In the ancient world of America's Mound Builders, the percentage of the population that reached 7 feet in height would have been even lower.'[90]

GIANT ARTEFACTS

Human skeletons are not the only remaining physical evidence indicative of an ancient race of giants existing in prehistory. Many accounts also reveal the discovery of giant artefacts, often weapons or tools, all of which add weight to the giant hypothesis.

Below are some articles from the past, documenting the presence of such unusually large artefacts:

History of Erie County, 1884

'The bones of a flathead were turned up in the same township some two years ago with a skull of unusual size. Relics of a former time have been gathered in that section by the panful, and among other curiosities a brass watch was found that was as big as a common saucer. An ancient graveyard was discovered in 1820, on the land now known as Dr. Carter and Dr. Dickinson places in Erie, which created quite a sensation at the time. Dr. Albert Thayer dug up some of the bones, and all indicated a race of beings of immense size.'

The following excerpt taken from *Nature Magazine*, June 1935 mentions a giant hand-axe found in Sheringham, Norfolk in England.

'An altogether remarkable and gigantic hand-axe discovered embedded in the beach below Beeston Hill, Sheringham, by Mr. J. P. T. Burchell, has been figured and described by Mr. J. Reid Moir (Proc. Prehistoric Soc. East Anglia). The implement measures in its greatest length 15 inches, in greatest width 6 inches, in greatest thickness 5 inches. Its weight is approximately 14lb. It was derived originally from the base of the Cromer Forest bed, which rests upon the surface of the chalk. The material of the axe is of flint, the colour of the flaked surfaces being jet black. The ridges and outstanding parts are abraded, and it is striated in places. Hand-axes showing these characteristics have been discovered not only in England but also widely distributed over the earth's surface. The numerous specimens discovered in the basement bed, belonging to the early Pleistocene epoch, are as highly specialised as are those of any later prehistoric period and represent a very definite and necessary stage in implemental development. No adequate explanation of the purpose which the gigantic size of the Sheringham axe could serve has been offered.'

A newspaper report, relating the discovery at the time it was first announced read:

'That a race of giants roamed the earth ages ago in the early Pleistocene era seems to be indicated by the discovery of a huge stone axe at Norfolk, England, which apparently was wielded by prehistoric man. As the great axe was found in strata that underlies glacial deposits, scientists are sure it was produced and used by a race that antedated the Ice Age.'

The following report from 1934 also details the discovery of an anomalously large axe unearthed in a farmer's field:

ALTON EVENING TELEGRAPH, MAY 3, 1934
Jersey Farmer Plows up Prehistoric Giant's Axe

One of the largest axes of prehistoric origin in the memory of residents here was uncovered the past week by Louis Houseman on the farm where he resides, seven miles northwest of Jerseyville. The axe was weighed at the post office and lacked but several ounces of 10 pounds. The field where the axe was uncovered had been in cultivation for a number of years, but Houseman has a reputation for plowing several inches deeper than the average farmer, and it was to his practice in this respect that the axe was brought to the surface. Houseman recently began farming the place where the find was made. The axe had been scratched on a former occasion by a plow share, a mark on one of its sides showed. The relic was brought to Jerseyville by Houseman and left at the Munsterman filling station on South State Street. He has received several offers for his find, but has refused them. Much speculation has arisen relative to the physique of the man who carried such a heavy weapon or instrument. Such a tool corresponds to some of the unusually large skeletons of prehistoric men that have been unearthed in western and southwestern Jersey County.

Reported in 1811 but published later in 1824, a county historical report called *A History of Livingston County, New York* included an account where 'rude medals, pipes and articles' were discovered alongside the remains of a giant 'of enormous size, the jawbone of which was so large that Adam Holslander placed it, mask-like over his own chin and jaw' inside an Indian mound on Mount Morris.

At a site in Cuxton, Kent, the University of Southampton unearthed over twenty flint hand axes during an important archaeological dig. Among the tools they discovered two of 'exceptional size and quality', one of which measured 30.7 cm, becoming the second largest flint axe ever found in Britain. In addition to its extreme size, the hand axe was described as displaying 'exquisite, almost flamboyant, workmanship.'

Found alongside it was a cleaver measuring 17.9 cm in length and 13.4 cm wide.

The Lower Palaeolithic period, which lasted from 600,000 to 250,000 BC in Britain, has not previously been associated with the clearly defined types of hand axe found here which reflect such a deliberate design. According to dig leader Dr Francis Wenban-Smith, "The sharp point, straight edges and symmetrical waist would not arrive except by design, indicating the ability to hold in the mind the idea of the intended shape, and suggesting that humans at that time were already capable of language."

The hand axe shown on the left comes from the Acheulian culture (Lower Palaeolithic, about 400,000 years ago) and was found at Furze Platt near Maidenhead, England. It measures 30.6 cm in length and weighs 2.8 kg.

In the 1990s, archaeologists discovered four giant stone hand axes (fig. 25) on the dry lake basin of Lake Makgadikgadi in Botswana. Measuring over 30 cm in length, these unusual finds have baffled scholars as to their purpose and origin and reveal an uncertain past in this part of the Kalahari.

In *Timeless Earth*, Peter Kolosimo mentions the discovery of five hundred double-edged axes weighing 8 kg each found by the French captain Lafanechère amongst an arsenal of other hunting weapons at Agadir in Morocco. Also in Moravia and Syria, giant bones were unearthed close to giant stone implements.

Fig. 25 Giant stone hand axes recovered from the dry lake basin of Lake Makgadikgadi, Botswana.

Dr. Louis Burkhalter, a French archaeologist and former delegate of the Société Préhistorique Française (French Prehistoric Society), wrote a paper on the large Moroccan artefacts discovered by Lafanechère, entitled *A Report on Gigantic Implements Found in South Morocco*.

Commenting on the 'gigantic' lithic stone tools unearthed at Sasnych in Syria which included bifaces of 'abnormal' dimensions weighing between 2.5 and 3.5 kg, Burkhalter wrote in the Revue du Musee de Beyrouth (National Museum of Beirut) in 1950, 'I want to make it clear that the existence of gigantic men in the Acheulian age (i.e. between about 75,000 and 150,000 years ago) must be considered a scientifically proven fact.'

Burkhalter theorised that one reason for both ancient and modern gigantism could be that biological mutations are caused by quantitative variations in the solar emission of infrared rays which affect the human body biochemically. Such a concept is in keeping with similar theories which connect solar activity and other environmental factors such as higher oxygen content, with the oversized growth of creatures during the Jurassic period. The science behind these ideas has not really been explored satisfactorily to date, but it is worth consideration.

Further afield in Australia, many more archaeological discoveries of giant artefacts have come to light which raise questions as to their exact purpose and origin. Amateur scientist and author Rex Gilroy found some remarkable giant tools and weapons in old Pleistocene river gravels near Bathurst, New South Wales.

The unusually large objects that Gilroy discovered over a wide area included hand axes, knives, clubs, pounders, adzes and chisels, all weighing between 3.6 and 11.3 kg. He also recounts the discovery of a large fossilized human molar which a fossil hunter found in the Winburndale Rivulet, north of Bathurst, whilst another giant molar was also recovered from ancient deposits near the Australian city of Dubbo.

He also claims that over the past forty years or so, New South Wales prospectors working in the Bathurst district frequently reported witnessing large human footprints in shoals of red jasper. 'Some of these have been rediscovered over the years and give every appearance of being of great antiquity,' wrote Gilroy.

Fig. 26 Rex Gilroy with the stone club found at Bathurst which weighs 21 lbs.

Half a mile away from the area where he found the many giant stone artefacts, Gilroy discovered a massive stone club weighing 21 lbs (fig.

26) which he described as 'displaying a handle chipped out to form a gripping surface and thumb rest for a mighty hand larger than any living man's.'

He would later recover another hand axe which even surpassed the Bathurst stone club by weighing an incredible 25 lbs. which Gilroy claims makes it the heaviest stone artefact ever found at Bathurst.

These bizarre discoveries prompted Gilroy to the assumption that Australia was once a land of giants, 'The point raised by these discoveries is that there once existed on the Australian continent giant tool-making hominids that preceded the aborigines by many thousands of years. For, it is certain that the aborigines were never the first inhabitants of this continent. Even they admit in their ancient folklore that this land was inhabited by many races of man, as well as giants, long before them.'[87]

Coinciding with global mythology, giant artefacts and skeletal remains have been found all over the world, in Sicily, Turkey, France, Russia, Egypt, Sardinia, Japan and Mexico among other countries.

Patagonia, a region which crosses Argentina and Chile, has always been synonymous with legends of giants. The name 'Patagonia' is considered by some to translate as 'Land of the Big Feet', although this assertion may not be wholly accurate. The first accounts of giant folk in South America originated in the 1520s with the voyages of Ferdinand Magellan, and for centuries afterwards the area continued to be associated with them.

Tales of giant Indians in the Amazon have been passed on through folklore in Brazil and neighbouring countries, and recent discoveries of giant skeletons in Ecuador and Peru have surfaced on the internet though confirmation of their validity is yet to surface. Such findings, should they prove genuine, would certainly correlate with old written chronicles that have been preserved from centuries ago.

In *A Brief Description of All the Land of Peru* written in 1595, Dominican cleric and chronicler, Reginaldo de Lizarraga claimed, 'There were once giants here, and the natives say that they don't know from whence they came; their houses were three leagues below the anchorage, made of two gables with very large beams.'

And at the crossroads of Western Asia and Eastern Europe, Georgia has played host to a number of giant discoveries over the years. One such discovery was made at a cave site near Gora Kazbek in the 1920's where a number of giant skeletons were reportedly found, and during summer of 2000, two amateur archaeologists claimed to have dug up a 4-metre long skeleton near the village of Udabno, a small, almost forgotten village located about 50 km from Tbilisi.

Another finding was made in 2008 near Borjomi in the Caucasus Mountains of Georgia, where the ancient bones of a giant male estimated to have been between 9 and 10 feet tall was unearthed along with a skull nearly three times larger than the average human's.

In conclusion, there doesn't appear to be any solid evidence available to us at this point in time which could conclusively prove beyond any doubt that the human race once had giants living in its midst. Despite the global presence of giant mythology and comparatively similar descriptions of giants in folklore worldwide, the sheer absence of skeletal remains available for public viewing does hinder the scientific process of connecting us with our mysterious past.

What we do have however is a vast array of reported giant discoveries which have been documented, printed and stored in the archives, some of which we have just encountered.

'There is no question in my mind that the findings from these excavations are genuine, as most if not all were unearthed within plain view of numerous, if not hundreds, of eyewitnesses. Many were widely documented at the time of their discovery.'[88]

Would it be foolish to suggest that our past may well have included a giant human race which for reasons unknown has been wiped from our collective consciousness? The sheer volume of reports worldwide certainly alludes to such a possibility, with the American reports in particular exhibiting an air of authenticity and plausibility which could in time prove to be significantly important as historical documents.

As long as the current paradigm regarding human evolution remains at the forefront of scientific acceptability, then any contradictory hypothesis will no doubt continue to remain on the fringes of public thinking, and any true consideration on the existence of giants in our past will continue to be undertaken by a small minority. Nevertheless, regardless of the lack of popularity of such ideas, the facts remain unaffected. Giants either lived as real as you and I, or they didn't.

As the evidence put forward in this chapter highlights, the reasons against believing such a possibility are less than the reasons for, as there appears to be some truth to the myths, and until we can completely disprove the notion entirely then one should keep an open mind and allow for even the strangest of realities to remain feasible. The presence of giant artefacts around the world certainly serves as compelling physical evidence to legitimise the whole concept.

Next we shall take a look at more evidence that history is missing important details suggestive of a forgotten chapter in our past, a past much more fascinating and advanced than we currently understand or are willing to accept, as we bring to the fore many anomalous physical objects which could force us to re-evaluate the history of our species.

Chapter Five

OUT OF TIME
AND PLACE

We have reached a crisis in the fields of anthropology, history and archaeology because the conventional theses are unable to solve an increasingly large number of anomalies.

Will Hart

MANY ANOMALOUS ARTEFACTS have been discovered over the years which raise severe questions concerning human origins and the rise of civilization. These out-of-place artefacts commonly referred to as OOParts, are manmade objects which have appeared either in a time which predates their official invention or in a place where they simply should not belong.

These seemingly impossible discoveries are often of interest to those refuting the theory of evolution, such as Creationists among others, and have been offered as evidence of forgotten and advanced ancient civilizations that harboured knowledge far exceeding what is presently perceived possible by the scientific and archaeological establishments.

Advocates of Creationism often use these unusual artefacts to substantiate their belief that the Earth itself was only formed as recently as 4004 BC, in keeping with the Biblical texts which declare such an unfeasibly young age for our existence. By disregarding established dating methods, and contradicting the science behind geological processes, those supporting these theories insist that rock strata, fossils, minerals, coal seams and other ancient natural formations have all formed within a few thousand years rather than billions as officialdom declares.

The anomalous items you are about to consider have been chosen to highlight the many inconsistencies inherent in the story of mankind. The mysterious nature of these bizarre discoveries suggests that our current understanding of the world and our place within it may be inaccurate to say the least. If even one of these incredible objects proves to be as authentic as it seems, then we must surely endeavour to revise our understanding of the past, especially regarding man's technological advancements.

If evidence exists of manmade objects that would under normal circumstances be considered to be the handiwork of a more recent civilized society, yet discovered somewhere obscure and unexpected, questions need to be answered as to why they were found out of time and place. If those answers cannot be satisfactorily agreed upon by studying the evidence at hand then we will continue to have unexplained anomalies in our midst. Like all mysteries, things only remain mysterious due to our current lack of understanding or perception.

Perhaps if the Library of Alexandria was still intact today and brimming with the manuscripts, scrolls, parchments and books which once filled its shelves, we would be so much clearer about our origins and meteoric rise to dominance from the nomadic days of hunting and gathering to the space-age technologically advanced era we find ourselves living in today.

BAGHDAD BATTERY

In June of 1936, a mysterious small yellow clay vase was discovered in an ancient tomb by workers excavating the ruins of the 2,000 year old village of Khujut Rabu'a, near the southeast of Baghdad in Iraq.
Archaeologists used other relics in the tomb to identify the artefact as belonging to the Parthian Empire whom, although nomadic and apparently illiterate, dominated the Fertile Crescent area near the banks of the Tigris and Euphrates rivers between 190 BC and 224 AD.

In 1938, the previously overlooked artefact which was gathering dust on a shelf at the National Museum of Iraq was examined by an assistant of the museum, archaeologist Dr. Wilhelm Koenig (or Konig), and what was at first perceived as a simple vase, not uncommon of the type found during that period, turned out to be much more than it initially appeared.

Fig. 27 The 2,000 year old Baghdad battery predates the 'official' invention of the electrical battery by Allesandro Volta in 1799.

The Baghdad or Parthian battery (fig. 27) is composed of clay with an asphalt stopper sealing the contents inside. An iron rod sticks through the asphalt and into a cylinder made of a sheet of high purity copper. The cylinder is 10 cm high with a diameter of one inch, and it sits inside the vase which measures 14 cm in height with the circular opening at the top of the vessel being 3.3 cm in diameter. The rod showed signs of corrosion from some form of acidic substance, the kind which would be necessary to generate a small electrical charge.

Dr. Paul Craddock, a metallurgy expert at the British Museum, told the BBC in 2003, "The batteries have always attracted interest as curios. They are a one-off. As far as we know, nobody else has found anything like these. They are odd things; they are one of life's enigmas."

The unusual artefact which is believed to be around 2,000 years old and originated from the Parthian period was actually not an isolated discovery. Professor Dr. Ernst Kuhnel, whilst director of the Staatliche Museum of Berlin, headed an expedition and discovered similar vases or 'batteries' with copper and iron parts at a site in Ctesiphon, also in the vicinity of Baghdad. These particular finds date from a later period than the Baghdad battery, during the period of the Sassanid Empire between 205 and 651 AD.

Despite the lack of evidence to support the theory, Dr. Koenig was the first to suggest a possible use for the Baghdad battery when he claimed that they could have been used in ancient times for electroplating gold onto silver objects, a method still in use in Iraq today. The vase when filled with an electrolyte solution such as vinegar was capable of producing between 1.5 and 2 volts of electricity between the copper and iron, which would make the clay artefact the first documented battery invention in history.

It is still possible however, that there may have been earlier examples of such technology as Dr. Koenig also found Sumerian copper vases plated with silver dating back to 2500 BC, although no actual Sumerian batteries have been discovered thus far. However, not everyone has been convinced of the battery theory. Professor of Archaeology at Stony Brook University, Elizabeth Stone disagrees completely and in a 2012 interview she stated as much:

"My recollection of it is that most people don't think it was a battery. It resembled other clay vessels . . . used for rituals, in terms of having multiple mouths to it. I think it's not a battery. I think the people who argue it's a battery are not scientists, basically. I don't know anybody who thinks it's a real battery in the field."[91]

German-American science writer and science historian Will Ley didn't see the ancient Iraqi vase serving any other purpose other than that proposed by Koenig in 1938, 'An assembly of this kind cannot very well have any other purpose than that of generating a weak electric current. If one remembers that it was found among undisturbed relics of the Parthian Kingdom - which existed from 250 B.C. to 224 A.D. - one naturally feels very reluctant to accept such an explanation, but there is really no alternative.'[92]

Ley went on to say, 'While the probable date of the invention is entirely open to conjecture, it seems likely that it was made in or near Baghdad, since all known finds were made in the vicinity of this city. It must be assumed, of course, that the subjects of the Sassanides had some use for them, and Dr. Koenig, the discoverer of the best preserved of all these vases, suggests that this use might still be in evidence in Baghdad itself. He found that the silversmiths of Baghdad use a primitive method of electroplating their wares. The origin of their method cannot be ascertained and seems to date back a number of years. Since galvanic batteries of the type found would generate a sufficiently powerful current for electrogilding small articles fashioned of silver, it might very well be that the origin of the method has to be sought in antiquity.'

History currently credits the Italian physicist and chemist Alessandro Volta as the inventor of the electrical battery, since he published results of his experiments with electrical currents in 1799. The 'voltaic pile' was the first electrical battery to harness the natural force and continuously provide an electric current to a circuit, thus becoming the first electrochemical cell.

Volta's battery consisted of two electrodes, one made of copper and the other zinc, whilst either sulphuric acid mixed with water or a saline solution provided the electrolyte that was required to transmit the current.

In 1940, Willard F.M. Gray, an engineer working for the General Electric High Voltage Laboratory in Pittsfield, Massachusetts, designed a replica of the Baghdad battery after having read Koenig's theory. Using a copper sulphate solution Gray's replica produced 0.5 volts of electricity, thus proving the viability of the original 2,000 year old vessel's purpose as a battery.

German Egyptologist Arne Eggebrecht also replicated the anomalous artefact in the 1970s, this time filling the vase with freshly pressed grape juice as he believed that Egyptians would have used the same substance thousands of years ago. Remarkably, Eggebrecht's version generated 0.87 volts, enough electricity to enable him to electroplate a silver statue with gold, just as Koenig had speculated decades earlier.

Hundreds of people around the world have reproduced the Baghdad battery since, all with incredible success, thus proving that in all likelihood electric battery technology was already invented, available, and in use almost 1,800 years before Volta's ingenious 'pile' came to fruition.

Speculation regarding the intended function of the ancient Iraqi vessel may continue to rumble on over the coming years as the concept of such an ancient battery changes our modern historical understanding of such a vital invention, but other evidence also exists which suggests electricity may well have been in use thousands of years ago.

Fig. 28 The Dendera 'light bulb' in the Hathor Temple, Egypt.

Some researchers cite the mysterious Dendera 'light bulb' (fig. 28) as proof of the use of electricity in ancient times. The unusual stone relief inside the Hathor Temple at the Dendera temple complex in Egypt certainly resembles a modern light bulb, despite the insistence of mainstream Egyptologists that the motif depicts a djed pillar and lotus flower spawning a snake inside, all symbolic of fertility and stability. Many theorists have questioned how the artwork could have been achieved in darkness underground without the use of artificial lighting, suggesting that firelight alone would have left traces of black smoke on the walls, of which there is none.

Regarding the use of electricity in the distant past, H.P. Blavatsky wrote in *Isis Unveiled*, 'It is generally asserted that neither the early inhabitants of the Mosaic times, nor even the more civilized nations of the Ptolemaic period were acquainted with electricity. If we remain undisturbed in this opinion, it is not for the lack of proofs to the contrary.'[93]

SAQQARA BIRD

A small bird-shaped artefact made from sycamore wood was discovered by a French archaeologist during the 1898 excavation of the Pa-di-Imen tomb in Saqqara, the City of the Dead, in Egypt. The wooden model was transported to the Cairo Museum along with the other finds from the dig, and it wasn't until 1969 that someone with an inquisitive eye for detail noticed that the wings didn't actually resemble those of a bird, as they were thicker towards the front edge before thinning out progressively towards rear edges and the tips of the wings.

Dated to approximately 200 BC, the unusual carved piece (fig. 29) which is now housed in the Museum of Egyptian Antiquities in Cairo has an uncanny resemblance to a modern aircraft, with its unnaturally straight wingspan and a tail feather resembling the vertical stabiliser found on planes, not in nature.

Weighing 39.12 g and with a wingspan of 7.1 inches, what this small object lacks in size it makes up for in mystery with its aeroplane features separating it from other more commonplace artefacts that imitate the natural world much more closely.

If the Saqqara Bird actually represents proof that the principles of aviation were already understood over 2,000 years ago as many people believe, it would predate the official invention of the aircraft by thousands of years.

Fig. 29 The design of the Saqqara Bird resembles a modern airplane despite being 2,200 years old.

Although the Wright Brothers are credited with the creation of the first self-powered and piloted airplane which flew on 17 December 1903, there are those who believe that they were wrongly given the honour. It has been noted that German aviation pioneer Gustav Weisskopf (who later changed his name to Whitehead on becoming an American citizen), was actually the first man to fly a plane. The 'Condor' which he had built himself was more of a flying car than just a plane, and the flight is said to have taken place as early as August 1901, beating the Wright Brothers by more than two years.

There are those who remain unconvinced that Orville and Wilbur Wright actually succeeded to take off at all in 1903, claiming that only one photograph exists to prove the legitimacy of the attempt of the 'Flyer' which only had an engine of 12 hp with no undercarriage to facilitate an independent take off. The meagre amount of spectators alleged to have been present that day were mostly employees of the Wrights' bicycle shop. It is the same people who claim that the Brazilian pioneering aviator Albertos Santos Dumont was the real inventor of the aeroplane, a contraption made of bamboo and piano wire, which he flew for 60 metres at a height of 3 metres off the ground on October 23, 1906 in Paris.

Khalil Messiha, an Egyptian archaeologist, physician and parapsychologist, firmly believes that the Saqqara Bird model proves that the ancient Egyptians developed the first aircraft, suggesting that it 'represents a diminutive of an original monoplane still present in Saqqara'.[94]

Messiha stressed that the model would function properly as a glider if it still had a horizontal tailplane or stabiliser, which he assumes had been lost, and stated that it was common for miniaturised representations of their technology to be placed in their tombs.

Messiha also insists that the reason the Saqqara Bird differs from the other models and statues of birds in the Cairo Museum is because of the shape of the tail which is so unlike a real bird's tail which appears more horizontal than that seen on the wooden model. The fact that it has no legs, and wings set at an angle which would assist in creating aerodynamic lift, seems also to verify the modern aircraft hypothesis.

This theory of the bird model representing a flying machine has not been accepted by either the mainstream or Egyptologists unsurprisingly, despite the fact that replica models have produced remarkable results when test flown.

Trying to prove the Saqqara Bird's flying capabilities, Messiha wrote 'I have already made a similar balsa wood model, and added the tailplane (which I suppose was lost) and was not astonished to find that it could sail in the air for a few yards when thrown by hand.'

In 2006, aviation and aerodynamics expert Simon Sanderson built a 5:1 scale model of the Saqqara Bird in an attempt to test the possibility that it was designed as a flying machine rather than simply an object paying homage to one of nature's creations. Using cutting edge technology developed by the University of Liverpool, Sanderson set out to recreate the environment needed to authenticate the glider theory which has confounded so many researchers. In a History Channel documentary on the subject Sanderson said, "The Saqqara bird is definitely the first step to understanding aerodynamics."

The tests which took place in an aerodynamic wind tunnel revealed that the dimensions and construction of the Saqqara artefact proved it to have all the characteristics of a glider, albeit without the vital rudder which would stabilise it and help maintain balance.

Closer inspection revealed that at the top edge of the tail rudder a segment had broken away at precisely the point where a tailplane would have attached to. So, Sanderson and his engineers initiated another experiment once he had attached the vital component to the rudder as required, to ascertain whether or not their assumptions regarding the missing piece were justified, thus enabling the model to fly.

The adjusted version was a success and 'the Saqqara Bird flew effortlessly high above the Egyptian plateau' in a flight simulator designed to replicate the dry and hot conditions of Egypt. The documentary declared that 'over 2,000 years after the ancient Egyptians carved this mysterious bird, modern technology has proved beyond doubt that it could have flown.'

Many ancient myths actually allude to man in flight, which only adds to the supposition that such a seemingly modern invention may have originated thousands of years earlier.

The following examples of 'flying machines' or 'Vimanas' which were extracted from the Indian texts the *Bhagavata Purana* and the *Mahabaratha*, are preserved for us to ponder on their true meaning:

'Oh you, Upicara Vasu, the spacious aerial flying machine will come to you – and you alone, of all the mortals, seated on that vehicle will look like a deity.'

'Visvakarma, the architect among the Gods, built aerial vehicles for the Gods.'

'He entered the favourite divine place of Indra and saw thousands of flying vehicles intended for the Gods lying at rest.'

'The Gods came in their respective flying vehicles to witness the battle between Kripacarya and Arjuna. Even Indra, the Lord of Heaven, came with a special type of flying vehicle which could accommodate 33 divine beings.'

As Graham Hancock wondered, 'Is it possible that the constant references in archaic literatures to something like aviation could be valid historical testimony concerning the achievements of a forgotten and remote technological age?'[95]

QUIMBAYA AEROPLANES

The plane-like bird effigies found at Saqqara aren't the only discoveries to have confounded researchers over the years due to their similarity to modern technology.

A grave site situated near the Magdalena River in Columbia was discovered during the early 20th century by opportunist tomb robbers who inadvertently stumbled upon the ancient location. Dating back to a civilization known as the Quimbaya from the Tolima region, 1,500 years ago in pre-Columbian times, the grave accommodated hundreds of funerary objects and among them were around a dozen small gold figurines two to three inches in size.

These particular objects, many of which were most likely meant to imitate insects and birds seem to exhibit the same anomalous aspects as the Saqqara Bird, in that they appear to resemble modern aircraft with features very close in appearance to aeroplane parts. This includes a fuselage, delta wings, horizontal stabilisers and what looks closer to a rudder or tail-fin than the natural tail of a bird or insect.

The tail-fin or vertical stabiliser, which is an essential component of any flying machine but is never found within nature, suggests that the creators of these artefacts may well have had more than the familiar creatures that surrounded them in the natural world for inspiration.

Even the way that the wings of the figurines sit at the bottom of the body in complete opposition to how wings within nature's flying creatures always attach to the top part of the body, is very unusual indeed.

Most propeller planes have the wings at the top of the fuselage but all modern jet engine planes have the wings attached to the bottom part, just as the Columbian pieces have (fig. 30). Such specific design details mirror perfectly those of all modern aircraft including the Concorde and even the space shuttle, leaving one to question whether this matching correspondence is the result of pure coincidence or deliberate design.

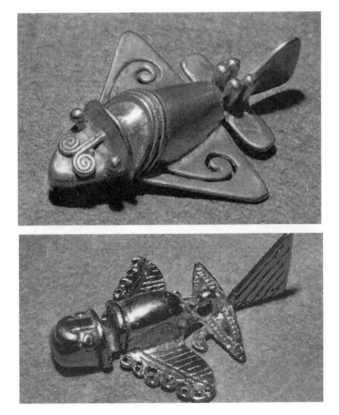

Fig. 30 Two examples of the 1,500 yr. old gold Quimbaya figurines discovered in Columbia, whose resemblance to modern aircraft cannot be ignored.

It is these anomalous features which seem to highlight the possibility that the Quimbaya were fully aware of the designs of modern aircraft and could well have understood the principles of flight despite the antiquity of the objects. Mainstream archaeology believes that the Quimbaya cultures lived in South America between 300 and 1550 AD, and were renowned for their precise gold and metalwork.

The majority of the gold pieces are said to have been made with a tumbaga alloy, a name given to an alloy consisting of a mixture of gold and copper by the Spaniards who discovered its widespread use right across pre-Columbian South America and Mesoamerica. Harder than copper but with a generous malleability, the alloy would have been easier to work with, especially due to the considerably lower melting point than copper and gold in their purest forms.

The artefacts which consist of around 30% copper are not dissimilar from accounts of the red-hued orichalcum alloy mentioned in Plato's *Critias* and *Timeaus* dialogues with regards to the lost city of Atlantis.

Plato wrote in *Critias*, 'In the first place, they dug out of the earth whatever was to be found there, solid as well as fusile, and that which is now only a name and was then something more than a name, orichalcum, was dug out of the earth in many parts of the island, being more precious in those days than anything except gold.' In fact ingots of the mythical metal orichalcum have been discovered on the sea floor near Sicily (fig. 31), bringing myth to life once more.

Mainstream archaeologists will undoubtedly take the stance that no culture that far back into antiquity could possibly have had the knowledge of modern flying machines. The sheer absence of modern engines and landing strips for the craft to employ, tallied alongside the fact that many of the Quimbaya artefacts do resemble insects, fish and birds, leads some to the conclusion that what might appear to be aircraft simply must be something else more explicable.

We know that they created artefacts based on interpretations of real life people, animals and objects, so the question is not whether the Quimbaya objects represent something they *have* seen in the outside world but *what* exactly was it that they chose to replicate?

Is it not also possible that these remarkable artworks could have been crafted to pay homage to incredible aircraft witnessed by the Quimbaya people? Could they have seen evidence of modern technology in ancient times and set out to memorialise such auspicious occasions which they must have revered?

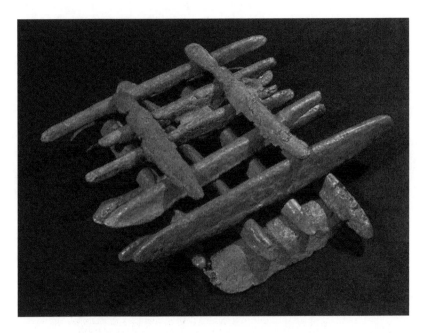

Fig. 31 Ingots of orichalcum discovered on the sea floor near Sicily.

We have seen examples of such reverence in modern times when remote cultures in Africa and South America have seen airplanes passing overhead. A shift in religious belief and practise has occurred on occasion, especially in one instance where South Pacific islanders constructed statues to imitate the planes they had witnessed in the skies above. Their religion became known as the Cargo Cult following investigation by anthropologists of their rituals after WWII planes had inadvertently dropped cargo onto their land from the American planes.

The tribesmen believed that the cargo was sent from some heavenly place so they began to build replicas of airplanes out of branches and twigs, whilst also imitating airplane sounds in hope that another heavenly shipment may drop from the sky. Runways were also built to encourage planes to land and endow them all with the riches which had once befallen them. So it is not difficult to understand how such technology bewilders the natives of ancient and remote tribes, considering their lack of knowledge and experience in these areas.

In order to prove that some of the Quimbaya artefacts were intended to replicate modern aircraft as they certainly appear to do at first glance, three German aeronautical engineers, Algund Eenboom, Peter Belting and Conrad Lubbers, built large scale radio-controlled models of two of the designs (fig. 32), the very first one was baptised 'Goldflyer I'.

Fig. 32 Peter Belting and Conrad Lubbers with their radio-controlled replica models of the Quimbaya aeroplanes.

Weighing 750g and measuring 90cm long with a wingspan of approximately one metre, Goldflyer I was built at a scale of 16:1, with the addition of a propeller on the nose of the plane and the necessary flaps and rolls attached to the wings. This simple design allowed the plane to have a stable flight path, and could land accurately and comfortably, leading the replica plane to behave as planes should, and fly with no problems.

'Goldflyer II' was the next to be developed, and was built following the exact same dimensions as the first but was equipped with a jet engine and landing gear this time. The team expected that the original artefacts would have been based upon a modern type of flying machine which would have included an engine such as the one they had attached to their larger model, as a propeller would not really have been a suitable means of propulsion going on the modern design of the Quimbaya planes.

Once these vital components were fixed on, Goldflyer II was a remarkable success. Just as the Saqqara Bird flew perfectly in simulated environments, the large replicas of Quimbaya craft flew with ease, thus proving the aerodynamically-sound structural design of the ancient objects.

In August 1997, Belting and Eenboom gave a flight demonstration of the Goldflyer II during the AAS Conference in Florida. The plane's impeccable behaviour in the air coupled with perfect landings impressed everybody, so 'insect' or 'plane', the aviation enthusiasts managed to prove the flight capabilities of the original designs regardless of their intended purpose.

One must question whether a simple bird or insect design alone if recreated in the same manner would have the capacity to achieve flight. It is highly unlikely as the specificity of plane design must meet certain requirements, and should any of those particulars not be met adequately, then flight would prove impossible.

The Germans have proved beyond reasonable doubt that what the Quimbaya have immortalised in their intricate statuettes were always meant to memorialise actual aircraft, and even though that may well be the case, we are still left with questions. Were they replicating their own craft, or the technology of others that they had witnessed, or did they make the items using historic knowledge given to them from a time gone by?

'Whenever, in the pride of some new discovery, we throw a look into the past, we find, to our dismay, certain vestiges which indicate the possibility, if not the certainty, that the alleged discovery was not totally unknown to the ancients,' wrote Blavatsky.

Many other bizarre artefacts connected with modern flight have been discovered across the globe, some of which show what appear to be figures wearing modern astronaut outfits, and others sitting in space shuttles or rocket-like vehicles such as one artefact which was hidden away in the Istanbul Archaeology Museum in Turkey for 25 years before it was eventually noticed.

This particular item (fig. 33), which many consider to be a hoax that was created in recent times due to the obvious modern rocket design, was excavated at the ancient city of Toprakkale, known as Tuspa in ancient times.

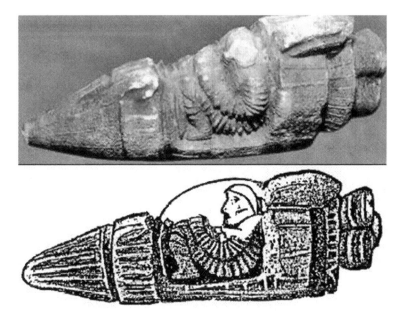

Fig. 33 Is this a genuine sculpted piece depicting an astronaut in a space shuttle?

Another man-in-rocket image can be seen on the tomb of Lord Pacal at Palenque in Mexico dating from around 675 AD, which some have interpreted as the King himself sitting in an upright rocket of some kind.

The existence of these extremely modern types which were created in ancient times, raises many questions once again, either suggesting that such technology was available in the past or possibly that other more advanced races than ourselves were witnessed by our ancestors and these objects were created in their likeness.

We shall leave this ancient astronaut hypothesis for another day as it will open up a can of worms as they say, and we do not have time to cover such concepts here, however, it must be deemed worthy of consideration in the light of the research on offer here and perhaps the reader might wish to investigate this theme further.

ANOMALIES IN COAL AND STONE

Coal was formed when buried plant material from swamps and peat bogs were buried by tectonic movements before being subjected to extreme high temperatures and pressures, thus causing the necessary physical and chemical changes required to transform the vegetation first into peat, before finally becoming coal.

Over vast amounts of time the coal changes state from lignite (brown coal) into 'sub-bituminous' coals, before eventually forming into the harder and blacker 'bituminous' coal that we are so familiar with. This process described by the World Coal Association began 360 to 290 million years ago.

With this in mind, it would seem absolutely impossible for any human artefacts to be found within this ancient substance but incredibly, many items *have* reportedly been found in such deposits, either buried inside the coal itself or found buried deep down within coal veins found only in the mines which have been tunnelled out far beneath the Earth's surface.

On June 11, 1891, an Illinois newspaper reported the unusual discovery of a modern artefact found embedded in a lump of coal that had originated from a South Illinois mine, which the Illinois State Geological Survey said had formed between 260 and 320 million years ago, at some time during the Carboniferous Period. The bizarre report printed in *The Morrisonville Times* went as follows:

'A curious find was brought to light by Mrs. S.W. Culp last Tuesday morning. As she was breaking a lump of coal preparatory to putting it in the scuttle, she discovered, as the lump fell apart, embedded in a circular shape a small gold chain about ten inches in length of antique and quaint workmanship.'

According to the report, Mrs. Culp initially suspected that the chain must have accidentally been dropped into the coal container, but as she went to pick up the chain she saw that it was actually still attached to the coal itself.

The news article read: 'the idea of its having been recently dropped was at once made fallacious, for as the lump of coal broke, it separated almost in the middle, and the circular position of the chain placed the two ends near to each other; and as the lump separated, the middle of the chain became loosened while each end remained fastened to the coal.'

Finding a human artefact such as this with the possibility of being crafted hundreds of millions of years ago raises the most unlikely of questions, should we choose to accept that a) the object was actually located inside the coal as reported and not simply discovered alongside it and b) the geological age of coal itself has been accurately dated. Should these two factors prove to be correct as they initially appear, one must then question civilized man's place in history.

As Michael Cremo suggests, 'this raises the possibility that culturally advanced human beings were present in North America during that time.'[96]

A remarkable iron pot (fig. 34) was allegedly found inside a large piece of coal in Oklahoma back in 1912, and is now being kept at the Creation Evidence Museum at Glen Rose, Texas.

On January 10, 1949, a photograph of the iron cup was sent to Frank L. Marsh of Andrews University, in Michigan, by Robert Nordling who wrote, 'I visited a friend's museum in southern Missouri. Among his curios, he had the iron cup pictured on the enclosed snapshot.'[97]

The iron cup had been displayed at the private museum along with the following signed affidavit made by Frank J. Kenwood in Sulphur Springs, Arkansas, on November 27, 1948:

'While I was working in the Municipal Electric Plant in Thomas, Okla[homa], in 1912, I came upon a solid chunk of coal which was too large to use. I broke it with a sledge hammer. This iron pot fell from the center, leaving the impression or mould of the pot in the piece of coal. Jim Stall (an employee of the company) witnessed the breaking of the coal, and saw the pot fall out. I traced the source of the coal, and found that it came from the Wilburton, Oklahoma Mines.' The Wilburton mine coal is about 312 million years old according to Robert O. Fay of the Oklahoma Geological Survey.

Fig. 34 The iron pot which was allegedly discovered inside a piece of coal.

Another bizarre and anomalous coal discovery was made in 1944 by Newton Richard Anderson who was ten years old at the time. Tasked with stoking the furnace at his home in Buckhannon, West Virginia, Anderson went down to the basement one evening and picked out a particularly large lump of coal which he placed onto his already loaded shovel. The large piece inevitably wobbled and fell to the ground, splitting in two as it hit the hard floor, and protruding from one of the broken halves was a slender metallic object; so setting aside the piece containing the unusual item, the curious boy threw the remainder into the furnace.

Using a croquet mallet, Anderson bashed the bituminous coal lump that had been mined in Upshur County not far from his house, and extracted what appeared to be a small and ornate brass bell with an iron clapper (fig. 35) before cleaning it with lye and a scrubbing brush. Again, the coal from that particular mine is supposed to date back to around 300 million years ago.

Fig. 35 An ornate brass bell was found in 300 million year old coal.

The strange find was kept in Anderson's possession until 2007 when he gave it to Dave Woetzal, the man responsible for running a Creationist website called Genesis Park, and soon after The Institute for Creation Research submitted the bell to the laboratories at the University of Oklahoma. The bell was then tested using neutron activation analysis (NAA), a nuclear process used for determining the concentrations of elements in various materials, and the results revealed that the metals which made up the bell were an unusual mix which included copper, tin, iodine, zinc and selenium, proving that ultimately they were different from any known modern alloy production. In order to validate his claims, that he did actually find the small metal bell *inside* the coal as he had claimed, Newton Anderson took a polygraph test (fig. 36) by L.S. Fulmer Inc. on May 11, 2007 which he passed comfortably.

REPORT ON POLYGRAPH EXAMINATION
Privileged - Confidential

On May 11, 2007, Newton R. Anderson voluntarily agreed to take a polygraph examination. Prior to the test Mr. Anderson signed a form stating he was taking the test voluntarily. This document has been retained in the examiner's file.

Mr. Anderson is approximately 73 years old. He has the medical conditions of narcolepsy and catalepsy, which he developed at a very early age. Mr. Anderson is currently taking the medication Ritalin and also medication for high blood pressure.

The main issue under consideration was to determine whether or not Mr. Anderson was truthful in his responses to the relevant test questions.

The following relevant test questions were used during the examination:

Did you find the bell in question encased in coal, as you described?
Response: Yes.

Is the bell you sold to David Woetzel the identical one you found encased in coal?
Response: Yes.

Did you give false information as to how you found the bell in question?
Response: No.

At this time a polygraph examination was administered to determine Mr. Anderson's truthfulness to the relevant test questions.

Examiner's Opinion: Mr. Newton R. Anderson was truthful to the relevant test questions. No deception was indicated.

L. Stan Fulmer
L. S. Fulmer, Inc.

P.O. BOX 681 • DAVIDSON, NORTH CAROLINA 28036 • CHARLOTTE (704) 527-1804 • CONCORD (704) 788-6782

Fig. 36 Newton Anderson's 2007polygraph test proves he was telling the truth about finding the bell inside encased in coal.

The figure atop the bell which Anderson discovered is strikingly similar to that of the Hindu deity Garuda which is commonly placed on top of

Ghanta bells used in Indian, Tibetan and Nepalese worship, Ghanta being a Sanskrit word for a temple bell used in either Hindi or Buddhist practices. These bells are generally made from brass and are usually adorned with a figure; if worshipping Lord Shiva the figure will represent Lord Nandi or if used to worship Vishnu or Krishna, it will most commonly depict Garuda.

The winged figure on both Anderson's bell and the Nepalese bell both reveal a stepped design with a ribbed grip and a Garuda on the platform praying in a kneeling position. The latter has been catalogued as originating somewhere between the 18th and 19th centuries.

Could the anomalous artefact discovered in a lump of coal possibly reveal the presence of a Vedic influence in North America hundreds of millions of years ago? It might seem completely implausible following the rigid framework of Darwinist thought but Vedic literature is in keeping with such timescales which span back into great antiquity.

The next two examples of OOParts discovered in coal are on a larger scale than the previous objects as on both occasions manmade walls have been reportedly found deep within coal mines where evidence of human manufacture should simply not be present.

A document recording his grandfather's account regarding a stone block wall that was exposed whilst mining for coal, was kept by W.W. McCormick of Albilene, Texas.

The document read, 'In the year 1928, I, Atlas Almon Mathis, was working in coal mine No. 5, located two miles north of Heavener, Oklahoma. This was a shaft mine, and they told us it was two miles deep.' It was in 'room 24' of this mine one evening where Mathis had blasted coal loose using explosives that he would discover physical proof of ancient civilized activity below the ground.

'The next morning there were several concrete blocks laying in the room. These blocks were 12-inch cubes and were so smooth and polished on the outside that all six sides could serve as mirrors', wrote Mathis.

Continuing he added, 'As I started to timber the room up, it caved in; and I barely escaped. When I came back after the cave-in, a solid wall of these polished blocks was left exposed. About 100 to 150 yards farther down our air core, another miner struck this same wall, or one very similar.'[98] If the coal was Carboniferous as would be expected, this would mean that the wall dates back to at least 286 million years.

Another wall-in-coal-mine story was reported by the author and astronomer M.K. Jessup, 'It is . . . reported that James Parsons, and his two sons, exhumed a slate wall in a coal mine at Hammondville, Ohio, in 1868. It was a large, smooth wall, disclosed when a great mass of coal fell away from it, and on its surface, carved in bold relief, were several lines of hieroglyphics.'[99]

Although documented stories like these are nigh on impossible to authenticate, they remain valuable research material which should be considered seriously first before being rejected. Being difficult to prove is not enough to dismiss such cases as fallacious, and the simple fact that men have reported these bizarre discoveries at all would suggest that there must be something to them, otherwise why would working class men with nothing to gain fabricate such claims?

If told in isolation, then one would might feel rightly inclined to ignore tales of modern artefacts found in ancient strata, but these accounts should be considered as part of a larger context that includes the many anomalies covered in this chapter, of which there must be countless more out there either undiscovered or unreported.

In 1844, a curious report appeared on June 22, in the *London Times* which mentioned the bizarre discovery of a gold artefact in Early Carboniferous stone dated between 320 and 360 million years old.

The newspaper report was as follows: 'A few days ago, as some workmen were employed in quarrying a rock close to the Tweed about a quarter of mile below Rutherford-mill, a gold thread was discovered embedded in the stone at a depth of eight feet.'

Eight years later, on June 5, 1852, another unusual report surfaced, this time appearing in the magazine *Scientific American*:

'A Relic of a Bygone Age – A few days ago a powerful blast was made in the rock at Meeting House Hill, in Dorchester, a few rods south of Rev. Mr. Hall's meeting house. The blast threw out an immense mass of rock, some of the pieces weighing several tons, and scattered fragments in all directions. Among them was picked up a metallic vessel in two parts, rent asunder by the explosion. On putting the two parts together it formed a bell-shaped vessel. . . On the other side there six figures of a flower, or a bouquet, beautifully inlaid with pure silver, and around the lower part of the vessel a vine, or wreath, also inlaid with silver. . . This curious and unknown, was blown out of the solid pudding stone, fifteen feet below the surface. . . The matter is worthy of investigation, as there is no deception in the case.'

Fig. 37 The Dorchester Pot was discovered in 600 million year old rock.

The object was said to find itself in the possession of Mr. John Kettell. A Dr. JVC Smith, who has examined hundreds of curious domestic utensils from during his time in the Far East, of which he has drawings, said that he had never seen anything of the kind. He made a drawing and took the exact dimensions of the object, in order to submit them to the scientists.

Now referred to as the Dorchester Pot (fig. 37), the bell-shaped vessel which many have described as a vase but is more likely a pipe-holder or candlestick, was 4.5 inches high with a diameter of 6.5 inches at the base and 2.5 inches at the top, with a thickness of about 3 mm.

Michael Cremo believed that the intricate artwork decorating the vessel is evidence of an advanced culture way back in antiquity and reveals the 'presence of artistic metal workers in North America over 600 million years ago'.

Others remain unconvinced that the Dorchester Pot actually fell from the stone in the first place. *Bad Archaeology* website owners and archaeologists Keith Fitzpatrick and James Doeser explained that 'it is difficult to understand why anyone might take this report seriously,' as they believe that the object is 'clearly a candlestick of obviously Victorian style', and asked the question 'why would anyone in 1852 believe that it was more than a few years old?'

Italian author Biagio Catalano pointed out that the 'vase' was almost identical in appearance and style, to an Indian pipe-holder which is being housed at the CSMVS (Chatrapati Shivaji Maharaj Vastu Sangrahalaya, formerly known as the Prince of Wales) Museum in Mumbai, India. The similarities between the Dorchester Pot and the Indian artefact are so striking that a link between the manufacturers of both must exist somehow, and it would still remain somewhat mysterious to find an Eastern relic beneath the ground in America during the 19th century.

The pudding stone, now called the Roxbury Conglomerate, is of Precambrian age according to a more recent U.S. Geological Survey map of the Boston-Dorchester area, dating the stone which allegedly contained the vase-like container to 600 million years old.

ANTIKYTHERA MECHANISM

Labelled as one of the most extraordinary finds in history, the Antikythera Mechanism (fig. 38) is a bronze artefact only 20 cm in height which was discovered on the sea floor near the Greek island of Antikythera in 1901. Found amongst the greatest horde of Greek treasures ever found, this ancient 2,000 year old analogue computer is the oldest in existence, and has altered the way we understand the technological capabilities of our ancient past.

Back in 1900, after sheltering from a storm, a team of sponge divers decided to try their luck underwater and it was here that they inadvertently discovered a Roman haul, the likes of which have never been found all in one place since. The incredible discovery was the result of an overloaded Roman galley, whose precious cargo included luxury items such as bronze and marble statuary and glassware. Spotting a bronze sculpted hand protruding from the seabed, the divers told the Greek authorities, and the following winter a proper archaeological search took place.

Fig. 38 At over 2,000 years old, the Antikythera Mechanism is the most sophisticated machine ever recovered from ancient times.

In 1976, famous French underwater explorer Jacques Cousteau revisited the site and discovered much more cargo which had been missed during the earlier dives back in 1900. Amongst the bronze figurines and remaining timber of the vessel, Cousteau and his team uncovered 36 silver coins along with some bronze coins, all of which would help date the ship and its cargo, whilst revealing the route of its last voyage.

It is generally accepted that the vessel received its cargo from areas in Asia Minor (now Turkey) and the Aegean, and was most likely heading west, maybe to Italy. Coin experts discovered that the majority of Cousteau's haul of coins had in fact originated from the ancient Greek cities of Pergamon and Ephesus, situated on the west coast of modern day Turkey, dating back to between 70-60 BC.

It was among the beautiful and precious Greek statues that the divers discovered what became labelled as *Item 15,087* in the Athens Museum, an item which had split into several pieces of badly corroded lumps of bronze. This rare and remarkable object only came to light once researchers discovered the small gear wheels hidden amongst the metal, and it was at this point that they began to realise the significance on the find.

For decades, scientists had to rely more on imagination than facts as they struggled to come to terms with the sheer sophistication and complexity of what would become known as the Antikythera Mechanism. Over the past fifty years however, scientific research began to reveal the once hidden secrets of the ancient machine.

Dated from around the end of the 2nd century BC, it is now considered to be the most sophisticated mechanism in the ancient world. Now understood to be a device built to monitor astronomical data and track the cycles of the solar system, nothing as complex as the Antikythera Mechanism is known for another thousand years.

But as author Charles Berlitz explained in his book on Atlantis, ancient writing has confirmed that astronomy had reached high levels of advancement in the distant past:

'The Babylonian texts, generally expressed in astrological language, seem to indicate that the astronomers of thousands of years ago were cognizant of cosmic phenomena and theory that we have 'discovered' only in the last 400 years and, in several cases, as recently as the last forty years. But a peculiar feature of ancient knowledge is that the further it goes back in time, the more extensive it seems to be.'[100]

In the year 2000, a team of international scientists was formed by astronomer Professor Mike Edmunds to further investigate the complexity of the ancient device. Edmunds said, "An ancient Greek scientist has done a truly remarkable thing, he found a way of using bronze gear wheels to track the complex movements of the Moon and probably all the planets as well. It was a mechanism of truly staggering genius."[101]

The team immediately turned to the pioneering work of physicist Derek de Solla Price, who was the first to examine the pieces of the mechanism in great detail using radiographs to bring the detail out of the bronze artefact. It was whilst employing this process that Price discovered for the first time that there were twenty-seven gears inside it, revealing a much more complicated device than had initially been suspected, after all there was no known object like it from the Hellenistic period; technology this advanced simply should not appear at this early stage of civilization.

In 1974, Price wrote, 'Perhaps the most spectacular aspect of the mechanism is that it incorporates the very sophisticated device of a differential gear assembly for taking the difference between two rotations, and one must now suppose that such complex gearing is more typical of the level of Greco-Roman mechanical proficiency than has been thought on the basis of merely textual evidence. Thus this singular artifact, the oldest existing relic of scientific technology, and the only complicated mechanical device we have from antiquity, quite changes our ideas about the Greeks and makes visible a more continuous historical evolution of one of the most important main lines that lead to our modern civilization.'[102]

The two-dimensional images acquired from the radiographs exposed the multitude of gear teeth attached to each gear, but counting them was a formidable task as each gear lay so close to another that visibility was seriously hampered.

It was Price who realised that the teeth count on the gears (should the figures correlate with already accepted astronomical numbers), could reveal some astronomical significance and purpose. And he was right. One wheel which included 127 teeth struck Price as a possible correlation with the movements of the moon. This was a revolutionary idea which Price found most disconcerting.

"Price was beginning to have sleepless nights worrying about the authenticity of the mechanism. If the ancient Greek scientists could produce these gear systems 2,000 years ago, the whole history of western technology would have to be rewritten," explains mathematician Tony Freeth.[103]

Price found that the number 235 was the mechanism's key to calculating the cycles of the moon, as the Greeks knew that 19 solar years matched exactly 235 lunar months, this is known as the Metonic cycle. This initial discovery led to scientists and scholars slowly coming to terms with the technological capabilities of this ancient computer.

Only once the team led by Prof. Edmunds contacted the specialist x-ray company X-Tec, did details of the rest of the gears truly come to light. In fact, x-ray engineer Roger Hadland built a prototype machine especially for the purpose of x-raying the Antikythera Mechanism, but due to the fragility of the ancient artefact, a decision was made to transport the 8-ton machine to Athens to perform the task.

The x-rays from Hadland's machine exposed detail never seen before and allowed the research team to accurately count the gears, teeth, and see all the hidden pieces which had eluded them to this point. Another piece of equipment was brought in at a later date which could photograph the mechanism from many different angles, allowing previously invisible surface writing to appear.

The team was now able to decipher the small ancient text inscribed on the surface that described the operation and construction of the device, which along with the incredible images they had produced, allowed the team to create a digital reconstruction of the Antikythera Mechanism.

It is believed that the device was housed inside a box and had external handles which could be turned to manoeuvre the internal gears in order to produce precise astronomical calculations based on mathematic principles developed by the ancient Greeks. By turning a handle to a particular date, the gears would spin round and once they stopped, a wealth of astronomical information would become available: the positions of the Sun, Moon, planets and stars, dates of upcoming solar eclipses and lunar phases, and even the speed of the Moon through the sky.

Freeth commented, "What we have realized is that the ancient Greeks had built a machine to predict the future. It was an extraordinary idea that you could take scientific theories of the time and mechanize them to see what their outputs would be many decades hence. It was essentially the first time that the human race had created a computer."

Fig. 39 A reconstructed model version of the Antikythera Mechanism reveals the complexity of the ancient device.

Remarkably, the mechanism's calendar dial was also built to compensate for the extra quarter-day in the astronomical year by turning the scale back one day every four years, thus managing to deal with leap years whose inclusion in the Julian calendar was not introduced until decades after the mechanism was apparently built.

Due to its small size, scholars believe that the object was probably intended to be portable, and most likely as a tool to teach astronomy to those with no knowledge of the subject, rather than as a navigational tool used at sea, as not only was the delicate composition of the object susceptible to the harsh salty air and water, its capacity to predict eclipses would serve no purpose to any seafarer.

THE MYSTERIOUS SABU DISC

On January 10th 1936, British Egyptologist Walter Bryan Emery found a mysterious and modern-looking disc inside the Mastaba of Sabu (the son of Pharoah Anedjib) which dates to around 3100-3000 BC, located at the plateau edge of North Saqqara, approximately 1.7 km north of Djoser's Step Pyramid.

The bizarre disc made from a metasedimentary rock called metasiltstone was originally found crushed, but once restored had a maximum diameter of 61 cm and a height of just 10 cm. This type of material would be extremely difficult to bend without fracturing even with the use of modern technology, but somehow the Sabu disc (fig. 40) was created by the ancient Egyptians to a high standard of workmanship.

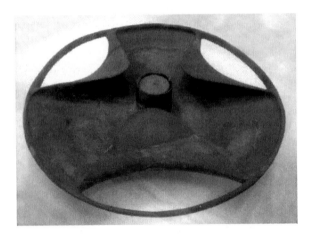

Fig. 40 The Sabu disc which the Cairo Museum claim is just a vase.

Now on display at the Cairo Museum, the purpose of the disc continues to be debated despite the official explanation described next to the exhibit: 'Vase of schist, of unique form, intended to be mounted on a post, and possibly intended to hold lotus flowers. First Dynasty, Saqqara. Tomb of Sabu. Emery, 1937.'

The idea of the disc being a vase for ornamental purposes alone seems rather simplistic considering the appearance of the object, with the three thinly carved lobes orientated at 120 degrees around the periphery and the small tube at the centre of the vessel.

Another theory suggests that the disc could be an instrument of megalithic energy, where water would be poured into the disc creating a specific resonance once in motion, causing the energy to be transferred from the three lobes.

'The Sabu disc is a generator for resonance wave pumping of energy in the physicochemical properties of Si-O bonds in silicon. The disc is a demonstration of how naturally existing processes can create megalithic energy.'[104]

Of course this is just one theory, the truth could be much simpler and less controversial, but it is certainly an extremely unusual object to discover in a 5,000 year old tomb.

THE GENETIC DISC

The following discovery remains somewhat controversial and has been heralded as a fake by some, and as an incredible artefact by others. The controversy over the object lies in the fact that very little is known of its initial discovery and that there doesn't appear to be anything else like it in the world, therefore no comparable artwork or artefact from the same artist in which to corroborate its existence. Nevertheless, a lack of evidential material to reinforce the likelihood of the objects' authenticity should not necessarily negate the possibility at least, that it is a genuinely anomalous artefact.

The Genetic (or embryonic) Disc (fig. 41) belongs to the collection of Columbian Professor Jaime Gutierrez Lega, who has been collecting unexplained ancient artefacts for years. The majority of artefacts in his collection have been discovered during explorations of Sutatausa, an almost inaccessible region of Cundinamarca in the Ubate province. Amongst his collection are stones with illustrations of people and animals with unknown symbols and inscriptions, but by far the most fascinating of them all is the Genetic Disc.

Fig. 41 The Genetic Disc shows details only seen under a microscope.

According to Professor Lega, the disc was in the possession of a local citizen who claims to have found it somewhere close to the city of Sutatausa, but other researchers (Von Daniken included) have proposed the idea that the stone object was most likely part of the incredible and rare collection of Father Carlos Crespi – an Italian missionary working in Cuenca, Ecuador. We shall be taking a closer look at the Crespi collection and its implications in a later chapter.

Many of the objects Crespi collected were believed to have been discovered in an ancient tunnel system 200 kilometres long spanning from Cuenca into the jungle, and despite never having categorised his collection formerly, many of the items reveal unknown languages and imagery which do not relate to any of the known ancient cultures of South America. It would therefore be of no surprise then if the Genetic Disc belonged to the same unknown culture responsible for many of the bizarre artefacts which made their way to the priest's door.

The disc is believed to have been constructed from lydite, a stone which was first mined in an ancient country called Lydia in the Western part of Malaysia, measuring 27 centimetres in diameter and weighing about 2 kilograms. Lydite is said to be of a similar hardness to granite, but with a layered constitution making it a very difficult medium to work with.

Also known as radiolarite, the bright coloured sedimentary rock has been used for manufacturing mosaics and jewels since ancient times, but as cutting designs into the surface is nigh on impossible - especially with the tools available in the past as the layered structure breaks upon contact with sharp implements - it has been suggested that the illustrations which fill both surfaces of the disc could well have been printed using some unknown technique, rather than carved.

The images depict the intrauterine foetal development in its different stages, which includes spermatozoids which could only be seen under a modern microscope, a feat which should have been impossible considering that some researchers have determined that the stone was designed around 6,000 years ago, in keeping with the ancient and unknown civilization where it allegedly originated. The dating of this particular artefact however must remain a speculative one, as stone cannot be dated and the actual origins of its discovery are still too vague.

But, if the disc *is* actually an ancient object from thousands of years ago, a feasible prospect which would correlate with the other remarkable and anomalous finds in both Crespi's and Lega's unusual collections, then questions must be asked regarding the technological capabilities of the distant and ancient cultures of South America.

The process of human beginnings is portrayed with unerring accuracy on the circumference of both sides of the disc, including depictions of the male and female reproductive organs, the moment of conception, foetal development inside the womb and the birth of the baby. One part shows sperm with no spermatozoids, another shows them together, illustrating the birth of the male seed, and another section reveals several completely formed spermatozoids.

But how could the creator responsible for the design of the artefact be capable of such intricate accuracies as these without the use of a microscope? The simple answer of course is that they could not.

The first man to make and use a modern-type microscope was the Dutch draper, scientist and pioneer of microscopy Anton van Leeuwenhoek in the late 17th century. He developed ways to make superior lenses than his contemporaries, and created a lens tube with a magnifying power of 270x which could view objects one millionth of a metre (compared to other microscopes of his day which rarely exceeded 50x magnification).

It was Van Leeuwenhoek who first witnessed and described bacteria, the circulation of blood corpuscles in capillaries, yeast plants and the miniscule life inside a droplet of water. And only in 1677, did he discover spermatozoids for the first time. He also proved the existence of single-cell organisms which had been completely unknown until that time.

If the Genetic Disc is as old as is speculated then it predates the invention of the microscope by thousands of years and suggests that maybe the art of microscopy was already in use in ancient times and has only been *re*discovered and not invented during the latter part of the 17th century.

THE DONETSK WHEEL

One curious find was discovered down a coal mine in the Ukrainian city of Donetsk in 2008, and has had to remain *in situ* as it could not be safely or successfully cut out due to the nature of the sandstone in which it was embedded. Whilst drilling the coal coking stratum named J3 'Sukhodolsky' at a depth of 900 metres from the surface, workers were surprised to find what appears to be the imprint of a wheel (fig. 42) above them in the sandstone roof of the tunnel that they had just excavated.

Thankfully, photographs of the unusual imprint were taken by the Deputy Chief V.V. Kruzhilin, and shared with the mine foreman S. Kasatkin who brought news of the find to light. Without being able to further explore the site and inspect the imprint at close hand, we are left with only the photographs as evidence of their existence (there was more than one imprint) and the word of a group of Ukrainian miners.

Without being able to definitively date the strata in which the fossilized wheel print was found, it has been noted that the Rostov region surrounding Donetsk is situated upon Carboniferous rock aged between 360-300 million years ago, and the widely distributed coking coals have derived from the middle to late Carboniferous, suggesting a possible age of the imprint at around 300 million years old. This would mean that an actual wheel became stuck millions of years ago and dissolved over time due to a process called diagenisis, where sediments are lithified into sedimentary rocks, as is common with fossil remains.

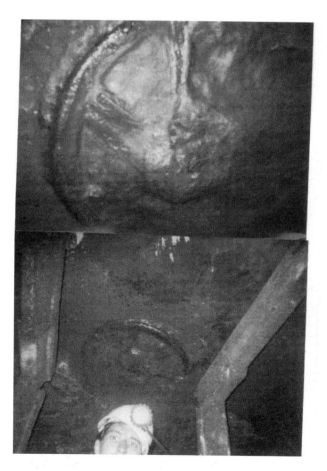

Fig. 42 A fossilised cartwheel discovered in a Ukrainian mine could be 300 million years old.

The following is an extract from a letter written by S. Kasatkin (translated from Ukrainian) in reference to his testimony of having being witness to the anomalous wheel imprint discovered by his team of miners in 2008:

'I'll tell you the history of this finding. At that time I worked as a mining foreman in VSE sector (Ventilation and Safety Engineering), specializing in Seismic Prognosis (dangerous coal and gas emissions forecast). Mine was listed as the one dangerous with sudden coal and gas emissions. I am not a beginner at the coal industry and fully recognize the responsibility for my own words.

This finding is not a PR action. In due time (2008), we as a team of engineers and workers asked the mine director to invite scientists for detailed examination of the object, but the director, following the instructions of the then owner of the mine, prohibited such talks and instead only ordered to accelerate work on passing through this section of lava and on fast 'charging' of the section with mining equipment.

Owing to that, this artefact and the smaller one found during the further work came to be in a tunnel blockage and could not be taken out and studied. It is good that there were people who in spite of the director's prohibition photographed this artefact.

I have connections with the people who first discovered these imprints and also with those who photographed them. We have more than a dozen witnesses. As you understand, the admission in the mine is strictly limited (it is dangerous on sudden emissions) and to obtain such permit is rather difficult.

The 'wheel' was printed on sandstone of the roof. Guys (drifters) tried to 'cut away' the find with pick hammers and to take it out to the surface, but sandstone was so strong (firm) that, having been afraid to damage a print, they have left it on the place. At present the mine is closed (officially since 2009) and access to the 'object' is impossible - the equipment is dismantled and the given layers are already flooded.'[105]

With only this written testimony and that of the other witnesses, the photographs remain the only proof of this anomalous imprint, but once again it must be deemed worthy of inclusion in the context of this work, despite any difficulties verifying the details beyond that which you have read. For, if the photographic evidence were indeed legitimate, then one must question how a manmade wheel became embedded in such ancient strata when according to scientific orthodoxy man had not even evolved yet.

ANCIENT TRACKS

Evidence for the existence of wheeled vehicles in antiquity has surfaced in other parts of the world, as petrified ancient tracks found in France, Spain, Italy, Malta, Kazakhstan, Ukraine and even North America reveal. A prehistoric site known formally as Misrah Ghar il-Kbir meaning the Great Cave in Maltese (and commonly referred to as Clapham Junction), is located at Siggiewi, near the Dingli Cliffs in Malta.

It is at this now famous site that what have been termed 'cart ruts' cut into the limestone have mystified all that have visited the area. Likewise, a number of unusual tracks in stone are also visible on the island of Sicily at the Greek amphitheatre called the Great Theatre of Syracuse. Interestingly, most archaeologists have suggested that the Maltese tracks were probably created by Sicilian settlers who travelled to Malta around 2000 BC at the start of the Bronze Age.

Yet more tracks are to be found in Turkey, some at Sofca cover an area roughly 45 by 10 miles, and also in Cappadocia where several pockets of tracks can be seen. The many ruts discovered around the world have caused a great deal of controversy as to their purpose, age and origin. These mysterious factors remain up for debate but due to the association and close proximity with megalithic structures, in Malta particularly, and due to the fact that many tracks are now submerged below the sea in that region, many researchers have concluded that the fossilised lines show signs of great antiquity.

Bizarrely, considering the anomalous wheel print discovered in Ukraine that we have just discussed, a medieval city-fortress in the Crimean Mountains of Ukraine called Chufut-Kale, lies in ruins but also plays host to a number of cart ruts in stone like those at the nearby site of Eski-Kermen.

Dr. Alexander Koltypin is a geologist and director of the Natural Science Research Centre at Moscow's International Independent

University of Ecology and Politology. He has spent a great deal of time visiting these sites and comparing them to one another in search of similarities.

'I first saw tracks in stone - fossilized car or terrain vehicle traces (usually called cart ruts) on Neogen plantation surface (peneplene in Phrygian) plain in May 2014 (Central Anatolia Turkey). They were situated in the field of development of Middle and Late Miocene tuffs and tuffites and according to age analysis of nearby volcanic rocks, had middle Miocene age of 12-14 million years.'

Fig. 43 Petrified cart ruts in the Phrygian Valley, Turkey.

This particular region which Koltypin has researched further is relatively unknown and the guide books offer nothing in the way of information. Whilst orthodox researchers claim that the tracks are simply the remnants of old petrified cart ruts from the kind of wheeled vehicles which donkeys or camels would have pulled, Koltypin has other ideas. 'I will never accept it,' he explained when confronted with the standard explanations. 'I myself will always remember . . . many other inhabitants of our planet wiped from our history.'

Upon measuring the width and length of the tracks at the Phrygian Valley site (fig. 43), he is convinced that they were created by vehicles of a similar length to modern cars but with tyres 9 inches wide. With the depth of the impressions of the tracks in stone exceeding that which one would associate with small carts, Koltypin maintains that the vehicles responsible must have been much heavier.

He theorises that whichever civilization drove the heavy vehicles that created the tracks were most likely responsible for the many different but identical roads, ruts and underground complexes which are scattered around the entire Mediterranean, more than 12 million years ago.

This single, widespread advanced prehistoric civilization has been wiped out by multiple tumultuous events which include flooding, tectonic shifts, tsunamis and volcanic activity. But he knows only too well that discovering who these people actually were will not be simple; 'Without significant additional studies by large groups of archaeologists, geologists, and experts in folklore it is impossible to answer the question, what was. . . [this] civilization?'

Aware that the process of petrification can occur within a relatively short period, Koltypin insists that the heavy mineral deposits which coat the tracks and the visible erosion are suggestive of a greater antiquity; along with the surrounding underground cities, irrigation systems, wells, and more, which also show signs of being millions of years old in his view.

Koltypin wrote on his website, 'We are dealing with extremely tough lithified (petrified) sediments, covered with a thick layer of weathering, that takes millions of years to develop, full of multiple cracks with newly developed minerals in them, which could only emerge in periods of high tectonic activity.'[106]

It is evident that much research is needed to clarify the age and origin of the many tracks that are being discovered at multiple geographical locations, and as easy as it is to simply state that they are the product of old carts which once trundled through these parts, further investigation may well reveal far more complex and remarkable explanations which could well correlate with the mysterious remnants of an unknown ancient civilization as postulated by Alexander Koltypin.

The sheer presence of the fossilised wheel found in the Ukraine is certainly suggestive of the fact that the ancients may have had access to more technology and knowhow than is currently accepted.

NAMPA FIGURINE

A small clay figurine was unearthed in Nampa, Idaho in 1889. It was discovered from the 300-foot level of a well boring.

The ancient sculpted piece shares a similarity with an Upper Paleolithic female figurine known as the Willendorf Venus which was discovered in 1908 in Willendorf, Austria, and dates back between 28,000-25,000 BCE.

According to the United States Geological Survey, the clay layer in which the Nampa figurine (fig.44) was found is 'probably of the Glenns Ferry Formation, upper Idaho Group, which is generally considered to be of Plio-Pleistocene age'. Should the object prove to have been found where it was claimed to have been, this would date the rare artefact at around 2 million years old.

Fig. 44 The Nampa Figurine could be up to 2 million years old.

George Frederick Wright, a geologist of Boston Society of Natural History, reported in his 1912 book *Origin and Antiquity of Man*, 'The record of the well shows that in reaching the stratum from which the image was brought up they had penetrated first about fifty feet of soil, then about fifteen feet of basalt, and afterwards passed through alternate beds of clay and quicksand. . . down to a depth of about three hundred feet when the sand pump began to bring up numerous clay balls, some of them more than two inches in diameter, densely coated with iron oxide. . . the image in question was brought up at a depth of three hundred and twenty feet.'

Describing the actual figurine Wright noted, 'The image in question is made of the same material as that of the clay balls mentioned, and is about an inch and a half long; and remarkable for the perfection with which it represents the human form. . . It was a female figure, and had the lifelike lineaments in the parts which were finished that would do credit to the classic centers of art.'

Professor Albert A. Wright of Oberlin College is an expert on such matters and believed the Nampa artefact to be the product of a true artist as opposed to a child or an amateur. Explaining the object in detail he wrote:

'Though badly battered by time, the doll's appearance is still distinct: it has a bulbous head, with barely discernible mouth and eyes; broad shoulders; short, thick arms; and long legs, the right leg broken off. There are also faint geometric markings on the figure, which represent either clothing patterns or jewellery - they are found mostly on the chest around the neck, and on the arms and wrists. The doll is the image of a person of a high civilization, artistically attired.'[107] Concerning the authenticity of this sensationally ancient piece of art which puts into question current theories of human development, how can we be sure that it was actually found at the depths below the ground as described above? G.F. Wright insists that he showed the object to Professor F.W. Putnam who immediately claimed 'the character of the incrustations of iron upon the surface as indicative of a relic of considerable antiquity.'

Wright wrote, 'There were patches of anhydrous red oxide of iron in protected places upon it, such as could not have been formed upon any fraudulent object.'

Upon visiting the locality of the recovery site in 1890, Wright took it upon himself to compare the discolouration of the oxide upon the figurine with that of the clay balls which were still lying among the debris from the well. They were nearly identical with one another, or as close to the same as is possible.

Wright remarked, 'These confirmatory evidences, in connection with the very satisfactory character of the evidence furnished by the parties who made the discovery, and confirmed by Mr. G. M. Cumming, of Boston (at that time superintendant of the division of the Oregon Short Line Railroad, and who knew all the parties, and was upon the ground a day or two after the discovery) placed the genuineness of the discovery beyond reasonable doubt.'

And according to Wright, the figurine conforms to numerous other relics of man that have been found on the Pacific coast beneath the lava deposits. He also remarked upon the resemblance to other 'Aurignacian figurines' found in prehistoric caverns in France, Belgium and Moravia.

So, is it possible that the Nampa figurine somehow slipped down from a higher level into the depths? Wright insists that such an idea can be ruled out by stating, '. . . it was impossible for anything to work in from the sides [of the tube]. The drill was not used after penetrating the lava deposit near the surface, but the tube was driven down, and the included material brought up from time to time by use of a sand pump.'

Author Michael Cremo explained the implications of such a find were it to be proved authentic, 'Other than *Homo sapiens sapiens*, no hominid is known to have fashioned works of art like the Nampa figurine. The evidence therefore suggests that humans of the modern type were living in America around 2 million years ago at the Plio-Pleistocene boundary.'[108] The Nampa artefact is now on exhibit at the Idaho State Historical Society in Boise.

FORBIDDEN ARCHAEOLOGY

Many more unexplained discoveries have surfaced through archaeological digs which have remained out of the public domain:

1. On a Babylonian clay tablet dating from around 1800-1600 BC is described the working methods of a pregnancy test. An herbal infused woollen tampon would be inserted into the vagina before being treated with an alum solution upon removal. The tampon would turn red if she was pregnant.
2. Metal fillings were used by the Maya of South America who knew how to drill teeth and repair cavities.

3. Excavation work at three burial sites at Sunghir, Russia, in 1964 revealed evidence that people were tailoring their own clothes as far back as 20,000 BC. Bodies were recovered which had worn hats, shirts, trousers and moccasins. Linen textile fragments, supposedly from a girl's skirt were excavated from a prehistoric mound at Çatal Hüyük in Turkey.

4. A cave drawing at La Marche, France and engravings found at the Grotte de Marsoulas and St Michel d'Arudy, show horses wearing bridles, suggesting that the domestication of horses in Europe was already in place as early as 15,000 BC.

5. There are 170,000 miles of underground aqueducts in Iran dating back thousands of years, as well as paved roads from prehistoric times in Yucatan, Kenya, Malta and New Zealand.

6. There are prehistoric copper mines and iron smelting furnaces found in many American states from California to New Jersey. In Zambia near Broken Hill, evidence of manganese mining was discovered. Charcoal at the site was carbon dated to over 28,000 years old.

7. More than 400 manmade cement cylinders, 40 to 75 inches in diameter were discovered by archaeologists excavating tumuli on New Caledonia and the Isle of Pies in the south-west Pacific. Speckled with silica and iron gravel, their purpose remains unknown, but carbon dating revealed they could be 13,000 years old.

8. In 1869, miners discovered an iron screw contained within a split granite boulder in a mine near Treasure City, Nevada. Similar iron nails were reportedly found embedded in the walls of a passageway in an Andean mine, during the conquest of Peru by Spanish invaders.

9. A remarkable golden animal figure which contained a system of mechanical gears was unearthed during excavation work in the jungle of Coclé in Panama. Such a technique was either forgotten or was never known by the succeeding Amerindian tribal nations.

Of course, artefacts such as those we have just covered will remain controversial and disputed by the vast majority within mainstream society, but this needn't affect the plausibility and likelihood that at least some of the aforementioned objects could be as authentically ancient as they appear. We have looked at a mere handful of OOParts in this chapter, and there are a great deal more that have surfaced throughout the years which also raise questions surrounding our current understanding of human history. It is likely that simple explanations can be given for some of the examples offered here but it only takes one truly genuine out of place artefact to rewrite history.

Next, we shall go one step further and see what evidence exists to suggest that our ancient ancestors may well have had access to technologies and knowledge which we consider modern, as we try to ascertain who these people were and where they got their knowledge from.

Chapter Six

ADVANCED ANCIENTS

The ancient Egyptians used advanced machining methods, which supports the deduction that their civilization, and perhaps others, was technologically advanced.

Christopher Dunn

W E HAVE ALREADY CONSIDERED some of the anomalous artefacts which have surfaced over the years so we are aware of the possibility that our ancient ancestors may have had the use, or at least the knowledge of more advanced technology than we currently give them credit for. But aside from these objects, what other evidence exists which is suggestive of a more technically able and knowledgeable ancient civilization in the remote past? And what do we mean when we use the term 'advanced'?

In this context 'advanced' does not necessarily have to share the same meaning as it might in today's climate. We know (or at least we presume) that our ancestors were incapable of building either skyscrapers or space shuttles among a plethora of modern technological achievements, but there is a vast amount of evidence which would suggest that their knowledge far exceeded that which modern historians are willing to attribute to them.

Understanding astronomy, geometry and mathematics before the rise of the ancient Greeks would be considered advanced, as too would circumnavigating the globe before it was believed to have been possible. The use of electricity and powered machinery in ancient times would show signs of extreme sophistication and knowledge, and would completely rewrite history were it proved a legitimate claim.

As much as we have advanced technologically, spiritually speaking it is evident to this author that the ancients were far more 'connected' than we are today and religious dogma aside, we seem more tuned into a materialistic existence than perhaps we once were. Our improved technologies have done nothing to change our ineptitude in this department, and the general disinterest in spiritual pursuits reflects this.

History as a discipline is an ongoing process which continually develops and changes whenever new information comes to light, either through archaeological discoveries, unearthed manuscripts or documentation which furthers our knowledge of the past. Civilization, as has been categorically accepted by the majority of the academic world, rose suddenly without precedent in the Fertile Crescent region of Mesopotamia in the Middle East.

But as author Martin Gray asserts, 'the currently popular 'scientific' notions concerning the origin, timing, order and locality of the development of the earliest civilization are little more than theories - tentative assumptions given the appearance of authority by the elitist posturing of the academic community - based upon less than two hundred years of piecemeal archaeological study.'[109]

GÖBEKLI TEPE AND PILLAR 43

It is in the Fertile Crescent, a term first coined by Egyptologist James Henry Breasted in his book *Ancient Times: A History of the Early World*, that we find the first evidence of agriculture, domesticated livestock and writing. But in the nearby hills of south-eastern Turkey, the relatively recent discovery of Göbekli Tepe, the oldest temple in the world which predates ancient Sumer by at least another four thousand years, has inconveniently placed a spanner in the works of conventional historical thinking.

The oldest part of the site has remarkably been dated to over eleven thousand years old, between 9130-8800 BC, which compared with Stonehenge built in 3,000 BC and the pyramids of Giza in 2,500 BC, is anomalously ancient.

The discovery of Göbekli Tepe has also opened up the possibility of an even older civilization stretching back into prehistory which left an indelible mark on the human psyche and whose influence and legacy can be seen at the many megalithic sites across the globe.

Did a fountainhead of civilization with superior levels of sophistication and technology exist in remotest antiquity? A forgotten world which has vanished with barely a trace, a world before our own whose confirmed existence would seriously challenge current paradigms of thought concerning the history and development of man.

We only have to look at ancient Egypt to see how every aspect of their knowledge such as their hieroglyphics system, architectural techniques and building capabilities, arose with almost no signs of development. Instead we see that the achievements of the earliest dynasties were far superior to anything created by the generations that followed. As author John Anthony West emphasised, "Egypt was at its height early in the Old Kingdom. Nothing produced by Egypt thereafter surpassed and seldom equalled the masterpieces of the Old Kingdom."[110]

The civilization responsible for building the Great Pyramid simply appeared from nowhere, and despite the academics' insistence that the step pyramid of Saqqara acts as proof of a precursor to later models, the evidence would suggest that 'Egyptian civilization was not a 'development' but a legacy,'[111] a legacy from some antediluvian civilization perhaps which has disappeared from both human memory and history itself.

Manetho the Mendesian, an Egyptian priest from Sebbenytus who lived during the early third century BC wrote that 'The Egyptians obtained their hieroglyphic writing from a drowned continent.' We shall look at the existence of such a continent and who might have been responsible for leaving such a legacy of high civilization in the following chapter.

One must consider how the Old Kingdom seemingly sprang up out of nowhere, with no precedent leading up to the start of Egyptian civilization. "It is generally accepted that all of the sciences – mathematics, astronomy, medicine, the hieroglyphs, the religious system – were all in place by Old Kingdom times, with no indication, or little indication of a period of development" states West.

Such a magnificent leap from Neolithic hunter-gatherers to the advanced culture which left its imprint on ancient Egypt is equivalent to going from "the first horseless carriage to the contemporary Porsche or Mercedes with effectively nothing in-between."[112]

So, how did such an advanced culture arise from primitive Neolithic settlements which produced crude pottery and agricultural implements, into the Kings of the Pyramid Age? And why does ancient Egypt decline instead of improve over thousands of years? Shouldn't we now have hundreds of great pyramids like those at Giza instead of a few? Why did the Old Kingdom culture make more precise constructions and more beautiful and stylised artwork than those who came after?

Since the discovery of the Turkish temple on the hill, a new model for the origins of civilization is required in order to accommodate the new archaeological findings, which have rocked the academic world to its very core. Could the ancient prehistoric temple complex in the Taurus Mountains of Turkey hold the key to understanding the origins of the progenitors responsible for leaving the legacy seen in ancient Egypt?

The remarkable discovery of Göbekli Tepe (Turkish for 'potbelly hill') alongside its even less known 'sister' site Karahan Tepe that remains unexcavated only 23 miles away, has forced the academic world to re-evaluate the origins of both religious practice, civilization and human history as a whole.

Stanford University's Ian Hodder said, "Göbekli Tepe changes everything," whilst David Lewis-Williams, Professor of Archaeology at Witwatersrand University in Johannesburg, believes that 'Göbekli Tepe is the most important archaeological site in the world.'

The site is so ancient that it predates everything in which man has achieved thus far. It is pre-pottery, pre-writing, pre-agriculture and pre-religion, yet according to mainstream thinking was built by Neolithic hunter-gatherers as a religious centre. If this is indeed the case, then our ancestors were far more advanced and unbelievably sophisticated than we have ever conceived them to be.

German archaeologist Professor Klaus Schmidt, who was responsible for the site after its initial discovery by a local Kurdish farmer in 1994, said "Gobekli Tepe is so stupefyingly old that it actually predates settled human life."

"It dates from 10,000 BC, before pottery and the wheel. Our excavations also show it is not a domestic site, it is religious – the world's oldest temple. This site proves that hunter-gatherers were capable of complex art and organised religion, something no-one imagined before," stated Schmidt.

As this cult megalithic complex built atop the hills near current day • anl•urfa revealed no evidence of permanent residence on the summit, it is now understood to have been a communal place to worship and practise religion, which is why Schmidt called it humanity's first "cathedral on a hill".

Both excavations and geomagnetic results have revealed that Göbekli Tepe consists of at least twenty individual installations, with over fifty percent of the entire site yet to be excavated. Based on what has been unearthed so far, the pattern principle seems to be that there are two huge monumental T-shaped pillars, weighing between 40-60 tons each and up to six metres high, in the centre of each installation which is surrounded by walls and enclosures, with smaller pillars slotted between the stones of the walls.

The T-shaped limestone pillars which give the site its unique appearance are anthropomorphic in their design, with elongated hands reaching around to the navel of the 'figures' where a belt can be seen adorning the waistline. These figures are certainly reminiscent of the Moai of Easter Island (fig. 45), whose stone bodies have been recently discovered extending far beneath the surface, where once the heads seen protruding above ground level were believed to be the complete statue.

Some of the carved reliefs on the Turkish stones include gazelles, bulls, lions, spiders and scorpions, whilst other symbols echo designs seen at other megalithic sites, namely the 'H' sign found on the fascinating stone blocks scattered around the ancient Bolivian site of Puma Punku, and also the mysterious 'handbag' motif which has resurfaced at many ancient locations across the globe. It is these striking similarities of design, whose appearance has not been hindered by the oceans and vast distances which separate them, that suggest a common heritage, a third-party civilization whose influence reached every continent in the distant past.

Fig. 45 Despite being separated by 16,826 km, the T-shaped pillars at Göbekli Tepe (Left) exhibit the precise placement of hands on the navel as the Moai of Easter Island (Right) when fully excavated.

Göbekli Tepe was built at the end of the last Ice Age following the final years of the Younger Dryas period, a climatic event which came to an end around 9600 BC, the precise date which Plato ascribes to the destruction and submergence of Atlantis.

At around 8000 BC, the monument builders for reasons unknown buried their megalithic temple beneath thousands of tons of earth, creating the artificial hills of the area and perfectly preserving the site until the present day. It is due to the nature of the burial that the archaeologists were fortunately able to accurately carbon-date specimens found *in situ* beneath the immense mounds of earth covering the entire complex.

This paradigm-busting discovery has only served to reinforce the notion put forward by alternative researchers, one which is still vehemently denied by mainstream academia, that a civilization predating ancient Egypt was capable of producing monumental structures such as the Sphinx which many consider to have been carved at a much earlier epoch than is currently accepted.

Göbekli Tepe has also raised the question of what came first, religion or agriculture. It has always been assumed that as hunter-gatherers were constantly on the move and too busy surviving, that both farming and religious practices would have been impossible undertakings. It is also believed that agriculture and the domestication of animals must have preceded any religious activity, but now that hypothesis has to be re-examined. If Göbekli Tepe *is* the oldest religious site on the planet and predates farming, then religion must have come first, contrary to the prevailing theory.

Prof. Schmidt believed that a correlation must exist between the beginnings of religious worship and agriculture; 'To build such a place as this, the hunters must have joined together in numbers. After they finished building, they probably congregated for worship. But then they found that they couldn't feed so many people with regular hunting and gathering. So I think they began cultivating the wild grasses on the hills. Religion motivated people to take up farming.'

This once fertile region is still considered to be the cradle of agriculture, with the cultivation of domestic cereals such as rye and oats originating here, alongside Einkorn wheat that was first grown on the hills near Göbekli Tepe, from which all species of wheat worldwide have descended.

The domestication of animals such as sheep, cattle and goats is also considered to have originated in eastern Turkey, with the world's first farmyard pigs being domesticated at Çayönü, a Neolithic settlement inhabited around 7200 to 6600 BC, which is only 60 miles away from Göbekli Tepe.

On the builders of the temple site Hancock wrote, '. . . their sudden venture into spectacular monumental architecture, closely followed by their equally spectacular 'invention' of agriculture, is very strange. Indeed it amounts to an almost inexplicable 'great leap forward' that cries out for a coherent explanation which archaeology has yet to provide.'[113]

Fig. 46 The astronomical bas-relief on Pillar 43 in Enclosure D at Göbekli Tepe, Turkey. Note the presence of the mysterious 'handbag' motif at the top.

What is even more astounding than simply the discovery of the site itself is the possibility that the builders had access to astronomical knowledge thousands of years before their time, as the stones have been found to include zodiacal symbols in the design work, and also alignments in the layout of the complex appear to have some astronomical significance.

Presently, the excavated areas of Göbekli Tepe consist of six enclosures which have been catalogued as A through to F. Located in the north-northwestern section of Enclosure D stands Pillar 43 (fig. 46) which is of particular interest due to the supposed celestial imagery which is carved into the limestone.

The proposed importance of Pillar 43, also referred to as the 'Vulture Stone', was first noticed by researcher Paul D. Burley who published his findings in his 2011 paper titled *Göbekli Tepe: Temples Communicating an Ancient Cosmic Geography*. In his paper Burley describes the details and significance of the pillar in Enclosure D:

'One of the limestone pillars includes a scene in bas relief on the upper portion of one of its sides. There is a bird with outstretched wings, two smaller birds, a scorpion, a snake, a circle, and a number of wavy lines and cord-like features. At first glance this lithified menagerie appears to be simply a hodgepodge of animals and geometrical designs randomly placed to fill in the broad side of the pillar.

The key to unlocking this early Neolithic puzzle is the circle situated at the centre of the scene. I am immediately reminded of the cosmic Father – the Sun. The next clues are the scorpion facing up toward the sun, and the large bird seemingly holding the sun upon an outstretched wing. In fact, the sun figure appears to be located accurately on the ecliptic with respect to the familiar constellation of Scorpio, although the scorpion depicted on the pillar occupies only the left portion, or head, of our modern conception of that constellation. As such, the sun symbol is located as close to the galactic centre as it can be on the ecliptic as it crosses the galactic plane.'[114]

Hancock responded, 'if Paul Burley is right, the reliefs on that pillar use symbolic language to depict the December solstice sun at the southern gate of the Milky Way between Sagittarius and Scorpio. In other words, those reliefs are speaking to our time. They are speaking to us.'[115]

Burley believes the moment represented on Pillar 43 portrays a time around 11,600 years in the future from when Göbekli Tepe was built, which roughly points to the epoch of 2012. The reason for suggesting this particular timeframe derives from the fact that it is only during our epoch, specifically in an 80-year window from 1960 to 2040, that the sun on the winter solstice (December 21) not only sits over the vulture's outstretched front wing (signifying the constellation of Sagittarius) but also highlights the dark rift or centre point of the Milky Way galaxy.

It is significant to note that the Maya of Mesoamerica, whose calendar famously panicked many overzealous folk into believing the end of the world would arrive in December 2012, also prophesised that the same 80-year window would later become a prominent landmark in human history worthy of memorialising in stone.

Precisely what this specific time actually signifies remains up for debate but some have suggested that it could foresee the coming of a comet which will impact the earth in the years ahead. Recent scientific research on the possibility of this somewhat grim scenario is presently being taken very seriously.

Should the theory proposed by Burley prove to be accurate, that our ancient ancestors in the Turkish hills were capable of predicting future cosmological events, then it reveals the hunter-gatherers of 12,000 years ago to have reached a quite extraordinary level of sophistication with an advanced knowledge of astronomical precession and the processes involved in tracking the movement of the stars over thousands of years.

As Burley explains, 'the similarity of the bas relief to the crossing of the ecliptic and galactic equator at the centre of the Milky Way is difficult to reject, supporting the possibility that humans recognized and documented the precession of the equinoxes thousands of years earlier than is generally accepted by scholars at this time. Göbekli Tepe was built as a symbolic sphere communicating a very ancient understanding of world and cosmic geography.'[116]

THE RIDDLE OF THE SPHINX

The Great Sphinx of Egypt remains the most enigmatic, majestic and mysterious piece of sculpted art to have survived millennia of tumultuous meteorological, cultural and societal changes from remotest antiquity to the present. This immense monolith carved out of the limestone bedrock of the Giza Plateau is 240 feet long, 38 feet wide across the shoulders and 66 feet high.

Many times during the thousands of years which the Sphinx has endured, the monument has been completely engulfed in sand, whilst at other times only the head has remained protruding above the desert surface. Separated by vast periods of time, different rulers have arranged for the sand to be cleared, and some have attempted to restore it to its former glory by adding blocks of masonry to its rock-hewn body. It was even painted red for a long period.

The name 'Sphinx' derives from Classical times as a corrupted Greek translation of the ancient Egyptian *Seshap-ankh Atum*, 'the living image of Atum'. But the ancient Egyptians also used the Harranian (from the sacred city of Harran which is located south of modern Turkey) derivation *Hwl*, the name of the God which the Sphinx represented, as seen on artefacts and commemorative stelae dating back to the early second millennium BC. The Sphinx was also referred to by the Egyptians as *Hu* or *Hor-em-Ahket*, which means 'Horus in the Horizon', after the first and original deity of the ancient Egyptian pantheon, *Atum-Re*. It could be said that the Egyptian word *Hu* put god into the word *hu*man.

Flinders Petrie, one of the founders of Egyptology, found evidence that the enigmatic Sphinx had originated in Ethiopia and therefore was not an Egyptian sculptural form at all.

The mystery surrounding the Great Sphinx and the reason for its inclusion here is down to the anomalous data which accompanies this ancient wonder. Firstly, the common consensus regarding its age and purpose appear to be highly disputable upon further investigation. The orthodox view which continues to be widely accepted by mainstream Egyptologists and historians alike is that the massive statue was initially carved during the 'Old Kingdom' on the orders of the Fourth Dynasty Pharaoh named Khafre (who would later be referred to as Chephren by the ancient Greeks) at some point during his reign between 2520 and 2494 BC. It is also claimed as fact that the face of the Sphinx was carved as a representation of Khafre himself, a fact which is not reinforced by hard evidence.

Referencing the *Encyclopaedia Brittanica*: '*Sphinx*, mythological creature with a lion's body and human head. . . The earliest and most famous example in art is the colossal recumbent Sphinx at Giza, Egypt, dating from the reign of King Khafre (4th dynasty, *c.*2575-2465 BC). This is known to be a portrait statue of the King. . .'

This assumption that the human head which adorns the body was designed in Khafre's likeness has become accepted like so many 'facts' which dwell so suspiciously within the realms of what is considered to be true history and no longer questioned.

Graham Hancock and Robert Bauval wrote in *The Message of the Sphinx*, 'none of us, not even distinguished Egyptologists, is really in a position to say whether or not the Sphinx is a portrait or likeness of Khafre. Since the Pharaoh's body has never been found we have nothing to go on except surviving statues (which might or might not have closely resembled the king himself.)'

In 1993, a senior forensic artist with the New York Police Department, Lieutenant Frank Domingo, was commissioned to make a detailed study of the points of similarity and difference between the Sphinx and the best known statue of Khafre which is carved out of a single piece of diorite and housed at the Cairo Museum. Domingo was not convinced in the slightest that the face on the lionine figure was designed to recall Khafre's image.

After comparing hundreds of photographs of both the diorite statue and the Sphinx, Domingo concluded, 'after reviewing my various drawings, schematics and measurements, my final conclusion concurs with my initial reaction, i.e. that the two works represent two separate individuals. The proportions in the frontal view, and especially the angles and facial protrusion in the lateral views convince me that the Sphinx is not Khafre.'[117]

Of course this is only the view of one man, but a man who is an expert in facial recognition with over twenty years of experience in his field. What does this prove? It doesn't prove anything but it does raise questions as to the legitimacy of claims suggesting the Great Sphinx was built with Khafre's orders and to memorialize the king himself. The official explanation therefore offers us both a rough time of construction and a reason as to why it was conceived in the first place. But what if Domingo is right? What if it wasn't meant to represent the Pharaoh? Then we no longer have a date or a purpose.

As has been well established by now, stone cannot be accurately dated unless accompanied by reliable contemporary texts which refer to their construction or something which can be carbon-dated like human or animal remains whose presence can be satisfactorily confirmed as being contemporaneous with the monument in question.

Egyptologist Mark Lehner is a known proponent of the Khafre supposition, but even he has managed to inadvertently concede and contradict himself by stating that 'there is no direct way to date the Sphinx itself because the Sphinx is carved right out of natural rock.'[118]

Writing in the *Cambridge Archaeological Journal*, Lehner wrote, 'Although we are certain that the Sphinx dates to the Fourth Dynasty, we are confronted by a complete absence of Old Kingdom texts which mention it.'

One must therefore question how such certainty over the age of the Sphinx has arisen if not one piece of evidence exists in which to place the monument but the hearsay and opinion of a few 'experts' from decades gone by.

As Hancock and Bauval reiterate, 'what confronts us at Giza is an entirely anonymous monument, carved out of undatable rock, about which, as the forthright Egyptologist Selim Hassan wrote in 1949, 'no definite facts are known'.'

So, aside from the alleged facial similarities between a couple of Khafre statues and the head of the Sphinx what else has led the Egyptologists to continually insist on attributing the Sphinx to Khafre's Fourth Dynasty?

One prime reason is down to a single syllable carved on the granite stela which stands between the front paws of the monument. Despite not being contemporaneous with the Sphinx itself, the stone stela was erected to commemorate the later work of Pharaoh Thutmosis IV (1401-1391 BC) who successfully resurrected the Sphinx from the deep sands which had swallowed it up, once more revealing the great symbol of Egypt which was described as the embodiment of 'a great magical power that existed in this place from the beginning of time.'[119]

On line 13 of the stela's inscription, which was already damaged by the time it was excavated by the Genoese explorer Gian Battista Caviglia in 1817, and has now completely flaked away, *Khaf* - the first syllable of the name Khafre was inscribed. Egyptologists such as Sir E. A. Wallis Budge took its presence to mean that the priests of Heliopolis, whose advice had led Thutmosis to clear the encroaching sands from around the great monument in the first place, must have believed that it was built by Khafre. But does that one syllable really prove that he did?

We only know of its existence because not long after the 1817 excavation of the stela, a facsimile of the inscription was made by Thomas Young, a leading expert in ancient Egyptian hieroglyphics, whose translation read as follows, '. . . which we bring for him: oxen . . . and all young vegetables; and we shall give praise to Wenofer . . . Khaf . . . the statue made for Atum-Hor-em-Ahket . . .'[120]

Young assumed that Khaf meant Khafre and subsequently added the syllable *Re* between square brackets to show his addition. This assumption has stood the test of time and has ultimately led to a long held association with the King, and if you were to ask any Egyptologist today why the experts believe the Sphinx was the brainchild of Khafre, they will no doubt point you in the direction of the Thutmosis Stela as proof of his involvement.

But aside from the fact that his name has never been discovered in its entirety in connection to either the Sphinx or 'his' pyramid at Giza, the absence of a cartouche of his name does not seem to have deterred the experts.

A 'cartouche' is an oval shaped sign or enclosure which was inscribed with the name of a king inside. From the very beginning of Pharaonic civilization to the very end, *every* inscription to include the name of a king in ancient Egypt has been inscribed in a cartouche. So why, if the stela did in fact refer to Khafre was it not in the form of a cartouche?

American Egyptologist James Henry Breasted was quick to point out this question upon closely studying Young's facsimile in 1905, 'This mention of King Khafre has been understood to indicate that the Sphinx was the work of this king – a conclusion which does not follow; [the facsimile of] Young has no trace of a cartouche . . .'[121]

As other detractors of the theory have commented, even if it *was* his name being referred to on the stela, does that necessarily mean that he built it or is it possible that he too was being commemorated for his restoration work?

In 1900, the Director of the Department of Antiquities at the Cairo Museum, Gaston Maspero wrote, 'The stela of the Sphinx bears, on line 13, the [name] of Khafre in the middle of a gap . . . There, I believe, is an indication of [a renovation and clearance] of the Sphinx carried out under this prince, and consequently the more or less certain proof that the Sphinx was already covered with sand during the time of his predecessors . . .'[122]

This is not an isolated idea, that the Sphinx was already ancient prior to Khafre's reign, as the text on the 'Inventory Stela' also discovered at Giza, states that even Khafre's predecessor Khufu – the alleged builder of the Great Pyramid – had already seen the Sphinx with his own eyes which would of course imply that Khafre had no part in its original construction.

It must be noted here that the Inventory Stela is considered by the majority of modern Egyptologists to be a work of fiction, maybe because the information contained therein disproves their own rigid theories on the origins of the Sphinx?

One man who remained objective despite considerable pressure from his peers was Selim Hassan, who clearly was not impressed by the ease of which his contemporaries were willing to board the bandwagon as far as the Khafre/Sphinx correlation was concerned.

In 1949, Hassan voiced his opinion on the matter in his classic work *The Sphinx: Its History in the Light of Recent Excavations*, 'Excepting for the mutilated line on the granite stela of Thothmosis IV, which proves nothing, there is not a single ancient inscription which connects the Sphinx with Khafre. So sound as it may appear, we must treat this evidence as circumstantial until such a time as a lucky turn of the spade will reveal to the world a definite reference to the erection of this statue.'

Although nothing new has been literally unearthed to assist solving this particular mystery, evidence has come to light which directly opposes the current hypothesis on both the age and purpose of the famous sculpture.

Firstly, the appearance of water erosion on both the Sphinx, the Sphinx enclosure and also the Sphinx Temple and the Valley Temple (which sit side by side situated due east of the Sphinx) and were built from the same limestone used to carve out the monument from the bedrock. It was R. A. Schwaller de Lubicz who first brought attention to this water erosion in his 1961 book *Sacred Science*. Best known for his meticulous studies of the Luxor Temple, Schwaller's observations which appeared to have either been ignored or simply gone unnoticed prior to his writings, challenged the Egyptological consensus placing the construction of the Sphinx to the reign of Khafre during the epoch of 2500 BC.

Schwaller wrote, 'A great civilization must have preceded the vast movements of water that passed over Egypt, which leads us to assume that the Sphinx already existed, sculpted in the rock of the west cliff at Giza, that Sphinx whose leonine body, except for the head shows indisputable signs of aquatic erosion.'[123]

It was the independent researcher and author John Anthony West who first brought Schwaller's observations regarding the Sphinx to light during the late 1970's, and who would subsequently reveal to the world what had previously gone under the radar.

West, suddenly illuminated by the notion and distinct possibility of some pre-pharaonic civilization having being responsible for the construction of the most famous sculpture in the world, realised that Schwaller had inadvertently found a way to 'virtually prove the existence of another, and perhaps greater civilization antedating dynastic Egypt – and all other known civilizations – by millennia.'[124]

West wrote, 'If the single fact of the water erosion of the Sphinx could be confirmed, it would in itself overthrow all accepted chronologies of the history of civilization; it would force a drastic re-evaluation of the assumptions of 'progress' – the assumption upon which the whole of modern education is based. It would be difficult to find a single, simple question with graver implications.'

So in order to try and prove the validity of this astounding discovery, West approached the highly respected geologist Professor Robert Schoch of Boston University, whose speciality in the weathering of soft rocks would serve them well in an investigation of the eroded limestone surrounding the Sphinx.

It soon became apparent that the water responsible for the erosion on the Sphinx enclosure (fig. 47) had been caused not by periodic flash flooding but by incessant precipitation over many, many years. As Schoch put it, 'only water, specifically precipitation, could produce the weathering. . .'

Fig. 47 Vertical fissures in the limestone Sphinx enclosure show signs of incessant precipitation not seen on the Giza Plateau for thousands of years.

It was the combination of deep vertical fissures and horizontal coves which Schoch described as 'a classic, textbook example of what happens to a limestone structure when you have rain beating down on it for thousands of years. . .'[125]

It is this geological evidence which Schoch insists proves 'that the Great Sphinx predates its traditional attribution of *circa* 2500 BC. . . I'm just following the science where it leads me, and it leads me to conclude that the Sphinx was built much earlier than previously thought.'

This piece of physical proof alone has seismic implications for the history of ancient Egypt and beyond, as the sheer volume of heavy rainfall that would be required to cause the limestone to erode in the way that it visibly has, ceased to fall on Egypt thousands of years before 2500 BC, re-dating the Sphinx to a much earlier epoch than is currently accepted. Schoch's initial geological observations led him to suggest a very conservative estimate of between 7,000 and 5,000 BC as a minimum.

Seismic testing of the ground around the Sphinx revealed that the rear end of the Sphinx was actually built later than the head and paws, estimated at around 2500 BC, during Khafre's reign, whilst the front end of the monument shows signs of ancient weathering ten times older than the back. So for the first time we see that the Sphinx was not built by one group during one time period, but was in reality the result of the work of different cultures separated by thousands of years, which appears to have commenced over ten thousand years ago.

During this period, so the Egyptologists tell us, the Nile Valley was populated with primitive hunter-gatherers whose only tools were made from flint and wood.

'If Schoch is right, therefore, then it follows that the Sphinx and its neighbouring temples (which are built out of hundreds of 200-ton limestone blocks) must be the work of an as yet unidentified advanced civilization of antiquity.'[126]

But instead of rewriting history and leading a torrent of researchers to follow the evidence further and advance our knowledge of the ancient past, Schoch's involvement only served to aggravate Dr. Zahi Hawass, the Egyptian Antiquities Organization's Director General of the Giza Pyramids. Hawass has a great understanding of Egyptology and is always quick to refute new ideas which may rock the 'academic boat' which has taken centuries to construct in order to protect that legacy.

On this particular occasion, Hawass suspended West, Schoch and the American film crew brought in by West to document the water erosion as part of the NBC documentary *The Mystery of the Sphinx*, which was presented by Charlton Heston and seen by millions of viewers. In reality, they were more than suspended from performing their duties but were virtually thrown off the site for what Hawass considered to be an 'unscientific mission', before he made a report which he presented to the 'permanent commission who rejected the mission's work in future . . .'[127]as he firmly believed that 'there is absolutely no scientific base for any of this.'

Hawass wasn't the only 'expert' to disagree with West and Schoch's hypothesis that on older civilization carved the gigantic lion at Giza, Carol Redmont, an archaeologist form Berkeley at the University of California had this to say on the matter, 'There is no way this could be true. The people of that region would not have the technology, the governing institutions or even the will to build such a structure thousands of years before Khafre's reign.'[128]

John Anthony West has become a bit of a thorn in the side of modern Egyptology as his pursuit of proof to vindicate his belief in a greater antiquity for the beginnings of the civilized world extends way beyond the conservative estimates in which geologist Schoch was prepared to announce.

'Schoch very deliberately takes the most conservative view allowed by the data . . . However I remain convinced that the Sphinx must predate the break-up of the last Ice Age. . .'[129] wrote West.

West's theory implies that we are looking as far back as before 15,000 years ago when the last Ice Age is known to have come to an end. Aside from the precipitation-induced weathering on the rocks, West considers the lack of other evidence of other high cultures during the time frame of 7,000-5,000 BC as per Schoch's estimates, to suggest that there was no one around at that time capable of producing an object like the Great Sphinx, leading him to the idea of a lost pre-Ice Age civilization which could have been.

Schwaller's research also led him to believe that the Sphinx was carved by an unknown ancient civilization, 'Schwaller was familiar with an occult tradition that the Sphinx was not built by ancient Egyptians, but by the survivors from the civilization of Atlantis, who had fled some time before the final catastrophe.'[130]

AS ABOVE, SO BELOW

It is no secret that the ancient Egyptians had an ever-consuming fascination with all things cosmological. Their reverence of the stars is reflected in their countless inscriptions and is epitomised in the gods of which they worshipped. The only surviving wonder of the ancient world, the Great Pyramid, exhibits astounding geodetical knowledge which is inherent in the measurements of its construction and also reveals a greater understanding of the stars above.

Astoundingly, the Great Pyramid encodes the dimensions of the Earth on a scale of 1:43,200. Multiplying the height of the Great Pyramid by 43,200 gives us the earth's polar circumference whilst multiplying the base perimeter of the Great Pyramid by 43,200 equals the equatorial circumference of the earth. The number 43,200 has not been picked at random here in order to attain some collaborative figures between the Earth and the pyramid in question, rather it is one of the sequence of precessional numbers used repeatedly throughout world mythology which has great significance.[1] We mention it here as a means to understanding the ingenuity and high sophistication shown by the ancient builders.

In fact, a number of ancient Egyptian local traditions actually attributed the building of the three Giza pyramids to a mythical antediluvian king who was informed that a deluge would reach Egypt and destroy it: 'And he engraved in these Pyramids all things that were told by wise men, as also all profound sciences – the science of Astrology, and of Arithmeticke, and of Geometry, and of Physicke. All

---

[1] For more in-depth analysis of this topic watch Randall Carlson's *Cosmic Patterns and Cycles of Catastrophe* presentation available at www.sacredgeometryinternational.com.

this may be interpreted by him that knows their characters and language . . .'[131]

The excerpt below was written on the mysterious Emerald Tablet or *Tabula Smaragdina*[132] which some believe to be an Arabic work written between the sixth and eighth centuries, that describes the concept of mirroring the cosmos on the ground.

> 'Heaven above, Heaven below;
> Stars above, Stars below;
> All that is over, under shall show.
> Happy thou who the riddle readest.'

Giza, Egypt.

Another aspect of the Sphinx mystery relates to an astronomical correlation between the constellations in the night sky and the floor plan of the Giza plateau, a theory first put forward by author Robert Bauval in 1983. Of course Bauval's theory was met with much derision and has been widely criticised and discredited by the scientific community who consider 'The Orion Correlation Theory' or 'OCT' to be the product of pseudoscience.

The theory suggests that the Pyramids of Giza were built according to an earth-sky plan which mirrors the constellation of Orion, with particular emphasis on the three stars Alnilam, Mintaka, and Alnitak which make up Orion's belt. Being one of the most prominent constellations in the night sky, Orion has been revered by ancient cultures around the world for thousands of years and what was originally named after the Greek demigod Orion in the 8th century BC is usually referred to as M42 by modern day astronomers.

Bauval realised that the third and slightly smaller star in the belt was slightly offset from the other two, just as the Pyramid of Menkaure lies offset from the two larger pyramids at Giza, and in 1989 he published his ideas for the first time in the journal *Discussions in Egyptology*.

Further analysis led to the discovery that the Nile River which runs alongside the Giza plateau appeared to mirror the Milky Way once the Pyramids/Orion's belt correlation was fixed in place. Bauval has also gone on to suggest that other lesser known pyramids in the vicinity were built to mirror other stars of Orion. The Fourth Dynasty 'Unfinished Pyramid' at Zawyet El Aryan situated south of Giza could represent the star Bellatrix, the pyramid of Djedefre which is often referred to as 'The Lost Pyramid' at Abu Rawash further north of Giza, represents Saiph, the sixth brightest star in the constellation of Orion, whilst the three pyramids at Abusir farther south correspond to the head of Orion.

Using computer software which can accurately show the placement of the constellations at specific time periods in the past, Bauval and co-author Hancock attempted to find a suitable match for the sky-ground correlation where the belt of Orion would align with the pyramids below. Remarkably, they were to discover that the correlation would only occur at one very specific point in time, a point which arrived at 10,500 BC according to the computer calculations.

Hancock wrote, 'the lowest (southernmost) point in the entire precessional cycle of Orion's belt – the 'First Time of Osiris' in allegorical terms – occurred in 10,500 BC. Most mysteriously, it is the precise disposition of these stars in the sky at that date that is frozen on the ground in the form of the three great Pyramids of Giza.'[133]

The period referred to here, occurred during the Upper Palaeolithic, a time which according to orthodoxy would have seen roaming hunter-gatherers and not civilized, advanced people with astronomical knowledge of the degree required to map an earthly imitation of the stars above. If such a supposition proves accurate in the years to come, it will prove that ancient astronomical knowledge was far more advanced than is currently understood.

'The world view of the ancient Egyptians, which they appear to have inherited intact and fully formed at the very beginning of their historical civilization some 5000 years ago, was profoundly dualistic and cosmological. . . the architecture of their temples and pyramid complexes, and even the land of Egypt itself and the Nile – all these were cosmological concepts to them. Indeed, they saw their cosmic environment as being bound together in perfect duality with their earthly environment.'[134]

It is also at around 10,500 BC that the Great Sphinx would have faced directly towards the Leo constellation, due east precisely as the sun rose on the spring equinox. Here, the lionine body of the Sphinx begins to make sense, as a definitive reference to both the Age and constellation of Leo. 'Its astronomical and leonine symbolism does not make sense unless it was built as an equinoctial marker for the Age of Leo.'[135]

In 2017, Bauval wrote of the Sphinx's position on the Giza plateau stating that 'in 10,500 BCE it was gazing at its own celestial counterpart, Leo, at the exact moment that the three stars of Orion's Belt correlated in the south with the three Giza pyramids on the ground. This, in my opinion, is extremely unlikely to be a coincidence.'

As the precipitation-induced weathering on the rock-hewn trench surrounding the monument is consistent with an age of more than 12,000 years in accordance with the ending of the last Ice Age, the geological features appear to match with the astronomical alignments of that proposed timeframe quite significantly.

As Hancock explained in *Fingerprints of the Gods*, '. . . we have demonstrated with a substantial body of evidence that the pattern of stars that is "frozen" on the ground at Giza in the form of the three pyramids and the Sphinx represents the disposition of the constellations of Orion and Leo as they looked at the moment of sunrise on the spring equinox during the astronomical "Age of Leo" (i.e., the epoch in which the Sun was "housed" by Leo on the spring equinox.) Like all precessional ages this was a 2,160-year period. It is generally calculated to have fallen between the Gregorian calendar dates of 10,970 and 8810 BC'.

If this theory is correct, along with the geological evidence on show, it implies that the Sphinx could well have been carved out during that incredibly early epoch as part of a ground-plan which also included the Pyramids/Orion correlation (fig. 48).

This does not however suggest that the Pyramids were also built at that remote time, 'It may have been the case that the ground-plan of the three great Pyramids was *physically established* in 10,500 BC – perhaps in the form of low platforms. Or it may have been that the precise astronomical records from that epoch were preserved and handed down to the astronomer-priests of Heliopolis by the 'Followers of Horus'. Either way, we are still reasonably certain that the Pyramids themselves were largely built in 2500 BC when Egyptologists say they were. We are also sure, however, that the site was already vastly ancient by then and had been the domain of the 'Followers' – the Sages, the 'Senior Ones' – for the previous 8000 years.'[136]

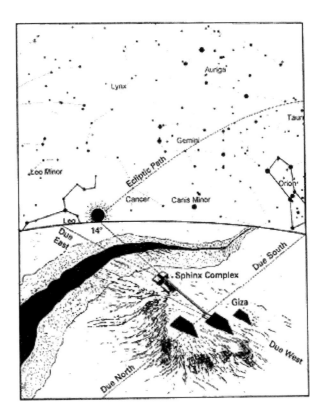

Fig. 48 The Sphinx faces due east towards the constellation of Leo at sunrise on the spring equinox during the Age of Leo over 10,000 years ago whilst the three pyramids of Giza align with Orion's Belt.

According to John Anthony West, many of Egypt's ancient monuments appear to have been built on top of pre-existing foundations of greater antiquity. The Red Pyramid (or North Pyramid) located at the Dashur necropolis in Cairo for example, could have been built to memorialise whatever stood there before. As West explains, 'I think it was a sacred spot to the very ancient Egyptians, and they built the whole Red Pyramid around it.' The Great Pyramid itself was built on top of a mound of bedrock.

In ancient times it was the Khafre (second) Pyramid that was revered the most and referred to as the Great Pyramid, and some scholars contend that it could have predated much of the developments on the Giza Plateau.

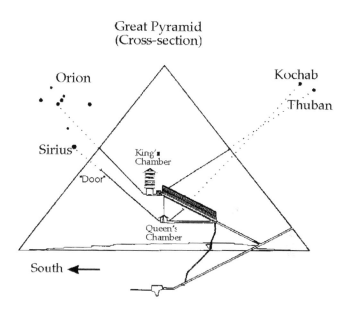

Great Pyramid
(Cross-section)

Fig. 49 Cross-section view of the Great Pyramid shows how the shafts aligned with revered constellations in the night sky.

The ancient Egyptians have always associated Orion with Osiris – the god of rebirth, afterlife, death and resurrection – whilst his sister Isis was associated with the 'Dog Star' Sirius. Fascinatingly, whoever built or designed the Great Pyramid of Giza also built shafts into the design which point to these important stars. The southern shaft in the so-called King's Chamber is thought to be aligned with Orion's belt whilst the southern shaft of the Queen's Chamber is aligned with Sirius (fig. 49).

This vision of 'as above, so below' despite being met with some derision from modern scholars, was clearly deliberate and calculated, as described in the ancient texts *The Hermetica*:

'Egypt is an image of the heavens,
and the whole Cosmos dwells here,
in this its sanctuary.'

Teotihuacán, Mexico.

Astonishingly, the Orion connection to the Pyramids of Giza is not an isolated case. More pyramids and formations in other parts of the world also mirror the constellation, revealing a global reverence of the famous star cluster.

In central Mexico, the ancient site at Teotihuacán, a Nahuatl name given to the city by the Aztecs which literally translates as 'the place where men become gods', also employs a sky-ground plan with astronomical numbers intrinsic to its entire design.

There are numerous similarities to the Egyptian pyramids which include the same mathematics as in the Giza plateau. Both the bases of the Great Pyramid and the Pyramid of the Sun in Mexico measure 750 square feet, whilst the Pyramid of the Sun is exactly half the height of the Great Pyramid.

All three major pyramids at Teotihuacán, which are conventionally believed to have been built much later than those at Giza, somewhere between 700 and 100 BC, are similar to their Egyptian counterparts in other ways too, including the correlation with Orion's Belt (fig. 50), whilst the Pyramid of the Sun is said to be aligned with the Pleiades, another constellation with great importance to the ancients. In fact the entire city of Teotihuacán seems to have been astronomically aligned.

The site is consistently oriented 15 to 25 degrees east of true north whilst the front wall of the Pyramid of the Sun is exactly perpendicular to the point on the horizon where the sun sets on the equinoxes. The straight axis of the 'Way of the Dead' points at the setting of the Pleiades, another alignment involves the 'Dog Star' Sirius, and the rest of the ceremonial buildings were laid out at right angles to the Pyramid of the Sun. Such consistent and accurate alignments were certainly deliberate and part of a preconceived blueprint by the ancient builders responsible.

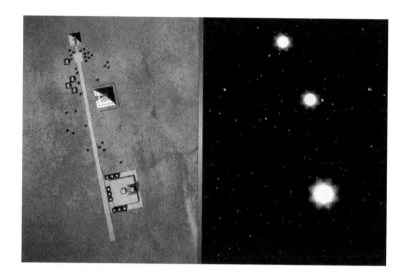

Fig. 50 Orion's Belt mirrors the three major pyramids at Teotihuacán.

The trajectory of the Way of the Dead targets the point of sunset on the western horizon on May 19 and July 25, the only two days of the year with such a specific astronomical significance on which, at noon, the sun passes vertically overhead through the zenith at the latitude of Teotihuacán (19.5 degrees north of the equator).

Some scholars have speculated that the Way of the Dead – which has also been known in certain traditions as the 'Way of the Stars' – could well have been designed to represent the Milky Way, serving as a metaphoric path on which 'spirits were believed to pass. . . between earth and the land of the souls amid the stars.'[137]

The ancient architects 'reproduced on earth a supposed celestial plan of the sky-world where dwelt the deities and spirits of the dead', claimed Stansbury Hagar, Secretary of the Department of Ethnology at the Brooklyn Institute of the Arts and Sciences during the 1920's.

Such remarkable correlations like the mimicking of Orion and the Milky Way, the alignments to specific days of the year in accordance with important celestial events and the memorialising of certain historic time-frames, highlights how knowledgeable and advanced the ancients were in this respect, and we can only look back in awe and wonder where such information originated.

As Hagar concluded his investigations, 'we have not realized either the importance, or the widespread distribution throughout ancient America, of the astronomical cult of which the celestial plan was a feature, and of which Teotihuacán was at least one of the principal centers.'[138]

Xi'an, China.

Much has been written already about both the pyramids at Giza and those at Teotihuacán, but less known is the fact that China also plays host to a great number of pyramids, three of which also imitate Orion's Belt. Despite rumours circulating for centuries that ancient pyramids that rivalled the size of those at Giza were to be found in the Shaanxi Province, the Chinese authorities have gone to extreme measures to guard their secrets.

It took a U.S. Air Force pilot who had inadvertently stumbled across a forbidden site at Xi'an due to engine troubles forcing him to navigate at a lower altitude during a return flight from China to Assam, India, before the world finally got to see what China had been hiding all of those years.

After having just photographed hostile troop movements, pilot James Gaussman flew three times around what would later be known as the 'White Pyramid' of Xi'an which is believed to be 300 metres high, taking pictures as he went. It was only later during his debriefing in Assam that he informed his intelligence officer of his discovery, saying that the world would be stunned when word got out about the gigantic monument.

Gaussman wrote, 'There was nothing around it, just this pyramid in the middle of nowhere. I think it's extremely ancient. Who built it? Why? What's inside? . . . Though I wanted to set my plane on the ground and investigate, there was no way I could land it on that terrain.'

Gaussman continued, 'I flew around a mountain and then we came to a valley. Directly below us was a gigantic white pyramid. It looked as if it were from a fairy tale. The pyramid was draped in shimmering white. It could have been metal, or some other form of stone. It was white on all sides. What was most curious about it was its capstone: a large piece of precious gem-like material. I was deeply moved by the colossal size of the thing.'

Developed and filed in a military archive, Gaussman's photograph (fig. 51) remained hidden for the next 40 years and only saw the light of day when Australian Brian Crowley published the photograph in his book.

Fig. 51 The White Pyramid of Xi'an taken by James Gaussman in 1945.

Finally, following years of resistance and political secrecy, we now have proof that sixteen pyramids were built within the Xi'an region of the Shaanxi Province and purposely concealed with a covering of indigenous cypress trees and other smaller trees.

Located about 40 miles southwest of Xi'an in the area designated as a Shensi, or a 'no-go area', a forbidden zone by the Communist authorities, the White Pyramid is the largest of sixteen pyramids in that area. Although it remains unknown exactly when the 'Great Pyramid' of China was actually constructed, some Chinese archaeologists have suggested that it was built during the Xia Dynasty from 2205 to 1766 B.C.

Details of the Xi'an Pyramid are preserved in ancient records stored in an old monastery near the Mongolian border, in which it was written that the structure measured 1,000 ft. in height, over twice the height of the Great Pyramid of Giza which is 450 ft. tall. The monastic documents reveal that the pyramid was already ancient at the time the records were made. According to the records, there were dozens of other pyramids in the valleys surrounding the Xi'an Pyramid, some of which reached similar heights.

American trader Fred Meyer Schroeder and Oscar Maman travelled to China in 1912, where they supplied the Mongolians with weapons and also dealt in tobacco and candles. As they travelled along the Chinese-Mongolian border, their monk guide Bogdo informed them that soon they would come across some ancient pyramids.

On seeing the pyramids for the first time Schroder wrote, 'In the past, they were apparently partly covered with stones, but those have disappeared. A few stones lie at the bottom. It is an earthen pyramid, with giant gullies on its sides. They were the reason why the stones loosened and fell down. Its sides are now partially covered with trees and shrubs. It almost looks a natural hill. We rode around the pyramid, but did not discover any stairways or doors.'

In the early 1990's, German researcher and explorer Hartwig Hausdorf travelled to China with his friend Peter Krassa where they saw at least fifteen pyramids in the area near the township of Xianyang, about 40 miles west of Xi'an.

The two men were surprised to see small trees planted along the sides of the pyramids, and Hausdorf reportedly commented, 'I had been told that, over the past four or five years, the Chinese had been planting fast growing conifers, a kind of Cypress tree on the slopes of these pyramids. I wondered briefly what they were trying to hide by making these extraordinary artefacts blend so completely with their surroundings.'

Resembling the pyramids found at Teotihuacán with stepped sides and flattened tops, and standing well over 200 ft. tall, the Xi'an pyramids also reveal an ancient knowledge of astronomical alignments and precessional numbers by whoever built them. It is believed that as many as one hundred pyramids were originally constructed, the majority of which are yet to be discovered.

Author and former pilot Bruce Cathie believes there is evidence linking the pyramids of China with those at Giza, and speculates that they could have been built by the same people despite the obvious differences in their appearance. He states that there are 16,944 minutes of arc between the longitude of the Great Pyramid of Giza and the tallest pyramid at Shensi, and also notes that the Chinese structures placement alongside the river is reminiscent of the Nile's proximity to their Egyptian counterparts.

Author Rand Flem-Ath discovered that in the past, when the Earth's poles were located differently from today, that the White Pyramid at Xi'an was at five degrees north, precisely the same latitude as Byblos, a city held sacred by both the Phoenicians and the Egyptians.

In an email describing his finds Flem-Ath wrote, 'It seems to me that the very position of the Chinese pyramids suggests an advanced knowledge of the Earth's dimensions, coupled with an ability to determine these distances within very small margins of error.'[139]

Hopi Reservation, Arizona, USA.

For over a thousand years the Hopi Indians, a Native American tribe, have lived on an area comprised of three mesas in the north-eastern part of Arizona. This landscape reflects their deep connection with the constellation of Orion, where they built and abandoned villages before finally settling down. Their reservation rests high above the Arizona desert and encompasses more than 1.5 million acres consisting of 12 villages.

The Hopi are said to have chosen this location, as the natural structure of the three mesas mirrors the three stars in the belt of Orion which features heavily in their cosmology and monuments. Here they can make contact with the gods in a place they believe to be the centre of their universe. Some researchers have speculated that Hopi monuments and landmarks around the southwest are connected in such a way that they map the entire constellation of Orion (fig. 52).

Of course, many sites around the world can be joined together in a dot-to-dot fashion in order to fit preconceived connections with any chosen constellation if one so desires, but the Hopi's location is worthy of inclusion here as it cannot be ruled out that such a correlation with Orion's Belt does in fact exist.

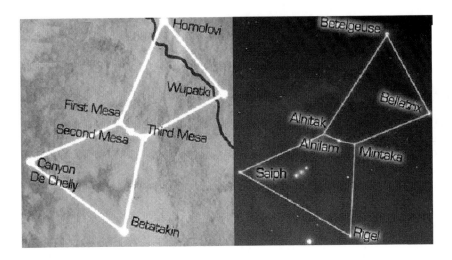

Fig. 52 Researchers speculate that the entire Hopi landscape appears to mirror the constellation of Orion.

At the Mesa Verde National Park in Colorado, some researchers have noted that the Sun Temple which is part of an 800-year-old ceremonial complex have also been constructed to mirror Orion's three belt stars. Although the stellar correlation appears possible when confronted with an overhead photograph of the temple, the alignment is not truly accurate between the three circular kivas built by Ancestral Pueblo peoples and the belt of Orion.

The reason for its brief inclusion in this segment is that due to the geometrical precision involved in the Sun Temple's construction, an Orion connection cannot be ruled out despite the minor off-placement of the kivas in this context, as the discovery alone of the geometrical qualities of this site were most unexpected.

The technical knowledge on show at Mesa Verde raises more questions regarding the capabilities and knowhow of the ancient Americans of this area. Dr. Sherry Towers, a physicist and statistician at Arizona State University wrote, 'These findings represent the first potential quantitative evidence of knowledge of advanced geometrical constructs in a prehistoric North American society, which is particularly remarkable given that the Ancestral Pueblo peoples had no written language or number system.'[140]

Thornborough Henges, England

Located near Chapel Hill east of West Tanfield village, between the national parks of the Yorkshire Dales and the North York Moors in England, lies the world's only triple henge complex. Thornborough Henges, sometimes referred to as 'The Stonehenge of the North' are believed to have been constructed somewhere between 4000 and 3500 BC as part of a religious pilgrimage point during Neolithic Britain. When it was a single earthwork the site was originally sixteen times bigger than Stonehenge.

The henges are circular ditches, each built 240 metres in diameter, with all three 'rings' joined to a cursus (two parallel linear ditches with internal banks) and closed off at the ends. The henges which originally consisted of external earth walls are the largest truly circular henges in Britain and are so precise in their design that they were considered by many archaeologists up until the 1940's to be of Roman origin. As researcher Mark Branagan wrote, 'Thornborough Henges bemused archaeologists, who were convinced that they were Roman amphitheatres.'[141]

Cursus are thought to be ceremonial causeways and are amongst the earliest ritual monuments in Britain, and the Thornborough Cursus was at least 1.2 miles long when it was first built and still remains close to a mile in length today.

Fascinatingly, it would appear that the relatively unknown Thornborough site could be part of a huge prehistoric ritual landscape based on the valley of the River Ure. This proposed landscape – the scared Vale of Mowbray (fig. 53) – starts further north at the Scorton Cursus and Catterick Henge,   before heading in a south-easterly direction through Thornborough towards the three monoliths known as the 'Devil's Arrows' at Boroughbridge, passing the Cana and Hutton Moor Henges and the destroyed Nunwick Henge en route.

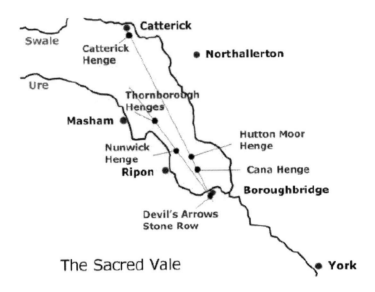

Fig. 53 The Vale of Mowbray in North Yorkshire, England could be the site of Britain's largest religious Neolithic monument complex.

Originally, it is thought that the henges at Thornborough, Hutton and Cana were possibly as large as 300 metres in diameter, built with an outer bank and inner segmented ditches that created multiple entrances, thus creating the largest concentration of henges in Britain. They could be part of the largest building project ever attempted during the Neolithic period.

Thornborough Henges (fig. 54) which predate the pyramids at the Giza plateau could in fact be the earliest evidence of an Orion correlation, as an article on the BBC website stated, 'Thornborough is unusual in that its stones are aligned with the three stars of Orion's belt' and 'Thornborough is the world's earliest Orion complex, predating the pyramids by 1,000 years.'

The three circular formations in England are actually a more accurate reflection of Orion's Belt than the Great Pyramids, which makes one wonder how such ancient people were capable of transferring what they saw in the night sky onto the ground in such a vast site as Thornborough.

Fig. 54 Thornborough Henges are the world's oldest Orion alignment.

Another question might also be *why* such reverence was given to Orion in an ancient culture like that occupying Neolithic Britain. Why does Orion matter so much to all of our ancient ancestors across the globe? Egypt's connection to Orion has been well documented in their own records as the home of the Gods, responsible for the creation of mankind and the civilizations that followed, but ancient Britons have left no such commentary for us to reflect upon.

Aside from the three belt stars mirroring the three henges, the Cursus connecting them together on the ground is aligned roughly east to west and according to the BBC website, 'it is to the west that the Cursus is thought to have aligned with the setting of Orion in 3,500 BC. The eastern alignment may well have been set to the midsummer solstice sunrise, for although the monument was built using straight lines, at its centre (the point under the central henge) it changes direction slightly: an adjustment for its eastern alignment - possibly the sunrise?'

Academics at Newcastle University have suggested a further relationship with Orion based on the alignment of the henge entrances, of which there are two per henge. Set on opposing sides of the perimeter of each henge, the entrances form an alignment approximately north to south, and when viewed from the centre of the henge 'the southern entrance frames the zenith of Orion at the time when Sirius is rising to the east.'

Nabta Playa, Egypt.

In 1973, whilst travelling through the remote Nabta Playa region of the Nubian Desert in southern Egypt, a team of archaeologists spotted potsherds by their feet prompting several seasons of digging in the years that followed. After what initially appeared to be simple outcrops of small rocks spread over the area, the team soon realised that they were in the presence of ancient megalithic standing stones.

Fred Wendorf, one of the archaeologists responsible for some of the excavation work at Nabta Playa dug up an abundance of artefacts which were later radiocarbon dated to between 10,000 BC and 3,000 BC, with the majority of items clustering around the 6,000 BC mark during an epoch with a climate much wetter than today's.

The team also excavated through the 8-12 feet of sediments laid down during this period and discovered that some of the megaliths had been buried intentionally, and here they also found evidence of great antiquity in the bedrock under the sediments where strange carvings were unearthed.

Not only is Nabta Playa one of the major Neolithic settlement regions of the Sahara, but spreading over a surface area of about 10 sq. km it is also the largest Neolithic ceremonial centre of the entire African continent.

West described the discovery, '. . . the crude egg-shaped stone circle and adjacent stone structures at Nabta Playa in the remote, uninhabited Nubian Sahara enshrine a wealth of complex astronomical information, some of it so sophisticated that only over the past few decades has it become available to contemporary astronomers.'[142]

Former NASA physicist Thomas Brophy reviewed the sparse data available to him and presented his findings on the astronomical significance of the site in his book *The Origin Map*. Using custom-engineered astronomy software, Brophy was able to decode the stone circle (the calendar circle) as well as the nearby megaliths which lay in six straight lines leading away from the central focal point, by tracking the star movements at Nabta Playa over thousands of years.

The blurb on the back cover of his book succinctly details the contents of Brophy's remarkable research, 'An insight into the meaning and use of the megaliths led to a step-by-step sequence of discoveries, verified by measure and calculation, revealing that the megalithic architecture at Nabta Playa is a unified and detailed astrophysical map of truly astonishing accuracy, with no less than staggering implications.'[143]

Much to his amazement, Brophy discovered that the calendar circle has a built-in meridian-line and a sight-line which indicated that the circle could well have been some kind of star-viewing platform. During the period between 6400—4900 BC, a night viewer could stand at the north end of the meridian axis and allow himself to be guided by the three stones at his feet, situated in the centre of the calendar circle, where he would be led to the constellation of Orion overhead.

In Brophy's words, 'A user of the calendar circle diagram, standing at the north end of the meridian sightline window, would look down on the stone diagram and see a representation of the stars of Orion's Belt just as they appear on the meridian in the sky when the user looked up.'[144]

Just like the other examples we have covered, another correspondence between ground and sky is self-evident here, where before the summer solstice the three stones within the outer circle are precisely laid out in the familiar formation of the stars of Orion's Belt. The southerly lines of the large megalithic stones emanating away from the main stone circle are aligned to the same stars represented in the calendar circle, during the epoch of 6270 BC.

Brophy also suggests that the other three stones inside the calendar circle are representative of the head and shoulder stars of Orion as they appeared in the sky at the winter solstice circa 16,500 BC, an almost unfeasibly ancient date which sceptics will have a hard time digesting.

In *Magical Egypt*, Chance Gardner explained that "Brophy follows the clues to a greater and greater realisation of a profoundly advanced knowledge of our universe, from a time when traditional dating shows human civilization had yet to begin."

Essentially, what Brophy infers in *The Origin Map* is that the ancient Africans who created the Nabta Playa site somehow had access to three aspects or levels of knowledge which, if his theory is correct, raises a multitude of questions concerning mankind's ancient understanding of the cosmos and our place within it. Below, written by Robert Schoch in the foreword to *The Origin Map*, are the three areas which Brophy highlights as being present at the site:

'1. Maps and markers denoting objects, alignments, and events that can be observed in the sky with the unaided (naked) eye.

2. Markers indicating celestial phenomena and events that cannot be observed (apparently) with the unaided eye.

3. Detailed astronomical and cosmological information, such as distances to stars, speeds at which stars are moving away from us, the structure of our galaxy (The Milky Way), and information (for example, concerning planetary systems around stars) that we do not even have available to us at the moment.'[145]

Some of the dates being bandied around by Thomas Brophy are difficult to comprehend, such as the 16,500 BC timeframe which he suggests is represented by the positioning of the head and shoulder stars of Orion as seen in the calendar circle. Is it even possible that our ancient ancestors could have mapped something so incredibly advanced in such a remote epoch? Brophy's calculations seem to confirm that it is.

By measuring the distances between the individual stones which make up the six long base-lines of megalithic stones spreading out from the central stone circle feature, he calculated that they indicate the vernal equinox heliacal rising point and the *actual* distance of each of the stars from the 'star-viewing diagram' in the calendar circle. These distances which are measured in light years have only recently been calculated.

How such a feat could be achieved is not presently known, but the possibility of light years having been accurately measured in greatest antiquity has to at least be considered, in the light of Brophy's remarkably detailed hypothesis. The proof lies in the numbers, of which Brophy as a former NASA physicist is more than qualified to assert as being correct following his thorough and detailed analysis. If his interpretation proves to be correct then it may well signal 'a radical paradigm shift in our understanding of our ancient past.'[146]

As West wrote, 'In one sense Brophy's work will seem radical; revolutionary. Yet in another it can be seen as just the latest (admittedly most dramatic) contribution to a reappraisal of an ancient history that has been lurching along by fits and starts for more than a century.'[147]

MASTER BUILDERS

We have seen how the ancients' reverie of the stars inspired them to commemorate the abode of the gods through imitation and mimicry at ground level, by constructing their monuments to suit a remarkably considered celestial blueprint. Such designs already show astounding astronomical knowhow which we would struggle to replicate today, but what is even more dumbfounding is the engineering technicality involved in some of the world's megalithic sites.

There are many stone artefacts from the ancient world made from the hardest stone on the planet such as granite and diorite, which have been cut and shaped with such quality, precision and accuracy that the standard explanations of their manufacture are simply inadequate.

Take the granite sarcophagus in the King's Chamber of the Great Pyramid for example, which has been hollowed out with such absolute precision that famed English Egyptologist Flinders Petrie firmly believed that the craftsmen present during Khufu's reign must have had access to tools '. . . such as we ourselves have only now reinvented.'[148]

Petrie was dumbfounded by the anomalously modern stone-cutting techniques on show in Egypt and wrote, 'The character of the work would certainly seem to point to diamond as being the cutting jewel; and only the considerations of its rarity in general, and its absence from Egypt, interfere with this conclusion. . .'[149]

The presence of such bizarrely fashioned stones dating back nearly five thousand years still remains a conundrum today, '. . . at the supposed dawn of human civilization, more than 4,500 years ago, the ancient Egyptians had acquired what sounded like industrial-age drills.'[150]

It isn't just the quality of the cutting which has baffled researchers, but the sheer immensity of some of the stones used to build the many monumental constructions has caused scholarly debate for centuries, and even today the experts struggle to explain how some of these massive bocks were cut, shifted and placed so perfectly into place.

We are talking of such enigmatic archaeological sites as Baalbek in Lebanon, Sacsayhuamán, Ollantaytambo and Machu Picchu in Peru, Tiahuanaco and Puma Punku in Bolivia, Easter Island, Stonehenge in England, and of course the Great Pyramids and temples of Egypt, to name but a few.

These structures all exhibit signs of ancient engineering skills which should not have been possible in such ancient times with the tools and knowledge which orthodox academics insist were available to them. We see evidence of heavy lifting which cannot be done today with the world's largest cranes, and holes and cavities in the hardest rock on earth that only diamond-tipped saws of the modern era should be capable of producing. How was any of this possible?

As Hancock remarks in *The Message of the Sphinx*, 'What we may be looking at here are the fingerprints of highly sophisticated and perhaps even technological people capable of awe-inspiring architectural and engineering feats at a time when no civilization of any kind is supposed to have existed anywhere on Earth.'

On the Giza plateau in front of the Great Sphinx are two temples built from the same limestone rock which was carved out of the horseshoe-shaped enclosure in which sits the Sphinx itself. Both the so-called 'Sphinx Temple' and the 'Valley Temple of Khafre' are built from massive limestone core-blocks, which were once fitted with granite casings inside and out.

Bewilderingly, the builders of these ancient and anonymous temples chose to stack stones of immense proportions, some of which are 30 ft. long, 12 ft. wide and 10 ft. high, and weigh in the region of 200 tons each. Even the smallest stones were still a mighty 50 tons apiece. Now the questions that arise today aside from *how* did these early civilizations manage to haul around such incredibly large stones, must be *why?* It would be so much easier to build with smaller blocks or bricks like we do in modern times, but for some unknown reason our ancestors chose the difficult option.

What they have succeeded in doing, apart from leaving behind physical evidence of their existence, is confounding us with their capabilities, with the mysteries of the master engineers remaining unsolved.

To get a sense of the sheer size and weight of a 200 ton block we can compare its dimensions to a locomotive train which as a general rule of thumb weighs in at 30-35 tons per axle, with the average 4-axle locomotive around 125 tons and a 6-axle locomotive around 200 tons. Imagine stacking the largest of these trains one on top of the other, it would be a logistical nightmare.

The standard cranes that we see in our cities on large construction sites can generally hoist a maximum load of 20 tons when the crane arm is at minimum span, but whilst outstretched to its maximum will only lift round 5 tons. Special cranes are required to lift loads exceeding 50 tons, with the most equipped cranes capable of dealing with a 200-ton load being few and far between. Only two land-based cranes in the United States are presently capable of such a feat.

'Built with structural steel members and powered with massive electric motors, the majority of these cranes have a load limit of under 100 tons' writes Hancock, and 'a commission to put together a temple out of 200 ton blocks would be a most unusual and very taxing job, even for modern heavy-load and crane specialists.'[151]

According to Egyptologists, the stones were raised 50 feet above the ground into position by employing a combination of ramps, levers and ropes alongside a huge amount of manpower. But mystified by conventional explanations, John Anthony West sought answers and visited a Long Island construction site to see for himself, precisely how a 200 ton weight could really be shifted.

It took twenty men working for six weeks to even prepare to lift a 200 ton boiler using one of the largest cranes in existence with a 220 ft. high boom and a counterweight made of concrete weighing an incredible 160 tons. A second crane was then brought in to precisely fit the boiler in place.

Discussing the construction of the Valley and Sphinx Temples, chief engineer Jesse Warren commented, "seeing how they moved these heavy 200 ton blocks, possibly thousands and thousands of years ago, I have no idea how they did this job. It's a mystery, and it'll probably always be a mystery to me."[152]

In the Beqaa Valley north of Beirut lie the remains of the ancient Phoenician city of Baalbek, (meaning Lord Baal of the Beqaa Valley), once referred to as Heliopolis or 'the City of the Sun' in what is now modern day Lebanon. In the ancient world as early as 9000 BC (although time may reveal the site to be much older), Baalbek became an important pilgrimage site for the worship of the Phoenician sky-god Baal and his consort Astarte, the Queen of Heaven.

At the heart of the city stood a grand temple dedicated to Astarte and Baal which today consists of a five million square foot platform built using some of the largest stones ever shaped by human hands. This immense ancient platform became the foundation for the later Roman temple complex which includes three separate temples dedicated to Jupiter, Bacchus and Venus respectively.

The stones used at this site are so enormous that they make the 200 ton blocks seen at the Giza temples look like toy bricks in comparison. Some of the blocks in the wall are around 400 tons each while the three hewn stones known as the 'trilithon' which lay in the base of the Jupiter

Baal Temple ruins, each weigh an estimated 800 tons. Officially, scholars attribute the shifting and cutting of these monstrous monoliths to the Romans circa 27 BC, but many researchers contest this idea, suggesting instead that they are the remnants of some other ancient civilization from a far earlier epoch altogether.

Hancock is one such dissident; 'the moving and positioning of three 800 ton megaliths to a height of 18 or 20 feet above the ground as is the case at Baalbek is a problem of a completely different order. I suggest this requires careful consideration rather than simply saying "the Romans did it" as archaeology is at present inclined to do.'[153]

The combined weight of the entire base at Baalbek is estimated at around five billion tons. Were the Romans capable of shifting such an amount of stone? It is hard to imagine, and no other evidence of Roman construction anywhere else supports such a theory.

A stone quarry site can be found not too far from the ruins, and it is here where the largest stones ever unearthed were discovered. Sticking out of the ground at a slight angle, a limestone monolith that was named 'Hajjar al-Hibla' in Arabic or 'the Stone of the Pregnant Woman' was found which weighs an approximate 1,200 tons (or six locomotives)!

Archaeologists agree that this huge monolith was left in the quarry simply because the quality of the stone block's edge proved too poor to transport as it could be too easily damaged.

In 2014, the Oriental Department of the German Archaeological Institute conducted more excavation work in the stone quarry trying to find new data about the mining techniques and the transporting of the megaliths. But what they found was an even larger monolith directly beside the first one (fig. 55) which had been covered up beneath the ground until that summer.

Measuring an astounding 19.6 metres (64 feet) in length, 6 metres (19.6 feet) wide and 5.5 metres (18 feet) high, this unbelievable find weighs 1,650 tons (nearly 1.5 million kilos) and is now the biggest known ancient stone block anywhere in the world. The archaeologists also concluded that due to the block's configuration and level of smoothness, it was most certainly being readied for transportation without being cut, and all at an altitude of around 1,170 metres.

Following the discovery of the second monolith Hancock wrote, 'I believe these huge megaliths long predate the construction of the Temple of Jupiter and are likely to be 12,000 or more years old — contemporaneous with the megalithic site of Gobekli Tepe in Turkey. I suggest we are looking at the handiwork of the survivors of a lost civilization, that the Romans built their Temple of Jupiter on a pre-existing, 12,000-years-old megalithic foundation, and that they were unaware of the giant hewn megaliths in the ancient quarry as these were covered by sediment in Roman times (as, indeed, the newly discovered block still was until very recently).'[154]

Fig. 55 The 1,650 ton block (right) remains *in situ* at the Baalbek quarry.

It remains unexplained how the Romans – or whoever was actually responsible for such an astounding feat of engineering – quarried, cut and transported the megaliths of Baalbek. And another mystery is why they left the largest blocks *in situ*. The mainstream answer is that they were simply too heavy to manoeuvre so were left in the ground, but they succeeded in shifting the 800 ton 'trilithon' blocks so why not the others? Even if they decided they were beyond the limits of their engineering capabilities, surely they would have cut them up into smaller, more manageable blocks in order to complete the temple constructions. 'It's really puzzling that they didn't do so and therefore the fact that these gigantic, almost finished blocks remain in the quarry and were never sliced up into smaller blocks and used in the general construction of the Temple of Jupiter, suggests to me very strongly that the Romans did not even know they were there,' explains Hancock.[155]

We may never know the answer to these questions, but we can still conjecture as to the technological means in manoeuvring the megalithic stones left around the world which continue to perplex us with their mystery.

Fig. 56 Immense megalithic blocks weighing thousands of tons in Siberia.

More recent discoveries have revealed even more megalithic stones, this time in Southern Siberia near the mountains of Gornaya Shoria. Georgy Sidorov found and photographed the 'super' megaliths (fig. 56) for the first time on an expedition to the Southern Siberian Mountains in 2014.

There are no accurate measurements given as of yet, but judging from the scale depicted by the human figures in some of the photographs, these Siberian megaliths hewn from granite could prove to be twice the weight of the largest known megaliths found at Baalbek, possibly in the region of between 3,000 and 4,000 tons each. How many more such discoveries lie in wait across the globe? And at what weight will these astoundingly immense stones reach?

Reports of the 2014 expedition claim that the geologists encountered some unexplained problems with their compasses when the arrows began deviating away from the megalithic blocks. It has been suggested that they may have experienced inexplicable phenomena of a negative geomagnetic field, leading to notions of the possible use of ancient antigravity technologies unknown to modern science.

LEVITATING THE STONES

Egyptologists recently discovered the remains of another ancient wooden boat buried beneath the sands at the foot of the Great Pyramid of Khufu. The previous boat which was unearthed in the same vicinity now stands in the Giza Solar Boat Museum on the plateau, erected in 1985. The reassembled boat was attributed to Khufu as a ceremonial boat which was constructed to safely transport the King to the afterlife.

The more recent discovery however, which has also been attributed to Khufu due to the carbon dating of 2600 BC, was apparently not built for ceremonial purposes but was allegedly intended for actual use, for shipping the limestone blocks which made up the outer facade of the Great Pyramid. Well, so the recent theory goes. The reasons as to why *this* boat is considered to have been for practical use and not the other is not exactly clear, neither is how the Egyptologists jumped to the conclusion that it was built to shift heavy stones down the Nile to the Giza plateau.

Despite any actual hard evidence, the assumption remains that Khufu ordered thousands of men to cut, transport and lift into place, massive blocks of white limestone for the outside casing, and even bigger blocks of granite for the internal structure of the pyramid. Using ramps, levers and ropes and a whole lot of manpower, the ancient Egyptians managed to construct the biggest manmade structure on Earth which would stand for over 4,500 years. At least that is what the mainstream academics contend.

The standard view presently in circulation insists that the Great Pyramid took twenty years to construct. With over two million stone blocks in the pyramid, this would mean that if the men worked 12 hours a day, 365 days a year for 20 years, they would have to quarry, carve, then lift one block every 2.5 minutes; and all this was achieved using nothing but copper chisels, stone mallets and hemp ropes.

This appears to be a staggeringly impossible supposition one would have to agree. The timeframe of two decades continues to be accepted, as the Egyptologists still insist that it was built for the pharaoh during his lifetime for him to finally be buried in. Considering that it took 150 years to build the pyramid at Teotihuacán which is only 216 ft. high compared with the 455.4 ft. of its Egyptian counterpart, that 20 year timeframe starts to look ridiculous.

'The truth is that, where the pyramids are concerned, there are no absolute certainties: only certain, established ideas that the 'experts' have agreed to accept because it is convenient to do so.'[156]

This is the same group of experts that continue to insist that is was built as a tomb for Khufu, despite the lack of circumstantial evidence to reinforce such a notion. Around 820 AD, after months of intensive labour, Arabs first bored into the Great Pyramid under the instruction of the Caliph of Baghdad, Abdullah Al Ma'mun, but they missed the actual entrance which was 24 feet to the east and ten courses higher then they had supposed. The men found nothing inside. No inscriptions, no funerary objects, no treasure or gold, just the granite sarcophagus which lies in the King's Chamber to this day.

'Finally the last block was removed. Up they went into the Grand Gallery. One or two stopped to examine and peer closely into the well. Into the Queen's chamber the men forged. Into the Ante-Chamber they went. Still the promised riches eluded them. Beneath the last, low-suspended stones they crawled, coming out into the beautiful King's chamber. Alas the coffer was empty.'[157]

According to one version of events, in order to pacify his disappointed men, Al Ma'mun had a treasure of gold hidden near the pyramid later that night, amounting to just the wages his team were owed, a coincidence which he explained came about through the wisdom of Allah.

The account states, 'That night under the cover of darkness, while his weary men slept soundly, Ma'mun, who was very rich, carried, with the aid of a few trusted officers, many gold coins to a spot adjacent to the pyramid and buried them securely. Next day he confronted his men and in his grandiose manner announced that in a vision during the night Allah had revealed to him where the wealth that they had been seeking really lay. The man dug at the spot directed by the Caliph, and soon uncovered the cache of gold.'[158]

The sheer lack of anything at all associated with either Khufu or his burial remains a complete mystery.

Researcher Rick Richards commented, 'For the ancient Egyptians to spend so much time, energy and money to build such a monument and not spend one ounce of time or energy to decorate it in their customary elaborate, ornate funeral-ritualistic style to depict the awe-inspiring structure as a tomb for their great Pharaoh makes no common sense at all, especially since that is one of the things the ancient Egyptians are so famous for!'

One only need venture to the Valley of the Kings to see how Tutankhamen was buried, in a tomb worthy of a King. Despite this particular tomb being dated to around 1323 BC, over a thousand years later than Khufu's dynasty, one would still expect to see at least inscriptions of some sort inside his pyramid if it was truly built with this purpose in mind. But as author Stephen Mehler explains, 'no inscriptions or reliefs either depicting or stating that *any* king was ever buried in a pyramid have ever been found.'

Only one cartouche with the King's name was discovered – in the highest part of the pyramid, the fifth relief chamber – and debate continues to rumble on concerning the authenticity of this one and only piece of evidence linking Khufu to the Great Pyramid.

The first relieving chamber was discovered by Nathaniel Davison in 1765, and no hieroglyphic inscriptions of any kind were found there. 72 years later, the famous Egyptologist Col. Howard Vyse discovered the rest of the chambers which were above 'Davison's Chamber', and they were the *only* parts of the complex to contain inscriptions of any sort, including the infamous Khufu cartouche. It is well established that Vyse was under pressure to find something remarkable, and find it he did. But is the cartouche which is set among the ancient graffiti genuine?

The point being made here is that many assumptions have been, and continue to be made regarding the enigmatic edifice built from over 2.3 million blocks of granite. To put the Great Pyramid into perspective, it remains the largest edifice ever built by man. At over six million tons, it contains more masonry than all the medieval cathedrals, churches and chapels built in Europe added together.

If the scholars are wrong about the pyramid's actual purpose, couldn't they also be wrong about the construction methods employed? And if not a tomb, then why was the pyramid built at all?

We have discussed how the 200 ton block stones found at the Valley and Sphinx temples were transported and set in place possibly as far back as 10,500 BC; blocks whose placement mystifies construction engineers today. The 1,650-ton monolith at the Baalbek quarry, as well as the possibility of up to 4000 ton cut granite blocks in Siberia serve as clues that maybe the mainstream archaeologists are wrong, maybe the megalithic structures and walls seen around the world were built using more than manpower and ingenuity alone. Hancock and West discussed this matter in 2016:

GH: "Are you open to the notion that the ancients perhaps had a different way of manipulating matter than we do?"

JAW: "It almost seems a prerequisite because it doesn't seem possible with anything that we know about moving and cutting stones. It raises more questions than it answers because a) how did they do this? That's a complete mystery . . . and then why do they even want to do this to that level of perfection? That's another huge mystery."[159]

Some researchers have suggested that a form of antigravity technology involving sound resonance could explain how such incredible and seemingly impossible feats of engineering could have taken place in ancient times. The ancient Egyptians were certainly aware of sound vibrations and acoustic principles, as they incorporated them into their architecture. One broken obelisk in Egypt resonates like a tuning fork when struck, ringing like a bell, and this has led some to purport that all of the obelisks were built with a particular resonance in mind, and not just as a means to hold commemorative inscriptions.

As author Brien Foerster stated, "the fact that this segment of an obelisk resonates to one specific frequency and one frequency only, backs up the theory that the original function of the obelisk was not something to be written on to glorify a Pharaoh or other kind of ruler, but in fact was designed to be tuned to a specific frequency because it was part of an ancient system of energy transmission of some kind."[160]

Even at the 12,000 year old site at Göbekli Tepe there is a limestone pillar in the centre of a circular shrine which 'sings' when smacked with the flat of a hand, and many other ancient sites use very specific stones which resonate when struck.

The Welsh bluestones used to build sections of Stonehenge in 2800 BC for example, which were transported over 140 miles from a site in Preseli, Wales to Amesbury in southwest England, also displayed musical properties. Modern stonemasons inspecting the quarry in Wales discovered that as many as one in ten of the unusual bluestones which were used, resonated when struck.

'Instead of the dull clunking sound of rocks struck with stone tools, these strange bluestones chimed like a bell, rang like a gong, or resounded like a drum when struck with small hammer-stones', wrote author Will Thomas. And generations later, a small Welsh village in the Preseli region of Wales was named Maenclochog to memorialise the 'ringing stones', as it translates in English.

The Battle of Jericho in the Bible speaks of how sound was used to destroy the great walls, 'And it shall come to pass that when they make a long blast with a ram's horn and when you hear the sound of the trumpet, all the people shall shout with a great shout and the walls of the city shall fall down flat.'

Chicago-based acoustical engineer Thomas Danley experimented with sound technology and described acoustic levitation as "a non-magical way of floating an object in midair using very loud sound".[161]

One of Danley's experiments involved levitating a small object the size of a pea using one or two sound sources and a reflector, where "the sound bounces off the reflector and on its way back down, two sound fields pass through each other".

"It is in that region where there's the interference of those two sound fields, there are little wells that you can actually levitate small objects", said Danley. However, the engineer believes that levitating the much larger objects like the 200 ton blocks hewn from the Sphinx enclosure, "is a little beyond what we can do currently."

Describing what would be necessary to lift such weights using sound technology, he explained that "the frequency required is much lower than we can produce at sufficient intensity and the reflector you'd have to have above the object would be approximately a quarter of a mile cross."[162]

Early Spanish travellers visiting the ruined Bolivian city of Tiahuanaco during the Spanish conquest (1519-1521) were curious as to the origins of what must have once been an amazing city. The chronicler Pedro Cieza de Leon wrote, 'I asked the natives whether these edifices were built in the time of the Inca. They laughed at the question, affirming that they were made long before the Inca reign and . . . that they heard from their forebears that everything to be seen there appeared suddenly in the course of a single night.'[163]

Another Spanish visitor of the same period recorded a tradition denoting that the gigantic stones had been lifted miraculously off the ground claiming that 'they were carried through the air to the sound of trumpets'.[164]

One Maya legend maintains that 'construction work was easy for them, all they had to do was whistle and heavy rocks would move into place.'[165]

And in *The Ancient Egyptian Book of the Dead*, a magician was said to have raised 'a huge vault of stone 200 cubits long and 50 cubits broad' into the air.

An article published in a German magazine detailed how Tibetan monks were also able to levitate large stones using an acoustic levitation technique that enabled them to build their monasteries on mountainsides which would otherwise be impossible to achieve.

The article revealed, "We know from the priests of the far east that they were able to lift heavy boulders up high mountains with the help of groups of various sounds. . . the knowledge of the various vibrations in the audio range demonstrates to a scientist of physics that a vibrating and condensed sound field can nullify the power of gravitation.'

Dr. Jarl, a Swedish doctor who studied at Oxford, travelled to Egypt for the English Scientific Society in 1939, where he was approached by a man acting as messenger who knew the young Tibetan student whom Jarl had befriended during his time in England. He was asked to travel to Tibet to urgently treat a high Lama.

It was in Tibet where Dr. Jarl was invited to stay for a prolonged period where he would learn some of the Tibetan secrets usually not shared with foreigners, the details of which were later published in *The Lost Techniques*, a book written by another friend of the Swedish doctor, a civil engineer and flight manager, Henry Kjellson.

According to Kjellson, Dr. Jarl accompanied his Tibetan friend to a place close to the monastery where he was shown a sloping meadow surrounded by high cliffs. At a height of about 250 metres in one of the rock walls, a big hole resembling the entrance to a cave could be seen. There was a platform in front of this 'cave' with the only access to it being from the top of the cliff. Using ropes, the monks lowered themselves down onto the platform where they were building a rock wall.

A polished slab of rock, with a bowl-like cavity in the centre, lay in the middle of a meadow which was situated about 250 metres from the cliff face. Yak oxen manoeuvred another block slab of stone, 1 x 1.5 metres in length, into the cavity of the bowl which had a diameter of one metre and a depth of 15 cm.

Next, 19 musical instruments consisting of 13 drums and 6 trumpets were set in an arc of 90 degrees at a distance of 63 metres from the stone slab, with the radius of 63 metres being measured out accurately, highlighting the importance of specific measurements for the undertaking of this task.

Everything had to be precise. All the trumpets were the same size with a length of 3.12 metres and an opening of 0.3 metres. The eight larger drums had a cross-section of one metre, and a length of one and one-half metres. Four medium-sized drums had a cross-section of 0.7 metres and a length of one metre and the only small drum had a cross-section of 0.2 metres and a length of 0.3 metres.

Weighing 150 kg each, the big drums were all made of sheet iron, 3 mm thick, and were built in five sections. All the trumpets and the big drums were fixed onto mounts which could be adjusted with staffs in the direction of the slab of stone.

A row of monks stood behind each instrument. Using big leather clubs the monks beat the drums which all had a metal bottom at one end and were open at the other. The technique was demonstrated in an illustration from his book (fig. 57).

Kjellson explained the process: 'When the stone was in position the monk behind the small drum gave a signal to start the concert. The small drum had a very sharp sound, and could be heard even with the other instruments making a terrible din. All the monks were singing and chanting a prayer, slowly increasing the tempo of this unbelievable noise. During the first four minutes nothing happened, then as the speed of the drumming, and the noise, increased, the big stone block started to rock and sway, and suddenly it took off into the air with an increasing speed in the direction of the platform in front of the cave hole 250 metres high. After three minutes of ascent it landed on the platform.'

Using this method the monks continuously transported between five and six blocks every hour, levitating the blocks on a 'parabolic flight track approximately 500 metres long and 250 metres high', removing the occasional split stone from the meadow.

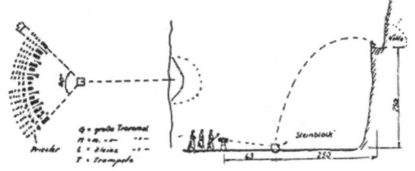

Fig. 57 Diagram from *The Lost Techniques* by Henry Kjellson shows monks lined up on the left, aiming the sound of the instruments towards the stone block in the centre.

Dr. Jarl was so amazed at what he was witnessing that he even wondered if he was the victim of mass-psychosis, so chose to record the incredible event on two separate films. The films revealed precisely what was described here, this was no illusion. Once Jarl shared the films with his employers at The English Society, they were subsequently confiscated and declared classified.

Of course, the legitimacy of this incident remains uncertain but it does offer the reader real food for thought as to how massive blocks can be shifted with relative ease, and would explain the presence of many anomalously large stones which have been used in ancient times to construct the megalithic structures which still stand firm after thousands of years.

It is important to note here that the methods used by the monks depended on the precise measurements involved and *not* the prayers which they chanted. The religious aspects of the ceremony were personal to that specific group and had no bearing on the actual outcome; it was the scientific knowledge of the high priests which caused the physical reaction to occur, showing that the Tibetan monks were fully conversant in the laws governing the structure of matter.

Researcher Bruce Cathie wrote, 'The secret is in the geometric placement of the musical instruments in relation to the stones to be levitated, and the harmonic tuning of the drums and trumpets. The combined loud chanting of the priests, using their voices at a certain pitch and rhythm most probably adds to the combined effect, but the subject matter of the chant, I believe, would be of no consequence.'

'The sound waves being generated by the combination were directed in such a way that an anti-gravitational effect was created at the centre of focus (position of the stones) and around the periphery, or the arc, of a third of a circle through which the stones moved', explains Cathie.

Details of the exact measurements, numbers and harmonics involved can be found following the link to Cathie's article in this endnote.[166]

We shall not delve too deep into the matter here as there is much to get through, but this example opens up the possibility of other means of manoeuvring heavy objects other than the labour intensive methods which are currently accepted as the only feasible means. If we were to understand how acoustic resonance and frequencies can affect gravity as the monks did, it would open up a myriad of new opportunities for our species and alter the way we perceive matter as a whole.

We already understand that all matter consists of atoms and molecules vibrating at various speeds, the slower the vibration, the more solid the matter appears. So is it really such a stretch of the imagination to consider how sound frequencies might alter how solid matter behaves?

In *Levitating the Stones*, author William Thomas questioned how the ancients accomplished such massive engineering projects such as the ruins which he witnessed firsthand on the Micronesian island of Kosrae. Asking a passing elder, "how did your ancestors ever lift those big stones so high?" the old woman replied, "they sang them into place". Such concepts certainly transcend Western thinking and exist all over the globe, as we find in this instance, even in the remotest and most inaccessible regions of the planet.

The Coral Castle in Florida (fig. 58) built singlehandedly by Latvian Edward Leedskalnin is a fascinating place, the construction of which still baffles people today. Built from 1,100 tons of oolite limestone and not coral as the name suggests, Leedskalnin somehow managed to cut and lift immense blocks of stone singlehandedly without the aid of heavy machinery or manpower. The biggest stone he lifted weighed 30 tons. Despite simple explanations involving pulley systems, gears and chains, what he achieved over a 28 year period is still remarkable.

Fig. 58 A child stands next to a doorway to the Coral Castle in Florida which was built singlehandedly out of limestone by Edward Leedskalnin.

According to a Florida website dedicated to him, 'When anyone asked Ed how he cut and moved the huge stones, Ed would state that he knew the secrets of the master stone cutters of Egypt, Peru, the Yucatán, etc. He also said that he understood the laws of weight and leverage'[167]

Many incredible stories surfaced surrounding the mystery of his building capabilities, for example, 'it has been reported that one night some children witnessed Ed "floating stones like hydrogen balloons"'.[168]

Also, 'There are a couple of credible accounts of adults witnessing strange occurrences as Ed worked. The man whom Ed hired to move the stones with his truck stated that he had forgotten his lunch box one morning and went back to the castle to get it. He had only been gone for a half-hour and when he arrived Ed already had several of the monolithic stones stacked on the rails of the trailer like cordwood. He never saw how Ed loaded them, just that Ed had absolutely no heavy machinery that should have been necessary to manipulate such heavy stones; especially that fast.'

What is clear when one looks more closely at the work of Edward Leedskalnin is that he understood more than he let on about the forces of gravity and its effects on solid matter. He used water, electric currents and magnetism to alter the way the huge blocks interacted with gravity and somehow succeeded in doing what no man since has managed without considerable assistance both manually and mechanically.

No doubt that he used ropes and chains to lift some of the stones with the use of the tripods which can be seen in the photographs and short film footage that he left behind, but no pulley can lift a 30 ton block over 10 feet in the air with nothing but the strength of one man.

Could he have been telling the truth when he claimed to know the secrets of how the ancients built the megalithic monuments we see today? Maybe our ancestors had access to knowledge which evades us in the present, technology which was once used and understood which has not filtered down to us as of yet. The available evidence left in the ruins and remnants of civilizations from antiquarian times certainly suggest this to be a very plausible idea.

GIZA POWER PLANT THEORY

If the purpose of the Great Pyramid of Giza was not to entomb the Pharaoh Khufu as Egyptologists contend, then aside from the possibility that they were meant as commemorative celestial markers, what other explanations exist to explain their presence?

The conventional date assigned to the beginning of construction is around 2470 BC. But Arab writer Abu Zeyd el Balkhy has suggested a date of 71,000 BC after reading from ancient scriptures that it was built at the time when the Lyre was in the constellation of Cancer. It would seem that nobody really knows for sure who and how 'the largest, most precisely built, and most accurately aligned building ever constructed in the world'[169] was actually built.

The word 'pyramid' is derived from the Greek words *pyramis* and *pyramidos*, whilst the meaning of the word 'pryamis' is obscure and may relate to the shape of a pyramid, 'pyramidos' has been translated as 'fire in the middle'. This unusual translation doesn't make a whole lot of sense in isolation, but it becomes a much more coherent translation when connected with the theory proposed by engineer Christopher Dunn which we are about to discuss.

According to researcher and author Stephen Mehler, the ancient Egyptians referred to their country as *KMT*, which has been written many different ways, *Kemet, Kemit, Khemet, Khem, Al Khem*, and the preferred form *Khemit*. Literally translated Khemit means 'the Black Land' which was a direct reference to the River Nile's rich, black soil deposits which were essential in order for the agricultural basis of the civilization to flourish. The indigenous tradition of Egypt tells us the civilization was called Khemit, so the people and their language were Khemitian.

Mehler, who considers himself a 'Khemitologist' as opposed to Egyptologist, explained that the ancient Khemitians used the term PR.NTR (Per-Neter) for pyramid, which in accordance with the indigenous traditions translates as 'House of Nature, House of Energy'. One of the main purposes of the Great Per-Neter was to generate, transform, and transmit energy.

The pyramid-as-tombs theory proposed by mainstream Egyptologists is based on the writings of Greek historians such as Herodotus, but Mehler contends that the Greek word 'pyramidos' is actually closer to the true meaning. And this idea of 'fire in the middle' appears to support Dunn's theory that the Great Pyramid was built as a power plant to harness electrical energy, if the energy reactions took place in the so-called Queen's and King's Chambers as Dunn proposes.

It is clear that we know very little about the historical period of the 'Pyramid Age' and even less about those responsible for the construction of the giant monuments, yet 'it seems obvious that the entire civilization underwent a drastic change, one so great that its technology was destroyed, with no hope of it being rebuilt', states the author. 'Hence a cloud of mystery had denied us a clear view of the nature of these people and their technological knowledge.'[170]

Like so many alternative researchers, Christopher Dunn finds the 'tomb' model for the pyramids to be lacking in evidence and somewhat impractical considering the size and precise dimensions involved in its construction.

As a master craftsman and engineer based in Manchester, England, Dunn has used his expertise to analyse the many anomalies which continue to appear at ancient sites around the world.

He is convinced that the ancient Egyptians must have used advanced power tools in which to cut, saw and drill some of the hard stone blocks and artefacts which they left behind, revealing that the technological capabilities available to them thousands of years ago have been lost to history.

Evidence which highlights the possibility of ancient machining can be seen on many artefacts around the world, with many examples available in Egypt such as the massive black sarcophagi housed at the Serapeum of Saqqara located northwest of the Pyramid of Djoser.

The Serapeum is a majestic ancient labyrinth which holds 25 megalithic stone 'boxes', assumed to be some form of sarcophagi, each weighing between 70 and 100 tons, and most of which are made from the extremely hard rock rose granite which was mined at a quarry about 800 kilometres from Saqqara. Other boxes were made from diorite, an even harder material that was brought from even further away. The precision of the boxes' construction with deviations registering in the thousandths of an inch reveals an extreme knowledge of engineering not consistent with the age of the objects themselves. The same can be said of the sole granite sarcophagus which adorns the King's Chamber inside the Pyramid of Khufu.

'The evidence carved into the granite artefacts in Egypt clearly points to manufacturing methods that involved the use of machinery such as lathes, milling machines, ultrasonic drilling machines, and high-speed saws,' claims Dunn.[171]

'They also possess attributes that cannot be produced without a system of measurement that is equal to the system of measurement we use today. Their accuracy was not produced by chance, but rather is repeated over and over again.'

This thinking led him to contemplate the energy source required to power such tools and machinery, eventually leading to the concept that the Great Pyramid of Giza could be the power plant which lay at the centre of an ancient, hi-tech national grid.

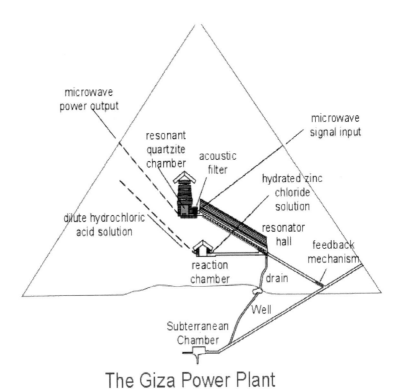

The Giza Power Plant

Fig. 59 Diagram illustrating Christopher Dunn's pyramid power plant theory. © Christopher P. Dunn

'I suspected that to account for the level of technology the pyramid builders seem to have achieved, he must have had an equally sophisticated energy system to support it', claims the engineer. So, after much consideration and in accordance with his belief that the Pyramid could in fact be a hydrogen-fuelled power plant, Dunn set out to reverse engineer its design.

Dunn commented, 'I began to see the drawings of the Great Pyramid, with its numerous chambers and passageways positioned with such deliberate accuracy, as the schematics of a very large machine.'[172]

Dunn's radical proposition which he believes to be 'supported by hard archaeological evidence', was calculated by considering the many facts and deductions based on the Great Pyramid's design and also the artefacts which have been found within. His premise suggests that the ancient Egyptians somehow converted vibrational energy into microwave energy, facilitated by hydrogen using the King's Chamber as its power centre (fig. 59).

As the author explains, 'For the power plant to function, the designers and operators had to induce vibration in the Great Pyramid that was in tune with the harmonic resonant vibrations of Earth. Once the pyramid was vibrating in tune with Earth's pulse, it became a coupled oscillator and could sustain the transfer of energy from the earth with little or no feedback.'[173]

According to Dunn's theory, the characteristics of the Queen's Chamber (which differ entirely from those of the King's Chamber) indicate that it was designed to produce the fuel required to allow the whole process to function. Salts found on the chamber walls could prove to be residual evidence that a chemical reaction took place there, whilst certain structural details and artefacts, such as that seen attached to Gantenbrink's 'door' at the end of one of the shafts, could reveal the true purpose of the pyramid.

Dunn believes that a supply of chemicals could have been pumped into the northern and southern shafts of the Queen's Chamber, until they were sufficiently full enough to have made contact with the grapnel hook and the electrodes which stick out of the 'door'. The chemicals then combined to produce hydrogen gas which filled the internal chambers and passageways of the entire structure, with the waste flowing along the horizontal passageway before exiting down the well shaft.

Through a series of tuned Helmholtz-type resonators housed in the grand gallery, vibrations from the pyramid coupled with the vibrations of the Earth, converted into airborne sound which was focused through the passage leading to the King's Chamber, after passing through some form of acoustic filter that was housed in the antechamber.

As Dunn explained, 'The King's Chamber was the heart of the Giza power plant, an impressive power centre comprising thousands of tons of granite containing 55 percent silicon-quartz. The chamber was designed to minimize any damping of vibration, and its dimensions created a resonant cavity that was in harmony with the incoming acoustical energy. As the granite vibrated in sympathy with the sound, it stressed the quartz in the rock and stimulated electrons to flow by what is known as the piezoelectric effect.'[174]

The hydrogen produced in the Queen's Chamber would then absorb the frequencies resonating in the King's Chamber, and ultimately once the process was complete, what first entered the chamber as a low energy signal transformed into 'a beam of immense power as it was collected in a microwave receiver housed in the south wall of the King's Chamber', before being directed to the outside of the pyramid through the metal-lined southern shaft. It was this beam which Dunn contends was 'the reason for all the science, technology, craftsmanship, and untold hours of work that went into designing, testing, and building the Giza power plant'.

Of course the Giza power plant hypothesis cannot be proven, and remains just another theory for us to consider, but it is certainly no less credible than the 'tomb theory' which continues to dominate the subject. With so many unexplained ancient anomalies continuing to bewilder researchers, is it not worthwhile considering alternative ideas which may help us to explain how our ancestors achieved the incredible feats of engineering that we see today?

Once we understand the implications involved in the creation of those mysterious anomalies, we can begin to place the technological knowhow available in the distant past into some form of historical context.

Admitting the existence of advanced techniques in antiquity could be the first in a series of important steps towards comprehending our murky past. As Dunn concludes, 'Western born Egyptology should not be immune from these scientific precepts, though its orthodox protectors' awkward attempt to force contradictory data to fit an unsupportable hypothesis gives little hope for the prospects of change.'

'. . . if the level of technology evident in the stones of Egypt are evaluated, completely understood and explained by appropriate experts, Egypt will give itself and the world, the greatest gift possible – an understanding of a glorious past with innumerable lessons for future generations.'

THE TEMPLE OF MAN

One man, whose study of ancient Egypt revealed the presence of a more advanced way of thinking, was the great mathematician, symbolist and philosopher R.A. Schwaller de Lubicz. In 1937, assisted by a highly trained team of architectural draftsman and surveyors, he began a fifteen year onsite study of the Luxor temple complex.

Realising that the unusual asymmetry of the site may actually have been an exercise in 'harmony' and 'proportion' as opposed to an architectural flaw, Schwaller sought to prove that these two supposedly Greek inventions were in fact already in place at Luxor, 'by showing that the Dynastic Egyptians possessed mathematics superior to that of the Pythagorean Greeks, whom they preceded by more than 1500 years, and that of the Europeans, whom they preceded by more than 3000.'[175]

Pythagoras is always credited with the discovery of the laws of harmony and the golden section, but once Schwaller and his team had analysed, recorded and precisely measured every column, stone, statue, inscription, chamber, and passageway in the entire Luxor complex, then a total re-examination of Egyptian thinking became necessary.

His seminal work would be published in the classic book *Le Temple de L'Homme* (*The Temple of Man*) in 1957, which has been described as 'the most important breakthrough in our understanding of ancient Egypt since the discovery of the Rosetta Stone'.[176]

Schwaller's exhaustive and authoritative study reveals the depths of the medical, metaphysical, and mathematical sophistication of ancient Egypt, by re-discovering how the Egyptians built this particular temple as a kind of 'architectural encyclopaedia' of what they understood of humanity and the universe, thousands of years before our time.

Using a kind of esoteric physiology, the entire complex structure was designed to tell the story of the creation of man and his relationship to the universe, by dichotomising the artwork on the wall friezes with the actual physical composition of the temple itself which embodies the very proportions of the idealised man in the floor plan, hence the Temple of Man.

But the temple is a masterpiece of symbolist teaching that did not just reflect the workings of the physical body – the architecture and the reliefs within the temple were created to reveal the occult or metaphysical anatomy of man.

As John Anthony West explained, "The various parts of the temple correspond to the main articulations of the human body and the symbolism of the friezes and the artwork, inscriptions and so on, reveal a lesson in esoteric physiology."[177]

Contemporary Egyptology continues to refute Schwaller's interpretation of the Luxor temple which was built in stages over the course of a thousand years, starting in around 1350 BC. Much of the construction which is still standing today was done by the prolific builder and 18th Dynasty Pharaoh Amenhotep III, and then completed by Tutankhamun and Horemheb. Rameses II eventually completed the Egyptian's input into the temple leaving Alexander the Great and also the Romans to contribute to the temple's final construction many years later.

At over 800 feet in length, this enormous asymmetric complex which was constructed over time upon three separate axes to a unique design, exhibiting sacred architecture at its very best, reveals that each contributor followed set architectural guidelines which must have been passed down through each generation, as all the building work adheres to a strict blueprint that originated thousands of years prior to its completion.

The asymmetry of the unusual axes had a purpose as Schwaller explains, 'In the Temple of Luxor we observe the use of several axes, which allows an action or 'movement', in the harmony of the construction. This is a subtle way of playing with the rigidity of matter.'

But what is it about the 'Temple of Man' that sets it apart from the other astounding temples of antiquity? The building was not simply designed as a place of worship or contemplation, but acts simultaneously as a three-dimensional representation of the male body, an encyclopaedic teaching aid, and a symbol of spiritual growth and understanding – a complex sacred teaching designed to be studied over time. Built into the very essence of the temple's construction lies an extraordinary synthesis of science, religion, philosophy and art, the likes of which is not equalled anywhere in the ancient or modern world.

West was fascinated by Schwaller's work and brought his discoveries to a new audience in his book *Serpent in the Sky* in which he wrote, 'Because there is nothing in our society that remotely corresponds to a Temple of Luxor, it is difficult to understand why Egypt should have exercised such infinite pains and genius on what is ultimately a symbolic gesture. It is even more difficult for us to understand the uses to which it was put and the effect it must have had on those exposed to it.'

In *The Temple of Man*, Schwaller superimposed a human skeleton over the entire Luxor temple complex (fig. 60) to show how each section of the temple correlates with the individual anatomical parts of the body. Although the first builders started with the 'head' section which represented the pituitary gland that is responsible for physical growth, visitors to the site enter through the 'feet' end first, into the 'Hall of Marchers', the final hall to have been built, and walk through the complex in the direction of the head which is located at the farthest end.

The actual journey through the temple itself is mimicked by 'the marchers' which are lined up on both sides of the hall, all with their left legs extended forward to denote an action or motion that represents the start of a journey of growth, both physically and spiritually. Each of the eighteen great stone figures, each representing Rameses, symbolises the movement forward into the world; humanity in action.

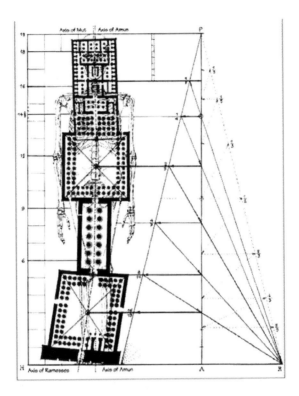

Fig. 60 The Temple at Luxor superimposed over a human skeleton with sacred geometric proportions as demonstrated by Schwaller.

The rest of the temple follows a straight axis, except the first hall where the asymmetric axis is mirrored by the angle of extension of the leg of the figures, a feature which can be seen in many other colossi across Egypt. Interestingly, this seemingly innocuous feature still influences temple and lodge rituals today, as witnessed by freemasons during public ceremonies where they step off with their left leg first.

Even the joints between the stones which make up the temple have been strategically placed to correlate with the room or area in which they were built. As the joints cross the section of the human form represented on the walls or columns, they serve as orientation aids in navigating the temple itself.

For example, if one ventures into the part of the temple which represents the knee, as seen by the male figure superimposed over the temple, the stones of the columns or walls in that particular section are cut through the knee joints of the figures in the friezes. So any student wishing to know which section he was now passing through would only have to look closely at the images around him to realise that he was among the knee section of the temple.

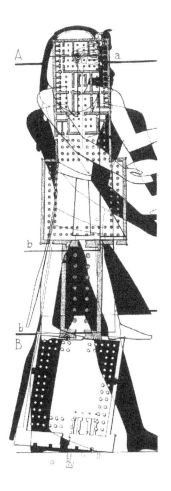

This 'joint' correlation runs seamlessly throughout the entire complex. This was one way in which the stonemasons fine-tuned the communication of the concepts being taught in any particular chamber.

Quite remarkably, as the temple grew over time, the stages of the temple's growth closely corresponded with the four stages of human growth, and the leg section in particular was added at a later date to denote the difference in height between boyhood and adulthood (fig. 61). Schwaller wrote, 'the temple of Luxor is conceived in its length as a sequence of phases of growth.'[178]

Fig. 61 The growth of the temple.

Moving into the 'thigh section', artwork symbolising the function of the femur, which is responsible for the manufacture of most of the blood's red corpuscles which feed the rest of the body, can be seen in the various friezes.

The essential nourishment of the whole system is produced in the femur, and this concept is externalised in the artwork on the walls of the 'thigh section' where depictions of figures are portrayed making offerings to the gods. These offerings symbolise the spiritual nourishment required to keep the whole spiritual enterprise moving, corresponding to the femur which provides the physical nourishment needed by the rest of the body in order to function properly. It is this dualism which typifies the Egyptian's esoteric school of thought, the 'as above, so below' theme which was so prevalent in ancient times.

Entering the 'Hall of Twelve Columns' which is situated where the eyes would be, the interplay between building and physiology continues, where the columns stand both as a symbol of the twelve hours of day and twelve hours of night, but more importantly represent the optic nerve which consists of twelve bundles of nerves. It is here at the centre of vision where consciousness is focused.

Other parts of the body are represented throughout the temple, lungs, mouth, vocal chords, heart and brain, each room as complex as the last, the details of which are too many to include here. In order to truly understand the knowledge and sophistication involved in such an undertaking as the construction and initial conception of the Luxor temple, one must begin to appreciate how advanced this great civilization really was.

Ancient Egypt is often misrepresented by the academics and mainstream Egyptologists as being more primitive, with the rulers portrayed as overtly religious, superstitious, egotistical megalomaniacs, self-obsessed and power hungry. But what we see at Luxor, among a multitude of stunning and monumental constructions all over the country, are signs that our ancient ancestors had access to cosmological knowledge and a greater understanding of our place within the universe.

West wrote, 'Egyptian science, medicine, mathematics and astronomy were all of an exponentially higher order of refinement and sophistication than modern scholars will acknowledge.'[179]

The symbolism inherent in the hieroglyphic system of writing has stood the test of time and transcends the use of the spoken language, which has done nothing but separate and divide what once was a unified means of communication. Our ineptitude to fully comprehend the complexity of ancient symbolism has led modern researchers to misinterpret large swathes of hieroglyphic text which remain intact inscribed in stone. 'If you do not see Egypt through 'symbolist' eyes, you do not see Egypt at all', insists West.

The ancient texts which fill the walls and columns of the tombs and temples of ancient Egypt were left for us to read and reconsider millennia after they were first inscribed, left for us to learn, remember and benefit from in future generations to come. Such a high civilization has never been recreated no matter how advanced we may consider ourselves to be in modern times, and the temples and inscriptions that adorn their walls will forever remind us of this fact.

As written in *The Hermetica*:

'So I, Thrice-Great Hermes,
The first of men
To attain All-Knowledge,
Have inscribed the secrets of the gods in sacred symbols and holy hieroglyphs,
On these stone tablets,
Which I have concealed
For a future world
That may seek our sacred wisdom.'[180]

MYSTERY OF THE ANCIENT MARINERS

Before concluding this chapter, let us now veer away from Egypt and focus our attention on the remarkably advanced maritime capabilities of ancient mariners as highlighted by the presence of anomalous maps from the past.

History tells us that on September 20, 1519, Ferdinand Magellan set out from the coast of Spain with his expedition, intent on being the first man in recorded history to successfully circumnavigate the world by sea. Despite many sources claiming that he succeeded in this immense task, the truth of this tale states that having become embroiled in a local war, Magellan was killed during battle on April 27, 1521. According to historic accounts, it was his personal slave Enrique of Malacca who ultimately succeeded where his master had failed, and managed to navigate the vast ocean the entire way around.

History speaks of many ancient crossings of both the Atlantic and Pacific Oceans in the past but evidence has come to light which extends the timeline of these activities thousands of years beyond the presently accepted figures.

Pitcairn Island, an isolated volcanic formation which lies 1,350 miles south-east of Tahiti in the Pacific Ocean, was first officially sighted in 1767. The population of Pitcairn today is made up of descendants from survivors of the 215-ton Royal Navy transport ship the HMS Bounty, which was the victim of a dramatic mutiny in 1789 by Master's Mate Fletcher Christian, who ultimately led his fellow mutineers to the island before disembarking then burning the famous ship. Here they established what they must have believed to have been the first colony in such a remote spot. But they were *not* the first. In 1820, a rock inscription written in the Libyan dialect of ancient Egyptian was reportedly discovered on Pitcairn Island that read:

Our crew, wrecked in a storm, made land thank God.
We are people from the Manu region. We worship Ra
in accordance with the scripture. We behold the sun
and give voice.

Manu is a highland area of Libya. So, the question remains how did such distant travellers reach these shores in ancient Egyptian times and why has this particular piece of evidence been ignored ever since? Is it because officially, no sailors ever crossed the Pacific that far back in history?

John L. Sorenson and Carl L. Johannessen studied evidence from archaeology, historical and linguistic sources, ancient art, and conventional botanical studies, which revealed 'conclusive evidence that nearly one hundred species of plants, a majority of them cultivars, were present in both the Eastern and Western Hemispheres prior to Columbus' first voyage to the Americas.'[181]

Their research paper *'Scientific Evidence for Pre-Columbian Transoceanic Voyages'* explains that many plant species, over half of which consisted of flora of American origin that spread to Eurasia or Oceania, can only have been distributed to foreign shores via transoceanic voyages led by ancient mariners.

'This distribution could not have been due merely to natural transfer mechanisms, nor can it be explained by early human migrations to the New World via the Bering Strait route,' state the authors.

Sorenson and Johannessen claim that, 'The only plausible explanation for these findings is that a considerable number of transoceanic voyages in both directions across both major oceans were completed between the 7th millennium BC and the European age of discovery.'[182]

Such controversial scientific findings contradict accepted notions of the plausible dates associated with transoceanic travel, but as the authors insist, 'Our growing knowledge of early maritime technology and its accomplishments gives us confidence that vessels and nautical skills capable of these long-distance travels were developed by the times indicated.'

Evidence which shows that ancient Egyptians had already crossed the Atlantic 3,000 years ago, long before Columbus in 1492, comes not only from the mimicking of cultural traditions as seen in Peru and the Canary Islands where evidence of trepanning and mummification has been found, but from the actual Egyptian mummies themselves.

Incredibly, in 1976, Dr. Michelle Lescott from the Museum of Natural History in Paris received a sample from the mummified remains of Egyptian Pharaoh Ramses the Great to study. Using an electron microscope she discovered grains of tobacco clinging to the fibres of his bandages.

This initial discovery was berated by the authorities and her senior colleagues insisted that she had simply observed "contamination from modern sources", maybe from some old archaeologist smoking a pipe in the vicinity, or perhaps she had found the traces of a workman's sneeze?

Tobacco first came to Europe from South America during the time of Columbus, 2700 years later, ruling out the possibility of tobacco being present during the reign of Ramses circa 1213 BC.

Some years later, Dr. Svelta Balabanova, a forensic toxologist at the Institute of Forensic Medicine at ULM, followed up on Dr. Lescott's findings with yet more intriguing evidence. In order to eliminate the possibility of contemporary contamination Dr. Balabanova obtained samples of intestinal tissue from deep inside Ramses, rather than the external layers of skin and cloth, and much to her amazement she discovered traces of cannabis, coca and tobacco, laid down in his body cells 'like rings on a tree'.

For her fellow researchers this still was not enough proof despite her excellent reputation, as such evidence contradicted conventional explanations of intercontinental contact thousands of years in the past. But, a decade later in 1992, seven ancient Egyptian mummies were flown from the Cairo Museum to Munich for further analysis.

Dr. Balabanova conducted a series of gas chromatography tests on samples of the seven mummies, and each individual revealed the presence of nicotine and cocaine. Both the mummies and the results were deemed entirely credible.

'It may be therefore implied that Egypt obtained these plants in trade with far flung urbanity from all over the ancient world', wrote author/researcher Dr. Alexander Sumach. 'Prepare to warm up to the plausible notion of intercontinental cultural contact that was either sustained, or else in play to some extent during every phase of human history.'[183]

Professor Martin Bernal, a historian at Cornell University is one of many scholars who conceded that ancient trade links which vastly predate present calculations must have existed; 'We're getting more and more evidence of world trade at an earlier stage.' Besides, he is not alone in his hypothesis.

More evidence of ancient mariners preceding the conventional timeframe of transoceanic travel can be found in the existence of ancient maps depicting an ice-free Antarctica. The detailed information recorded on the maps has confounded researchers and scientists alike, but they cannot be dismissed out of hand and demand closer inspection. Charles H. Hapgood studied the maps in detail and published his findings in *Maps of the Ancient Sea Kings*.

The maps in question are:

1. The Piri Re'is map of 1513
2. The Oronteus Finaeus (Oronce Finé) map of 1531
3. The Hadji Ahmed map of 1559
4. The Mercator map from 1569
5. The Athanasius Kircher map of 1665
6. The Buache map of 1737

The preface to Hapgood's book reads, 'It becomes clear that the ancient voyagers travelled from pole to pole. Unbelievable as it may appear, the evidence nevertheless indicates that some ancient people explored the coasts of Antarctica when its coasts were free of ice. It is clear too, that they had an instrument of navigation for accurately finding the longitudes of places that was far superior to anything possessed by the people of ancient, medieval, or modern times until the second half of the 18th century. This evidence of a lost technology will support and give credence to many other evidences that have been brought forward in the last century or more to support the hypothesis of a lost civilization in remote times. Scholars have been able to dismiss most of that evidence as mere myth, but here we have evidence that cannot be dismissed.'[184]

So what evidence is contained within those maps which led Hapgood, once an American college professor, to such strong assertions concerning advanced cultures in remotest antiquity? If we consider that we only developed a practical means of finding longitude during the 18th century, the same period when the circumference of the earth was first measured accurately, and recall that it wasn't until the 19th century that we sent out ships into the Arctic and Antarctic Seas for either whaling or exploration, with the first sighting of Antarctica coming around 1820.

No one single person can lay claim to the first confirmed sighting of the southern continent, but various sources claim that within days or months of each other, three individuals all spotted the ice shelf or coastlines of the frozen land. The three men that history tells us were the first to lay eyes on Antarctica are: Fabian Gottlieb von Bellingshausen (a captain in the Russian Imperial Navy), Nathaniel Palmer (an American sealer from Connecticut) and Captain Edward Bransfield of the Royal Navy.

What was previously referred to as Terra Australis Incognita, meaning 'Unknown Southern Land', remained unknown until the first ships reached the icy shorelines during the late 18th century, but it wasn't until January 26, 1853 that Captain Mercator Cooper sailed close enough to the ice shelf to climb out and make 'the first adequately documented continental landing' on the mainland of East Antarctica on an area now known as the Oates Coast of Victoria Land.

So how can an unknown continent not seen until recent centuries appear on a map dating from 1513? Drawn on gazelle skin and half missing, the Piri Re'is map which was rediscovered in rubble at Istanbul's Topkapi Palace in 1929, shows the north coast of Antarctica three hundred years before it was even recognised as a landmass. So who made this map and how?

Piri Re'is (real name Ahmet Muhiddin) was a Turkish Admiral who was executed in Egypt in 1554 under orders of Emperor Suleiman after the Governor of Egypt, one of the Admiral's political opponents, misrepresented the facts of Re'is' last voyage. The Governor reported that 'Piri Re'is had returned with only two ships though he sailed at the beginning with thirty-one'. He failed to mention however, that the large haul of treasures Re'is had taken from the Islanders of Hurmuz in the Persian Gulf actually filled all of the returned vessels.

Piri Re'is claims that he was not responsible for the original surveying and cartography of the map, instead claiming to have drawn up the map by compiling several different source maps, some made by contemporary sailors and others being charts of great antiquity which he collected on his various voyages.

Somehow, the ancient source maps that he had acquired over the years depicted the subglacial topography of Queen Maud Land, Antarctica – the true profile of the coastline as seen beneath the ice – a profile which has not been visible since 4000 BC when the ice sheet finally covered the area.

It wasn't until 1949 that a joint British-Swedish scientific reconnaissance team carried out a comprehensive seismic survey of Queen Maud Land that the area was revealed again for the first time in over 6000 years. The Oronteus Finaeus map which was printed in a book in 1531 also reveals estuaries, inlets and rivers along the coastal regions of the Antarctic continent before it became glaciated 6000 years ago.

Researchers at the Carnegie Institute in Washington DC were able to establish beyond reasonable doubt that great rivers flowed in Antarctica until about 6000 years ago. It was only after that date, around 4000 BC, 'that the glacial kind of sediment began to be deposited on the Ross Sea bottom . . . The cores indicate that warm conditions had prevailed for a long period before that.'[185]

Hapgood remarked on the accuracies of the fifty geographical points on the map which proved precise when re-projected, stating that 'the mathematical probability against this being accidental is astronomical.'[186]

As well as showing Antarctica in an ice-free state, the Piri Re'is map also includes Africa, Europe and South America all at the correct relative longitudes, which is 'theoretically an impossible feat for science of the time.'[187] This remarkable accomplishment was achieved centuries before John Harrison's invention of a long-sought-after marine chronometer in 1730, the Sea Clock which he built for solving the problem of calculating longitude while at sea.

Used by Captain James Cook in the 1770s once Harrison's invention had been tried and tested thoroughly, his maps of the Pacific rank among 'the very first examples of the precise cartography of our modern era.'[188]

'This brilliant invention made it possible for cartographers to fix longitude precisely, something that the Sumerians, the ancient

Egyptians, the Greeks and the Romans, and indeed all other civilizations before the eighteenth century were supposedly unable to do. It is therefore surprising and unsettling to come across vastly older maps which give latitudes and longitudes with modern precision.'[189]

After a long study of the Piri Re'is map in 1953, Arlington H. Mallery, an authority on ancient maps, discovered the projection method used then made a grid and transferred the map onto a globe, only to find that the map was totally accurate. The map was so accurate that the U.S. Navy Hydrographic Bureau, who had sent the map to Mallery, actually amended some errors on present day maps using the information on the Piri Re'is.

Mallery was so astounded by the precision exhibited by such ancient cartographers that he bewilderingly stated that the only way to draw a map of such accuracy would be by the use of aerial surveying, an unexplainable fact which contradicts the technological achievements of human history.

In order to precisely determine the longitudinal coordinates, the use of spheroid trigonometry is required, a process supposedly unknown until the middle of the 18th century. This means that not only did the original mapmakers known that the earth was round but also had knowledge of its true circumference to within fifty miles, and of course must have known about the curvature of the earth also.

Charles Hapgood later discovered that a cartographic document copied by an even older source was carved onto a rock column in China from 1137 which shows the same grid method and use of spheroid trigonometry as the western charts.

There are many more maps from antiquity which reveal that our ancient ancestors must have understood geodetics, geography, and the methods required to accurately determine longitudes and latitudes at a time when history insists we were incapable of such feats. The 'Dulcert Portolano' of 1339, the Zeno Map of 1380, and the Portolano of Iehudi Ibn Ben Zara all reflect an advanced level of geographical knowledge not available until the 20th century.

In acknowledgement of Hapgood's detailed research of the ancient maps, Lorenzo W. Burroughs – Captain of the USAF and Chief of the

Cartographic Section – replied in a letter dated 14 August, 1961: 'We are convinced that the findings made by you and your associates are valid, and that they raise extremely important questions affecting geology and ancient history, questions which certainly require further investigation.'[190]

These ancient maps serve as undeniable evidence that over 6000 years ago, there existed a culture capable of astonishing feats contrary to popular misconceptions still rife within modern society. Could we really be capable of aerial surveys at such a remote period in our history? How would this be possible? How could we have circumnavigated the world by sea nearly 6000 years before Magellan's failed voyages set sail? And the most pertinent of all these mysteries is why are such facts, like those which are evident in the cartography of our ancestors, not commonly known in the public arena? Shouldn't academic institutions be revelling in such mysteries, questioning how an ice-free Antarctica was accurately mapped at a time when no human on the face of the planet had any inkling that such a southerly continent even existed.

Hancock suggested that one reason that the ancient navigators were so obsessed with charting the gradual glaciation of Antarctica from 14,000 to around 5,000 BC, could be that they were making a permanent cartographical record of the slow obliteration of what was once their homeland. Could this frozen wasteland have once been the Atlantis of ancient mythology?

The questions raised by these mysterious maps will not be answered any time soon, but using rational thinking and further analytical research we can speculate and ponder such matters with a reasonable amount of conviction.

'The evidence presented by the ancient maps appears to suggest the existence in remote times, before the rise of any of the known cultures, of a true civilization, of a comparatively advanced sort, which either was localized in one area but had worldwide commerce, or was in a real sense, a *worldwide* culture.'[191]

This civilization that Hapgood suggests must have been responsible for the implementation of high knowledge during ancient times no longer exists, and according to mainstream academia, never did. But mythologies around the world all speak of a lost civilization, whose influence spread to both the western shores of Europe and Africa, and across the Atlantic to the Americas, all before its untimely demise into oblivion.

Is this the same ancient society that helped build Göbekli Tepe, the Great Sphinx, the megaliths at Baalbek, and the ground plan of the Giza plateau? Did they influence the Mesopotamians, the Mesoamericans, the ancient Egyptians and even the Easter Islanders?

Deeper research suggests that there once existed a relatively advanced civilization before the last Ice Age came to an end, a third-party civilization which imparted great wisdom onto those great civilizations that followed, whose existence remains shrouded in mystery.

Sceptics will continue to refute such a possibility as is their want, but without an unkown and mysterious ancient civilization, how do we explain the countless anomalies that we have covered throughout this book? The details may be murky, the remaining physical evidence still waiting to be discovered, but following the trail of clues left behind by the numerous cultures that arose from the ashes of this lost continent, maybe we can bring their long lost memories to the forefront of our minds once again.

Chapter Seven

THE LOST CONTINENT

It may be, as some indeed suspect, that the science we see as the dawn of recorded history was not at its dawn, but represents the remnants of a science of some great and as yet untraced civilization.

S.R.K. Glanville

MUCH OF THE EVIDENCE accumulated throughout this book points to the existence of an unknown civilization in prehistory, which according to world mythology was destroyed by some unseen cataclysm. The name of this mysterious lost culture is not really as significant as proving its historical reality but nevertheless, rumours of a lost land have come down to us through myth and folk tradition, and the name which continues to resurface is Atlantis.

To many, Atlantis is a dirty word, immediately invoking groans of disapproval from those of a sceptical disposition. The mere mention of the 'A' word in most social circles brings about thoughts of folklore, mythology and oral traditions as opposed to the serious consideration which we shall afford the topic here. This subject remains as controversial today as it was in the past and much is still up for debate. Most people still question the feasibility of a civilized nation existing so far back in antiquity, whilst others accept the possibility of its existence but question the location.

Understandably, after years of disinformation and ridicule, fringe subjects suggesting the possibility of a lost ancient civilization continue to be mocked and frowned upon, most notably within scientific or scholarly environments, as the history and origins of civilization has already been agreed upon. However, these are changing times and every day more and more information comes to light which forces us to re-evaluate the situation.

The anomalous artefacts, the unexplained feats of engineering, the astronomical and geophysical knowledge, the advanced cartography and the many, many other mysteries which confound us are all hanging like huge question marks demanding to be answered.

The existence of an Atlantis, or whatever other names were used in the distant past, answers many of those questions and solves most of those puzzles, for without a previous culture capable of passing on the advanced knowledge and skills previously mentioned, none of these mysteries would even exist.

As author Charles Berlitz summarised, 'the concept of one or more prior civilizations – such as Atlantis – on Earth lends itself to the explanation of archaeological artefacts that otherwise seem to defy historical logic.'[192]

Whether city, country or continent, the size of such a prehistoric civilization is not as important as the influence and impact it had on future generations and its vital role in the development of mankind. The Edfu Building Texts found in the ancient Egyptian Temple of Horus claim that a former world preceding their own once existed, whose influence was paramount in the construction of ancient Egypt: 'An ancient world, after having been constituted, was destroyed, and as a dead world it came to be the basis of a new period of creation which at first was the re-creation and resurrection of what once had existed in the past.'

But what evidence is there which reinforces the possibility that an Atlantis of some kind once existed in our remote past, in a time forgotten to all but the survivors who shared the tale of its demise? Research indicates that a common cultural source connects the ancient societies from continents on opposite sides of the Atlantic Ocean. The influence of this shared commonality is evident in the religion, language, writing, pyramid building and ritual practises seen on both sides of the Atlantic divide, in the Americas and the Middle East.

'The ancient South Americans and their counterparts in Egypt also practised many of the same rituals. Ritual mummification of the dead was practised in Egypt and the ancient Middle East as well as in all of Latin America.'[193]

This concept of a knowledge transfer from an unknown source is not a modern one, as in 250 BC Manetho the Mendesian wrote, 'The Egyptians obtained their hieroglyphic writing from a drowned continent.' Was Manetho referring to Atlantis? Even if he was not, he was still claiming that a lost culture was responsible for the advanced written language of the ancient Egyptians, a theory which does not sit well with contemporary Egyptology.

So, how could two opposing continents separated by an expanse of water thousands of miles across, inexplicably exhibit similar traits and influences if they had never been in contact with one another? Logic would suggest one of the following three scenarios:

1. Ancient mariners from countries such as Egypt, Sumer, Babylon and Turkey, crossed the Atlantic and colonized the Americas.
2. Vice versa - ancient cultures from the Americas traversed the vastness of the ocean to colonize North Africa and the Middle East.
3. Both sides derived their traditions from some unknown third party culture.

No writing, legends or archaeological finds support the first two hypotheses. Alternatively, there are literally hundreds of ancient, written references which 'attest to a primal civilization on an island continent that ended its history beneath the waters.' In fact, we actually see that 'tribal legends on both sides of the Atlantic describe the same place and the same story.'[194]

Sceptics would denounce all this evidence as 'coincidental' and look no further, but that approach will not bring us any closer to the truth about our past, nor shall it sufficiently explain the countless similarities expressed through folklore and mythology from all over the ancient world.

'Everything we've been taught about the origins of civilization may be wrong. Old stories about Atlantis and other great civilizations of prehistory, long dismissed as myths by archaeologists, look set to be proved true.'[195]

In *The Secret Doctrine*, Helen Blavatsky wrote about the sinking of a landmass upon which 'the Atlanteans' lived, and it was her understanding that over a long period of time waves of colonists were sent from Atlantis to most parts of the world before the island was finally submerged. Blavatsky also believed that Atlantis was originally seeded by extraterrestrials that were responsible for the influx of information and the onset of civilized man, an outlandish theory which although shared by others remains impossible to authenticate. But for now, let us first consider the origins of the Atlantis myth and the earliest written records which have survived millennia.

PLATO'S ATLANTIS

The tale of Atlantis originated in ancient Egypt, a story passed down from generation to generation which finally made its way to Greece, where the early fifth-century BC historian Hellanicus of Lesbos became the first scholar to discuss the lost continent in his work which is now lost to history but was quoted in part by subsequent writers.

Composed about twenty-five years before the birth of Plato, Atlantis was also included in fragmentary form in the Oxyrhynchus Papyri which was only discovered in 1882 at el-Bahnasa (the former ancient Oxyrhynchus), an Egyptian city approximately 100 miles away from Cairo. Plato later transcribed the available information in his Socratic dialogues *Critias* and *Timaeus* in around 360 BC, but he never completed the work which mysteriously cuts off mid-sentence. The dialogues take place between two politicians Critias (Plato's uncle) and Hermocrates, along with his former teacher Socrates and the philosopher Timeaus of Locri.

Plato (fig. 62), whose real name was Aristocles, was born in Athens in 427 BC, and earned the nickname Plat•n, meaning 'broad', either in reference to his wide shoulders (he was said to have been an excellent athlete) or his large forehead. Some speculate that his nickname derived from his sturdy literary style or his varied and wide-ranging interests. Either way, he became a pupil of one of the greatest ever philosophers to have lived, fellow Athenian Socrates.

Fig. 62 Plato, one of the great philosophers of ancient Greece popularised the story of Atlantis in 360 BC.

In Plato's version of events, Critias explains that Poseidon named the five pairs of male twins which he begat, as he divided the island of Atlantis into ten portions, 'And he named them all; the eldest, who was the first king, he named Atlas, and after him the whole island and the ocean were called Atlantic.'

So it is generally accepted that the name *Atlantis* originated in Greece meaning 'Island of Atlas', and subsequently the Atlantic ocean was named after Atlas, just as the Indian Ocean derives from India and the China Sea from China, but the word itself derives from much earlier sources.

American 19th century congressman and writer on Atlantis, Ignatius Donnelly states that the words *Atlas* and *Atlantic* actually have no satisfactory etymology in any known language in the whole of Europe. He claims that the words are neither Greek nor belong to any known language of the 'Old World', but instead insists that they originated in the ancient Nahuatl language from Mexico.

'In the Nahuatl language we find immediately the radical *a*, *atl*, which signifies water, war, and the top of the head. From this comes a series of words, such as *atlan* – on the border of or amid the water – from which we have the adjective *Atlantic*. We have also *atlaça*, to combat, or be in agony; it means likewise to hurl or dart from the water, and in the preterit makes *Atlaz*. A city named *Atlan* existed when the continent was discovered by Columbus, at the entrance of the Gulf of Uraba, in Darien . . . it is now reduced to an unimportant pueblo named *Acla*.'[196]

Author Manly P. Hall also suggested a South American origin for the name Atlantis, "*Atl* was one of the month names of the Mayas. It also has more than just a name significance; its' glyph or its' symbol is a deluge. This seems then to give us the real basis of our word. We are dealing with a term that represents a world experience . . . and the name that has survived to us today is probably based upon the records of the western hemisphere."[197]

Considering the nature of the demise of the alleged ancient Atlantean empire, it is interesting to note that the earliest derivations of the name Atlantis are all associated with water, whether 'deluge' or 'flood', 'amid the water', or to 'dart from the water'.

In *Timaeus*, the first of three projected dialogues, Critias in conversation with Socrates says, 'Then listen, Socrates, to a tale which, though strange, is certainly true, having been attested by Solon, who was the wisest of the seven sages. He was a relative and a dear friend of my great-grandfather, Dropides, as he himself says in many passages of his poems; and he told the story to Critias, my grandfather, who remembered and repeated it to us.'[198]

Socrates replied, 'And what other, Critias . . . has the very great advantage of being a fact and not a fiction? . . . which, though unrecorded in history, Critias declared, on the authority of Solon to be an actual fact?'

Critias then begins to share the tale told to Solon, a revered Greek statesman and lawgiver who during his travels visited the district of Sais in the Egyptian Delta, 'To this city came Solon, and was received there with great honour; he asked the priests who were most skilful in such matters, about antiquity, and made the discovery that neither he nor any other Hellene knew anything worth mentioning about the times of old.'[199]

Plato's text explains that the rise and fall of the Atlantean Empire was documented on a hieroglyphic pillar made from orichalcum in the temple of the goddess Neith, the divine patroness of history, situated in Sais. It was in Sais, where Solon was told by one of the priests that 'there is no old opinion handed down . . . by ancient tradition, nor any science which is hoary with age' because 'there have been, and will be again, many destructions of mankind arising out of many causes.'

Solon was informed that his people, namely the ancient Greeks known as the Hellenes, were too young to remember their true ancestry, and that their history had been forgotten because of the cataclysms which took place and eradicated much of the past:

'In the first place you remember a single deluge only, but there were many previous ones; in the next place, you do not know that there formerly dwelt in your land the fairest and noblest race of men which ever lived, and that you and your whole city are descended from a small seed or remnant of them which survived. And this was unknown to you, because for many generations, the survivors of that destruction died, leaving no written word.'

Although Plato does not mention the name of the elderly priest who divulges the forgotten history of Atlantis to Solon, the Greek biographer and essayist Plutarch (46-120 AD) suggests in *Life of Solon* that the priest's name was Sonchis:

'Near Nilus' mouth, by fair Canopus' shores, and spent some time in study with Psenophis of Heliopolis, and Sonchis the Saïte, the most learned of all the priests; from whom, as Plato says, getting knowledge of the Atlantic story, he put it into a poem, and proposed to bring it to the knowledge of the Greeks.'

Plato offered a detailed description of the location of this lost world in *Timeaus*:

' . . . for in those days the Atlantic was navigable; and there was an island situated in front of the straits which are by you called the pillars of Heracles; the island was larger than Libya and Asia put together, and was the way to other islands, and from these you might pass to the whole of the opposite continent which surrounded the true ocean; for this sea which is within the Straits of Heracles is only a harbour, having a narrow entrance, but that other is a real sea, and the surrounding land may be most truly called a boundless continent. Now in this island of Atlantis there was a great and wonderful empire which had rule over the whole island and several others, and over parts of the continent, and, furthermore, the men of Atlantis had subjected the parts of Libya within the columns of Heracles as far as Egypt, and of Europe as far as Tyrrhenia'.

It has been well established that the Pillars of Heracles (Greek for Hercules) represent the Straits of Gibraltar, the gateway to the Mediterranean Sea, the gap separating Spain from Morocco – the 'limit of the known world'. Although it must be noted that the Strait of Messina between Italy and Sicily could well have been the original Pillars of Hercules in ancient times before the third century BC, as Eratosthenes of Cyrene 'moved them to Gibraltar to balance the boundaries of the Greek world to that on the opposite side (to the east) has widened with the conquests of Alexander the Great.'[200]

Regarding the size of Plato's Atlantis, the text refers to Libya as Africa, and Asia (Minor) is understood to mean Turkey, so we are looking at an island of some considerable size and not just a city. Atlantis was considered to be an empire, which ruled over several other islands as well as parts of Europe and Africa.

Critias describes the physical landscape as an arrangement of concentric circles of alternating land and water, with extravagant architecture, baths, barracks and harbour installations. Canals and a perfectly engineered irrigation system led in and out of the city which was controlled by kings and a civil administration, and protected by an organised and strong military presence.

The story has it that war broke out between 'those who dwelt outside the pillars of Heracles and all who dwelt within them', where on one side 'the city of Athens was reported to have been the leader and to have fought out the war; the combatants on the other side were commanded by the kings of Atlantis.'[201]

Though a much smaller city-state, Athens stood alone against the might of the Atlantean forces but defeated the enemy against all the odds and ultimately triumphed over the invaders. It was following this destructive period of battling that natural disaster struck, and epic floods sank Atlantis beneath the waves and violent earthquakes wiped out the Athenian warriors, all around the date 9600 BC, a significant and poignant date which correlates with the end of the last Ice Age.

As Plato wrote, 'afterward there occurred violent earthquakes and floods, and in a single day and night of rain all your warlike men in a body sank into the earth, and the island of Atlantis in like manner disappeared beneath the sea. For which reason the sea in those parts is impassable and impenetrable, because there is a shoal of mud in the way; and this was caused by the subsidence of the island.'

But an Atlantean-Athenian war would not be possible according to official history, simply because Athens did not exist at the time. Archaeological evidence thus far has shown no sign of human occupation on the site of the Acropolis before 3000 BC, when a quite sophisticated Neolithic settlement was believed to have lived on the site in Athens. Data such as this contradicts Plato's tale and suggests that his Atlantis or certain elements at least, must have either been fabricated or somewhat embellished. In fact many problems arise when discussing Atlantis.

There are those who are convinced that Plato was describing a myth, not the history of real people, places and events. Freelance writer and Latinist N.S. Gill for example, believes that 'The Atlantis story is clearly a parable: Plato's myth is of two cities which compete with each other, not on legal grounds but rather cultural and political confrontation and ultimately war', and he insists that 'Atlantis as a tale really should be considered a myth, and one that closely correlates with Plato's notions of *The Republic* examining the deteriorating cycle of life in a state.'[202]

The editors of the Böllingen edition of Plato assert that he was 'resting his mind . . . making up a fairy tale, the most wonderful island that could be imagined'. But if it was indeed intended as a fictitious narrative then why did Plato first mention Atlantis in the *Timeaus*, his account of the creation of the universe described by Benjamin Jowett as 'the greatest effort of the human mind to conceive the world as a whole'?

'Plato's infamous Atlantis legend, in all its precise detail, sits there, thumbing its nose at all modern attempts to write it off as still another instance of the inflamed and disordered ancient imagination.'[203]

Some of Plato's critics denounce certain facts in his account, such as the timeframe of 9,600 BC for the destruction of the great empire. Some mainstream academics claim that he must have meant months instead of years when he wrote about the cataclysm taking place 9,000 years before Solon, but author Hancock is not convinced, "This was Plato, when he said years, he meant years. Solon was his own ancestor; he received this story through Solon. He was reporting, what for him was a very strong and definite fact, that there had been an event that destroyed a great civilization."[204]

Perhaps the most influential critic of Plato's narrative, whose influence indirectly continues to hinder and affect any serious investigation of the lost civilization today, was his most famous student Aristotle. Referring to the incomplete and sudden cut-off at the end of Plato's account, Aristotle remarked, "He who invented it destroyed it." But despite having succeeded, in his own mind at least, in destroying the concept of a 'real' Atlantis, Aristotle inadvertently contributed to the legend when he conceded that Carthaginian and Phoenician mariners *did* know of a great island in the Atlantic which they called Antilia. It would appear that he chose to remain blissfully unaware of the close resemblance between the two names Atlantis and Antilia.

Some researchers remain unaffected by the sceptics and insist that the way the dialogues are written suggests the tale to be true. Critias himself speaks of the whole affair as being based in reality, 'Socrates, I am ready to tell you the whole tale. The city and citizens, which you yesterday described to us in fiction, we will now transfer to the world of reality.'[205]

Atlantis researcher and author Richard Wingate also thinks that the legend was based on fact, 'The style that Plato used, indeed, indicates that he meant his references to Atlantis as factual history. It is dry and matter-of-fact, contrasting markedly with the elegance of his philosophic dialogues.'[206]

And likewise, Ignatius Donnelly also firmly believed the history of Atlantis to have been borne out of fact, 'There are in Plato's narrative no marvels; no myths; no tales of gods, gorgons, hobgoblins, or giants. It is a plain and reasonable history of a people who built temples, ships, and canals; who lived by agriculture and commerce; who, in pursuit of trade, reached out to all the countries around them. The early history of most nations begins with gods and demons, while here we have nothing of the kind.'[207]

Plato endorsed and preserved many catastrophic accounts in his writings, which Aristotle would later reclassify as 'mythical', 'non-historical' and 'unscientific'. Catastrophist Immanuel Velikovsky disagreed with Aristotle's view on Plato and wrote, 'one function of myth in Plato was to communicate a truth that could not readily be communicated in any other way; 'myth' was not a dirty word to Plato. Another function of myth was to preserve an account of past historical events: such an account was basically factual, not fictional.'[208]

Perhaps Velikovsky hit the nail on the head when he described Plato's account as 'basically factual'. Is it not possible that Plato embellished the tale he had heard, employing literary devices to improve and maybe even 'fill out' the actual story for the benefit of his readers? Need we discount the entire story as myth knowing that aspects of the tale simply are not historically feasible? He was certainly very keen to assert that his words should be taken seriously as fact not fantasy, and there are many elements of Plato's version that *are* plausible under closer scrutiny.

Written within Plato's account is a detailed description of the country that enveloped the city and beyond, and Solon was told that 'because of the greatness of the empire many things were brought to them from foreign countries, and the island itself provided most of what was required by them for the uses of life.'[209] This passage suggests that although mostly self sufficient, Atlantis was part of a trade route, meaning that other pre-Ice Age nations were already adept sea farers as we briefly summarised at the end of the previous chapter.

The island was apparently large enough to sustain many different species of animals too; 'there were a great number of elephants in the island; for as there was provision for all other sorts of animals, both for those who live in lakes and marshes and rivers, and also for those who live in mountains and on plains, so there was for the animal which is the largest and most voracious of all.'[210]

Interestingly, physical evidence has been discovered which reinforces the possibility of elephant herds somewhere out in the Atlantic just as Plato proposed. In 1967, oceanographers hauled up hundreds of elephant bones from the ocean floor, 250 miles off the coast of Portugal. Using bottom-profiling, a submerged land-bridge was discovered which extended from the Atlantic shores of Morocco out into what was formerly dry land.

'These important discoveries not only tended to verify the *Critias*, but showed that a peninsula once extended from the coast of northwest Africa, over which herds of elephants crossed far out into the Atlantic Ocean,'[211] declared author Frank Joseph.

He claims that seismic activity and sea level rising through mass flooding were responsible for the loss of land, 'leaving the animals stranded on surviving dry territories, now islands, one of them much later known as Atlantis.'

In fact, according to a scientific paper published in 1967, the remains of elephants off the coast of America have also been discovered below the Atlantic Ocean:

'The evidence indicates that the present continental shelf was a broad coastal plain about 15,000 years ago, and that it gradually submerged as water from glacial ice returned to the ocean. The distribution pattern of elephant teeth on the sea floor off the Atlantic coast shows three concentrations: Georges Bank, off New York City, and off the mouth of Chesapeake Bay. Occurrence of the teeth as far as 300 km from the present shore and their wide distribution show that the proboscideans lived on the shelf. One may assume, therefore, that this region was well covered with land vegetation.'[212]

Plato's Atlantis thrived in a different world than today. The climate would have been more temperate worldwide all year round, allowing for two harvests every year as Plato suggested. This consistently warm weather would create abundant luxuriant vegetation which could have supported large browsers like elephant herds which Plato claimed roamed Atlantean open plains.

One of the last surviving classical Greek philosophers was named Proclus Lycaeus or Diadochus Proclus (412-485 AD) and he studied at the Platonic Academy founded by Plato around 387 BC. Proclus wrote a commentary on *Timaeus* which revealed his conviction that Atlantis had indeed been an authentically historical land in ancient times.

Describing the geography of the island continent Proclus wrote: 'That an island of such nature and size once existed is evident from what is said by certain authors who investigated the things around the outer sea. For according to them, there were seven islands in that time, sacred to Persephone, and also three others of enormous size, one of which was sacred to Hades, another to Ammon, and another one between them to Poseidon, the extent of which was a thousand stadia (200 km) and the inhabitants of it – they add – preserved the remembrance from their ancestors of the immeasurably large island of Atlantis which had really existed there and which for many ages had reigned over all islands in the Atlantic sea and which itself had like-wise been sacred to Poseidon.'[213]

Scottish author and folklorist Lewis Spence sought to continue researching the Atlantis myth following in the footsteps of Ignatius Donnelly, by looking for clues of a cultural link between the early civilizations of the Old and New Worlds, which would highlight the existence of an earlier culture lost to history that must have been responsible for the striking parallel influences.

Like Donnelly, Spence also speculated that the sunken island was in all likelihood a Bronze Age civilization and firmly believed Atlantis to have been a historical reality, despite the rejection of his theories by mainstream scholars which only seemed to fan the flames of his conviction.

In his 1927 study *The History of Atlantis*, Spence wrote: 'What, after all, do we know of the ancient world so far, so as to permit us to adopt an attitude of negation to the deep-rooted traditional statement, so oft-repeated in the most venerable chronicles, that in a period almost transcending the imagination, a civilization of a high order, from which all the cultures of this planet proceeded, shone, flickered, and like a shattered sun, cast its broken lights upon the dark places of our world? If we can discover no material proof of that civilization, is it not because it remains asleep beneath the Atlantic? But we can surely infer with confidence from its last fragments in Europe, Africa and America, appearing suddenly, and having no roots therein, as well from its well-authenticated tradition that it assuredly existed.'

Charles Berlitz explains why the story remains mythical, an 'understandable reason for Atlantis' status as a myth or legend is that its memory, although well preserved in racial and tribal traditions around the circle of the Atlantic and elsewhere, has come down through spoken and then transcribed legends from a very distant past.'[214]

'Legends become transformed in the retelling; kings and leaders become gods and demigods, endowed with divine powers. Geographical locations become uncertain and, in the case of Atlantis, indistinctly perceived through the mists of the sea.'

THE SLEEPING PROPHET

Another name synonymous with the legendary Atlantis is the American mystic Edgar Cayce (1877-1945). A simple, uneducated Kentucky man, Cayce (fig. 63) found himself capable of entering a trance state and making pronouncements about the ancient past as well as giving predictions for the future.

At the age of 12 whilst reading the Bible in his hut in the woods, the young Cayce claimed to have 'seen' a woman with wings, who explained that his prayers would be answered should he know precisely what it is that he wants. He replied that he wanted to be a missionary and help others, sick children in particular.

Fig. 63 Edgar Cayce, the 'Sleeping Prophet' dedicated many of his psychic readings to the subject of Atlantis.

It was at this tender age that he first discovered his gift, following an incident with his father who had knocked him out of his chair after failing to succeed in his spelling tests. Cayce 'heard' the angelic woman's voice telling him that 'they' could help him if he could sleep a little, so he asked to be allowed to rest, which he did with his head on top of the spelling book. Much to his father's amazement, when he returned to wake his son and test him once more, Edgar knew all of the answers and could recall anything from that book. From that day on he learned all of his knowledge from his school books using that technique.

At school shortly after, the young Cayce was struck by a ball on the base of the spine and was sent to bed due to the strange behaviour which he exhibited following the incident. It was during his sleep when he apparently diagnosed a cure for his injury that his family subsequently prepared and which cured him whilst he slept. His father became very proud of his son's sleeping gifts and declared that Edgar was "the greatest fellow in the world when he's asleep." As Cayce himself said "Dreams are today's answers to tomorrow's questions."

He later became known as the 'Sleeping Prophet' as his psychic readings also came about during a sleep state. From 1923 onwards, a young stenographer named Gladys Davis was hired by Cayce to record every single trance session and psychic reading from then on, which she would copy for each client and keep a permanent record of for future reference.

In 1931, Cayce founded the Association for Research and Enlightenment (A.R.E.), to help explore and research a variety of subjects including ancient mysteries, dream interpretation, holistic health, spirituality, reincarnation and philosophy. It is at the A.R.E. headquarters in Virginia Beach, Virginia where all of Cayce's records are kept to this day. 14,306 readings of his that were all typed and recorded by the meticulous Davis are catalogued and archived there, making them the largest collection of recorded material by a single individual, as quite remarkably he conducted at least two readings every day for 43 years until his death.

Cayce also gave readings for a number of very famous people including Woodrow Wilson, Thomas Edison, Nelson Rockefller and George Gershwin. Some of his prophecies which came to light included the onset of WWII, the stock market crash of 1929, the life of the Essenes prior to the discovery of the Dead Sea Scrolls, and the shifting of the Earth's poles.

In a number of readings Cayce claimed that "What is now the Sahara was an inhabited land and very fertile" (364-13), an idea which would later be proved correct when satellite images revealed the ruins of a long-lost civilization beneath the African sands.

In areas of desert which appear empty today, the images showed that there was once extensive and advanced development which was built by the vanished 'Garamantes' culture. Professor of Archaeology at Leicester University, David Mattingly commented on the significance of these discoveries, "It is like someone coming to England and suddenly discovering all the medieval castles."

What the Romans considered as 'barbarian nomads' couldn't have been further from the truth, "In fact, they were highly civilized, living in large-scale fortified settlements . . . It was an organized state with towns and villages, a written language and state of the art technologies."

Lots of evidence has come to light in recent times which confirms that thousands of years ago the Sahara region was indeed a green and fertile land, teaming with life and animals such as giraffe, elephants, aurochs, antelope and hippopotami, just as depicted in prehistoric Saharan rock art.

Cayce biographer Sidney Kirkpatrick wrote, 'In Edgar Cayce's lifetime much of what he said about lost civilizations, ancient worlds, was regarded as science fiction. It really wasn't until this century and literally the discovery of the Dead Sea Scrolls that people have begun to look much harder and realistically at his readings as perhaps, maybe these aren't so far-fetched.'[215]

There is no doubt that Edgar Cayce had special intuitive abilities, and was always way ahead of his time as his interest and knowledge of so many fringe subjects is testament to, but it is his fascination with Atlantis which we shall explore here. According to Cayce, Atlantis which was destroyed in a final catastrophic event *circa* 10,000 B.C. extended from the Gulf of Mexico to Gibraltar.

In 1932, Cayce spoke about the location of the lost continent:

"The position . . . the continent of Atlantis occupied is between the Gulf of Mexico on the one hand and the Mediterranean upon the other. Evidences of this lost civilization are to be found in the Pyrenees and Morocco, British Honduras, Yucatán and America. There are some protruding portions . . . that must have at one time or another been a portion of this great continent. The British West Indies, or the Bahamas, are a portion of same that may be seen in present. If the geological survey would be made in some of these especially, or notably in Bimini and in the Gulf Stream through this vicinity, these may be even yet determined." (364-3)

It was during psychic readings for certain clients whom he claimed were descendants of the ancient Atlanteans where he gave out a great deal of information on the sunken empire. In the following extracts he mentions advanced technologies available to the Atlanteans, with communications and transportation evidently as highly developed and widespread as today, a concept which is in keeping with many of the anomalies featured in this book:

"in Atlantean land during those periods of greater expansion as to ways, means and manners of applying greater conveniences for the people of the land – things of transportation, the aeroplane as called today, but then as ships of the air, for they sailed not only in the air but in other elements also." (2437-1; Jan. 23, 1941)

He also said "when peoples understood the law of universal forces entity able to carry messages through space to the other lands, guided crafts of that period." (2494-1; Feb. 7, 1930)

Other readings also emphasised technical developments available to the Atlanteans which rivalled and often exceeded those of present times: "Had to do with mechanics, machinery, application of electrical forces, radiation and heating, commercial application; of same as would be called today." (1003-1; March 6, 1937)

"As indicated, the entity as associated with those who dealt with mechanical appliances and their application, during the experience. And so we find, it was a period when there was much that has not even been thought of yet, in the present experience." (1440-5; Dec. 20, 1933)

During many different sessions, Cayce spoke of an exodus from the destruction of the ill-fated Atlantis to opposing continents on both the eastern and western shores.

". . . in Atlantis during periods of the breaking up of the land. Set sail for Egypt, but ended up in the Pyrenees in what are now Portuguese, French and Spanish lands. In Calais may still be seen the marks in the chalk cliffs of the entity's followers as attempts [were made] to create a temple activity for the followers of the Law of One." (315-4; June 13, 1934)

The marks in the cliffs which he refers to in the previous excerpt still existed in 1934 when the reading was given. The following reading reveals the influence of eastern practices being discovered in the Americas.

"In Atlantean land during period of egress before final destruction – coordinated departure activities – journeyed to Central America where some of the temples are being uncovered today [1935] – began practice of cremation, ashes may be found in one of temples prepared for same." (914-1; May 1, 1935)

Interestingly, at the time of the reading in 1935, Man was only believed to have been present in the Americas for a few thousand years, so the presence of an anomalously ancient civilization in that part of the world was ground-breaking. In fact, a *Washington Herald* newspaper article from February 10, 1935, reported the recent discoveries of noted British explorer F.A. Mitchell-Hedges, a name forever associated with one of the famous crystal skulls.

The article revealed that he had found traces of an unknown civilization on islands off the coast of Central America which Mitchell-Hedges claimed "may be a remnant of the fabled Atlantis." The British Museum, of which he was a member, avoided any mention of Atlantis but did state that 'this is an early culture from which the early forms of culture were diffused over Central America.'

The National Museum of the American Indian in New York wrote to Mitchell-Hedges to express their concurrence on the matter:

'Your own observations and the U.S. Government surveys in Nicaragua prove conclusively that at some remote period a tremendous earth movement of cataclysmic force must have taken place in that part of the world – and your excavations have actually unearthed the cultural artefacts of a prehistoric people that existed prior to that earth movement – your discoveries open up an entirely new vista in regard to the ancient civilizations of the American continent.'[216]

Later discoveries of archaeological sites in Columbia, which included unusual statues among the found relics, were described as 'an archaeological mystery for which no definite chronological or cultural links to other known civilizations have been established.'[217]

HALL OF RECORDS

Among Cayce's many readings were mentions of the existence of a library of sorts which contained records and wisdom of the lost civilization, written by survivors of the cataclysm. This 'hall of records' not only contained the collected wisdom of their race but also included the true history of the human race as a whole.

According to the readings, the Atlanteans, aware that their civilization was about to be destroyed, hid identical records of the civilization of Atlantis in three locations; the Bahamas, Egypt and the Yucatán. One is believed to be found at Bimini where Cayce claimed certain discoveries would be made in around 1968, the other he states lies beneath one of the paws of the Great Sphinx on the Giza plateau, and Piedras Negras in Guatemala has been touted as a possible site for the third hall of records.

"It would be well if this entity were to seek either of the three phases of the ways and means in which those records of the activities of individuals were preserved – the one in the Atlantean land, that sank, which will rise and is rising again; another in the place of the records that leadeth from the Sphinx to the hall of records, in the Egyptian land; and another in the Aryan or Yucatán land, where the temple there is overshadowing same." (Cayce; Sept. 25, 1939)

"A record of Atlantis from the beginnings of those periods when the Spirit took form or began the encasements in that land, and the developments of the peoples throughout their sojourn, with the record of the first destruction and the changes that took place in the land. . . This in position lies, as the sun rises from the waters, the line of the shadow (or light) falls between the paws of the Sphinx, that was later set as the sentinel or guard, and which may not be entered from the connecting chambers from the Sphinx's paw (right paw) until the TIME has been fulfilled when the changes must be active in this sphere of man's experience. Between, then, the Sphinx and the river. . ." (Cayce; 378-16)

"As given, that temple was destroyed at the time there was the last destruction in Atlantis. Yet, as time draws nigh when changes are to come about, there may be the opening of those three places where the records are one, to those that are the initiates in the knowledge of the One God: The temple by Iltar will then rise again. Also there will be the opening of the temple or hall of records in Egypt, and those records that were put into the heart of the Atlantean land may also be found there - that have been kept, for those that are of that group. The RECORDS are ONE." (Cayce; 5750-1)

The study and search for the Hall of Records is considered by many mainstream academics to be pseudo-archaeology, with no scientific basis for the research in the first place. This may well be the case but it hasn't stopped some interested parties from investigating Cayce's claims further.

Beneath the Sphinx

Back in 1991, Dr. Robert Schoch and Dr. Thomas Dobecki began initial seismic tests around the area of the Giza Plateau suggested in Cayce's readings. In 2003, Schoch wrote, 'The seismic analysis Dr. Thomas Dobecki and I performed around the Sphinx in 1991 revealed what might be a chamber or room carved into the limestone under the left paw of the Sphinx, hailed by some as "The Hall of Records" of the lost continent of Atlantis. To the best of my knowledge, this cavity has never been probed or explored, so we don't know what it might contain, if anything.'[218]

Cayce prophesised that one hall of records would be rediscovered and opened between 1996 and 1998, and sure enough in May of 1996 more intensive seismographic and radar surveys were undertaken at Giza in search of proof of such a library.

The survey was performed by the Schor Foundation in collaboration with the Florida State University after having being granted a license by the Supreme Council of Antiquities in Egypt. Dr. Schor was a member of the A.R.E. and wrote on May 24th, 1994 of his personal interest in corroborating, 'the Cayce records which indicated that the culture which led to the building of the Pyramids dates to 10,400 BC', whilst also wishing 'to further delineate that civilization.'

However, on April 11th, 1996 Dr. Schor was quick to assert to the mainstream media that any association with Cayce was irrelevant in the context of his project, "We do not work for the Edgar Cayce Group . . . The major purpose of the Schor Foundation and the Florida State University is to aid in the preservation and restoration of the Pyramids and Sphinx. In addition, we are surveying the underground of the Giza Plateau to find faults and chasms that might collapse. This will increase the safety of the plateau . . ."

Regardless of intent, the team succeeded in discovering a tunnel which runs some 40 feet below the rump of the Great Sphinx, as well as a tunnel leading from the Queen's Pyramid towards the Great Pyramid's eastern flank. Radar readings also confirmed the possibility of a large rectangular chamber under the front paws of the Sphinx as previously acknowledged by Schoch.

Despite the absence of definitive proof that any kind of hall or library may exist within any of these cavities, author Robert Bauval wrote that 'Dr. Schor, however, is adamant that his radar survey around the Sphinx virtually confirms the existence of an underground network of tunnels and chambers.'[219]

A short video filmed by Boris Said at the end of 1995 and produced in early 1996, was also financed by Dr. Schor. Fascinatingly, the film opens with the infamous Dr. Zahi Hawass scrambling into a tunnel leading underneath the Sphinx. On reaching the bottom Hawass turns to face the camera and whispers to the viewer, "Even Indiana Jones will never dream to be here. Can you believe it? We are now inside the Sphinx in this tunnel. This tunnel has never been opened before. No-one really knows what's inside this tunnel. But we are going to open it for the first time."

In commentary, the film's narrator goes on to state, "Edgar Cayce, America's famous 'Sleeping Prophet', predicted that a chamber would be discovered beneath the Sphinx – a chamber containing the recorded history of human civilization. For the first time we'll show you what lies beneath this great statue . . . a chamber which will be opened tonight, live, for our television cameras." For some reason this never happened and still nobody knows what remains inside.

Dr. Zahi Hawass announced to the Egyptian press on April 14th, 1996 that under the Sphinx and around the Pyramids there were secret tunnels which he believed would prove to "carry many secrets of the building of the Pyramids." Hawass remains a controversial figure due to the sheer inconsistency of his comments throughout the years and his innate unwillingness to challenge the current status quo regarding Egyptology. As we see here, Hawass is openly discussing the discovery of underground tunnels and chambers, yet years after making these public claims he began denying their existence once more.

A 1999 Fox documentary film shows Hawass down in the chamber with the sarcophagus, a story which is relatively unknown these days and should be front page news considering the implications of such a remarkable discovery. The film footage reveals the three levels below the surface (fig. 64), with a burial chamber which includes six individual rooms cut out of the rock, and two red granite sarcophagi along with pottery and bones which Hawass claims date back to around 500 BC.

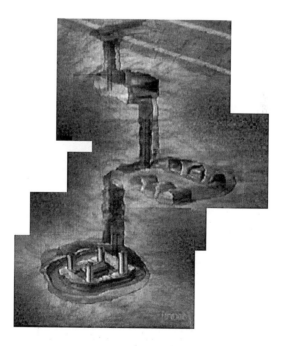

Fig. 64 Fox TV artist's depiction of the shaft's three levels, with the 'tomb of Osiris' on the third level surrounded by four pillars.

As researcher Philip Coppens pointed out, 'red granite is not native to the Giza Plateau; the only source is Aswan, hundreds of miles to the south. The very presence of red granite, discovered in 1980 in the vicinity of the Sphinx, proves that there is something underneath the Giza Plateau. And if Hawass says anything different, it should first be seen as a case of "methinketh he protesteth too much".'[220]

Descending down again to a third subterranean level, located between four inscribed pillars, Hawass and his team uncovered another sarcophagus (fig. 65), 9 feet in length and estimated to weigh between 11 and 12 tons. These startling discoveries somehow have gone under the radar despite being aired on the *Fox* television network at the end of the 1990s.

Fig. 65 Zahi Hawass stands beside the sarcophagus inside the 'Tomb of Osiris' on the third level beneath the Great Sphinx.

In a Danish publication from 1999, Hawass commented, "I have found a shaft, going down 29 metres (95 feet, approximately) vertically down into the ground, exactly halfway between the Chefren Pyramid and the Sphinx. At the bottom, which was filled with water, we have found a burial chamber with four pillars. In the middle is a large granite sarcophagus which I expect to be the grave of Osiris, the god."[221]

A German researcher going by the name 'Ananda' who explored the tomb site below Giza with his colleague Randolph Barolet in February 2010, confirmed the information offered by Hawass in the *Fox* documentary, and claimed that 'underneath the sarcophagus was a huge cleared vertical shaft that was submerged in water'.[222]

Ananda also claimed that, 'upon later research, [it] showed that some astounding discoveries had been made under the water, and that the scanning work of Dr. Boris Said of an underground tunnel leading to the Sphinx, has not only been confirmed, but thoroughly explored.'[223]

Zahi Hawass, standing at the entrance to a mysterious horizontal tunnel situated on the third level beside the 'tomb of Osiris', replied to the question of whether the tunnel could lead to Cayce's Hall of Records; "Edgar Cayce and lost civilization[s], it's a legend, it's a myth. The Arabs in the last century, they talked about all of this, and [the] psychic brought it to us back. But, to be fair, I did not excavate this tunnel yet, and really I don't know where it leads us. But, I always say that you never know what the sand and the tunnels of Egypt may hide."[224]

Another tunnel heads in the opposite direction, and one would expect that the tunnel system links the Sphinx complex with the pyramids, as Ananda confirmed, 'There were tunnels going west to the middle pyramid, and east to the Sphinx,'[225] but could one of the tunnels possibly lead to the Hall of Records?

Is this the area which Edgar Cayce spoke about in 1937? It certainly fits the description perfectly: "records that are yet to be discovered or yet to be had of those activities in the Atlantean land, and for the preservation of data that is yet to be found from the chambers of the way between the Sphinx and the pyramid of records." (1486-1 Nov. 26, 1937)

In fact, the Greek historian Herodotus was among the first to mention the existence of a hall of records, 'This I have actually seen, a work beyond words. For if anyone put together the buildings of the Greeks and display of their labours, they would seem lesser in both effort and expense to this labyrinth . . . Even the pyramids are beyond words, and each was equal to many and mighty works of the Greeks. Yet the labyrinth surpasses even the pyramids.'[226]

It is widely believed that Herodotus was not actually referring to the underground complex between the Sphinx and the Pyramid of Khafre however, but a site beside the Pyramid of Amenemhat III at Hawara, less than 100 km from Cairo, discovered in 2008 by a group of Egyptian and Belgian researchers led by Louis De Cordier.

This fascinating archaeological discovery which remains concealed and unexplored to this day could prove to be the location of such a vast 'temple of records', as Cayce once referred to them as, but only time (and an honest and public investigation) will reveal this to us.

The Bahamian Stones

One of the locations Cayce claimed would house one of the three sets of Atlantean records was at Bimini in the Bahamas. Rather than chains of islands, a vast 'island' was in the area before the end of the last Ice Age when the ocean levels were at least 300 feet below their current levels. According to Cayce, Bimini was one of the mountaintops of ancient Atlantis, while today the island cannot be considered a mountain, it was once one of the highest points in the region some 12,000-years ago. Both Bimini and Andros Island used to be part of the same island back then, which Cayce referred to as the "Poseidia" temple that is covered by "the slime of ages" and sunk in 10,000 B.C.

In one reading, he revealed that some of the ruins of Atlantis would be discovered there at the end of the 1960's, "Poseidia will be among the first portions of Atlantis to rise again – expect it '68 and '69 – not so far away." (958; June 28, 1940)

Nearly three decades later and Cayce's prophecy came true, as in 1968, a fishing guide named Bonefish Sam led underwater explorer and archaeologist Dr. J. Manson Valentine to a site where a 'road' of enormous neatly placed stones were laid in the shallow waters near the island of Bimini, fifty miles east of Miami. Located a mere 20 ft. below the surface, the 'Bimini Road' (fig. 66) is a formation of flat limestone rocks measuring up to 13 ft. across, seemingly cut at right angles and set in a straight line stretching for half a mile, before hooking off at the end. However, it is not widely known that a portion of the Bimini Road was removed after a hurricane in 1926.

Fig. 66 Top and bottom left: Sections of the 'Bimini Road' limestone rock formations lie in shallow waters only 20 ft. below the surface. Bottom right: More unusual rock formations in the same vicinity.

Upon his initial discovery, Valentine concluded that the stones were most likely part of a ceremonial road leading to a sacred site, which he believed must have been built by 'the people who made the big spheres of Central America, the huge platforms in Lebanon, Malta in the

Mediterranean, Stonehenge in England, the walls of Ollantaytambo in Peru, the standing stone avenues of Brittany, the colossal ruins of Tiahuanaco in Bolivia, and the statues of Easter Island – this was a prehistoric race that could transport and position cyclopean stones in a way that remains a mystery to us.'[227]

Others are less convinced that the rock formations are anything more than natural stones which have been shaped by weathering, erosion and tidal currents over millennia, but in 2005, American TV channel *NBC* set up a new expedition and conducted its own investigation of the area. On the expedition, author Dr. Greg Little and his wife Dr. Lora Little were accompanied by archaeologist William Donato, Doris Van Auken and two dive operators at Bimini. Photos and video were taken both on the surface and underwater and the results were published in a 29-page internet article and a 73-minute DVD documentary.

The sceptics believe that the Bimini Road is simply the formation of natural sedimentary limestone (beachrock) that fractured in place, a conclusion based on less than twenty core rock samples, which led the geologists to the premature assumption that because the stones seemed similar in their structure, they must therefore be natural formations.

But of course this wasn't their only gripe, as Dr. Greg Little explained in an article for *Atlantis Rising Magazine*, four of the critical components of their argument were:

'1. That nowhere at the site are any blocks resting on the top of other blocks — they assert that there is not even a single example of this.
2. That all the blocks are lying on the bedrock bottom or on sand.
3. That no prop stones are present under the blocks.
4. That no human ancient artefacts or tool marks are present on the site.'[228]

The 2005 Bimini expedition dealt with all of these concerns with an extremely thorough examination of the mysterious rock formation. Little reported their findings in his article:

Issue 1—Multiple Tiers of Blocks Resting on Blocks. Over a dozen multiple tiers of stone blocks were quickly found in direct contradiction to the geologists' claims. These were found primarily in an area of the formation that has a large amount of coral and plant growth. Massive schools of fish were present in this area to such a degree that it was difficult to actually see through the many fish. Sharks are often present in this area of the formation, and it can be speculated that the sceptics may have avoided this area or simply viewed it from the surface.

Issue 2—All the Blocks Rest on the Bottom. The May 2005 trip was Bill Donato's 17th Bimini expedition, while it was only our fourth. The two perspectives at the site (snorkelling from the surface versus diving on the bottom) yield vastly different views. In many areas, the surface view clearly showed that in all areas relatively clear of sand, there are many tiers of stone blocks present.

Issue 3—No Underlying Prop Stones are Present. Prop stones were used in the construction of ancient Mediterranean harbours to level the top layers of blocks forming breakwaters. At Bimini, numerous cube-like prop stones were found under many blocks. Sceptics who have addressed the presence of these blocks have asserted that they were dumped by modern or historic ships. When these blocks were first encountered during the 2005 expedition, they were intriguing, but we immediately realized there was no proof where they came from or when they were placed there. In brief, the idea that they were dumped was initially the most logical explanation. However, during the time we inspected under massive blocks, we were astonished to find many of these rectangular slabs under the larger stones. In all these cases, the massive blocks visible from the surface were literally resting on top of the smaller rectangular slabs. In several cases, we found rectangular slabs literally stacked on top of each other essentially levelling the massive block on top of them. There is no way that these slabs could have been dumped from ships. It was one of the most important discoveries and totally contradicts the sceptics' assertion that there are no prop stones present there.

354 THE MYTH OF MAN

Issue 4—No artefacts or tool marks are present at Bimini. A bottom surface search confined to small areas yielded many artifactual finds. A unique "u-shaped" mortise cut into a 3-foot square stone was discovered. It is possible it could be natural, but a few ancient stone anchors found in the Mediterranean are virtually identical to it. In addition, we discovered a 3-feet-long, plumb-bob-shaped stone with a large hole bored through its middle. On both ends groove marks were clearly discernible where a rope had been attached. The stone is identical to several ancient stone anchors that have been recovered at Thera. It was covered with a deep layer of coral and carbonate crust on the exposed side and was found just to the outside of the main J-shape, toward land. Lora Little also discovered another stone anchor within the main J-shaped formation. It was a large circular stone about 4 feet in diameter with a large hole drilled through the middle.'[229]

About seven miles north of Bimini, divers also discovered a load of scattered granite blocks sitting on the sea floor about thirty feet below the surface. This 'well-worn, coral encrusted, human engineered granite' were remnants of a much larger amount which was obtained by an American underwater salvager named Captain Webster, who located the large quantities of cut ancient granite while searching for wrecks on the Moselle Shoal.

According to locals who remember Webster, he salvaged at least 11 or 12 double barge loads of Bimini granite which he hauled up for jetty stone construction to make the Government Cut jetty in Miami and the Jupiter Inlet jetty farther north.

"Captain Webster had two barges – one was one hundred feet long and the other was about eighty feet. They was pulled by a big black tugboat", said local man Mr. Sherman who also claimed that the captain "lost two barges on the Moselle Shoal and two more barges in the Gulf Stream" due to the inclement weather "when the waves was rough."[230]

Author Richard Wingate realised, that if Webster had raised up to twelve double barge loads of trimmed and dressed granite over three and a half years, and with hundreds of tons still lying on the Shoal, maybe it was possible that he had been quarrying the remains of an ancient sunken building.

In 2007, Dr. Greg Little also examined the site and describing the stones wrote; 'These rectangular forms lie uniformly on a ridge running for at least a mile and a 10-foot drop-off is adjacent to them. This drop-off leads to a narrow flat area that then descends quickly. Found about 10 feet above the 10,000 B.C. shoreline, they raise intriguing possibilities related to Cayce's statements about Atlantis and Bimini.'[231]

Wingate went to investigate and examined the granite jetties in and around Miami where Webster was said to have taken the sunken granite, and he was amazed to discover evidence of human activity among the ancient stones.

He wrote, 'The Bimini granite is extremely weathered in contrast to the more modern sharp-edged quarried stone from the United States. This ancient stone displays eroded tool marks, drill holes, carving, and extensive evidence of ancient engineering.'[232]

Closer inspection of the Bimini granite used at the jetties revealed the edges of the rectangles, squares, and pyramid-shaped stones to be lined with 'finger-sized half holes which were usually one to one and a half inches apart'. These 'half-holes' resembled ancient carved holes for the purpose of inserting soft wooden plugs which would crack the granite when water-expanded. Other perfectly drilled holes were six inches across and bored through blocks between four and twelve feet thick. It has been suggested that these holes would have held wooden dowel pegs to be used to sight stars along the rows, like at Stonehenge.

Some blocks had holes aligned in rows of thirteen and others revealed shallow drilled holes forming a perfect 'X' shape. At Fort Lauderdale jetties, more dressed Bimini granite was discovered among the freshly quarried American granite, and a perfectly cut five-pointed star was discovered that had clearly outlined tips which had been drilled through a twelve foot long block.

Other stars were found a few inches apart in diagonal rows, all with weathered edges suggesting a great antiquity. As ocean levels rose between 3 and 600 feet about 10,500 years ago, these shapes must have been made prior to that, as granite doesn't erode underwater and it was already eroding before the Great Flood.

The five-pointed star was a symbol used by the Algonquin Indian Micmac tribe who were unusually European looking, being taller and slightly lighter than other tribes. They called themselves the 'Wabanaki' meaning the 'men from the East', and as most of them lived on the east coast of America, east to them refers to the Atlantic. Their written language included at least 2,000 known symbols that are also Egyptian hieroglyphics, with the five-pointed star representing 'God' or 'Heaven' in both the Algonquian and Egyptian cultures.

Could these drilled holes and ancient symbols which were cut into the Bimini granite, originally discovered beneath the Bahamian shores, be evidence of a long lost ancient civilization? Perhaps, under closer scrutiny, the most likely explanation for the Bimini Road formation could be that it was once an ancient harbour wall perhaps, whilst the granite blocks are more likely to be remnants of an extremely ancient building which sank beneath the waters following a cataclysmic flood which occurred in the distant past.

Wingate concluded, 'Since ocean levels rose 10,500 years ago, and since this granite was ancient when it was inundated by that worldwide flooding which the Bible distortedly remembers, the Bimini material and that discovered over the entire Bahamas bank must be the oldest known structures in the world.'[233]

In May 2007, Drs. Greg and Lora Little made a weeklong expedition to explore the small islands just north of Andros in the Bahamas and conducted a wide, systematic survey of the Great Bahama Bank, accompanied by boat/dive operators Krista and Eslie Brown. A local resident told them about a massive wall located in the shallow waters off the small chain of islands called Joulter's Cays which is about seven miles north of Andros.

Reaching the site by boat proved extremely difficult as they had to speed over a mile of water no more than a foot deep, but once they found the 'wall' they spent four entire days at the site, filming and photographing the unusual formation, which is positioned in a small and narrow bay that appears to lie between two islands.

Greg Little wrote, 'The wall is primarily made from square and rectangular limestone blocks that range in length from 3-6-feet, a width of 2-3-feet, and a thickness of 6-inches to 3-feet – with some blocks far larger. The blocks are obviously cut and roughly dressed and rough tool marks are clearly visible on many. There are some smaller, cube-like stones, about a foot square, occasionally found in portions of the intact wall and in places on the bottom. One area of the wall remains fairly intact and is found in water about 6-feet deep.'[234]

Another section of the wall which is formed by huge blocks stacked on top of each other, with three vertical layers visibly exposed, extends about 30 ft. in length with another 50 or so large stone blocks widely scattered in the area.

'The initial impression is that it might have been a retaining wall of some sort, but the entire area is so shallow that the bringing in of large boats or barges is simply impossible. We have also done extensive research in journals and magazines from the Bahamas, but it remains a mystery – an intriguing one,' wrote Little.

The limestone 'road' and the ancient granite blocks at Bimini, along with the mysterious underwater 'wall' in the shallows at Joulter's Cays are just a few examples of anomalous stone structures discovered beneath the waves in the Bahamas. These are just a few sites which have been discovered, and there are thousands more scattered worldwide, remnants of pre-flood civilizations which have disappeared from both view and human memory. When Cayce mentioned the Bahamas as one of the sites containing a hidden hall of records and referenced the area as part of the Atlantean empire, one wonders whether such archaeological discoveries could prove to be the physical traces of such a lost world.

Piedras Negras and the Yucatán

Cayce stated that the Yucatán Hall of Records was put in place by a small group of Atlanteans whom he claimed were led by a priest named Iltar. Initially, they travelled to coastal regions of Yucatán before finally heading inland, whilst other Atlanteans allegedly fled to Central and South America simultaneously.

Many researchers believe that Piedras Negras, a ruined pre-Columbian Mayan city on the north bank of the Usumacinta River in the Petén region of Guatemala, may have been what Cayce referred to during his readings. Others have disputed this idea, as he only claimed that the records had been carried "to what is now Yucatán" and never mentioned Guatemala at all. But it must be remembered that the reading was given during Cayce's era when the whole Maya region was commonly referred to as Yucatán. Back in the 1800s, Yucatán was actually portrayed on maps covering the whole of Guatemala as opposed to just the peninsula as it is today.

Piedras Negras ('black stones') is a fascinating archaeological site which was populated from as early as 2,700 years ago but only rediscovered at the end of the 19th century by the Italian-born explorer Teoberto Maler. Between 1914 and 1931, the Carnegie Institute paid for four visits to the site before undertaking a five year excavation project which ended in 1936.

The first to decipher the Mayan inscriptions on the monuments at Piedras Negras was Tatiana Proskouriakoff, whose thorough examination and reconstruction of the site remains the most detailed analysis of the area still available today. Such was her love for the place that she requested that her ashes be scattered at the highest point of the site, known as the Acropolis, following her death at 74 years of age in 1985.

There are thirteen pyramids in total at Piedras Negras, five of which are located in the oldest section of the site that is referred to as the South Group. Situated in front of the Acropolis and directly in line with Pyramid K-5 sits Altar I, a broken stone table first discovered by Maler. One of five large altars uncovered there, Altar I sits on one side of the prominent Acropolis whilst Altar II, a stone shaped as a jaguar paw, remains in place on the opposite side of the Acropolis.

"In his readings on the Yucatán Hall of Records, Cayce related that the stones which were being uncovered at the site were actually altars. Their presence at the base of the Acropolis may somehow point to the location of the Hall of Records" said Dr. Greg Little.

Cayce described this location as being "in the Aryan or Yucatán land, where the temple there is overshadowing same." This information has led to the suggestion that the multi-tiered temple J-29 positioned at the base of the Acropolis, which is overshadowed by another temple higher up among the Acropolis temples, could be the site of the Hall of Records. The researchers have speculated that a tunnel system joins the pyramids O-13, K-5 and J-29, and would have been the ideal location to safely conceal such important documents.

Fig. 67 Altar I at the ancient pre-Columbian Mayan ruined city of Piedras Negras, Guatemala.

Inscribed on Altar I (fig.67) is the Mayan creation date of 3114 BC, a date which is only inscribed on five known monuments throughout the Mayan world, but which is mirrored in other areas of the site. This date also has connections with Orion's Belt, just as we have seen to be the case in other ancient cultures around the world.

As Dr. Lora Little explained, "What we found was that the Belt of Orion rises over the top of one of the pyramids in the morning, right at the date August the 12th 3114, which is the Mayan creation date . . . and even more interesting when we look at how the Belt of Orion sits; it can be aligned by the same pyramids setting on the day that is considered the ending of the era, December the 12th 2012."[235]

During excavation work the site yielded many incredible objects such as clumps of iron, a number of crystals, and sculptures which some experts believe to be the best examples of sculpted art anywhere in the ancient world, most of which are now on view in the Guatemala Archaeological Museum of Guatemala City.

Also on display is a very unusual artefact that was unearthed at the end of the 1990's from Tikal, another Mayan site just over 100 miles to the east of Piedras Negras. The object shows a six-pointed 'Star of David' intricately engraved on a circular shell, and is very similar to another star design engraved on a sun disc at Uxmal, discovered in the 1800s and reported by the Bureau of Ethnology. This same symbol which has become synonymous with Judaism was discovered on the Bimini stones by Richard Wingate and could well have its origins in antiquity, despite the oldest conventional example being cited as being on the front cover of the Leningrad Codex dated to around 1008 AD.

Interestingly, over 70 years ago Edgar Cayce disputed the conventional 'into America' thesis, which asserts that the first humans to migrate into the Americas entered from Siberia via the Bering Strait Land Bridge around 9,500 BC. Lately this theory is being debunked due to the ever increasing physical evidence which contradicts these outdated claims, such as human remains found in Monte Verde, Chile in 1997, which point to the fact that at least 12,500 years ago, long before the possibility of migration through the ice-covered Arctic regions of North America, the Americas was already populated. And let us not forget the controversial stone tools discovered at Hueyatlaco in Mexico which were firmly dated as 250,000 years old, and some of the other anomalously ancient human remains also discovered in the Americas such as the 1.5 million year old skull found in Buenos Aires.

Cayce controversially stated that the first people in South America actually entered the continent from the "South Pacific" as far back as 50,000 BC, an idea which American archaeologists insist is both ridiculous and impossible and lacking supportive anthropological evidence.

However, contrary to the hundreds of museum displays around the U.S. depicting the standard Siberian migration theory, an educational display in the Guatemala Archaeological Museum reinforces Cayce's reading and portrays the first people entering the Americas from the South Pacific just as he had claimed decades earlier. Dr. Greg Little wrote, 'the "official" Guatemalan archaeological display seems to show they are more interested in discovering the truth about ancient America than maintaining academic dogma.'

Could Cayce's insights actually have some credibility to them? Much of the published information he has shared over the years has yielded interesting results thus far, enough to remain open-minded on the subject at least.

Regarding Cayce's claims that part of Atlantis was in the Bahamas and one of three sets of historical records were placed in Yucatán before the untimely demise of the great Atlantic empire, one major flaw in his assertions has been a lack of archaeological finds definitively placing humans in the area earlier than 4000-6000 BC.

But archaeologists from Florida State University's Underwater Archaeology Department (FSU) found the remnants of human settlements along the continental shelf off Florida – dated to around 10,000 BC. According to the FSU, in that area of the Bahamas in 10,500 B.C 'the water levels were only about 100 feet lower than today. But areas of human occupation on these ancient shores tend to cluster at depths around the 45-foot level.' The human remains they discovered were consistently found in 45 feet of water.

In 2001-02, a team of underwater scientists led by Mexican archaeologist and director of the Desert Museum in Saltillo, Arturo Gonzáles, officially discovered the oldest human skeleton ever found in the Americas. The female skeleton named 'Eva de Naharon' was found along with three others in underwater caves along the Caribbean coast off the Yucatán Peninsula. Charcoal samples found with Eva were carbon-dated to 13,600 years old by the University of California and the three other skeletons were given a date range of 11,000 to 14,000 years ago.

González said, "We don't know how [the people whose remains were found in the caves] arrived and whether they came from the Atlantic, the jungle, or inside the continent . . . but we believe these finds are the oldest yet to be found in the Americas and may influence our theories of how the first people arrived."[236]

These rare discoveries suddenly legitimise Cayce's claims of an Atlantean occupation in the Yucatán during that early period, as Dr. Greg Little declared, 'The Yucatán find now confirms that humans were in the region where the Cayce readings state that Atlanteans went just prior to the final destruction, which occurred circa 10,500 BC'.

THE CRESPI COLLECTION

More physical evidence connecting the Americas with the East can be found in the astonishing collection of an Italian priest who spent his life in rural South America. Some of the objects discovered within this remarkable treasure trove of ancient artefacts are highly suggestive of a third party pre-diluvian culture whose influence reached both sides of the Atlantic.

The enigmatic story of Father Carlos Crespi (1891-1982) is quite incredible, and remains both mysterious and controversial. The priest housed his collection of anomalous artefacts in remote, dusty rooms beside the village church; objects which are highly indicative of an unknown lost civilization. Author Frank Joseph wrote, 'the Crespi Collection is persuasive testimony to regular contacts between the Old World and the New thousands of years ago.'

Richard Wingate visited the priest in the 1970s and managed to photograph some of the rare collection for publication in his book *Lost Outpost of Atlantis*, and described the situation in his introduction:

"In a dusty, cramped shed on the side porch of the Church of Maria Auxiliadora in Cuenca, Ecuador, lies the most valuable archaeological treasure on earth. More than one million dollars worth of dazzling gold is cached here, and much silver, yet the hard money value of this forgotten hoard is not its principal worth. There are ancient artefacts identified as Assyrian, Egyptian, Chinese, and African so perfect in workmanship and beauty that any museum director would regard them as first-class acquisitions. Since this treasure is the strangest collection of ancient archaeological objects in existence, its value lies in the historical questions it poses, and demands answers to. Yet it is unknown to historians and deliberately neglected in the journals of orthodox archaeology."[237]

Father Crespi (fig. 68) was a man with a big heart and a deep fascination of the ancient past who spent most of his life living and working in Cuenca, Ecuador. Since the early 1920s he was assigned to work among the Indian Shuar community as the Cuenca parish priest at the Catholic Church of Maria Auxiliadora in the obscure Ecuadorian village, high in the Andes.

Fig. 68 Italian priest Father Carlos Crespi, who spent his life working in Cuenca, Ecuador.

He had a great interest in many subjects including anthropology, art, botany, cinematography, music, exploration and humanitarianism, and he was so revered by the local population that upon his death an impressive sculpture was erected in Cuenca in his honour.

Father Crespi was not simply an amateur collector of random artefacts as some sceptics presume, but a serious scholar who had a

Masters Degree in Anthropology and Doctorates in Natural Sciences, Engineering and Music. As an intern in the 1920s he gathered artefacts from Ecuador for exposition in Rome, and exhibited artefacts in New York City in 1928-9. He was Director of the Colegio Cornelio Merchán, and also founded both the Agricultural School in Yanuncay and the Instituto Orientalista of Cuenca. In 1956, he was awarded the illustrious 'Son of Cuenca' medal and in 1982 Italy conferred upon him the 'Medal of Merit of the Republic'.

It is important to understand the intelligence of this man in context with the unusual artefacts which he began receiving and collecting during his long stay in Cuenca. He was a humanitarian with a great intellect who gained the trust of the local community, and the religious celebrations over which he presided brought a host of Indians who attended them in baptism, marriage, and death, bearing gifts for him.

Crespi had collected books and pictures of Phoenician, Egyptian, Babylonian and other Old World cultures and shown them to the natives saying, "If you ever find anything like this, bring it to me, and I will reward you." Over fifty years his collection steadily grew and grew, until eventually it filled many large rooms containing some 70,000 artefacts.

Originally, much of the collection was kept in the courtyard of the Maria Auxiliadora church until finally the Vatican gave him permission to build a museum in which to house the collection, but in 1962 many of the artefacts were destroyed in a fire. Fortunately, a large part of the collection survived long enough to be photographed and documented before the Vatican among other institutions took possession of the hoard following Crespi's death in April 1982.

When asked where the Indians got the artefacts from Crespi nonchalantly replied, "Oh, they get them from the caves and subterranean chambers in the jungles." "There are over 200 kilometres of tunnels starting here in Cuenca. They run from the mountains down to the Eastern lowlands near the Amazon."

If this were true, it would be quite remarkable to consider how a vast array of ancient and anomalous artefacts came to be stored in subterranean chambers and caves of the Amazon. Where did these objects originate? And how did they manage to arrive at such remote destinations?

In 1925, the explorer Colonel Percy Fawcett went missing somewhere in the Amazon jungle, never to reappear, but before leaving for his final trip he wrote these prophetic words, 'Whether we succeed in penetrating the jungle, and come out alive, or whether we leave our bones there, of this I am certain – the key to the mystery of ancient South America and perhaps the whole of prehistory can be found if we are able to locate these old cities of the solar civilization and open them up to science.'[238]

In 1976, a landmark expedition to the caves of the Tayos Indians in Ecuador was organized by Scottish engineer Stan Hall, with the first man on the moon Neil Armstrong, as Honorary President and participant. A mixed team of British and International explorers associated with the Royal Academy of Science successfully mapped hundreds of miles of underground caves and tunnels in search of the mysterious 'Metallic Library' and other relics of Atlantis.

Could the 'Metallic Library' and other ancient objects be truly authentic remnants of a lost civilization in the Americas? We know that some of the unusual items stored by Father Crespi were fakes, as many a sceptic is quick to highlight, but this was something that the priest was very aware of (he actually kept a room dedicated to the obvious fakes and bogus material). The problem was, he just couldn't resist aiding those in need and once word got out that he was willing to pay for *any* artefacts offered to him, it encouraged forgers to try their luck with counterfeit items. It is due to this 'muddied water', that many of his detractors declare *all* of the artefacts to be counterfeit.

Many have questioned the authenticity of Crespi's collection due to his admittance of purchasing fake artefacts in order to support those less fortunate than himself, as an interviewer once asked, "Is it certain that Padre Crespi has been sold things that have no scientific value, that they swindle you?" To which the reply was, "in summary, permit me, don't put that down. In Cuenca there are still many people who experience hunger. And Padre Crespi knows."

But as author Frank Joseph highlights, 'because Cuenca, anciently Tomebamba (*tumi-pampa*, "plain of the knife in Quechua, language of the Incas), functioned as northern capital of the Inca Empire under three monarchs, it is not an unlikely place for antiquities treasured from the past millennia to survive.'[239]

Fig. 69 The depiction of an African animal on the 'Elephant Stela' found in Ecuador is as anomalous as the Libyan script inscribed beneath.

So what kind of artefacts are we talking about? The list is long. His collection of curios and antiquities included: plaques made of gold, silver, bronze and brass, gold masks, metal flasks, and plates of various metallic compositions with unique inscriptions, symbols, pictographs and hieroglyphs. Stone tablets, shelves of dusty ceramics from floor to ceiling, idols, jewellery, tools, shields, helmets and implements of war like spears, axes, clubs of wood, metal and stone. Many animals were also represented in the collection, both extinct and still living.

Despite being based thousands of miles to the east on the vast African plains, elephants were also represented on some pieces, such as the 'Elephant Stela' (fig. 69) which was photographed by J. Manson Valentine and published by Charles Berlitz in 1972. It had been found in Cuenca during construction of the airport according to Crespi.

The Libyan script inscribed upon the stela translates as, 'The Elephant that supports the Earth and therefore is the cause of the Earthquake.' Despite the unknown whereabouts of the piece today, Frank Joseph asserted, 'That it once existed is beyond doubt, and that anyone in Ecuador prior to 1972 could have counterfeited it stretches credulity.'[240]

Fig. 70 The Masinissa Plaque – one of Crespi's mysterious metal objects from South America depicting an Egyptian pyramid.

The 'Masinissa Plaque' (fig. 70) was another of the artefacts in the collection, a 'gold-coloured, roller-stamped', rectangular metal plaque that was inscribed with a sun atop a pyramid, flanked by a cat on either side, with a row of unknown inscriptions written along the base of the pyramid. Note also the inclusion of elephants again in the bottom corners of the piece. Dr. Barry Fell of Harvard University concluded that the unknown text was written in a Libyan-Egyptian language which announced the death of Masinissa, King of Libyan-Egyptians who died in 148 BC, and the ascension of his son to the throne of a united Egypt.

One of Crespi's personal favourites was a metallic plaque weighing about 44 lbs, measuring 20.5 inches high, 5.5 inches wide and 1.5 inches in thickness. This particular piece (fig. 71) is imprinted with 56 different characters which remain undeciphered to this day, and since the Incas had no recorded form of writing, they couldn't have been responsible for its creation. These letters have been compared to characters used by the ancient Sumerians in their cuneiform tablets, and those used by the Magyars of the Carpathian Mountains.

In a letter to his son Brian, Percy Fawcett wrote that, "Judging by inscriptions found in many parts of Brazil, the inhabitants used an alphabetical writing allied to many ancient European and Asian scripts", thus offering more confirmation of a link between the two continents which may well have come about by a mysterious third-party culture such as Atlantis.

Fig. 71 A metallic plaque from the Crespi Collection with unknown characters which still remain undeciphered.

This is not to say that the authentic artefacts amongst Crespi's treasures were created by Atlanteans, but that the knowledge imbued within them such as the writing, symbolism, style, influence and content, may well have derived from survivors of the lost continent before being passed on to the Mesoamericans in ancient times.

Crespi himself was convinced that due to the Egyptian, Babylonian, and Phoenician appearance of some of the objects he had in his possession, that there must have been Mediterranean contacts with

Ecuador thousands of years ago, or perhaps we are seeing evidence of a shared influence which affected both continents.

In the late 70s, J. Golden Barton visited Crespi in Cuenca with Dr. Paul Cheesman and described the scene once the doors were opened to Crespi's collection: "Father Crespi's mysterious room seemed overburdened with the treasures of an unknown antiquity. It literally over-flowed with bizarre artefacts, many wrought in precious metals. Most intriguing were the innumerable plates of bronze, brass and gold. Many bore strange inscriptions and hieroglyphic symbols. Others were replete with the engravings of incongruous animals – elephants, snakes, jaguars, wild beasts of every kind."

Describing some of the objects he said, "We photographed a plate inscribed with representations of what appeared to be Egypt's step pyramid . . . Still more plates contained artwork with what looked like Assyrian or Babylonian symbols. We grew dizzy with the gleaming opulence and historical anomaly all around us."

Analysing photographs of the Crespi artefacts, leading South American scholar Professor Miloslav Stingl wrote, 'If these pictures are genuine, and everything indicates that they are, because no one makes forgeries in gold, at any rate not on such a large scale, this is the biggest archaeological sensation since the discovery of Troy.'

Frank Joseph believed a portion of the collection to have been genuine and of historical interest and concluded that, 'some of Crespi's unique relics should be considered authentically ancient on the basis of internal evidence. Who in Ecuador would be capable of counterfeiting inscriptions in Cypriot or Phoenician, for which no published sources are known to exist? That the Padre obtained them from Europe is improbable, considering that some of them translate in Quechua. The many large slabs at Zuchay [south of Cuenca], bearing recognizable Cypriot letters within grids, are so heavy as to discount the modern-import theory. The inference is that at some time in the past, Andean artisans had access to knowledge of Mediterranean scripts.'[241]

It is this South American access to Mediterranean artefacts, language, symbolism and religious custom which is anomalous. We now know that some contact between the opposing continents looks credible judging by an array of evidential data which includes the ancient maps of Antarctica that we previously covered, and also the cocaine mummies of ancient Egypt, but it is also possible that Crespi's curios derived from an unknown source which was in contact with both sides of the Atlantic.

Barton described one object as "a large piece of metal that had been moulded and hammered into a long sheet. It looked like it might be made of gold. The sheet was inscribed with a curious artwork beyond identification." This description is in keeping with accounts of huge stone Peruvian buildings which housed priests and nobles, thousands and thousands of years ago, all of which were 'wallpapered with silver and gold metallic sheets'.[242]

Barton returned to Cuenca in hope of showing the artefacts to his two sons, but was disappointed to hear that Crespi had died and his collection was no longer available for public view, and in spite of Barton's efforts to convince the young priest who had replaced Crespi that they had travelled a long distance and would appreciate one last viewing, the priest "insisted that the room with the artefacts could not be shown on orders from the Vatican."

In January 1980, there commenced the implementation of a decision made when Crespi was critically ill the previous March. For 13 million sucres (£310,000) which equates to around £1,250,000 in today's money, the Museo del Banco Central purchased and took charge of the Crespi Collection. Once recovered following the removal of a cancerous prostate, Father Crespi discovered that behind closed doors to prevent his intervention, the sale and sorting of many of his artefacts was taking place. As reported by Dr. Warren L. Cook of Castleton State University, upon meeting personally with the 90 year old Crespi in June 1981, when asked if they could photograph his collection he replied, "Ay, eso me lo han robado todo!" meaning "Ay, they have robbed me of all that!"

Archaeologists Dr. Gustavo Reinoso Hermidia from Cuenca, and Dr. Olaf Holm, director of the Museo del Banco Central of Guavaquil, were appointed to separate 'the wheat from the chaff' from Crespi's collection. Reinoso estimated that about a third of the ceramics were valuable, including hundreds of high quality examples, leading to some 8,000 pieces of ceramics being transferred to the Museo for cataloguing, storage and if deemed worthy, eventual exhibition. The bulk of the collection was (allegedly) judged to be worthless, with an array of rock artefacts and carved stones being discarded, and many metal sheets were described as "only worth melting down."

All we are left with today are a small selection of books and photographs which serve as a record of a quite incredible man and his most unusual collection of ancient artefacts. The mystery and controversy surrounding Crespi will forever remain, as it appears that following his death a great deal of the genuine treasures he kept stored away for decades have either been 'discarded' or simply removed by the Ecuadorian authorities, without his consent one might add, and where all of the most valuable pieces have been taken, nobody really knows.

What we do know for sure, thanks to the scholarly input of people such as Dr. Fell and Dr. Cheesman is that there were genuinely authentic exhibits amongst the modern imitations found in Crespi's dusty, church store rooms.

It is those examples which need to be remembered and considered as legitimate evidence of either contact between two opposing continents at a time when academics insist was impossible, or even more remarkably, physical proof of a lost civilization whose influence reached both shores of the Atlantic – a reminder of a lost culture possibly predating Göbekli Tepe by centuries, and even thousands of years before ancient Egypt sprang mysteriously into life.

On the rare objects contained within the Crespi Collection, Joseph concluded, 'Whether still available or known only through photographs, they have cracked open a bit wider a door slammed shut when Rome destroyed Carthage and then subjugated the Libyan-Egyptians, obscuring from us a significant chunk of knowledge of the past.'[243]

Other artefacts prove that ancient seafarers travelled between Africa and South America in the remote past. The Fuente Magna Bowl (fig. 72) for example, is a large stone vessel which resembles a libation bowl which was discovered in the surrounding areas of Lake Titicaca in Bolivia, around 75 km from the city of La Paz. The bowl is beautifully engraved inside and out with anthropomorphic characters and zoological motifs, but what is of importance here is the cuneiform writing imprinted on the inside. Dr. Clyde A. Winters wrote in 2002, 'when I recognized cuneiform writing on the Fuente Bowl I hypothesized that the other symbols on the bowl might be Proto-Sumerian, my subsequent reading of the inscriptions confirmed the hypothesis.'

Fig. 72 The Fuente Magna Bowl found near Lake Titicaca in Bolivia reveals proto-Sumerian writing on the inside.

This acts as further evidence of contact between East and West, in this case between the Sumerians and the Andeans, confirming theories suggesting that ancient Sumerians crossed the Atlantic to reach Bolivia in search of tin and other metals. This particular example, which is not an isolated one, may well explain how some of the Mesopotamian artefacts reached Ecuador and eventually found themselves amongst the Crespi Collection.

Probably the most fascinating of all of Crespi's objects are the representations of the Apkallus (fig. 73) from the Mesopotamia region based around modern day Iraq and Syria; home to the ancient cultures of Sumer, Babylon, Assyria, Akkadia and Phoenicia. The Apkallus or Seven Sages were said to have been created by the god Enki or Ea, to give civilization to mankind and to establish culture.

Fig. 73 Left: Apkallu from the Temple of Ninurta in the ancient city of Nimrud, Mesopotamia. Right: Apkallu figure bought by Carlos Crespi in Cuenca, Ecuador.

The examples sold to Father Crespi differ slightly from their Mesopotamian counterparts and are either imitation Sumerian reliefs made in South America, or actually originated in ancient Sumer and were brought across the ocean. Either way, their presence in Ecuador is anomalous enough, especially if it is true that they were indeed found in the subterranean tunnels and caves of the Amazon as the Shuar insist.

The Apkallus are often dressed in fish garbs representing the Oannes figure (fig. 74) who emerged from the sea to civilize the people, whereas the two examples on the previous page are winged. With either the head of a fish or an eagle; both hold the mysterious pine cone in one hand, most likely representing the pineal gland (although some researchers suggest they represent maize), and in the other hand they grasp the mysterious 'handbag' which has recently appeared carved on the ancient monuments at Göbekli Tepe. The modern 'wristwatch' looking item worn around the wrists of the Apkallus is another unexplained feature which consistently appears.

A GOD-FISH.

Fig. 74 Left and centre: Two reliefs from ancient Iraq show the same stylised figure of Oannes (Right) but one wears the fish garb instead of having wings.

Just like the 'H' symbol, the 'handbag' or 'bucket' symbol continues to resurface in ancient art around the world and it is the sheer cultural displacement of these ancient motifs that insinuates a global connection in the past, a connection with its roots in antiquity possibly stretching back to Atlantis or another similar antediluvian civilization which has disappeared from the historical record.

Other Eastern artefacts discovered in the Ecuadoran tunnels by the Shuar Indians which found their way into Crespi's remarkable and eclectic collection were similar in their size and design. The Sumerian/Assyrian lamassu (fig. 75) is a protective deity most commonly depicted with a human head with the body of a winged bull or lion. In sculptural form, Lamassi are usually depicted as 'double-aspect' figures, appearing to possess five legs when viewed from an oblique angle. The reason for this is to allow for two depictions simultaneously: 1. standing guard, when viewed from the front; and 2. striding forward, when viewed from the side.

In the image below we can compare the Crespi artefact found in South America with the statue excavated at Nimrud in ancient Iraq which dates to around 883-859 BC.

Fig. 75 Left: A lamassu from Crespi's collection. Right: Lamassu statue from ancient Mesopotamia.

ZEP TEPI

At Edfu, forty miles north of Aswan, on the walls of the Temple of Horus, texts referring to 'Seshu Hor' refer to an advanced people who brought knowledge and civilization in prehistoric times when they entered Khemit. The ancient Egyptians themselves believed that these ancestors were the real progenitors of the Egyptian civilization.

The 'Building Texts' inscribed on the walls in the Edfu temple describe the 'First Occasion' which the ancient Egyptians also referred to as the 'First Time' or 'Zep Tepi', which represented a distant epoch where the bringers and preservers of knowledge originated.

The records also describe the Zep Tepi as actual historic peoples, who after having arrived in the Nile valley from the south proceeded to rule and civilize the natives. They survived a disaster in their former home before seeking refuge in the Nile valley, and went on to build the Great Sphinx and the Giza pyramid complex, according to the Egyptian records. As Plato wrote, 'Egypt has recorded and kept eternally the wisdom of the old times. . . all coming from time immemorial when gods governed the earth in the dawn of civilization.'

The Edfu Building Texts reveal that ancient Egypt as we know it was indeed a legacy; 'An ancient world, after having been constituted, was destroyed, and as a dead world it came to be the basis of a new period of creation which at first was the re-creation and resurrection of what once had existed in the past.'

The peoples described in the texts were also referred to as the 'Ancestors' and the 'Sages', some of whom include Osiris and Thoth. The slouching lion epitomised in the image of the Sphinx represents these 'Sages' as well as the Age of Leo (approx. 12,000 years ago). As the peoples from an antediluvian culture which predated the Great Flood, they are also associated with water.

Zep Tepi was the time of the very first prehistoric Egyptian civilization which was founded by the 'Seven Sages', divine beings whom originated from an island referred to as the 'Homeland of the Primeval Ones', an island which sank during a catastrophic flood, 'an island which, in part, was covered with reeds and stood in the midst of the primeval water . . .'[244]

Could this 'homeland' refer to Atlantis? The Egyptian version of events is remarkably similar to Plato's and we know that his tale also originated in Egypt.

'At a certain point during the primeval age, however, this blessed 'former world' was overwhelmed, suddenly and totally, by a great flood, the majority of its 'divine inhabitants' were drowned and the 'mansions of the gods were inundated.'[245]

The Seven Sages described in ancient Egyptian texts mirror the 'Seven Apkallu' revered by all the ancient Mesopotamian cultures. The Apkallu were led by the civilizing hero Oannes who is often depicted as a 'fish-garbed figure' who came from the waters following a cataclysmic global deluge. The Babylonian, Sumerian, Akkadian and Assyrian traditions all share similar themes of a worldwide flood destroying a former paradise and a new world which was civilized by the wise sages who survived the disaster.

The Edfu texts state that the few who survived became 'the Builder Gods' who re-established civilization following the flood, and just like the Apkallu, brought knowledge of agriculture, arts, morality, architectural, building and engineering skills to the fledgling post-flood world. The Egyptians believe that the ground plan for many of their temples was already designed and put in place by the sages in the remote and distant past.

If Zep Tepi represents a pre-flood golden era whose survivors re-civilized the world upon their arrival in Egypt, it therefore appears that the writings carved upon the walls inside the Temple of Horus are in all probability a direct reference to the lost island of Atlantis.

ATLANTIS DERIVATIONS

It is interesting to compare the associated names given by ancient peoples located in regions surrounding the North Atlantic Ocean, as place names and cultures associated with Atlantis exist in a variety of locations, all of which must have seen contact in the past with either survivors or descendants of Atlantis. As Donnelly wrote, 'We find allusions to the Atlanteans in the most ancient tradition of many different races.'[246]

Despite not mentioning Atlantis by name, legends from even the remotest Pacific Islands speak of great land masses sinking when the earth shook, a time when islands disappeared into the sea and large islands became smaller ones.

In Greek tradition, Olympus was situated 'in the far west', 'in the ocean beyond Africa', 'on the western boundary of the known world', 'where the sun shone when it had ceased to shine on Greece', and where the mighty Atlas 'held up the heavens'. Plato tells us that Atlas and Poseidon ruled the land that was Atlantis, and according to the traditions of the Phoenicians, Atlas lived in the Gardens of Hesperides which 'were in the remote west'. The region of Hades known as Tartarus, the gloomy home of the dead, was also located 'under the mountains of an island in the midst of the ocean in the remote west.'

Donnelly speculated that the name 'Olympus', the land of the Gods in Greek mythology, may well have derived from the word 'Atlantis':

'May we not even suppose that the very word "Olympus" is a transformation from "Atlantis", in accordance with the laws that regulate the changes of letters of the same class into each other? Olympus was written by the Greeks "Olumpos". The letter *A* in Atlantis was sounded by the ancient world broad and full, like the *A* in our words *all* or *altar*; in these words it approximates very closely to the sound of *O*. It is not far to convert Atlantis into Oluntos, and this into Olumpos. We may, therefore, suppose that when the Greeks said that their gods dwelt in "Olympus", it was the same as if they said that they dwelt in "Atlantis".[247]

Donnelly could well have been clutching at straws here, but then again, language does change in such ways over time that his proposition could also prove valid. In his thorough studies on Atlantis, Donnelly also highlighted the anomalous ancient connection between place names on opposing continents of the East and West, a theme which continues to resurface. In Ptolemy's *Geography of Asia Minor*, he lists five cities in Armenia Major in A.D. 140 which had their counterparts in the names of Central American localities:

Armenian Cities	*Central American Localities*
Chol	Chol-ula
Colua	Colua-can
Zuivana	Zuivan
Cholima	Colima
Zalissa	Xalisco

Such clear links between these vastly separated lands is one of many examples of common origin across the great divide of the Atlantic. We find connections between the Guanches, the early inhabitants of the Canary Islands and Chichen Itza in Mexico's Yucatán Peninsula. Likewise, we find shared motifs and stone figures on view in the middle of the Pacific Ocean on Easter Island and at Göbekli Tepe in the hills of Southern Turkey. This hidden but evident influence remains uncategorised by conventional historians, but its existence is out there for all to see, and we can but speculate as to how these commonalities came about and where they may have originated. Atlantis remains a very plausible possibility, it is certainly ancient and civilized enough and would explain how such distant cultures show apparent similarities which according to orthodoxy should not exist.

Ancient writers referred to the tribes of north-western Africa near the Atlantic coast as *Atalantes*, *Atarantes*, and *Atlantioi* as 'remnants of Atlantean colonists or colonial populations'.[248] According to the Berber tribes of North Africa, their own legends describe a warlike kingdom off the African coast called *Attala*. Said to have sent gold, silver and tin to Africa, which they had in abundant mines, Attala also sent conquering armies onto African soil. Attala is now under the sea but will one day reappear according to prophecy.

The British Celts and the Welsh believed that their ancestors came from the lost paradisiacal island continent *Avalon* that sank into the Western Sea, a concept shared by both the ancient Gauls and the Irish.

The Basques in south-western France and northern Spain are thought to be a remnant of the earliest inhabitants of Western Europe, and Basque genes are understood to be unique, originating over 7000 years ago. The Basque language has long been considered to represent the culture which occupied Europe before the wide spread dissemination of Indo-European languages, and the Basques themselves believe they are the descendants of a lost island continent which they call *Atlaintika*.[249]

In Nahuatl, the language of the Aztecs, the mythical place of origin is *Aztlán*. Words or expressions spoken in Nahuatl can be interpreted in three different ways which include literal, syncretic and connotative meanings. Due to the plumage colour of herons, the connotative meaning of Aztlán is 'Place of Whiteness'. Mythical descriptions of Aztlán describe it as an island, or a land of paradise, and it is understood that eventually those who inhabited Aztlán became known as the Aztecs who then migrated from Aztlán to the Valley of Mexico.

In a letter to the King of Spain, the infamous Spanish conquistador Hernando Cortés recounted a conversation between Montezuma, the ninth ruler of Tenochtitlán, and himself atop the Temple of the Sun. Montezuma told Cortés about the island homeland of the Aztecs' ancestors, 'Our fathers dwelt in that happy and prosperous place they called Aztlán, which means whiteness.'[250]

In the *Codex Aubin*, a textual and pictorial history of the Aztecs starting from the migration from Aztlán through the Spanish conquest to the early colonization of the Spanish, the Aztecs fled Aztlán following a destructive flood and according to the legend, they were forbidden from using the name Azteca by the god Huitzilopochtli and instead would now be known as Mexica. This Aztec migration from Aztlán to Tenochtitlán remains a very important piece of Aztec history and was said to have begun on May 24, 1064, which became the first Aztec solar year.

What is of interest to us here is the place name Aztlán with its obvious similarities to Atlantis, but as we can see in the Aztec mythology of the 'Place of Whiteness', the migration didn't take place until 1064 which does not fit the chronology of Plato's submerged continent in the slightest. Is it not possible that the Aztec version of events is merely a distant recollection of a much more ancient story which was passed down to them over subsequent generations?

If Aztlán was the only derivative place name then maybe nothing more should be made of the matter, but the truth is that there exists a myriad more, in fact early explorers in Wisconsin discovered a fortified village near Lake Michigan which was called *Azatlán* by its inhabitants.[251]

A French abbé named Charles Étienne Brasseur de Bourbourg travelled to Guatemala and found the *Popol Vuh*, the sacred book of the Quiché Indians, which he translated into French and published in

1864. He also discovered a Mayan religious book known as the *Troano Codex* (or the *Madrid Codex* as it is currently housed at the Museo de América in Madrid) which is one of only three surviving pre-Columbian Maya books of Mesoamerican chronology, considered by the Spanish museum curators as the most important piece in their collection. It was originally owned by a descendant of Cortés, whose army defeated and destroyed the Aztec empire following his arrival in Mexico in March 1519.

Brasseur learned from a descendant of the Aztec King Montezuma that a great cataclysm is described in the *Codex* in the language of the Nahuatl tribe. The descriptions in the *Codex*, along with oral traditions told to Brasseur by natives he met, speak of the destruction of a great continent in the Atlantic Ocean which led him to speculate that the civilizations of both Egypt and South America had originated from Atlantis.

Brasseur suggested that Quetzalcoatl, the bearded white god who emerged from the sea, was an inhabitant of the lost Atlantis. In the *Chimalpopoca Codex*, another manuscript also written in Nahuatl, Brasseur first discovered that the catastrophe had occurred around 10,500 BC – but was not an isolated event, rather a series of at least four upheavals, each caused by a temporary shifting of the earth's axis.

One of the oldest Hindu Puranas called the Vishnu Purana speaks of a place called *Atala*, meaning 'The White Island'. Referred to as one of the seven Dwipas (islands), the ancient text places Atala in the 'seventh zone' which according to the translator Francis Wilford (1808) places the island in the same latitude as the Canary Islands off the coast of Africa.

The names *Sveta Dwipa* and *Saka Dwipa* are also used in the Puranas in the same way as Atala, and as described in the Sanskrit Dictionary (1974), Saka Dwipa means 'island of fair skinned people'. The Mahabharata (circa 600 BC) also refers to 'Atala, The White Island', which it describes as an 'island of great splendour', stating that 'the men that inhabit that island have complexions as white as the rays of the moon and they are devoted to Narayana . . . indeed, the denizens of White Island believe and worship only one god.'[252]

The similarities between Plato's Atlantis and the Indian Atala are not just in the name either, as Atala had a capital city called Tripura which consisted of three concentric circles, just as the capital of Atlantis was said to have been divided by concentric canals.

Book 12 of the Mahabharata, the Santi Parva, claims that Atala was inhabited by men who never sleep or eat, an interesting citation mirrored by the Greek historian Herodotus (450 BC) who describes a race of people called the *Atlantes* that 'are said to eat no living creature, and never to dream.'

The Atlantes are synonymous with another nation described by the later Greek historian Diodorus Siculus (8 BC) in his *Bibliotheca Historica*. The *Atlantioi*, were said to have been the 'most civilized men among the inhabitants of those regions', who inhabited 'the regions which lie along the shore of the ocean.' The Atlantioi lived on the western Saharan coast of Africa, most likely descendants of Atlantean survivors, and they 'dealt in a prosperous country and possessed great cities' among which 'mythology places the birth of the gods.'

The Mahabharata also describes a ten-year war which finally ended with the island of Atala and all its inhabitants sinking into the 'Western Ocean'. It is worth noting that the Atlantic Ocean was occasionally referred to as the 'Western Ocean' in ancient Egyptian, Greek, Sanskrit and even Latin sources. And more references to a white island in the Atlantic were mentioned in *Greek Religion* (1985) by Walter Burkert, who wrote that 'Achilles is transported to the White Isle, which may refer to Mount Teide on Tenerife, whose volcano is often snow-capped and as the island was sometimes called the white isle by explorers.'

If you recall, it was Aristotle, one of Plato's earliest detractors, who claimed that a large island in the Atlantic was known to the Carthaginians, and the Phoenicians also referred to a huge Atlantic island as *Antilia*. A chart/map produced by Paulo Toscanelli in 1474 shows Antilia as an island west of the Canaries in the mid-Atlantic, just south of the Azores. And in 1492, German mapmaker and navigator Martin Behaim devised the earliest extant terrestrial globe which he called the 'Nürnberg Terrestrial Globe', now known as the 'Erdapfel'.

Depicted on Behaim's globe is 'Insula Antilia Septa Citida' which translates as 'The Island of Antilia of the Seven Cities'. The legend of the Seven Cities is cited in numerous sources at slightly different locations ranging from the Azores to the West Indies.

An old manuscript called the *Oera Linda Book* was written in the West Germanic language Old Frisian, and purports to cover mythological, historical, and religious aspects of remote antiquity from 2194 BC to 803 AD. The manuscript included the history of the people of a large island called *Atland* that was destroyed by a terrible cataclysm of a cosmic scale:

'During the whole summer, the sun hid itself behind the clouds, as if unwilling to shine upon the earth. In the middle of the quietude, the earth began to quake as if it was dying. The mountains opened up to vomit forth fire and flames. Some of them sunk under the earth while in other places mountains rose out of the plains... Atland disappeared, and the wild waves rose so high over the hills and dales that everything was buried under the seas. Many people were swallowed up by the earth, and others who had escaped the fire perished in the waters.'

The place names mentioned above are not definitive evidence of the existence of Atlantis, but they do serve as historical data correlating the stories and myths from varied sources across the world. If such a place did exist, one would expect to find many name similarities dispersed far and wide, and we are certainly not lacking in this regard.

As Berlitz wrote, 'All of these similar names for an island continent or lost homeland do not constitute a determining proof that it once existed. They do, however, strongly indicate that Atlantis was not a literary device of Plato. These legends are of great antiquity and come from widely separated parts of the world that were not in communication with one another within the time we count as history.'

LOCATION HYPOTHESES

There are many suggested locations for the lost sunken continent ranging from South America to Santorini. As David Hatcher Childress commented, 'When it comes to questions regarding the actual physical location of the fabled lost civilization of Atlantis, the answers usually depend on with whom you are speaking. Everyone seems to have a favourite candidate for which a convincing case can be made. Whether in Antarctica or the Aegean, the Bahamas or the North Atlantic, intriguing clues are to be found everywhere, and sorting it all out can be confusing.'[253]

Atlantic Ocean

Taking Plato's account literally, a mid-Atlantic location beyond the Straits of Gibraltar would seem the most logical choice. The remnants of the fabled isle may possibly be revealed by the presence of the Azores and maybe the Canaries nearer mainland Spain, stretching across the sea to the Bahamas and even potentially Cuba.

According to author Charles Berlitz, it is still the current belief among the Portuguese that Atlantis (*Atlantida*) once existed near Portugal, and remnants of the fabled continent can be seen in the Azores Islands, whose presence is visible as only the peaks of the former land. This idea of the Azores being the remains of at least part of the Atlantic empire is not an isolated one:

'Deep under the ocean's waters Atlantis is now reposing and only its highest summits are still visible in the shape of the Azores. . . The great island rose in steep cliffs from the sea. . . Its cold and hot springs described by the ancient authors are still there as they flowed many millenniums ago. The mountain-lakes of Atlantis have been transformed now into submerged ones. . . If we follow exactly Plato's indications and seek the site of Poseidonis among the half submerged summits of the Azores, we will find it to the south of the Dollabarata. There, upon an eminence, in the middle of a large and comparatively straight valley, well protected from the winds, stood its splendid capital, the 'city of the golden gates.' . . . It is strange that the scientists have sought Atlantis everywhere, but have given the least attention to this spot, which after all was clearly indicated by Plato.'[254]

The hot springs mentioned by Plato could well prove to be those seen in the Vale da Furnas near São Miguel in the Azores.

In March 1974, the Russian vessel *Academician Petrovsky* underwent an expedition to examine the Ampere and Josephine Seamounts southwest of the Azores. These seamounts or underwater mountains rise from a depth of 10,000 feet or more to a summit which reaches several hundred feet below the surface. Underwater photographs taken during the expedition revealed a stone wall which included cut stone blocks scattered on both sides, which may represent evidence of buildings on the ocean floor in the precise area indicated by Plato as the location of Atlantis.

What appear to be artificial steps partially covered with lava were photographed on the flat summit of the Ampere Seamount, which led Soviet scientist Professor Aksyonov to proclaim, 'In my opinion these structures once stood on the surface.'

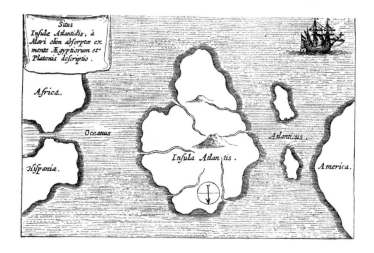

Fig. 76 The Athanasius Kircher map from 1665 (with South at the top) places Atlantis between Africa and America in the middle of the Atlantic Ocean.

Frank Joseph believes that this underwater region seems to fit Plato's description very well; 'Unlike any other site on Earth, the Horseshoe Seamounts fit the basic criteria for Atlantis set out in Plato's two dialogues: they compromise a ring of high mountains lying outside the Straits of Gibraltar; their foremost peak, Mount Ampere, stands to the south – the same position assumed by Mount Atlas. Mount Ampere stood above sea level as an island until it collapsed beneath the surface within the past 10,000 years. . . The bones of numerous elephants have been dredged up from the area, corroborating Plato's observation that these creatures inhabited the island of Atlantis.'[255]

Remarkably, a NOAA (National Oceanic and Atmospheric Administration) underwater image (fig. 77) has revealed the presence of what has been described as a canal system, measuring approximately 165 km east to west and 120 km north to south. This anomalous discovery is located to the east of the Madeira Abyssal Plain, 1,750 km west-southwest of the Strait of Gibraltar near the Canary Islands, 750 km south of the Azores, and 650 km nearly due west of Madeira.

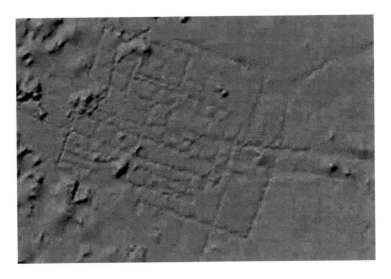

Fig. 77 An underwater anomaly on the sea floor photographed by the NOAA could be the canal system described by Plato in *Critias*.

This extraordinary find closely correlates with Plato's account of the Atlantis canal system in *Critias*; 'It was rectangular, and for the most part straight and oblong. . . It was excavated to the depth of a hundred feet, and its breadth was a stadium [equivalent to 185 metres] everywhere; it was carried around the whole of the plain, and was ten thousand stadia in length. . . The depth and width and length of this ditch were incredible and gave the impression that such a work, in addition to so many other works, could hardly have been wrought by the hand of man. It received streams which came down from the mountains, and winding round the plain, and touching the city at various points, was there left off into the sea. . . From above, likewise, straight canals of a hundred feet in width were cut into the plain, and again let off into the ditch toward the sea; these canals were at intervals of a hundred stadia, . . .cutting transverse passages from one canal into another, and to the city.'

The distance between the submerged canals seen in the image varies, but measurements taken of the span between two major east-west canals measures 15 km which equates to roughly 85 stadia (5.666 stadia equals 1 km). Thus, Plato's description of 100 stadia between the canals is very similar to what is lying on the sea floor in the Atlantic. And the overall length of the canal system, if laid end to end, is calculated to be 1,775 km, which translates to nearly 9,600 stadia – within 4% of Plato's description. It is highly likely that the highland region in the west, which is the eastern extent of the Mid-Atlantic ridge, was the source of the canals' water.

A faint outline of this anomalous rectangular shape can be seen by following the coordinates on Google Earth (24.4°W, 31.3°N), and to the right of this bizarre formation lies a straight line on the ocean floor which extends for thousands of miles before changing course and continuing for thousands more. What caused these immense marks remains inconclusive, but its close proximity to what could well prove to be the Atlantis canal system certainly suggests some kind of connection between the two.

This unexplained rectangular shape beneath the sea may be the kind of evidence we have been searching for all these years, the smoking gun of Atlantology perhaps? The location fits neatly with the Greek descriptions written over two millennia ago, and considering that whatever of wherever Atlantis once was; it *should* be deep below the sea today if we are to take Plato's tale into account. But some researchers have other ideas.

388 THE MYTH OF MAN

Santorini

In the Aegean, some distance from the Atlantic, Santorini continues to be touted as a possible location because of the Minoan Eruption (or Thera Eruption) of 1640 BC that 'wiped out the Minoan civilization on the north coast of Crete and deposited a layer of white pumice and ash nearly ten metres thick over the whole island group.'[256]

However, despite many attempting to jiggle Plato's words in a manner more befitting that particular scenario, the historical reality does not seem to correlate in any other fashion other than that a cataclysmic event destroyed an ancient civilization.

Despite the fact that Plato would have been aware the volcanic explosion as it occurred more than a millennium before he was born, evidence reveals that the eruption was not as sudden as the event which Plato spoke of, giving the inhabitants enough warning to completely evacuate the region prior to the final destruction, and of course the timeline does not match the 9600 BC date cited in *Timeaus*.

'However, the sequence of events and the eruption in Thera, as also documented by the excavations and differently from Plato's writings, exclude the theory of sudden cataclysm. In fact, in all houses brought to light in Akrotiri there are no human remains, no jewels, no precious objects, as if the inhabitants had had the time to gather their goods and run away. Tools and supplies of food were found in the basements of houses, perhaps in order to protect them from tremors: practice that suggests the habit of islanders to earthquakes.'[257]

Remarkably, the Minoan city of Akrotiri, which is the only archaeological site still standing on the island, shows signs of extreme sophistication for such an ancient complex built in the Bronze Age. With open streets, three-storey buildings, modern looking windows, and earthquake resistant structures in place, Akrotiri reveals a modern style of housing construction thousands of years ahead of its time. They even had flush toilets, sewer systems, aqueducts and plumbing, all dating back to a staggering 3600 years ago, so it is no surprise that Atlantis continue to be associated with such an advanced culture that disappeared in a heartbeat.

Much of the tourist literature in Greece continues to suggest that Atlantis was destroyed at the same time as Crete following the volcanic eruption of the Aegean island, despite the implausibility of the region being the true location of Atlantis which Plato describes as being in the west, whilst Santorini lies in the east. And let us not forget that he never mentions a volcanic eruption whatsoever.

Malta

Malta is a fascinating possibility as a site for the lost civilization. With over fifty ancient free standing structures and temples, along with the mysterious fossilised cart ruts, some of which seem to lead straight into the sea, it is clear that what is now a small island was once much larger and attached to the mainland. Marine scientists at the University of Malta discovered in 2013 that the Maltese islands were connected to Sicily via a land bridge 20,000 years ago.

Malta's oldest prehistoric site is the Ghar Dalam cave, whose discovery was the key to understanding Malta's history by decoding the stratigraphy of the site. The lowest strata was dated at over half a million years old during the Pleistocene and contained fossilised remains of dwarf elephants and hippopotami among other species. Some theorists advocating the 'Malta as Atlantis' theory may suggest that the existence of elephants on Malta corroborates with Plato's version of events, but once again, the timeline here refutes any correlation. The top layer inside Ghar Dalam referred to as the 'cultural layer' holds evidence of the first human habitation of Malta dated to around 5400 BC, again this is thousands of years later than the 9600 BC date given for the destruction of the land in Plato's dialogues.

An underwater site on a plateau approximately 2 km off the coast of St Julian's in Malta, was discovered on July 13, 1999 by brothers Shaun and Kurt Arrigo working for retired German real estate investor Hubert Zeitlmair. 19 metres below sea level, the underwater plateau is 900 x 500 metres and contains large boulders which Zeitlmair considers to have been manufactured as opposed to being natural formations.

The site which is now referred to as 'Gebel gol-Banar' which means 'Stones in the Sea' in Maltese, consists of a cluster of three stone circles

390 THE MYTH OF MAN

with 'rooms' measuring a diameter of 9-11 metres, with some sections reaching between 6 and 10 metres in height. With an 'avenue' leading up to the structure's east facing entrance, and more tracks resembling cart ruts around the site, it is most likely a prehistoric megalithic temple.[2] The idea of an Atlantis/Malta connection is not a new one either, as in 1854, Maltese architect Giorgio Grongnet de Vasse had already proposed that the Maltese Islands, or more specifically the Gulf of Gabes off the Tunisian coast, could be the remnants of the fabled land.

Sardinia

Sardinia lies a stone's throw away from the Strait of Messina that separates Italy from Sicily, which some researchers have suggested could have represented the 'Pillars of Heracles' in ancient times before the Straits of Gibraltar. 3,500 years ago an ancient civilization thrived on the island of Sardinia, and thousands of ruins remain as testament to this once great culture.

American Robert Ishoy, from the Society for Historical Exploration, has studied the Sardinian ruins for decades and believes that they could prove to be remnants of the lost continent. Discussing the ruins at Nuraghe Losa he said, "This culture here on Sardinia, matches everything Plato describes about Atlantis. He talked about the culture being a very advanced culture, look at the architecture, this is very advanced technique. The circular aspects of the buildings, Plato said everything was round . . . and they built pillars."[258]

Well, Sardinia certainly has plenty of pillars or stone towers on view, but what else could correlate with the Greek written accounts? Regarding the flood and earthquakes as mentioned in the Greek texts, Sardinia has had its fair share of flooding, and just off the coastline of Nora, on the southern end of the country lays a major fault.

---

[2] Zeitlmair was so convinced of Malta's association with Atlantis that he dedicated an entire book to the subject called *Die Säulen von Atlantis - Malta: Handschrift einer verschwundenen Hochkultur* (The pillars of Atlantis - Malta: Manuscript of a vanished high culture).

Plato describes three different coloured rocks which were quarried from underneath the centre island, 'one kind was white, another black, and a third red', and also hot and cold springs, all of which are found across Sardinia. The largest complex found on Sardinia is Su Nuraxi (fig. 78) in the Italian municipality of Brumini. The oldest part of this archaeological site consists of five towers; a large central tower surrounded by four smaller outer towers which match the compass of north, east, south and west, all built from blocks of basalt between the 1700-1300 BC. Despite its considerable height, Su Nuraxi was only fully excavated between 1950 and 1957 under the direction of Giovanni Lilliu, as it was completely concealed beneath a layer of mud. Its round 'Nuraghes' or towers are certainly reminiscent of the Atlantean archetypes described in Plato's work.

Fig. 78 Su Nuraxi in Sardinia was inhabited by the Nuragic civilization nearly 4,000 years ago.

And right at the heart of Sardinia lies Santuario Nuragico di Santa Vittoria, an ancient temple site which was surrounded by a moat in ancient times, dedicated to a water deity, located high on a hill and overlooking the open plains below; suitably matching Plato's temple of Poseidon 'which was situated in the middle of the island'.

All of the evidence available on Sardinia is enough to convince Robert Ishoy that this location matches the lost world of antiquity: "If you give the description given by Plato, of all the different things about Atlantis; the geography, the island itself, the civilization, there is no other place on this earth that fits it better than Sardinia."[259]

This hypothesis certainly remains a possibility, but one of a number of problems when considering Sardinia is that the Nuragic civilization which arose during the Bronze Age around 1800 BC came about almost as a consequence of the Santorini eruption which had already devastated Crete centuries earlier. Once again, the timeline doesn't fit well, and let us not ignore the fact that Atlantis is said to have been submerged beneath the waves, and therefore should not still remain standing on high ground. Maybe Santorini's inhabitants were inspired by tales of Atlantis and imitated the lost culture by incorporating some of the Atlantean designs into their own constructions.

Spain

A massive 5000 year old site, one kilometre in diameter, lies buried beneath more modern constructions at Jaen in Southern Spain. This Copper Age settlement which was once inhabited by 40,000 people also shares similarities with the buildings described in Plato's story.

The architecture includes concentric circles, with canals and individual circular homes, and over 60,000 artefacts were unearthed during excavation work. The city grew from a central point, expanding outwards in a series of concentric circles with moats and linked walls, leading some archaeologists to believe that the construction methods employed at this particular site mirror those described in the *Timeaus*.

The Motilla del Azuer (fig. 79) site in the central area of the Iberian Peninsula may be far too inland to be considered a true possibility for the drowned world of Atlantis but it has some incredible ancient structures that are remarkably similar to the nuraghes on Sardinia. Found throughout the plain of La Mancha, these artificial mounds known as 'motillas' which rise to 4-10 metres high and tend to be situated less than 5 km from one another; date to between 2200 and 1500 BC. Here lies the oldest well ever found in the Iberian Peninsula:

"Recent studies show that the 'motilla' sites from the Bronze Age in La Mancha may be the most ancient system of groundwater collection in the Iberian Peninsula"[260]

Fig. 79 The Motilla del Azuer in Spain is reminiscent of the nuraghes in Sardinia. Did a common source influence both these cultures?

In Andalusia, southern Spain, another area of interest to those seeking Atlantis is the nature reserve Doñana National Park, due to its strategic location between the continents of Europe and Africa and its proximity to the Pillars of Hercules. Nowadays the region is all marshland but it used to be an open bay situated adjacent to the Strait of Gibraltar.

About 50 km north of the city of Cadiz, satellite photos of the salt marshland Marisma de Hinojos have revealed two rectangular structures beneath the mud and sections of concentric rings that could have once surrounded them. Dr Rainier Kuehne told *BBC News Online*, "Plato wrote of an island of five stades [in] diameter that was surrounded by several circular structures – concentric rings – some consisting of earth and the others of water. We have in the photos concentric rings just as Plato described."

In fact it was lecturer and Atlantis enthusiast Werner Wickboldt who first noticed the formations in the images, leading him to believe that they could represent the ruins of the forgotten land; "This is the only place that seems to fit [Plato's] description."

But Tony Wilkinson, an expert in remote sensing in archaeology, warned against reaching premature conclusions, "We use the imagery to recognise certain types of imprint on the ground and then do [in the field] verification on them. Based on what we see on the ground we make an interpretation. What we need here is a date range. Otherwise, you're just dealing with morphology. But the [features] are interesting."[261]

But Kuehne's theory isn't based solely on the satellite images, "Plato also wrote that Atlantis is rich in copper and other metals. Copper is found in abundance in the mines of the Sierra Morena," explained Dr Kuehne.

Interestingly, a mud shoal in the Strait of Gibraltar called Spartel Island, sank into the sea approximately 12,000 years ago believed to have been caused by the rising ocean levels, and in 2001 Jacques Collina-Girard, a French geologist, discovered that it was not a coral reef as had been previously proposed but the remains of a large submerged island.

Not far from Spartel Island, six stone anchors were discovered by divers during the filming of the documentary *Atlantis Rising*. Such rare discoveries reveal that large ships were stopping off in the area thousands of years ago, suggesting that an ancient port existed near the Pillars of Hercules at the entrance to the Atlantic Ocean, right where Plato insisted was the gateway to the lost continent.

Discussing one of the marine artefacts, Professor Richard Freund of the University of Hartford said, "It's a really amazing find. This anchor you can get very excited about. This is a 3,000, 4,000-year old anchor that is massive for a very large boat, which shows us that ancient large boats were sailing into this area 4,000 years ago,"[262]

Presenter Simcha Jacobovici concurred saying, "These anchors could be 3,500 to 4,000 years old and establish a harbour in the Atlantic, where I didn't even dare dream to find anchors. If we found six on a few dives, there must be thousands out there, confirming Plato's report of a port just past the Pillars of Hercules."

So it is possible that traces of Atlantis may be discovered around the south of Spain, and certainly some of the ancient construction methods already found do appear to correlate reasonably with Platonic accounts. Maybe we are seeing traces of the forgotten civilization, whose survivors and descendants dispersed further and further east into the Mediterranean. Maybe the true location will continue to evade us, should the ancient account be factual in the first place. "Southern Spain may have been the centre of a civilization which spread to Malta, Santorini or all the other places we have investigated," said Jacobovici.

Antarctica

Perhaps the most intriguing site to have been cited as a possible Atlantis location is today concealed beneath thick ice and remains the world's least explored or inhabited continent – Antarctica.

'It is to icy Antarctica that we look to find answers to the very roots of civilization – answers which may yet be preserved in the frozen depths of the forgotten island continent.'[263]

Antarctica as Atlantis was originally suggested by Professor Charles Hapgood in the 1950s, and originated following his extensive work on the anomalous ancient maps which we discussed at the end of the previous chapter. Realising that an ice-free Antarctica had once been surveyed and mapped in the distant past, Hapgood began to consider the possibility that this isolated continent may well be concealing traces of a lost civilization beneath its frozen exterior.

Another reason for his hypothesis stems from the fact that his research revealed that the desolate Antarctic wasteland was once in a far more temperate zone and only reached its present geographical position due to crustal displacement, a theory which posits the Earth's entire crust shifted like the orange peel might move over the orange if sufficiently loose.

In his 1958 book *The Earth's Shifting Crust*, Hapgood speculated that the Earth's rotational balance was disrupted by the accumulation of ice at the poles which destabilized the outer crust and led to its slippage. He proposed that around 9,600 BC, a 15° pole shift occurred which led to great cataclysms taking place that wiped out the vast majority of animal species in North America at the end of the Last Glacial Maximum, highlighted by the quick demise of the mammoths who were found in their thousands frozen in Siberia, with their stomach contents of buttercups and other temperate zone flora still undigested.

Librarians Rand and Rose Flem-Ath took Hapgood's findings even further in *When The Sky Fell*, and presented a plethora of reasons to believe the 'Antarctica as Atlantis' theory.

'We believe that the account given in Plato's Timaeus is an accurate southern hemisphere 'global' view of the earth as it did in fact appear 12,000 years ago. Further, we believe that the previous Temperate Zone of Antarctica was capable of supporting human settlements prior to the earth crust displacement. We believe that the lost continent of Atlantis was our generally ignored lost island continent of Antarctica. In addition, we believe that Atlantis was an advanced civilization (possibly a world culture) which possessed an accurate advanced geographic view of the total planet.'[264]

The Flem-Aths highlight the fact that at 6,500 feet, Antarctica is the highest continent in the world, a fact which is in keeping with Solon's account, as recounted by Plato, 'To begin with the whole region as a whole was said to be high above the level of the sea, from which it rose precipitously . . . [and the mountains] were celebrated as being more numerous, higher and more beautiful than any that exist today.'[265]

The following description of the geology of Antarctica comes from *Whitaker's Almanack* (1992): 'The most conspicuous physical features of the continent are its high inland plateau (much of it over 10,000 ft.), the Transantarctic Mountains . . . and the mountainous Antarctic Peninsula and off-lying islands. The continental shelf averages 20 miles in width (half the global mean, and in places it is non-existent) . . .'[266]

The Antarctica hypothesis is as problematic as it is possible. The sheer fact that it remains the least explored of the world's continents, and the immense amount of ice which dominates the frozen landscape could well be concealing evidence of a former civilization make it a fascinating supposition, but many details recorded in ancient myths do not correlate with the geological position of the giant landmass.

When the Egyptians speak of their civilizers coming from the west, whilst the Mesoamericans claim that they came from the east, where does Antarctica fit in to those descriptions? And more poignantly, how can Antarctica be the site of Atlantis which was swallowed by the sea, if the southern continent is still very much above sea level?

The Flem-Aths suggest that 'the present shape of Antarctica as depicted is based upon the current ocean level, not that of 11,600 years ago. Atlantis did not actually sink beneath the waves. Instead, as the old ice caps melted, the ocean level rose, covering some of the continent's permutations.'[267]

One might say that such an explanation remains a feasible, albeit not altogether convincing argument, yet the most interesting connection however must be the references to the colour of the island which the ancient Indians described as Atala, the 'White Island' and the Aztecs called Aztlán the 'Place of Whiteness'. If white was associated with the actual colour of the landscape and not the race of men inhabiting the continent, then a snow covered land would make sense were it not for the fact that no mention of snow was ever mentioned in ancient texts, and also the premise that Antarctica was once free of ice as it was in a much more temperate zone thousands of years in the past.

Still, the authors of *When The Sky Fell* continue to believe that the most southerly land on Earth could prove to be the missing continent: 'Antarctica sits, like the mythological homeland of the Okanagan, in the "middle of the ocean". Like the Aztec's "Aztlán", Antarctica is "white". Like Iran's lost paradise, Antarctica is covered "with a thick sheet of ice". And like the "first land" of Japanese mythology, it is close to one of the earth's poles. This last-explored continent may well have been the lost island paradise of world mythology.'[268]

References to a frozen lost continent can be found in both India and Iran. Bal Gangadhar Tilak, the first leader of the Indian Independence Movement, a man imprisoned in Bombay in 1897 for 'seditious writings', retired to the mountains upon his release and in 1903 wrote his great work, *The Arctic Home in the Vedas*. In his book, Tilak speculated that beneath the Arctic Ocean could be found the remains of an island paradise which he argues became a frozen wasteland, 'It was the advent of the Ice Age that destroyed the mild climate of the original home and covered it into an ice-bound land unfit for habitation.'

Here Tilak also summarized a key passage in the *Zend-Avesta*, the oldest saga in Iran, 'Ahura Mazda warns Yima, the first king of men, of the approach of a dire winter, which is to destroy every living creature by covering the land with a thick sheet of ice, and advises Yima to build a Vara, or an enclosure, to preserve the seeds of every kind of animal and plant. The meeting is said to have taken place in the Airyana Vaêjo, or Paradise of the Iranians.'

The Iranian tale is strangely reminiscent of the Biblical story of Noah and the Ark, replacing the boat with a Vara in order to preserve all life, but does this 'dire winter' have any associations with the cataclysm responsible for the demise of a once great civilization?

With so many location hypotheses being bandied around by an ever growing number of Atlantis enthusiasts, it can be troublesome dredging up any true facts which may help us in our quest to gain some clarity on the matter. The simple truth is, nobody really knows a great deal about Atlantis or its possible whereabouts. Hence, it remains both a myth and a mystery.

What it is reasonable to declare however, is that the sheer volume of information which somehow or other relates to a lost pre-Ice Age civilization, whether in the form of ancient texts, poems or mythology, or perhaps the anomalous artefacts, underwater ruins and the unexplained physical remnants of past cultures remaining on land, do offer us a tantalising glimpse of a forgotten episode in our distant past. Whether or not there once existed a land precisely matching Plato's description remains to be seen, but it certainly appears from all of the evidence so far covered in this book, that civilization did not begin when orthodox historians claim it did.

Ancient Egypt was a legacy from an earlier epoch which they refer to as Zep Tepi. The knowledge and sophistication inherent in the construction of Göbekli Tepe was transferred to them from their ancestors, who in turn received it from theirs.

The world as we see it today is not the result of a gradual linear development which is currently peaking in modern times. It is a far different world from the one which once existed before most of mankind and the animal kingdom were wiped clean from the face of the earth by a cataclysmic force so terrifying it has being erased from the human collective consciousness.

This forgotten memory remains only in whispers, traces of its destruction are only today being recognised, and the myriad of stone ruins that lay unseen below today's high sea level are testament to the fact that the world was once a very different place. What extinction level event could be so immense and powerful that it erased our land, animals, civilization, and much of mankind from our planet and our memory? There can only be one culprit – the Great Flood of antiquity.

Chapter Eight

THE WORLDWIDE FLOOD

Deluge myths are universal around the world, and the mythologies of widely separated peoples tell, over and over again, variations of the same story of global cataclysm.

John Anthony West

I F AT SOME TIME IN THE REMOTE PAST we actually reached high levels of civilization and technology, could some cataclysmic global event be responsible for the demise of our ancestral heritage, therefore validating the 'Great Flood' stories which appear throughout world mythology and folklore?

The Great Flood myth which is encapsulated in the biblical story of Noah's Ark, has its roots in antiquity, but remains consistent enough throughout the many different versions across the world to warrant further investigation, as 'the myth of the destruction of mankind by a flood is to be found in some form or other in every part of the world.'[269]

Incredibly, more than 500 deluge myth legends are known around the world, and in a survey of 86 of these stories undertaken by specialist researcher Dr Richard Andree, 62 of them were entirely independent of the oldest flood myths ever discovered which originated from Mesopotamian and Hebrew accounts.

Today, it is the common consensus that mass flooding caused by the melting of glacial ice is responsible for the *gradual* rising of ocean levels, and evidence of such inundations can be seen around the globe with the submergence of coastal regions. We know Britain wasn't always an island, Siberia was attached to Alaska via the Bering Land Bridge, and countless other countries have witnessed the shrinking of their landmass as the waters have risen higher than the coastline.

But, this current paradigm does not include the existence of a worldwide flood in antiquity. In fact, the process by which the flooding occurred according to orthodoxy took thousands of years as a series of more localized floods, rather than a sudden, devastating 'megaflood' which befits the flood mythologies shared around the world.

This notion of gradually melting glaciers and icecaps only originated as recently as two hundred years ago when geologists determined that there never had been a worldwide flood. The origin of this scientific paradigm dates back to the 19th century when scientists set out to prove whether there was any truth to the flood myths which permeate so many cultures worldwide.

As they travelled to various parts of Europe, the geologists discovered that the sediments carried by floodwaters, known as diluvial deposits, were the result of multiple events in the distant past. We are told that the many erratics (out of place boulders) scattered across the landscape were all transported by moving glaciers as opposed to a mass inundation of water, and also the absence of a common event in the diluvial records was enough to prove that there had never been one single worldwide flood.

Among the key figures influencing the whole debate was the Reverend Adam Sedgwick, a former president of the Geological Society of London and Professor at Cambridge University. Once a believer in a single flood, Sedgwick chose to recant his belief during his farewell presidential address at the society's meeting in 1831:

'The vast masses of diluvial gravel . . . do not belong to one violent and transitory period. It was indeed a most unwarranted conclusion when we assumed the contemporaneity of all the superficial gravel on earth. . . Having been myself a believer [in a worldwide flood], and, to the best of my power, a propagator of what I now regard as a philosophic heresy . . . I think it right . . . thus publicly to read my recantation.'

By only looking on land for signs of a single flood mechanism capable of reaching far and wide to affect the many regions that reported the cataclysmic events in their own mythology, the early geologists were missing vital evidence which is available to us today. Affected by the common assumption that all of the water present on earth today has always been there, they failed to consider the possibility that 'now-submerged landscapes were at one time exposed but were later inundated as a result of some unknown event.'[270] As author Michael Jaye rightly points out, 'the early geologists' precise conclusion from the evidence should have been that a worldwide flood did not inundate *presently* exposed landscapes.'[271]

Because of this simplistic conclusion based on scant evidence and even less research, science remains blinded by outdated concepts of our planets' geological past, and the incorrect conclusion made over two hundred years ago was so widely accepted that it has become entrenched in the scientific paradigm of our time and remains a fundamental belief today which continues to hinder our present understanding of human history.

'Culturally independent, ubiquitous accounts of a worldwide flood that have been discounted or dismissed due to geology's fundamental error are instead factual, corroborating accounts by survivors.'[272]

GLOBAL FLOOD MYTHS

When considering stories of a great flood in ancient times most of us will immediately think of Noah's Ark, as it is by far the most well-known flood story in the world and is often taught to children from an early age. Its inclusion in the Old Testament does not lend any credence to the story, especially for those without religious inclinations and therefore is widely believed to be a myth, a story of morality and consequence perhaps, but not an accurate record of a real cataclysmic event.

Undoubtedly, many people will assume that all other versions of the flood myth must have derived from the biblical tale; however this is simply not the case. The Hebrew story of Noah comes from the Book of Genesis in the Old Testament but the date for the story's origin remains unknown and continues to be debated. What we do know is that the oldest piece of epic literature in the world, which predates the writings of Homer by 1500 years, is the great Sumerian/Babylonian poetic work *The Epic of Gilgamesh* which was written sometime between 2150 and 1400 BC.

This may be the oldest flood myth ever retrieved but it is by no means an isolated story, as references to a cataclysmic flood occur in 230 different cultures worldwide. It is certainly possible that each flood myth was influenced by the one which preceded it, the similarities between many of the accounts would warrant such a conclusion, but the distances separating some of the cultures around the world harbouring such myths suggests a lack of contact between many of the tales, therefore negating the possibility of outside influences.

"Myths are largely event-based, in that they are triggered to a large part by an event, or combination of events, that catastrophically impact society," said environmental archaeologist Bruce Masse. "Then these myths provide a window upon those events that can be recovered, retrieved and even dated."

Before we begin our search for evidence of the existence of a worldwide flood, let us briefly revisit some of the flood stories which have survived centuries and even millennia to reach us in modern times. The sheer number and consistency of these tales from around the globe may prove to be more than just creation myths and shared folk tales to tell the grandchildren. They may have been written to memorialise the greatest geological catastrophe that mankind has ever had to endure, and the survivors who lived to tell the tale could be, as so many contend, the progenitors of civilization as we understand it today.

As we shall see, the chronology of the various Mesopotamian flood myths can be difficult to ascertain as it appears that variations of the tale with different heroes, villains and gods all recount the same story which must have derived from the original tale dating back thousands of years, long before the Hebrews conceived the Old Testament.

The Epic of Gilgamesh

Originating from the ancient civilizations of Mesopotamia and dating back over 4,000 years, the Babylonian legend of the deluge was included in the *Gilgamesh Epic* found on an ancient clay tablet known today as Tablet XI. Written in cuneiform script in the form of an epic poem called *The Epic of Gilgamesh*, the Babylonian version of the flood is believed by some scholars to have been added to Tablet XI by an editor who borrowed the tale from the earlier *Epic of Atrahasis*.

'The story itself 'evolved' so to speak. The earliest copies of *Gilgamesh* are Sumerian and may be as old as the third millennium BC. Also, the earliest versions of this epic did not even include a flood story. That was added toward the end of the second millennium and was deliberately adopted from *Atrahasis*.'[273]

The actual tablets date back to around 650 BC but we know that they are not originals, since fragments of the flood story have been found on much older tablets leading experts to date the actual text itself to around 2100 BC. The poem described as the oldest known complete story ever found was only discovered by Assyriologist Hormuzd Rassam in 1853 in the ruins of the great library at Nineveh, and is considered by scholars today to be a foundational text in world literature.

The tale preserved on twelve tablets essentially follows the story of Gilgamesh, the mythological hero-king of Uruk, and his friend Enkidu, as they undertake a series of adventures and dangerous quests, and following the death of Enkidu, Gilgamesh searches for the secret of immortality and goes on a journey to find his relative Utnapishtim (meaning 'he found life').

The story recounts how the great sage Utnapishtim builds a vast circular-shaped boat called 'Preserver of Life'. Reinforced with tar and pitch it carries his relatives, grains and animals after having been forewarned of an imminent flood which the wrathful gods lead by Enlil, were about to unleash.

It was the god Ea who warned Utnapishtim about the coming flood and told him to build a large boat and load it with supplies and animals, and just like the Noah legend, this boat also survived the flood and finally came to rest on a mountain before the waters eventually receded and humanity could begin again. Utnapishtim also sent out a dove to seek dry land before attempting to leave the safety of the boat. Other correlations between the Hebrew and Babylonian versions can be seen in the extracts below taken from *The Epic of Gilgamesh*:

'The time was fulfilled, the evening came, the rider of the storm sent down the rain. I looked out at the weather and it was terrible, so I too boarded the boat and battened her down.

Then the gods of the abyss rose up; Nergal pulled out the dams of the nether waters, Ninurta the war-lord threw down the dykes, and the seven judges of hell, the Annunaki, raised their torches, lighting the land with their livid flame. A stupor of despair went up to heaven when the god of the storm turned daylight to darkness, when he smashed the land like a cup.

Even the gods were terrified at the flood, they fled to the highest heaven, the firmament of Anu; they crouched against the walls, cowering like curs. Then Ishtar the sweet-voiced Queen of Heaven cried out like a woman in travail: "Alas the days of old are turned to dust because I commanded evil; why did I command thus evil in the council of all the gods? I commanded wars to destroy the people, but are they not my people, for I brought them forth? Now like the spawn of fish they float in the ocean."'

For six days and six nights the winds blew, torrent and tempest and flood overwhelmed the world, tempest and flood raged together like warring hosts. When the seventh day dawned the storm from the south subsided, the sea grew calm, the flood was stilled; I looked at the face of the world and there was silence, all mankind was turned to clay. The surface of the sea stretched as flat as a roof-top; I opened a hatch and the light fell on my face. Then I bowed low, I sat down and I wept, the tears streamed down my face for, on every side was the waste of water.'[274]

The Eridu Genesis

The Eridu Genesis was discovered on an ancient Sumerian tablet from Nippur which describes 'the oldest account of the Great Flood and the creation of both humans and animals on our planet and records the names of Antediluvian cities on earth and their respective rulers'.

The Eridu Genesis contains the Sumerian creation myth which covers the creation of the world, invention of cities and the flood, and is dated by its script to a period during the Old Babylonian Empire, around 1600 BC. Published in 1914 by Arno Poebel, the text tells the story of King Ziusudra or (Zin-Suddu) of Shuruppak (modern day Tell Fara in Iraq) who is listed as the last king of Sumer prior to the deluge in the WB 62[3] Sumerian King List. He is subsequently recorded as the hero of the Sumerian flood epic.

The line following Ziusudra in WB 62 reads, 'Then the flood swept over' followed by 'after the flood swept over, kingship descended from heaven; the kingship was in Kish.' Soon after an archaeologically attested river flood in Shuruppak, which has been radiocarbon dated to around 2900 BC,[275] the city of Kish (among other Sumerian cities) began to flourish.

The timeline reflected in this particular area of archaeological research does not match the worldwide flood scenario, which as we shall discuss further in the chapter appears to coincide with the end of the last Ice Age, but it does legitimise this ancient account as recorded factual content rather than just a mythical tale.

After a missing section in the tablet, we learn that just like many other flood myths, the gods decided to send a flood to destroy mankind.

---

[3] WB 62 is a small clay tablet that is part of the 'Weld-Blundell Collection', donated by Herbert Weld Blundell to the Ashmolean Museum. Discovered in Larsa, dating to around 2000 BC, it is the oldest source containing the Sumerian King List.

The water-god Enki (the Sumerian equivalent of the Babylonian god Ea) warns Ziusudra, a pious, god-fearing, humble king and ruler of Shuruppak, to build a very large boat. The long passage giving the details of the construction of the boat is destroyed, and the next section of legible text resumes in the midst of describing the flood:

'All the windstorms, exceedingly powerful, attacked as one, the deluge raged over the surface of the earth.
After, for 7 days and 7 nights,
The deluge had raged in the land,
And the huge boat had been tossed about on the great waters,
Uttu (sun-god) came forth, who sheds light on heaven and earth.
Ziusudra opened a window of the huge boat,
Ziusudra, the king,
Before Uttu prostrated himself,
The king kills an ox, slaughters a sheep.'

The Atrahasis Epic

Centred in the city of Akkad (modern day Iraq), the Akkadian Empire (c.2334-2154 BC) was the first ancient Semitic-speaking empire of Mesopotamia. During the first millennium BC, Akkad was used as a name not only for the northern half of Babylonia, but also for Sumer.

The Akkadian version of the flood is the fullest account found in ancient Mesopotamian literature and the text is known from several versions; two were written by Assyrian scribes (one in the Assyrian, the other in the Babylonian dialect), a third version was written on three tablets during the reign of King Ammi-Saduqa of Babylonia (1647-1626 BCE) and as we have already covered, parts are quoted in Tablet XI of the *Epic of Gilgamesh*.

The Babyloniaca by the Babylonian writer Berossus which was written in three books sometime around 290–278 BC, also contains a mixture of references to various Mesopotamian flood myths. Berossus claimed he was making available to Greek readers books preserved at Babylon containing 'the histories of heaven (and of earth) and sea and the first birth and the kings and their deeds', according to the preface of his book.

'Cronus appeared to Xisouthros in a dream and revealed that on the fifteenth day of the month Daisios (May) mankind would be destroyed by a flood. Therefore, he ordered Xisouthros to bury the beginnings and the middles and the ends of all writings in Sippar, the City of the Sun.

[On the third day] after the flood had come and swiftly receded, Xisouthros released some of the birds [to determine if they might see somewhere land which had arisen from the waters. But finding neither food nor a place on which to alight, the birds returned to the ship. After a few days Xisouthros again released the birds and these again returned to the ship but with their feet covered with mud. On being released a third time, they did not again return to the ship. Xisouthros understood that land had reappeared.'[276]

In the Akkadian *Atrahasis Epic*, it is the god Enki once again who warns the hero Atrahasis (meaning 'extremely wise') to escape the flood, by building a boat following the decision of the god Enlil to cull the population in an attempt to reduce the numbers. So, just as with the other versions of the account, he built the boat, took on board the animals along with his family, sealed the door and eventually survived the flood after seven days had passed.

'The flood came out.
No one could see anyone else.
They could not be recognized in the catastrophe.
The flood roared like a bull.
Like a wild ass screaming, the winds howled.
The darkness was total, there was no sun.'[277]

The Zoroastrian Flood
Approximately 3500 years ago, Zoroastrianism was founded by the prophet Zoroaster (or Zarathustra) in ancient Iran. Dated to around 1323 CE, the sacred book of Zoroastrianism which contains the

teachings of Zarathustra and the cosmogony, law, and liturgy of the religion is called the *Avesta* or *Zend Avesta*. In the opening section of the *Zend Avesta*, known as the *Vendidad*, the verses speak of a primordial father figure called Yima, who is the first man, the first king and the founder of civilization.

The first chapter is a dualistic creation myth, followed by the description of a destructive winter comparable with the great floods of various other mythologies. Some claim this 'destructive winter' or 'evil winter' is a reference to the last glacial period which ended around 15,000 years ago.

Upon realising that the world had become overwhelmed by the constant multiplication of its immortal beings, and following a meeting of gods and men called by Ahura Mazda, the creator god of Zoroastrianism, and the king Yima, it was decided that the population of the earth must be reduced. To achieve this, a series of severe winters must take place, with one particularly harsh one which would be followed by flooding once the snow had melted.

With the imminent approach of the dire winter which would destroy every living creature, Yima was advised to build a Vara, a kind of underground fortress, in order to 'keep there the finest representatives of every kind of animals and plants' alive during the winter. As written in the *Zend Avesta*:

'And the beasts that live in the wilderness, and those that live on the tops of the mountains, and those that live in the bosom of the dale shall take shelter in underground abodes.

Before that winter, the country would bear plenty of grass for cattle, before the waters had flooded it. Now after the melting of the snow, O Yima, a place wherein the footprint of a sheep may be seen will be a wonder of the world.'[278]

'He brought the seeds of men and women. . . There he brought the seeds of every kind of tree [and] . . . every kind of fruit . . . All those seeds he brought, two of every kind, to be kept inexhaustible there, so long as those men shall stay in the Vara. . .'[279]

All was destroyed except for Yima's Vara and its inhabitants, and only when Yima opened his doors once the flood had subsided was the world inhabited again. The Ark in the Hebrew version is replaced here by an underground shelter, but the underlying theme of survival from a cataclysmic event remains the same. Is this simply a myth or does it have historically grounded roots? Graham Hancock leans towards the story having truthful origins:

'The Zoroastrian texts leave us in no doubt that these conditions posed a deadly threat to the future survival of civilization. It was for this reason that Ahura Mazda came to Yima with his warning and his instruction to build an underground shelter where some remnant of humanity could take refuge, keeping safe the seeds of all animals and plants, until the thousand-year winter had passed and spring returned to the world. Moreover the account reveals very little that seems 'mythical' or that obviously derives from flights of religious fancy. Rather the whole thing has about it an atmosphere of hard-headed practical planning that adds a chilling note of veracity.'[280]

Manu and the Fish

Hindu mythology from India contains one of the oldest and most interesting flood accounts ever recorded. Like the Mesopotamian flood stories, the Hindu flood myth can be traced to several different sources. The earliest account is believed to have been written in the Vedic *Satapatha Brahmana*, with later accounts found in the *Mahabharata* as well as in the *Puranas*, which include the *Bhagavata Purana* and the *Matsya Purana*. Each of the accounts include Manu Vaivasvata as the main character of the flood story who, like Noah, is described as a virtuous individual. As written in the *Satapatha Brahmana*, 'There lived in ancient times a holy man . . . called Manu, who, by penances and prayers . . . had won the favour of the lord of heaven.'

The story goes that whilst performing ablutions with river water, a small fish came into his hands and spoke to Manu, asking him to save its life. He kept the fish in a jar of water until the fish outgrew it and had to be thrown back into the Ganges River before heading to the sea. The fish then revealed itself as Matsya, the fish incarnation of Lord Vishnu as written in the *Puranas* (in the *Mahabharata* the fish is identified with the god Brahma).

Vishnu predicted that a huge flood lasting seven days would end the world and requested Manu to build a huge boat and take seven sages, four worlds, the seeds of all plants and one animal of each type.

'Then he warned Manu of a coming deluge. He sent him a large ship, with orders to load it with two of every living species and the seeds of every plant, and then to go on board himself.'[281]

Manu was told that Vishnu would appear again as a fish to propel the boat to Mt. Himavan to survive the flood and to take them to the next Yuga (the Indian name for an Age).

The Lord appeared after seven days and Manu tied the boat to the fish's horn by using the royal serpent Vasuki, and the fish took all of them to Mt. Himavan and kept them there until the flood receded. Then, like Noah he started procreation of the human race, but as Manu was the sole human survivor he had to perform a sacrifice that involved pouring oblations of butter and sour milk into the waters. One year later a woman who announced herself as 'the daughter of Manu' was born from the waters. Together they became the ancestors of a new human race to replenish the earth. Manu's survival led him to be considered as the progenitor of mankind and placed at the head of the genealogy of Indian kings.

The Great Flood of British Columbia

A Native American story also recounting a great flood was told by elders of the Coast Salish, a group of indigenous peoples of the Pacific Northwest Coast (living in the Canadian state of British Columbia and the American states of Washington and Oregon). Related through their ethnic and linguistic heritage, their folktale also tells a similar tale to that of Noah. Stephen Sindoni shared the story told to him by the Salish elders:

"In ancient times there were so many people in the land that they lived everywhere. Soon hunting became bad and food scarce, so that the people quarrelled over hunting territories. . . In dreams their wise old men could see the future, and there came a time when they all had similar bad dreams that kept coming to them, over and over again.

The dreams warned of a great flood – this troubled the wise men who told each other about their dreams. They found that they all had dreams that the rain fell for such a long time, or that the river rose causing a great flood so that the people were drowned. Those who believed in the dreams decided to build a huge raft.

Soon after the raft was ready, huge raindrops started falling, rivers overflowed and the valleys were flooded. They lived on the raft many days and could see nothing but water, even the mountain tops disappeared beneath the flood."

The Punishing Wave

There is a Buddhist version of the flood story called *The Tale of the Merchants at Sea* which was written in the *Samudda-Vanija Jataka* (454). The Buddha told this story while staying at Jetavana. The elaborate account tells the story of a group of unhappy carpenters who decided to move to another place. They built a mighty ship from cut down trees, and sailed out of the Ganges River until they reached a bountiful island in the middle of the sea.

Once settled into island life many of the inhabitants would get drunk, misbehave and slowly the island paradise became polluted and unsightly. The spirits became enraged at the behaviour of the islanders until one day one of them decided to create a wave so large it would utterly destroy them all.

"Let's create a great wave which will completely sweep over the island. That way, we can wash away the filth and get rid of these obnoxious creatures at the same time," shouted an impetuous deva. Someone else suggested they "do it on the next full moon" and the others agreed. But another deva, who had been quietly listening to the conversation, pondered the situation then withdrew from the others.

"These human beings are thoughtless and foolish, but they are not all hopeless. I cannot bear to see them all destroyed so cruelly." Then, filled with compassion, he decided to warn the settlers, so one night he appeared above their heads in a blaze of light and spoke in a sternly voice saying, "the devas are angry with you for getting drunk and fouling our paradise. In just two weeks, the moon will be full. At that time, the devas are planning to create a great wave which will sweep over the island and destroy you, one and all. You must flee from here and save your lives! Mark my words! As the next full moon rises in the sky, a mighty flood will overwhelm this entire island. You are in great danger."

A third deva told the people not to worry, all would be fine and to carry on as they were. Those who believed him would later regret their decision, as only the good and righteous who had listened to the warning would survive the ensuing flood.

Sure enough, on the day of the full moon a series of ever-growing waves hit the island. The first was not very deep, the second reached their waists, the third wave was much stronger and reaching chest height it swept away the children. The fourth wave reached the tops of the palm trees and drowned the remaining adults who stayed on the island with only those who heeded the warning sailing away to safety. And finally the fifth wave, the Punishing Wave, rose as high as the mountains and sweeping over the whole island washed away everything in its path.

Buddha later clarified some details within the story, "At that time, Devadatta was the foolish carpenter; Kokalika was the unrighteous deva who lied to the carpenters; Sariputta was the compassionate deva who warned them of danger; and I was the wise carpenter."

Is this tale of consequence and punishment by water also a flood memory from time immemorial? It certainly echoes similar themes as those we have already encountered.

Deucalion and Pyrrha

The Greek flood myth derives from Hesiod's *Theogony* in which he describes the five 'ages of man' as the Gold, Silver and Bronze Ages followed by the Age of Heroes and the Iron Age. According to Hesiod, Zeus became disappointed with the aggressive Bronze men who worshipped the god Ares, and destroyed one another, so sent a great flood to eradicate mankind as punishment for their actions, a familiar narrative replicated throughout most flood myths.

On this occasion, the immortal Titan Prometheus warned his son Deucalion about the forthcoming disaster and advised him to build an ark in order to survive the flood which would put an end to the Bronze Age and bring about the Age of Heroes. Along with his wife (also his cousin) Pyrrha, Deucalion survived for nine days on the rising waters which submerged the whole earth except for Mount Olympus and Mount Parnassus where they finally came to rest.

Once the water receded, the two survivors were commanded by the sun god Apollo to repopulate the world with worthy inhabitants, which they did by casting behind them 'bones of their mother', which Deucalion interpreted as stones that they must throw.

So the couple tossed stones over their shoulders as soon as they left the oracle, and all the stones that Deucalion threw became men, whilst those of Pyrrha became women, and the descendants of Deucalion and Pyrrha would later become the Greeks.

Aztec Flood Myths

Aztec mythology also tells the tale of a great flood which only Coxcox and his wife Xochiquetzal survived by taking refuge in the hollow trunk of a cypress tree which floated them to safety on a mountain in Culhuacán.

Another Aztec account states that the god of rains warned a devout couple, Tata and his wife Nena, about the ensuing flood which he was about to unleash as the people had become wicked and no longer worshipped the gods. He instructed them to hollow out a great log and take two ears of corn for each of them to eat, and nothing more.

'So Tata and Nena entered the tree trunk with the two ears of corn, and it began to rain. When the rains subsided and Tata and Nena's log landed on dry land, they were so happy that they caught a fish and ate it, contrary to the orders of Tlaloc.'[282] Their disobedience led to the destruction of the world and the ushering in of the present era of the Fifth Sun.

Other Flood Legends

The Quran also includes a flood story comparable with the biblical version, where Nuh (the Arabic form of Noah) is the chosen one. Noah is also represented in Hawaiian folklore as Nuu who finally finds himself atop the highest mountain in Hawaii, Mauna Kea.

Taken from *The Prose Edda* by Snorri Sturluson (1179-1241), Norse mythology also includes a flood myth. When Ymir, the first of the mountain giants (jotuns) turned evil, three young gods called Ville, Ve and Odin were forced to kill him. The flood in this ancient Scandinavian tale was caused by the blood of Ymir which drowned almost every tribe of jotuns, accept for two that had survived by building an ark. The survivors once again were a man, in this case Ymir's grandson Bergelmir, and his wife who would later go on to bring forth new families of jotuns.

In inland China, the Miao tribes talk about the wickedness of humanity, and God created a flood that covered the entire earth which only one family, 'the family of Fuhi' survived. This family consisted of one man and his wife, three sons and three daughters, all of whom stayed alive in a boat. The Chinese account says that it poured for forty days, and then it flooded, followed by forty-five days of misting and drizzle. On this occasion, the righteous person who was saved was called Nuah, who built a very wide and vast boat, which saved his family along with male and female pairs of animals.

In Australia the Aborigines speak of a Dreamtime flood called Woramba, where the Ark Gumana carries Noah and the Aboriginal people along with their animals south where they come to rest in the flood plain of Djilinbadu.[283]

The Karens of Burma also have traditions of a global deluge in which two brothers survive the cataclysm on a raft. And in Vietnam, a brother and sister stayed alive in a great wooden chest which also contained every kind of animal in pairs.

Some Japanese traditions claim that the Pacific Islands of Oceania were only formed once the flood waters of a great deluge had receded, and in Oceania itself, the Hawaiian natives believe the world was destroyed by a flood before being recreated by a god named Tangaloa. Likewise, the Samoans also believe that mankind was almost annihilated by a great inundation which only two humans survived as they were sent out into the sea in a boat which finally landed in the Samoan archipelago.

And finally, even the ancient Egyptians had a flood story which they place at the onset of their civilization. Inscribed on the stone walls inside the Temple of Edfu, the Edfu Building Texts refer to an upheaval 'so violent it destroyed the sacred land . . . The Primeval water . . . submerged the island . . . and the island became the tomb of the original divine inhabitants . . . the Homeland ended in darkness beneath the primeval waters.'

We are told that the survivors from this sacred island – the 'Homeland of the Primeval Ones' – set sail in their ships to 'wander' the world in order to 'recreate and revivify the essence of their homeland.'[284] This, according to the Edfu texts, was the very beginning of Egyptian civilization which was built as 'the re-creation and resurrection of what once had existed in the past.'[285]

It is apparent from the plethora of folk traditions denoting a historic flood of disastrous proportions that the likelihood of the flood myths being solely fictitious seems fairly low considering how far reaching the myths are. With so many different cultures around the world sharing such similar tales, it seems reasonable to assume that there must be at least a kernel of truth within each story.

'To take these myths seriously, and especially to countenance the possibility that they might be telling the truth, would be a risky posture for any modern scholar to adopt, inviting ridicule and rebuke from colleagues. The academic consensus today, and for a century, has been that the myths are either pure fantasy or the fantastic elaboration of local and limited deluges – caused for example by rivers overflowing, or tidal waves.'[286]

If the reality was simply that local flooding had affected certain regions then we would not be witnessing the globally shared experience as we do. Only a worldwide flood large enough to wipe out much of life on Earth would explain the consistency and severity of the flood traditions, what else would be worth memorializing over thousands of years from generation to generation?

'Perhaps paradoxically, as a 'no flood, ever' consequence, we must believe that ancients from around the planet paddled their canoes thousands of miles to some centralised myth-making conference, where they conjured the fabulous flood story to confuse the thinking of future generations; and that after attaining consensus on the story, they paddled their canoes back to their homelands and, upon return, convinced their kinsfolk to accept and propagate the story for hundreds of generations. Which is the more absurd; that the conference was a success or that there was a flood? Put another way: ought not the many worldwide flood accounts have us questioning geologists and their fundamental belief? Could there exist an error in the science?'[287]

If we are to believe the mythology of so many global traditions, what physical evidence exists which verifies the worldwide flood scenario? We are actually living in very exciting times in this regard, as new scientific evidence is coming to the fore which is beginning to shed more light on the whole situation. The proof which is only now beginning to surface explains a lot which has either been previously misunderstood or completely dismissed.

Records of the past are slowly being rewritten due to the recent advent of underwater archaeology, but one piece of evidence has been highlighted by Michael Jaye, who took full advantage of modern technology and discovered submerged ancient river systems using Google Earth as a tool. He succeeded in bringing to light the existence of submarine canyons and former river tributary systems in the deep sea, whose existence 'remains essentially beyond our understanding'.[288] Such meandering channels could only have been formed when they were above sea level and using new map data, Jaye revealed in his book *The Worldwide Flood* that these submerged rivers which are undeniable in their structure are now lying beneath more than two miles of water below the sea.

'The new maps unequivocally reveal well-preserved drainages under more than two miles of water, and they are ubiquitous. Their existence implies that there must have been a worldwide flood,' claims Jaye.

'The new data should evoke new thinking, which in our case would result in the restoration of the belief that the Earth suffered a devastating flood. That geologists have failed to review their fundamental belief in the presence of this new data is yet another powerful testament to the constraining effect that 'no flood, ever' holds over science, related disciplines, and rational thought.'[289]

The inundation of such an immense volume of water could only have been caused by a cosmic source according to Jaye, 'A cosmic impact nearly 13,000 years ago before present, introduced more than 3 km of water to the earth's ocean basins and ecosystem. By causing the submersion of vast formerly exposed landscapes, by displacing the atmosphere, and by inducing what we call the Younger Dryas ecosystem changes, the worldwide flood forever changed the planet. The impact ushered in a new geologic era, the Post-Diluvian.'[290]

THE YOUNGER DRYAS CLIMATE EVENT

What cosmic impact was Jaye referring to exactly? A group of scientists now hypothesise that multiple fragments of a large comet collided with the earth during the Younger Dryas, a geological period between 12,800 and 11,600 years ago.

The name Younger Dryas derived from Swedish and Danish pollen records in the late 1800s that indicated the cold-tolerant plant *Dryas octopetala* had returned following a warm interval.

The period has always been considered mysterious because when it first began 12,800 years ago, the earth had spent approximately 10,000 years emerging from the Ice Age with steadily rising temperatures worldwide as the ice caps slowly melted, before taking a sudden and previously unexplained dramatic return to colder conditions, reaching similar freezing temperatures as those at the peak of the Ice Age 21,000 years ago. It is thought the ensuing floods and tidal waves threw up vast clouds of dust into the upper atmosphere which enshrouded the earth, preventing sunlight from reaching the surface which in turn initiated the sudden global deep freeze at the onset of the Younger Dryas.

Lasting 1,200 years until 11,600 years ago, the deep freeze rapidly began to heat up once more until the rising global temperatures were hot enough to melt the remaining ice caps in such a short space of time that sea levels rose massively due to the influx of fresh water being dumped into the oceans, ultimately cooling the seas to such an extent that the Gulf Stream and other essential ocean currents became ineffectual.

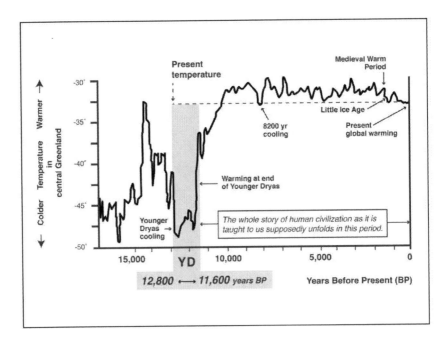

Fig. 80 12,800 years ago there was a sudden plunge in global temperatures as measured in the Greenland ice cores. Then 11,600 years ago there was an equally steep rise in global temperatures bringing an abrupt end to both the Younger Dryas interlude and the Ice Age.

The cataclysm responsible for the massive temperature fluctuations, immense floods and vast wildfires was not a single event but an epoch with two pronounced nodes of disaster. The first stage which occurred at the onset of the Younger Dryas around 12,800 years ago marked the start of a humungous flood followed by extreme global cooling. Then, 11,600 years ago, another cataclysmic flood occurred which was to be accompanied by abrupt, extreme global warming (fig. 80). This second period of flooding which occurred around 9,600 BC could also be connected to the intense precipitation which left its geological footprint on the Sphinx enclosure at the Giza Plateau, if Robert Schoch's theories are correct.

The episodes of immense global flooding at both ends of the Younger Dryas are referred to as Meltwater Pulse A and 1B, and are the result of remnant ice caps in North America and northern Europe which collapsed simultaneously amidst worldwide global warming.

The sudden flooding of the world's oceans is captured with this data which also correlates with the Greenland ice core data that shows spikes in temperature at precisely the same periods. Cesare Emiliani, a Professor from the Department of Geological Sciences at the University of Miami discovered hard evidence of cataclysmic global flooding 'between 12,000 and 11,000 years ago' whilst examining isotopic analysis of deep-sea sediments. But what exactly caused such upheavals?

In order to answer that question the Younger Dryas Impact Hypothesis (YDIH) is a theory proposed by the Comet Research Group, part of a non-profit, charitable corporation collaborating with 63 scientists from 55 universities in 16 countries. The group set out to scientifically assess the effects of comet impacts on human history and to educate the public around the world of their findings, with the ultimate goal of providing enough data which could protect us from possible future comet impacts on Earth.

The YDIH suggests that the impact from a fragmented comet 'instantaneously melted millions of square miles of ice which caused the global deluge that is commemorated in myths across the globe,'[291] but as the impact hit the North American icecap in Canada, no crater depression was left on the earth's surface.

How do we know the comet hit Canada if no impact crater has been found? An article in the *New Scientist* explains, 'Levels of the extraterrestrial debris, for example, are highest at the Gainey archaeological site in Michigan, just beyond the southern reach of North America's primary ice sheet 12,900 years ago. Moreover, levels decrease the further you go from Gainey, suggesting that the comet blew up largely over Canada.'

More proof of this cataclysmic event comes from a variety of sources, all coinciding with various other events which have confounded academics for decades. It is during the Younger Dryas climate event that we find the mysterious extinction of mammoths and megafauna, as we shall see shortly. Also the Clovis culture of North America vanished completely from the archaeological record during the Younger Dryas period between 12,800 and 11,600 years ago.

Evidence of the rapidity of the sudden global warming at the end of the Younger Dryas comes from Greenland ice core data, sediment core data and moon data, which all indicate that the 9700 BC warming was instantaneous; "At 9700 BC we have incredible climatic change going from deep Ice Age to modern warming, and this literally, now based on what they call micro-stratigraphy from Greenland ice cores, can be dated within . . . weeks to days, so this happened, we are talking virtually overnight."[292]

Proof of a gigantic cometary impact over northern Canada roughly 12,800 years ago is indicated by the discovery of around 10 million tons of microspherules, carbon spherules, glass-like carbon (containing nanodiamonds and fullerenes) which were deposited across nearly 50 million square kilometres over North, Central and South America, a large portion of the Atlantic Ocean, North Africa and the Middle East, and most of Europe. Seen only through microscopes, all of these molecules which act as impact markers, reveal characteristics which are inconsistent with any known meteorites, suggesting that the impact was made by a previously unobserved, possibly extrasolar body (from outside of the solar system).

'A cosmic impact event at the onset of the Younger Dryas cooling episode is the only hypothesis capable of explaining the simultaneous deposition of peak abundances in nanodiamonds, magnetic and glassy spherules, melt-glass, platinum and/or other proxies across at least four continents (approaching 50 million square kilometres). The evidence strongly supports a cosmic impact 12,800 years ago.'[293]

The YDIH states that a comet which originated in the Oort Cloud – 'an extended shell of icy objects that exist in the outermost reaches of the solar system'[294] that contains trillions of comets – arrived in our solar system around 20,000 years ago before going into an orbit which crosses the Earth's orbit twice a year. Earth passes through the 30 million km wide orbit called the Taurid Meteor Stream, once in June/early July and once in November, taking twelve days to pass through on each occasion. According to the YDIH, data suggests that it was the fragments of a cataclysmic comet 62 miles in diameter which struck the Laurentide Ice Sheet in Canada, an absolute colossus compared with the 6 mile wide comet that decimated the dinosaurs 65 million years ago.

The most recent impact from a meteorite in the Taurid Meteor Stream hit Tunguska in Siberia at the end of June in 1908. That particular object was only 100 metres in diameter which actually exploded in the sky about 5 km above the ground, but still managed to flatten 80 million trees across 2,000 sq. km, an area the size of London.

The proposed cosmic impact was immediately followed by the appearance of a carbon-rich black layer caused by nationwide wild fires at many sites across the Unites States including 15 Carolina Bays (elliptical impact crater depressions along the Atlantic coast), with the *in situ* bones of extinct megafauna and Clovis tools being discovered beneath the back layer, not above or within it.

To this day, scientists have only discovered two layers of sediment which are broadly distributed across many continents; one layer was found 12,800 years, and the other was at the Cretaceous-Tertiary boundary 65 million years ago where a gigantic meteorite impacted the Gulf of Mexico and sent the dinosaurs and most of the earth's living things into oblivion.

'The concentration of impact markers peaks near the Great Lakes and their unusually high water content suggests that a 4.6 km-wide comet fragmented and exploded over the Laurentide Ice Sheet creating numerous craters that now persist at the bottom of the Great Lakes. The coincidence of this impact, the onset of Younger Dryas cooling, extinction of the megafauna, and the appearance of a black mat strongly suggests that all these events are directly related.'[295]

The data led the scientists of the Comet Research Group to the conclusion that 'the YD event resulted from multiple ET airbursts along with surface impacts. We further suggest that the catastrophic effects of this ET event and associated biomass burning led to abrupt YD cooling, contributed to the late Pleistocene megafaunal extinction, promoted human cultural changes, and led to immediate decline in some post-Clovis human populations. The evidence is more consistent with an impactor that was carbon-rich, nickel–iron-poor, and therefore, most likely a comet.'[296]

Fig. 81 The largest and best examples of giant ripple marks deposited by the Ice Age floods are at the Camas Prairie, Washington.

More fingerprints of the worldwide flooding during the Younger Dryas can be witnessed at the remarkable area of the Channelled Scablands in Washington State. The scabs which gave the area its name are huge clumps of rock which litter the landscape where the torrents of glacial melt water eroded away the different rock types, leaving the harder stone in raised scab-like formations whilst washing away the softer stone entirely.

Scattered over 'Boulder Park', Washington State, we find glacial erratics, some weighing in excess of 10,000 tons, whilst at Camas Prairie (fig. 81) we find giant current ripple marks, some more than fifty feet high, which cover the plains of what was once the bottom of Lake Missoula.

Fig. 82 The ancient Dry Falls cataract in Washington was created 12,800 years ago during a fortnight of immense flooding.

The extinct cataract (horseshoe shaped waterfall) of Dry Falls in Grant County, Washington (fig. 82) is an ancient fossilised waterfall dating back 12,800 years which dwarfs Niagara Falls in size being 2.5 times higher. It once carried several thousand times more water than Niagara Falls, whose discharge of water falling over its ledge reaches a maximum of roughly 200,000 cubic feet per second. In comparison, during the global flood of 12,800 years ago the 400 ft. high precipice of the Upper Grand Coulee at Dry Falls reached a discharge of somewhere between 3 and 400 million cubic feet per second or in other words, "somewhere between 10 and 20 times the combined flow of every river on Earth flowing all at once."[297]

Quite incredibly, the immense cataract at Dry Falls formed during less than two weeks of flooding compared to Niagara which is the result of 12,000 or more years of fast flowing river water. The information on this ancient terrain really brings into focus the sheer magnitude of the worldwide flood, and one really needs to see the images to get any idea of the scale of this event.

The common consensus from geologists regarding the Scablands and all of its features (which include the cataracts, coulees, dry flood channels, erratic fields and ripple plains) is that they came about as a result of a few thousand years of gradually melting ice sheets which slowly eroded away the landscape and left its indelible footprint over vast areas of the region. The reason for insisting upon such a long timeframe has always been down to the fact that nobody had ever presented a reasonable hypothesis on what could be capable of heating up the glaciers quick enough to release the meltwaters suddenly within a matter of weeks. But more recent studies from the Comet Research Group have finally found the smoking gun in the form of a cosmic impact large enough and hot enough to have caused such a cataclysmic meltdown.

Graham Hancock explained the details in an interview: 'There were two significant episodes of impacts from fragments of a single giant comet, which broke up into multiple fragments. The first set of impact was 12,800 years ago, and the second set of impact of 11,600 years ago. The second set of impacts, in particular, was associated with very large scale, rapid sea level rise, which in a sense, in a very real sense, was a global flood. All of the world's oceans are interlinked. You can't dump millions of square miles of ice water into any single ocean without affecting the level of all the world's oceans, and we know that at the end of the last ice age – and 11,600 years ago really is taken as the end of the last Ice Age – we know that sea levels rose 400 feet. 10 million square miles of land, roughly the equivalent in size to Europe and China added together was submerged by rising sea levels at the end of the last Ice Age. These are facts, and it sounds like a global flood to me.'[298]

Despite the overwhelming physical evidence in favour of the YDIH, scientists continue to react negatively and often contemptuously towards catastrophic theories, exposing their fervent and almost religious fixation on gradualism and the uniformitarian paradigm. This reaction to new revolutionary thinking is of course nothing new. Giordano Bruno was burned at the stake for suggesting a heliocentric solar system, and Alfred Wegener, the first to propose plate tectonics and continental drift, was heavily berated and criticised for his theories, although compared with Bruno he got off lightly.

It is worth noting that the comet impact hypothesis is only one theory and alternative suggestions are also beginning to surface such as the theory proposed by geologist Robert Schoch who believes that solar flares, or coronal mass ejections, were responsible for ending the last Ice Age. His findings are in keeping with the data which revealed that signs of intense heat were responsible for the global flooding during the Younger Dryas, but he doesn't believe that an object actually struck Earth as has been suggested, rather that the rapid fluctuations in global temperature and melting of the glacial ice came about through solar activity.

He suggests that it is entirely possible that comet debris actually struck the Sun which ultimately caused the immense and sudden outbursts of heat. "I am coming to conclude that it wasn't a physical object that hit us, it was a solar outburst," explained Schoch. "There are indications that comets diving into the Sun actually cause coronal mass ejections . . . so in some cases you'll have the Comet Group talking about how we go through these comet streams periodically, I agree . . . so it could be that comets are affecting the Sun which is then affecting the Earth."[299]

Whatever triggered the Younger Dryas climate event, the result of this extinction level flood was a rise in sea-levels so dramatic that around 10 million sq. miles of the Earth's surface became submerged at the end of the last Ice Age. Such a voluminous amount of water has concealed so much land that the disappearance of Atlantis among other post-flood civilizations seems incredibly likely, and as underwater archaeology improves over the coming decades, and hopefully with sufficient funding, many submerged ancient sites will be discovered which can improve our knowledge of our long forgotten past.

Another fascinating aspect of the Younger Dryas climate event is the timeline and its connotations. The end date of 11,600 years ago is accepted by geologists as the 'official' end of the last Ice Age – the end of the Pleistocene and the beginning of our current epoch – the Holocene, and the emergence of the flood data recorded as Meltwater Pulse A and B.

Intriguingly, 11,600 years ago also coincides with the 9600 BC date given by Plato for the destruction of Atlantis which was swallowed by the sea at the same time period that scientists have now proven that immense floods occurred. Writer Paul La Violette suggested, that 'there may be much truth to the many flood cataclysm stories that have been handed down to modern times in virtually every culture of the world. In particular, the 9600 BC date that Plato's *Timaeus* gives for the time of the deluge happens to fall at the beginning of the Preboreal at the time of the upsurge of meltwater discharge.'[300]

Despite this seeming coincidence between a date written by Plato over 2,000 years ago and the recent revelation that this exact date marks the time of immense glacial flooding, mainstream scholars are still averse to admitting any direct connection, and remain unlikely to investigate further using the advanced technologies of marine archaeology.

Back in 2002, before the Meltwater A and B flood data had been retrieved, Graham Hancock wrote, 'historians and archaeologists will go through Houdini-like contortions of reason and common sense rather than consider the possibility that their paradigm of prehistory might be wrong – so I am not surprised that they have never attempted to investigate at face value the Atlantis tradition of a devastating flood 11,600 years ago.'[301]

9600 BC is also the date given by Klaus Schmidt and the German Archaeological Institute, for the foundation of the megalithic site of Göbekli Tepe in Turkey. Civilization was rebooted following the last great deluge, and evidence of this is evident with the sudden appearance of unprecedented megalithic architecture in the form of stone circles at Göbekli Tepe. Schmidt himself was quick to realise the correlation between the ending of the last Ice Age and the Younger Dryas, and the dawn of civilization; "How likely is it to be an accident that the monumental phase at Göbekli Tepe starts in 9600 BC, when the climate of the whole world has taken a sudden turn for the better and there's an explosion in nature and in possibilities?"

The emergence of a Stone Age culture capable of such advanced stonework would remain mysterious if we discounted the possibility of pre-flood civilizations that had thousands of years in which to perfect their building skills and astronomical knowledge. It seems most plausible that this seemingly 'new' civilization arose from the ashes of a former world, a transfer of knowledge from the survivors of a great extinction level event which has been captured in the Younger Dryas scientific data. The temple on the hill in south-eastern Turkey 'could only have been conceived and implemented by people with extensive prior experience of megalithic architecture.'[302]

The carved reliefs on the pillars serve as reminders that these people, whoever they were, felt the need to memorialise recent events which had such a massive impact on world cultures and the survival of mankind as a species. As Dr. Martin Sweatman of the University of Edinburgh's School of Engineering remarked, "One of its pillars seems to have served as a memorial to this devastating event – probably the worst day in history since the end of the Ice Age."[303]

THE MEGAFAUNAL EXTINCTION

Between 11,000 and 9,000 BC, the vast majority of more than 40 million animals were obliterated from existence, a figure which includes more than 70 genera of large animals – all of which became extinct between 15,000 and 8,000 BC. To put this into perspective, only 20 genera had disappeared during the previous 300,000 years.[304]

Coinciding with the Younger Dryas timeframe of 1,200 years, we find that 35 genera of mammals (with each genus consisting of several species) simultaneously became extinct. Previously it has been thought that North America's giant mammals, or megafauna, were decimated due to human hunting, a theory first proposed by geoscientist Paul Martin over forty years ago known as the 'overkill hypothesis'.

This theory which is still heavily favoured today, came about partly due to the advances in radiocarbon dating which suggested a correlation between the arrival of the first humans in North America and the demise of the great mammals, but the evidence shows that only the mammoth and the mastodon actually exhibit clear signs of having being hunted, as the stone tool mark cuts on their bones testify.

Presently however, the timing of the extinctions with the dramatic temperature fluctuations at the end of the last Ice Age suggests a different cause for the sudden disappearance of the megafauna, 'The impact event, followed by extensive fires and sudden climate change, likely contributed together to the rapid extinction of the megafauna and many other animals.'[305]

The data taken from over 170 sites around the world indicates that an astounding 10 percent of the Earth's land surface, which equates to around 10 million sq. km, was eventually consumed by fires which may be what left the black mat layers that were discovered.

Radiocarbon dating also suggests that the North American megafauna actually underwent two major declines before finally reaching extinction, the first being 14,100 years ago before the first human migration into the area according to orthodoxy, in which case the animal population seemed to recover after about 500 years. The second period which began around 12,700 years ago saw the second and final population crash, at a time when the archaeological record reveals that Palaeo-Indians had just arrived in the region. But writer Michael Balter claims that the animals were already on their way out as 'between 75% and 90% of the north-eastern megafauna were gone before humans ever came on the scene.'[306]

Even during this 1,000 year overlap between human and mammal occupation, there is no evidence for hunting as neither of the megafaunal sites in the northeast nor those of the Palaeo-Indians contained bones showing signs of butchering or modification by human hand. So a more recent hypothesis revolves around the notion that the megafaunal extinction at the end of the Pleistocene derived from the cataclysmic changes during the Younger Dryas, and the thousands upon thousands of frozen mammoths discovered in Siberia reveal that whatever caused their demise happened in a heartbeat.

The mammoths were discovered frozen in time with undigested wild meadow flora in their stomachs, as Ivan T. Sanderson noted, 'The mammoths died suddenly, in intense cold and in great numbers. Death came so quickly that the swallowed vegetation is yet undigested . . . Grasses, bluebells, buttercups, tender sages, and wild beans have been found, yet identifiable and undeteriorated, in their mouths and stomachs.'[307]

The Siberian mammoths were found with dislocated bones as if they were literally swept off their feet with unimaginable force and dumped in piles before a sudden deep freeze arrived and encapsulated them in ice, preserving them for prosperity.

A recent scientific paper written by the Comet Research Group read, 'Increasing evidence suggests that the extinction of many mammalian and avian taxa occurred abruptly and perhaps catastrophically at the onset of the YD, and this extinction was pronounced in North America where at least 35 mammal genera disappeared, including mammoths, mastodons, ground sloths, horses, and camels, along with birds and smaller mammals. At Murray Springs, AZ, a well known Clovis site, mammoth bones and Clovis-age stone tools lie directly beneath the black layer where 'the sudden extinction of the Pleistocene megafauna would be dramatically revealed by explaining that all were gone an instant before the black mat was deposited."[308]

Of the 34 species living in Siberia prior to the catastrophic extinction event, 28 of them were adapted only to temperate conditions as opposed to arctic conditions, as the presence of the buttercups reveals. French zoologist Georges Cuvier wrote, 'this eternal frost did not previously exist in those parts in which the animals were frozen, for they could not have survived in such a temperature. The same instant that those creatures were bereft of life, the country which they inhabited became frozen.'[309]

Just like the Siberian mammoth graveyards (fig. 83), Alaska too witnessed this great extinction event and the frozen wastelands also contained thousands of *in situ* animal remains which suffered the same fate as their Siberian counterparts. Found in the Alaskan muck lies evidence of the worldwide flood and the cataclysmic force which claimed millions of lives in a geological instant.

Fig. 83 Thousands of scattered mammoth bones at the 'mammoth cemetery' in Berelekh, Northern Siberia. Two radiocarbon dates place the occupation of the site at around 11,500 BC.

As Professor Hibben of the University of New Mexico describes, in the Alaskan muck 'lie the twisted parts of animals and trees intermingled with lenses of ice and layers of peat and mosses . . . Bison, horses, wolves, bears, lions . . . Whole herds of animals were apparently killed together, overcome by some common power . . . Such piles of bodies of animals or men simply do not occur by any ordinary means.'[310]

The sheer numbers and the extreme and unparalleled violent nature of the megafaunal mass deaths is highly indicative of an unprecedented inundation of water, the likes of which we can barely imagine, that was so powerful and unforgiving that mammals weighing many tons were simply ripped apart and tossed around like leaves in the breeze. To better understand the severity of the deluge, a description from *The Path of the Pole* leaves little to the imagination:

'Mammoth and bison alike were torn and twisted as though by a cosmic hand in Godly rage. In one place we can find the foreleg and shoulder of a mammoth with portions of the flesh and toenails and hair still clinging to the blackened bones. Close by is the neck and skull of a bison with the vertebrae clinging together with tendons and ligaments . . . There is no mark of knife or cutting instrument [as there would be if human hunters had been involved]. The animals were simply torn apart and scattered over the landscape like things of straw and string, even though some of them weighed several tons. Mixed with piles of bones are trees, also twisted and torn and piled in tangled groups; and the whole is covered with a fine sifting muck, then frozen solid.'

Charles Darwin was also aware that some unknown earth upheaval must have been responsible for the decimation of large populations of megafauna, many to the point of extinction, and writing on his long voyage aboard the ship Beagle, he wrote in his journal pondering the possibilities:

'It is impossible to reflect on the changed state of the American continent without the deepest astonishment. . . What, then, has exterminated so many species and whole genera? The mind at first is irresistibly hurried into the belief of some great catastrophe; but thus to destroy animals, both large and small, in Southern Patagonia, in Brazil, on the Cordillera of Peru, in North America up to the Behring's Straits, we must shake the entire framework of the globe.'

The sheer presence and amount of frozen mammoths discovered in Alaska and Siberia has always been at the centre of much controversy, but the general consensus rests with the conclusion that the root cause responsible for their demise was due to gradual deglaciation. Were this true then we would be left with less evidence for the worldwide flood; an event which the data reveals was much more rapid than conventional science is willing to concede.

Sometimes referred to as the 'founding father of palaeontology', and one of the proponents of catastrophism, Georges Cuvier realised that what lay frozen in the northern regions of the planet were firm reminders that the cataclysm responsible must have been rapid and not slow and gradual as the academics contend.

'These repeated irruptions and retreats of the sea have neither been slow or gradual; most of the catastrophes which have occasioned them have been sudden; and this is easily proved, especially with regard to the last of them, the traces of which are most conspicuous. In the northern regions it has left the carcasses of some large quadrupeds which the ice had arrested, and which are preserved even to the present day with their skin, their hair, and their flesh. If they had not been frozen as soon as killed they must quickly have been decomposed by putrefaction. But this eternal frost could not have taken possession of the regions which these animals inhabited except by the same cause which destroyed them; this cause, therefore must have been as sudden as its effect.'[311]

AGRICULTURAL ORIGINS

As well as the megafaunal extinctions, the sudden disappearance of the Clovis culture in North America, and the coincidental date of 9600 BC which correlates with the second great flood at the end of the Younger Dryas, the destruction of Atlantis in the Platonic accounts, and the rise of the most ancient manmade construction on the planet discovered to date at Göbekli Tepe, this period of human history at the end of the last Ice Age also saw the emergence of agriculture and the first Neolithic civilizations.

The Flem-Aths wrote that 'all around the globe the sudden rise of early agricultural experiments date to the very century (9600 BC) during which the Egyptian priest says Atlantis fell.'[312]

Today, one would associate farming and agriculture with open fields on low-lying lands, as accessibility and practicality is a fundamental aspect of product efficiency. Travelling up mountains to maintain and harvest crops seems most unproductive and impractical so why do we find that agricultural origins were discovered worldwide in highland regions? Why choose the harder option of cultivation in tougher highlands which are often subject to extreme changes in weather as opposed to the more suitable plains below the mountain ranges?

The conclusive data which reveals the highland origins of agriculture only truly makes sense when one considers the worldwide flood scenario as historic fact. It is the rising ocean levels which forced civilizations higher towards safety and away from the usual habitats of human occupation around the shorelines where the oceans provided unlimited supplies of food.

Plato wrote, 'When . . . the gods purge your earth with a deluge of water, the survivors in your country are herdsman and shepherds who dwell on the mountains, but those, who like you, live in cities are carried by the rivers into the sea.'

Soviet botanist and geneticist Nikolai Ivanovich Vavilov (1887-1943) collected over 50,000 wild plants from all over the world, and in doing so he 'located eight independent centres of origin' of the world's most important cultivated plants which he showed related to the earth's highest mountain ranges. His research proved that the most important cultivated plants were initially developed in a zone which lies between 20 and 45° north latitude, near the highest mountain ranges; the Andes, the Hindu Kush, the Balkans, the Italian Apennines and of course the Himalayas. Likewise, animal domestication is also believed to have originated in highland regions of the planet.

'Most domesticated plants and animals were originally domesticated in centres 1,500 metres above ocean level. Agriculture was *re*born [italics added] in these mountains 11,500 years ago. Survivors of the Great Flood were terrified of descending to the lowlands in case another earthquake would cause a flood to destroy their world. Only after many generations were the survivors brave enough to bring their plants and animals from the highlands to lower elevations. The earliest civilizations were often found downriver from high mountains.'[313]

We find that as rice was being domesticated at Spirit Cave in the highlands of Thailand, on the opposite side of the globe tropical agriculture was in its infancy at Lake Titicaca in Peru at approximately the same time. Despite the timeline of the domestication of staples such as rice and maize still being contested, we do find correlations between the agricultural origins on opposing continents relatively shortly after the end of the Younger Dryas. This raises questions as to how and why cultures separated by thousands of miles inexplicably discovered the seemingly brand new techniques required to domesticate plants and animals alike.

'After hundreds of thousands of years of living by hunting and gathering, humankind turned to experimenting with agriculture on opposite sides of the earth at the same time. Is this likely without the intervention of some outside force?'[314]

As with the advanced building techniques and astronomical knowledge inherent in many of the ancient megalithic designs around the world, we can only speculate as to how this level of sophistication arose without precedent, just as farming did around the same time. So how did primitive Stone Age 'savages' progress from hunter-gatherers into the first farmers virtually overnight? Are we talking about a transfer of knowledge from survivors of the deluge? Is this evidence of the rebirth of agriculture as opposed to its origins?

'Many of the 'myths' contain telling details. In Genesis Chapter 9, the beginnings of agriculture, and in particular the cultivation of the vine, are attributed to Noah, suggesting that farming was not the natural development of a linear evolution, but rather a skill carried over by the survivors of the great disaster. In this context, it is interesting to note that the earliest indications of farming activity worldwide are, almost without exception, found on high ground, exactly what we would expect if we were dealing with a gradually receding flood.'[315]

Perhaps even more remarkable than the coincidental implementation of advanced farming methodologies at far removed locations is the manner in which these hunter-gatherers successfully transformed wild plants into domesticated ones, and domesticated wild animals too – an incredible initial output that produced sheep, goats, cattle and pigs, chicken and water buffalo. The four major strains of domesticated cattle in India, Africa, Europe and the Near East all appeared rather suddenly according to the genetic evidence.

As well as turning predominantly inedible wild plants – many of which were first discovered in the Fertile Crescent[4] – into staple edibles such as wheat, barley, rice, millet and yams, across the Atlantic in the New World of Mesoamerica came maize ('the gift of the gods'), squash, vicuna, peppers, beans, tomatoes and potatoes. So, how did these primitive farmers succeed in turning wild grasses, grains and cereals into easy to manage and highly nutritious domesticated foods which would continue to feed mankind to the present day?

'Not only did those primitive hunter-gatherers convert to farming (which meant somehow acquiring all the specialized knowledge that entails), they also became top-notch geneticists and botanists', wrote Lloyd Pye. It is a confounding mystery that '. . . the incredible scientific skills those straight-from-the-Stone-Age 'geniuses' displayed, [are] skills still unmatched by the geneticists and botanists of today.'[316]

In order to create nutritious and edible versions of the wild plants available to them, these early farmers inexplicably managed to double, triple and in some cases, quadruple the number of chromosomes in the wild plants! Official theory declares that between 5 and 10,000 years ago the earliest American Indians took a wild perennial that was finger-sized, and transformed it into the forearm-sized staple we know today as maize.

Controversial scholar Zecharia Sitchin highlights this anomaly, 'Scholars are agreed that agriculture began . . . with the harvesting of 'wild ancestors' of wheat and barley some 12,000 years ago (10,000 BC), but are baffled by the genetic uniformity of those early grain grasses; and they are totally at a loss to explain the botano-genetic feat whereby – within a mere 2,000 years (8,000 BC) – such wild emmers doubled, trebled and quadrupled their chromosome pairs to become the cultivable wheat and barley of outstanding nutritional value with the incredible ability to grow anywhere, and with the unusual twice-a-year crops.'[317]

---

[4] The term 'Fertile Crescent' was first coined by Egyptologist James Henry Breasted in his book *Ancient Times: A History of the Early World.*

Under normal circumstances nature would require thousands of generations to acquire even a modest degree of sophistication, whereas evidence of such a gradual and prolonged evolutionary process is nowhere to be found anywhere on Earth.

The origins of domesticated wheat can be traced back to the Turkish hills of the Karacadag range in the heart of the Fertile Crescent; in fact 64 km northwest of Göbekli Tepe, Nevalý Çori is presently accepted as the first place in the world where large scale wheat cultivation first occurred. It was here in the Karacadag Mountains that Neolithic people began manipulating strands of wild wheat coinciding with their change in lifestyle from nomadic hunters to farmers and settlers in communities.

'For over 100,000 years we walked across the great Savannas, made way through the jungles, camped in Arctic tundra, and hunted and foraged in the forests of this planet. Then, a little over 10,000 years ago, a blip in the timeline of our species, we started laying down our satchels, building our shelters with a sense of permanence, and began cultivating the grains and animals in our surroundings. This great event, perhaps the largest shift in human cultural evolution happened around a great temple now called Göbekli Tepe in south-eastern Turkey.'[318]

So following a cataclysmic flood which decimated large populations of people and megafauna alike, we find that at the onset of civilization (albeit a re-emergence of previous world culture) around 9600 BC, that both religion and agriculture appear relatively simultaneously in the exact same region where the oldest temple construction in the world (and the oldest surviving manmade structure if we neglect the possible ancient dating of the Great Sphinx) was discovered. This narrative which is starting to take shape now contradicts the previous version.

Klaus Schmidt from the German Archaeological Institute commented, "The origins of domesticated wheat can be traced exactly here to this region. All the cultivated wheat has some fingerprints which match the fingerprint that the wild forms of wheat have in this region. Now it is getting quite clear that the same people who were building Göbekli Tepe were the same people who were domesticating the wheat. There is lots of equipment for grinding here, so they processed the wild cereals here, it is clear."

Schmidt hypothesised that the increase in population as people gathered at Göbekli Tepe may have led to an increased demand for a sustainable food supply to feed the masses both during and after the construction of the ancient temple site. "Domestication had originally been in connection with feasting," Klaus claimed. "So the feasting and the need for a good food supply were influencing the domestication. So now we need very good food, we need the cereals, we need a lot of the cereals and so on."

As the cultivation of wheat in the region was contemporaneous with the building of Göbekli Tepe it would appear likely that during this "full scale revolution" one influenced the other, and the site which would have initially have been used by hunter-gatherers would later also be used by the revolutionary farmers.

Interestingly, it has been suggested that food may actually have been a secondary consideration, as Schmidt stated, "There are now ideas that the beginning of cereal domestication was not so much in connection with bread and with food, but with beer making, for brewing. It is easy to do it, it is not like our beer, all you need is water and if let to stand in some container it will start to produce alcohol. So maybe it was beer making at the beginning."[319]

Whatever the actual reasons for the rise of civilization, agriculture and religion, we know that all of these essential aspects of human existence all began following a catastrophic worldwide flood which came about during a time of great upheaval and unstable climate temperature fluctuations. The sheer abruptness and coincidence of the timing involved with these human 'revolutions' is certainly suggestive of new beginnings which one would expect to find after an extinction level event. Moreover, it is more likely that their sudden emergence is the result of a knowledge transfer rather than simply a lucky break conceived by some fortuitous inspiration.

SWALLOWED BY THE SEA

Finally, as we search for proof of the global deluge responsible for the destruction of former prehistoric civilizations, let us take a glimpse at some of the manmade structures which remain submerged beneath the waters that were swallowed by the sea since the last Ice Age.

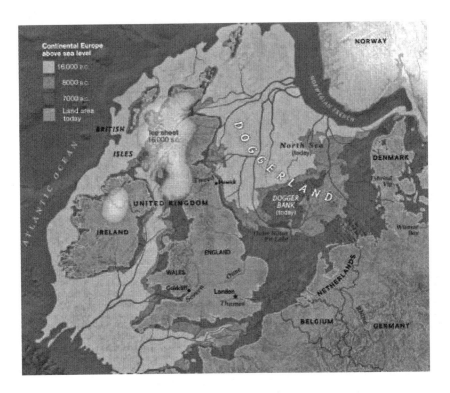

Fig. 84 Doggerland used to connect Great Britain with mainland Europe.

We already know that nearly five percent of the earth's surface, which equates to around 10 million sq. miles or the equivalent of the areas of the United States and South America combined, were engulfed by rising sea-levels at the end of the Ice Age according to mainstream geology. We also know that the evidence indicates that the present continental shelf – the underwater landmasses which extend from each continent and have become known as 'shelf seas' due to the relatively shallow waters – were broad coastal plains about 15,000 years ago before the glacial ice began its return to the ocean.

Approximately 12,000 years ago near the end of the last Ice Age, the North Sea between the eastern coast of Britain and mainland Europe was an area with 'gently sloping hills, marshland, heavily wooded valleys, and swampy lagoons' known as Doggerland (fig. 84). It is believed that around 6,000 years ago, the Mesolithic Doggerlanders were forced onto higher ground in what is today England and the Netherlands, as glacial meltwaters surged into the area and engulfed their low-lying settlements.

Ancient bones and tools dating to around 9,000 years ago were discovered by fishermen in modern times which revealed the presence of this submerged land that lay silently anonymous below the depths. 'Doggerland, like the fabled Atlantis, is just a sunken and mostly forgotten Stone Age culture, its only evidence being decayed artefacts and fossils of its people.'[320]

The highest part of this ancient landscape at a depth of between 30 and 40 metres is today referred to as Dogger Bank, and it is here as well as in the English Channel where 'bones of many Pleistocene mammals, including mammoths, have long been reported by fishermen'.[321]

According to Bruce Heezen, an oceanographer from the Lamont Geological Observatory, the sea-level rose between 100 and 150 metres worldwide around 11,600 years ago, a level that was sufficient to drown the majority of low-lying coastal regions of the planet.

We know that a land-bridge once joined Alaska and Siberia via what is now the Bering Strait, Malta was attached to Sicily, Sardinia and Corsica were part of one huge island, and Sri Lanka was joined to mainland India. Sometime between 14,000 and 11,000 years ago 'Sundaland', an antediluvian continent which contained Malaysia, Indonesia and the Philippines reaching as far north as Japan, was rapidly submerged. And the three main islands of Japan once formed a continuous landmass until about 12,000 years ago, a date which once again correlates to the end of the Younger Dryas and the disappearance of Atlantis at 9,600 BC.

Australia, Tasmania and New Guinea once formed a gigantic Ice Age continent called Sahul before the rising waters divided them into separate countries; and all of the shelves off the coast of Florida all the way south to Yucatán and even further to Nicaragua, were formerly exposed until the inundation changed things dramatically.

Regarding the discovery of submerged sites around the world, despite the advancements in marine archaeology and aside from Robert Ballard's Black Sea survey for the National Geographic Society back in 2000, very little has been done to further our knowledge of previous civilizations which now rest beneath the waves; 'marine archaeology simply has not concerned itself with the possibility that the post-glacial floods might in any way be connected to the problem of the rise of civilization.'[322]

Gulf of Cambay

On the north-western coast of India during late 2001, oceanographers from India's National Institute of Ocean Technology (NIOT) who were conducting a pollution survey 25 miles offshore from the Gulf of Cambay (now the Gulf of Khambhat) discovered archaeological remains of two ancient cities under 120 feet of water. Covering large areas of the sea floor, huge foundations with massive walls and plazas were found which predated the Harappan Civilization (3300-1300 BC) of the Indus Valley during the Bronze Age, characterised by such ruined cities as Mohenjo-daro, Harappa and Dholavira.

Dr. S. Badrinarayan, geological consultant for the NIOT, said that "it looks like a twin city, or a twin metropolis of ancient times. One city is about more than 8 km long, other one is almost 9 km. Both of them appear to be along river courses."

Found alongside construction material debris recovered from the site were manufactured items such as pottery, stone hand tools, beads, jewels, ornaments and sculpture; as well as the discovery of human bones and teeth, a piece of ancient wood was carbon dated to nearly 9,500 years old. The intricate detail and inherent beauty of some of the artefacts found reveal the great skill of a lost culture which lived along the shoreline of northern India at the end of the Ice Age.

This anomalously ancient date predates the oldest known remains in the subcontinent by more than 5,000 years. Sub-bottom profiling, a technique which detects objects beneath the seabed, revealed the cities massive foundations, whilst side-scan sonar exposed sophisticated geometric structures which included steps, square shapes, right angles and platform-like features.

'The sonar images showed regular geometric patterns in one palaeo channel over a length of 9 km in the sea about 20 km west of Hazira coastal area. Associated with this on either side of the palaeo channel, basement-like features in a grid pattern were observed at a water depth of 20-40m. These resemble an urban habitation site where pit-like structures are seen. Another palaeo channel over 9.2 km was detected off the Suvali coastal area. Here also similar features were observed. In general the basement-like features were located in a linear east-west direction on either side of the palaeo channel,' wrote Badrinaryan, chief geologist with the scientific team from NIOT responsible for the underwater surveys in the Gulf of Cambay.

'There were also evidences of water conducting systems like canals, etc. All these point to a properly planned township, with a high level of knowledge and practice by the ancients.'

All the evidence clearly establishes the existence of an ancient Indian civilization which was inundated over 10,000 years ago, and could well prove to be the remnants of another flood victim from Meltwater Pulse B 11,600 years ago.

Badrinaryan concluded, 'So, from the foregoing it is very evident the prehistoric civilization that matured and developed in the present day Gulf of Cambay was the forerunner and model to the subsequent advanced Harrapan civilization known to history. This wonderful twin prehistoric metropolis of Cambay lasted from about 13,000 BP to about 3,000 BP making it the most ancient and largest city civilization not only in Asia but also in the entire world.'[323]

The Yonaguni Monument

The Yonaguni Monument is located just off shore on the south side of Yonaguni Island, one of the Yaeyama Islands and the westernmost inhabited island of Japan. It is the last of the islands in the Ryukyu Islands chain, and lies 67 miles from the east coast of Taiwan, between the Pacific Ocean and the East China Sea.

Whilst diving in the waters off the southern shore of Yonaguni island in 1986-7, local resident and dive-master Kihachiro Aratake discovered some large and extremely unusual underwater stone structures which he named Iseki ('monument') Point. Despite the apparent artificial appearance of the bizarre looking terraces, platforms and steps, outside interest in the Monument did not surface until 1996 once Professor Masaaki Kimura from the University of the Ryukyus decided to survey the sunken site.

Consisting of both sandstone and mudstone deposited about 20 million years ago, most of the Monument's formations appear to have been carved from one underlying rock mass, and the stepped, straight-edged and almost pyramidal appearance of the structure would suggest that it may be a vast monolith carved by man. Other features suggestive of human manufacture are the presence of round holes; two on the edge of the Triangle Pool feature, and also a straight row of smaller holes which some have interpreted as an abandoned attempt to split off a section of the rock by means of wedges, as would be seen in ancient quarries.

From a layman's perspective, it is very difficult to imagine the Yonaguni site (fig. 85) as anything but artificial, with its huge symmetrical straight-edged steps, smooth paths, terraces and platforms, both square and round holes and also long corridors with some form of guttering running adjacent. Another mysterious feature is the placement of two parallel standing megaliths which lay directly opposite a stone tunnel formation.

The official Yonaguni study from 2000 stated: 'Diving operations revealed two big rectangular blocks measuring 6 metres in height, about 2.5 metres in width (both) and 4.9 metres thickness which have been located towards the western side of Iseki Point. . . These rectangular blocks are designated by Japanese workers as megaliths. These blocks have been located between two natural rock outcrops. The approach way to these megaliths is through a tunnel measuring about 3m long,

Fig. 85 Top: Illustration of the entire Yonaguni Monument. Centre: Divers show the scale of the immense step formations. Bottom: Close-up details.

1m high and 1m in width. The shape, size and positioning of these megaliths suggests that they are manmade.'[324]

The report also noted the presence of what they claimed resembled a monolith human head; 'A large monolith that looks like a human head with two eyes and a mouth was studied at Tatigami Iwa Point. A human-cut large platform in the same monolith extends outwards at the base of the head. An approach way leads to this platform from the shore-side. The surrounding basal platform is quite large (about 2500m²), and could easily have accommodated more than two thousand persons sitting. The human head and associated platform with an approach road are suggestive of an area of worship or community gatherings.'

Dating the coralline algae growing on the monument to around 4,000 BC, we can safely assume that if it proves to be the product of civilized man that it must have been on land much, much earlier than that. Whilst many geologists and scholars alike continue to debunk the notion of Yonaguni having been carved by human hand, Kimura remains convinced that it is clear evidence of a forgotten advanced civilization from prehistory. Prof. Kimura stated "if this has been made by nature it is very difficult to explain."[325]

"These are ruins, and to me, the fact has already been proved. The scientific conclusion is that the ruins are indeed artificial. A school of Japanese marine geologists agreed on this outcome. We found that the ruins are at least 6,000 years old. It could go back another 4,000 years when we consider the length of time before they sank into the water."[326]

Geologist Wolf Wichmann however, remains unconvinced, "Taking into account that there have been four or five different forces of weathering and erosion, you will find an explanation for almost every feature. . . What I saw up to now could be explained by natural forces."[327]

One reason archaeologists are unwilling to accept the manmade hypothesis is due to their perception that the societies existing in that area of Japan at the end of the last Ice Age were considered primitive and therefore incapable of such complex construction work.

Paradoxically, the same archaeologists agree that the ancient cultures of prehistoric Japan that they insist were primitive, were responsible for the technically advanced and artistic Dogu humanoid and animal figurines made during the late J•mon period (14,000 – 400 BC). The J•mon were actually proto-Caucasoids, fair-skinned with prominent noses and full, light-coloured beards, not of typical East Asian descent. Such similarities are indicative of a connection between them and ancient Americans and northern Europeans. According to mainstream archaeologists they were the first culture on Earth to develop pottery, with examples stretching back to 16,000 BC.

Despite opposition to the contrary, Sundaresh, a senior marine archaeologist at the NIOT, believes that the ancients must have cut into the existing rock, and regarding some of the small step formations rising from the bottom of the structure Sundaresh remarked, "Definitely that is manmade. I don't think it's natural." He undertook the first and only official scientific evaluation of the underwater structures in September 2000, in which he suggested that perhaps the Yonaguni Monument could have acted as a harbour.

'The length of the canal appears to be more than 250 m, while the canal has a width of 25 m. The purpose or utility of this canal structure is intriguing. Our observation all along the canal indicates that the western end of the structure begins underwater opening away from the terraced structure to the open sea. The width, height and terraced north side of the canal force us to suggest that the canal structure might have served as a channel for small boats communicating with the Arakawabana headland.'[328]

Remarkably, astronomical calculations reveal that Yonaguni was built along a very significant latitude, as it would have been exactly on the ancient Tropic of Cancer – a circle around the northern half of the Earth – connecting all points where the Sun stands directly overhead at midday on the summer solstice.

Kerama Stone Circles

Just three miles offshore from the nearest of the Kerama Islands to mainland Japan, at depths between 27 and 33 metres can be found what appears to be prehistoric stone circles. The area used to be a few kilometres inland before it became fully submerged sometime during the last 10,000 years when sea levels were much lower and it was connected to the main island of Okinawa.

Divers at the island of Aka, 40 km west of Okinawa, have known about a series of submerged stone circles for years, all of which seem to have been cut and worked by human hands. Resting at a depth of approximately 27 metres is the central circle with a diameter of 20 metres. The stone circle in its entirety has a much larger diameter of around 150 metres.

In his quest to find evidence of a pre-flood civilization, Graham Hancock dived frequently at Kerama and had become all too familiar with the mysterious stone circles which sat silently on the sea bed as testimony to a time long since forgotten, 'Every instinct in my body, for years now, had convinced me that these structures *must* be manmade, or at any rate could not have been made entirely by nature – they were simply too bizarre, unique and 'designed'.'[329]

Seeing as these mysterious submerged rock formations strongly resemble other stone circles found on land, and because historians accept that the ancient J•mon culture dating back to the Ice Age 16,000 years ago were actually known to have made stone circles, it doesn't take a great leap of imagination to consider that such an ancient civilization could have been responsible for the Kerama stone circles. After all, 'It would have been around this time, 9000-10,000 years ago, that Kerama's stone circles would have been inundated.'[330]

Aside from the organized placement of the stones with pathways between the boulders being perfectly suited to human movement to and from the site, the shaping of the monolithic stones themselves matches the shape of the adjacent paths; 'the monolith appeared to have been smoothly and perfectly cut down from top to bottom with a beautiful curve incorporated into it to match the curve of the pathways that were defined on either side of it and the curve of the central upright.'[331]

Aside from the few we have covered here, many other stone formations and structures rest beneath the waves at other sites across the globe, all acting as reminders that distant forgotten and unrecognized cultures once thrived and to left their indelible imprint; "Such monuments hint at highly organized human societies that flourished along coastlines all around the world at the end of the Ice Age."[332]

Working off the coast of Cuba, marine biologists Pauline Zalitzki and Paul Weinzweig obtained photographs taken by a submersible robot which revealed several giant pyramids and sphinxes sitting on the sea bed 600 feet below the surface, just inside the boundaries of the Bermuda Triangle. According to journalist Luis Mariano Fernandez, research into this collection of massive underwater structures which was first discovered decades ago, was halted due to the Cuban Missile Crisis.

"The U.S. Government discovered the alleged place during the Cuban Missile Crisis in the sixties, nuclear submarines cruising in the Gulf (in deep sea) met pyramid structures. They immediately shut down the site and took control of him and the objects, in order that it will not come to Russian hands."[333] But the research team led by Zalitzki and Weinzweig re-discovered the ruins, and they estimated the underwater pyramids to be of a similar size to the Egyptian pyramids at Giza as they believe that the submerged constructions were also built using stones that weigh several hundred tons.

By comparing the symbols and inscriptions found on the anomalous underwater ruins to relics of other ancient civilizations, the scientists suggested that the structures could have been constructed by the ancient and mysterious Olmec culture of Mexico that could have travelled to Cuba when it was still attached to the mainland near Cancún. Further information on these discoveries is difficult to attain, so speculation regarding the authenticity of these finds will continue to grow, but it is certainly worthy of consideration.

As is evident from the accumulation of evidence amassed throughout this book, our current understanding of human history is outdated, rigidly formatted, and in dire need of new impetus and a severe paradigm shift. Of course many of the subjects we have investigated remain mysterious and unexplained, but it is paramount that we at least acknowledge their existence and consider alternative views of our hidden past in order to understand that what we are taught is not always as factual as the experts let on.

The recent flood data and proof of an unprecedented cataclysmic event which occurred less than 13,000 years ago has reopened a window on a history long forgotten by mankind, whose state of amnesia and inherent neuroses are indicative of a species trying desperately to forget such a devastating period of their past.

With so much evidence of past civilizations still submerged beneath the oceans, buried beneath desert sands and concealed by thousands of years of dense vegetal growth which cover the great jungles of the world, we can say with complete conviction that there is so much more of our historic past to unveil that currently we base our knowledge purely on the scant evidence we have so far unearthed.

The prevailing narratives of the history of humankind have been written based upon such evidence, a fact which is admirable considering how little we have truly discovered at this point in history, but what is less admirable is the reluctance of the scholarly and scientific communities to embrace new ideas with a readiness to create new and more accurate narratives.

Recent topographical surveys using the high tech cameras of 'space archaeology' have revealed the presence of endless cities throughout Egypt which the ancient sands have buried beyond our sight, and likewise, covered by the thick, tangled Amazonian canopy of South America, we are only now discovering the ruinous signs of civilizations which spread over hundreds of miles where nobody ever thought to look. If we could drain all the oceans of the world, remove the sands of time and strip back the jungle layers just for a while, we would be astounded by what we would find. History would have to be completely rewritten, chronologies of civilizations renewed, and questions as to how we failed to see what was under our noses for millennia would inevitably be asked.

We have learned that the prevailing theories on our origins are extremely dubious and therefore must continue to be questioned as we discover previously suppressed information that exposes the greater antiquity of our genus. Further research into the creation and origins of

DNA must be undertaken as we come to terms with the fact that our existence on this planet remains inexplicable following established scientific means, as the data shows that the very blueprints of all material lifeforms must in actuality derive from either a divine, cosmic, or potentially even an extraterrestrial source.

The possible ancestral lineage between the ancient hominids and the present day living Sasquatch cannot be so easily dismissed, and likewise, the existence of a former race of giants in prehistory is discernible by studying the many reports of huge skeletal remains discovered all over the world. Along with all the anomalous objects and telltale signs of advanced societies across the globe, we can start to realise, if we are willing and able to break free from the shackles of domineering convention, that we know so very little of the true history of humankind.

Maybe by listening closer to the myths and legends that have somehow survived the ravages of time to communicate with us in the modern world, thousands of years after our near destruction as a species, we can sift fact from fiction and follow the clues left behind by the greatest minds of our past. With so many questions still unanswered, isn't it time for us to reassess how we perceive our ancient ancestors and the tales they fought so stoically to preserve?

There is clearly knowledge and wisdom contained within the lines of creative expression which we should take on board, as modern science continues to catch up with some of the advanced knowledge exhibited throughout the ancient world. As Plato told us over two thousand years ago, 'and so you have to begin all over again like children, and know nothing of what happened in ancient times, either among us or among yourselves.'

If he was right, as the evidence suggests, that we have forgotten the traumatic human experiences caused by past cataclysms, then all we can do is persevere with the search for our true hidden history as a species, and hope that the clarity and knowledge we have been seeking for millenia may finally emerge through the mists of time and expose the myth of man.

ABOUT THE AUTHOR

Jamie Paul Robinson was born in Beverley on the East Yorkshire coast of England in 1975. He first became fascinated in the mysteries of the world when he began considering the possibility of UFOs and extraterrestrial beings in his late teens during the early 90's; the last decade before the explosion of the internet.

His research then led him to consider the unexplained mysteries of ancient history, and inspired by the research of such luminaries as Graham Hancock and John Anthony West, his interest in mankind's forgotten past soon took hold.

He began honing his writing skills as a keen singer-songwriter for the best part of two decades and following five years of study in Contemporary Photography right through to degree level at Northumbria University, he developed his ability to research extensively and applied this to his dissertation where he received a first with honours. Back in 1998, his work was recommended for a commissioned piece in *The Guardian*.

During a period as a self-employed freelance photographer he decided it was time to accumulate all of his knowledge and in 2016 he published his first nonfiction book *The Alien Enigma* followed by *The Myth of Man* two years later.

He is currently living in Hull with fiancé Frowynke and his daughters Amelie and Aiyana, where he is working on his third book which investigates the paranormal and the reality of life after death.

For more information please visit www.jp-robinson.com

If you enjoyed this book, why not support the author and share your views by leaving a short review on Amazon.

Also available from J.P. Robinson

The Alien Enigma
Extraterrestrials: Science Fiction or Science Fact?

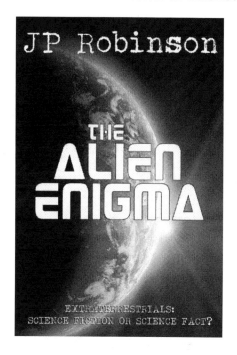

The Alien Enigma is a non-fiction book which closely examines evidence of the existence of extraterrestrial life on this planet. J.P. Robinson weaves together a wealth of astounding and suppressed material in this comprehensive work covering the many complex subjects associated with alien activity. In this intricate and expansive overview of the ET scenario here on Earth, Robinson exposes the government conspiracy to conceal essential information from the public regarding the alien presence and the already well established diplomatic relationship between them and us. Each chapter of *The Alien Enigma* offers a great insight into separate topics connected with the alien hypothesis, such as UFOs, abductions, crop circles, contactees, cattle mutilations, the NASA conspiracy and more.

'This book is destined to be a classic of its kind.'
Phenomena Magazine

BIBLIOGRAPHY

Berlitz, Charles. *Atlantis: The Lost Continent Revealed*

Butler, Alan and Knight, Christopher. *Before the Pyramids: Cracking Archaeology's Greatest Mystery*

Brennan, Herbie. *The Atlantis Enigma*

Brophy, Thomas. *The Origin Map: Discovery of a Prehistoric, Megalithic, Astrophysical Map and Sculpture of the Universe*

Carlson, A.E. *The Younger Dryas Climate Event. In: Elias S.A. (ed.) The Encyclopedia of Quaternary Science, vol. 3, pp. 126-134., 2013*

Cremo, Michael A. *Human Devolution*

Cremo, Michael A. and Thompson, Richard L. *The Hidden History of the Human Race*

Charles, R.H. (Translated by). *The Book of Enoch*

Chouinard, Patrick. *Lost Race of Giants*

Coppens, Philip. *The Ancient Alien Question*

Dewhurst, Richard J. *The Ancient Giants Who Ruled America: The Missing Skeletons and the Great Smithsonian Cover-Up*

De Santillana, Giorgio and Von Dechen, Hertha. *Hamlet's Mill: An Essay Investigating the origins of Human Knowledge and its Transmission through Myth*

Donnelly, Ignatius. *Atlantis: The Antediluvian World*

Dunn, Christopher. *The Giza Power Plant: Technologies of Ancient Egypt*

Firestone, Richard B. *The Case for the Younger Dryas Extraterrestrial Impact Event: Mammoth, Megafauna, and Clovis Extinction, 12,900 Years Ago.* Journal of Cosmology, 2009, Vol 2, pages 256-285. Cosmology, October 27, 2009

Flem-Ath, Rand and Wilson, Colin. *The Atlantis Blueprint*

Flem-Ath, Rand and Rose. *When the Sky Fell*

Freke, Timothy and Gandy, Peter. *The Hermetica: The Lost Wisdom of the Pharoahs*

Hall, Stan. *Tayos Gold: The Archives of Atlantis*

Hancock, Graham. *Fingerprints of the Gods*
　　　　　　　　　Heaven's Mirror
　　　　　　　　　Underworld: Flooded Kingdoms of the Ice Age
　　　　　　　　　Magicians of the Gods

Hancock, Graham and Bauval, Robert. *The Message of the Sphinx: A Quest for the Hidden Legacy of Mankind*

Hapgood, Charles H. *Maps of the Ancient Sea Kings*

Huxley, Thomas. *Man's Place in Nature*

Jaye, Michael. *The Worldwide Flood: Uncovering and Correcting the Most Profound Error in the History of Science*

Jones, Marie D. and Flaxman, Larry. *Viral Mythology*

Joseph, Frank. *Before Atlantis*

Kenyon, Douglas. *Forbidden History*

Kolosimo, Peter. *Timeless Earth*, 1968.

Marin, Diego, Minella, Ivan and Schievenin, Erik. *The Three Ages of Atlantis: The Great Floods that Destroyed Civilization*

Meyer, Stephen C. *Darwin's Doubt*

Milton, Richard. *Shattering the Myths of Darwinism*

Norvill, Roy. *Giants: The Vanished Race of Mighty Men*

Plochmann, George Kimball. *Plato*

Pye, Lloyd. *Everything You Know Is Wrong*

Rawicz, Slavomir. *The Long Walk*

Schwaller De Lubiscz, R.A. *The Temple Of Man*

Shackley, Myra. *Still Living? – Yeti, Sasquatch and the Neanderthal Enigma*

St. Rain, Tédd. *Mystery of America: Book 1 Enigmatic Mysteries and Anomalous Artifacts of North America: A Connection to the Ancient Past*, Lost Arts Media, 1997

Sykes, Bryan. *The Nature of the Beast – The First Scientific Evidence on the Survival of Apemen into Modern Times*

Velikovsky, Immanuel. *Mankind in Amnesia*

Weidenreich, Franz. *Apes, Giants and Man*, University of Chicago Press

West, John Anthony. *Serpent in the Sky: High Wisdom of Ancient Egypt*

Wilson, Colin. *From Atlantis to the Sphinx*

Wingate, Richard. *Atlantis in the Amazon*
           Lost Outpost of Atlantis

REFERENCES

PREFACE: MYTH MATTERS

[1] Hancock, Graham - *Fingerprints of the Gods,* 1995.
[2] E.O. James - *Creation and Cosmology: A Historical and Comparative Inquiry*
[3] Flaxman, Larry and Jones, Marie D. – *Viral Mythology: How the Truth of the Ancients Was Passed Down Through Legend, Art and Architecture*, New Page Books, 2014.
[4] De Santillana, Giorgio and Von Dechend, Hertha - *Hamlet's Mill: An Essay Investigating the Origins of Human Knowledge and its Transmission through Myth,* 1969.
[5] Magical Egypt DVD series.
[6] Flaxman, Larry and Jones, Marie D. – *Viral Mythology: How the Truth of the Ancients Was Passed Down Through Legend, Art and Architecture*, New Page Books, 2014.
[7] Schwaller De Lubiscz, R.A. – *The Temple Of Man*, Inner Traditions, 1998.
[8] Flaxman, Larry and Jones, Marie D. – Viral Mythology: *How the Truth of the Ancients Was Passed Down Through Legend, Art and Architecture*, New Page Books, 2014.

INTRODUCTION

[9] Flem-Ath, Rand and Wilson, Colin – *The Atlantis Blueprint,* 2000.
[10] Steiger, Brad – *Worlds Before Our Own,* 1978.
[11] Huxley, Aldous – *Proper Studies,* 1927.
[12] Hapgood, Charles H. – *Maps of the Ancient Sea Kings*, Adventures Unlimited Press, Illinois, 1996.

1 THE DEATH OF DARWINISM

[13] Lewin, Roger – *Human Evolution,* 1984.
[14] Cremo, Michael A. and Thompson, Richard L. – *The Hidden History of The Human Race*, Bhaktivedanta Book Publishing, 1996
[15] Barringer, David – *"Raining on Evolution's Parade"*, I.D. Magazine. March/April 2006.
[16] Gould, Stephen Jay – *Wonderful Life:'The Iconography of an Expectation'*
[17] Darwin, Charles – *On the Origin of Species*

[18] Pye, Lloyd – *Everything You Know Is Wrong: Book One: Human Origins*, 1997

[19] Ibid

[20] Ibid

[21] Ibid

[22] "Generalisation", from *Harijan* (6 July 1940). Quoted in *Teachings of Mahatma Gandhi* (1945), edited by Jag Parvesh Chander, Indian Printing Works, pages 243-244.

[23] Levinton, Jeffrey S. - "The Big Bang of Animal Evolution," Scientific American 267 (November, 1992): 84-91.

[24] Darwin, Charles – *On the Origin of Species*, 1859.

[25] Ibid

[26] Wallace, Alfred Russel – *Contributions to the Theory of Natural Selection, A Series of Essays*, Macmillan, 1870

[27] Barrow, John D. and Tipler, Frank J. – *The Cosmological Anthropic Principle*, Oxford University Press, 1996.

[28] Ibid

[29] http://www.intelligentdesign.org/whatisid.php

[30] *Darwin's Dilemma: The Mystery of the Cambrian Fossil Record*, Illustra Media, 2010

[31] Behe, Michael – Experimental support foe regarding functional classes of proteins to be highly isolated from each other. In Buell, J. and Hearn, G., eds. *Darwinism: Science or Philosophy*. 1994

[32] Polanyi, Michael – 'Life's Irreducible Structure', Science Magazine, 1967

[33] Meyer, Stephen C. - The Origin of Life: DNA by Design, Lecture presented by Koinonia House, 2014

[34] Cremo, Michael A. – *Human Devolution: A Vedic Alternative to Darwin's Theory*, Torchlight Publishing, 2013

[35] Behe, Michael – *Darwin's Black Box: The Biochemical Challenge to Evolution*, New York, Free Press, 1996.

2   BONES AND STONES

[36] Cremo, Michael A. and Thompson, Richard L. – *The Hidden History of The Human Race*, Bhaktivedanta Book Publishing, 1996

[37] Milton, Richard – *Shattering the Myths of Evolution*, Fourth Estate, 1992.

[38] Video Presentation- *The Hidden Truth About Human Origins & History* - Michael Cremo, Forbidden Archaeology, 1994

[39] Video Documentary - *Mysterious Origins of Man*, History Channel.

[40] Hancock, Graham – *Magicians of the Gods*, Coronet, 2015

[41] Prestwich, John – On the primitive character of the flint implements of the Chalk Plateau of Kent, with reference to the question of their glacial or pre-glacial age. Journal of the Royal Anthropological Institute of Great Britain and Ireland, 1892

[42] *Natural History*, 1921, v.21, p.56

[43] Rutot, A – Eolithes et pseudoeolithes. *Societe d'Anthroplogie de Bruxelles, Bulletin et Memoires,* 1906

[44] Cremo, Michael A. and Thompson, Richard L. – *The Hidden History of The Human Race,* Bhaktivedanta Book Publishing, 1996

[45] Ibid

[46] Weidenrich, Franz – *Apes, Giants and Man,* The University of Chicago Press, 1946.

[47] Cremo, Michael A. and Thompson, Richard L. – *The Hidden History of The Human Race,* Bhaktivedanta Book Publishing, 1996.

[48] Wyatt, Newsletter Five

[49] Cremo, Michael A. and Thompson, Richard L. – *The Hidden History of The Human Race,* Bhaktivedanta Book Publishing, 1996

[50] Keith, Arthur – The Antiquity of Man, Vol. 1, 1928

[51] Ragazzoni, Giuseppe – La collina di Castenedolo, solto il rapporto antropologico, geologico ed agronomico, 1880.

[52] Sergi, Giuseppe – L'uomo terziario in Lombardia *Archivio per L'Antropologia e la Etnologia,* 1884.

[53] Cremo, Michael A. and Thompson, Richard L. – *The Hidden History of The Human Race,* Bhaktivedanta Book Publishing, 1996.

3   LIVING HOMINIDS

[54] Shackley, Myra – Still Living? - *Yeti, Sasquatch and the Neanderthal Enigma,* Thames & Hudson, 1983.

[55] Originally printed in the Western Bigfoot Society Newsletter, "The Track Record". Excerpted from "Legends Beyond Psychology" by Henry James Franzoni III.

[56] Sanderson, Ivan T. – True Magazine, December 1959.

[57] Napier, Dr. John - *Bigfoot, the Yeti and Sasquatch in Myth & Reality,* 1972.

[58] Quoted in Hunter and Dahinden, 1973.

[59] Bigfoot Investigation: Documentary on Sasquatch Video Evidence and Footprints.

[60] Napier, Dr. John - *Bigfoot, the Yeti and Sasquatch in Myth & Reality,* 1972.

[61] Pye, Lloyd – *Everything You Know Is Wrong- Book One: Human Origins,* Authors Choice Press, 1997.

[62] *The Columbian,* Friday March 3, 1989.

[63] Bigfoot Investigation: Documentary on Sasquatch Video Evidence and Footprints.

[64] Pye, Lloyd – *Everything You Know Is Wrong - Book One: Human Origins,* Authors Choice Press, 1997.

[65] https://www.youtube.com/watch?v=7VLWnt5UTGc.

[66] Sanderson, Ivan T. – *Abominable Snowman – Legend Come To Life,* 1961.

[67] Shackley, Myra – Still Living? - *Yeti, Sasquatch and the Neanderthal Enigma,* Thames & Hudson, 1983.

[68] http://cryptomundo.com/cryptozoo-news/shipton-cast/

69 Shackley, Myra – *Still Living? - Yeti, Sasquatch and the Neanderthal Enigma*, Thames & Hudson, 1983.

70 Sykes, Bryan - The Nature of the Beast – *the first scientific evidence on the survival of apemen into modern times*, Coronet, 2015.

71 Cremo, Michael A. and Thompson, Richard L. – *The Hidden History of The Human Race*, Bhaktivedanta Book Publishing, 1996.

72 Pye, Lloyd – *Everything You Know Is Wrong - Book One: Human Origins*, Authors Choice Press, 1997.

73 Shackley, Myra – Still Living? - *Yeti, Sasquatch and the Neanderthal Enigma*, Thames & Hudson, 1983.

74 'Again the Snowman', article on Almas sightings from the early 1970s printed in bi-monthly magazine *Mongolie*, 1980.

75 Pye, Lloyd – *Everything You Know Is Wrong - Book One: Human Origins*, Authors Choice Press, 1997.

76 Napier, Dr. John - Bigfoot, *the Yeti and Sasquatch in Myth & Reality*, 1972.

4   THE FORGOTTEN RACE

77 http://www.ocregister.com/articles/kosen-263666-johnson-dentist.html

78 Chris L. Lesley, *Historical, Topographical, and Descriptive View of the County of Northumberland*, 1825.

79 The Megalithic Giants: The Lost History of a Forgotten Race, lecture by Hugh Newman.

80 Chris L. Lesley, *Historical, Topographical, and Descriptive View of the County of Northumberland*, 1825.

81 Wilkins, *Fate Magazine*, January, 1952.

82 https://www.si.edu/about/history

83 *The Worthington Advance*, November 18, 1897.

84 https://grahamhancock.com/vieiranewman1/

85 *Mystery of America: Book 1 - Enigmatic Mysteries and Anomalous Artefacts of American History: A Connection to the Ancient Past*. Presented by Tédd St. Rain.

86 Dr. Greg Little, *The truth about giant skeletons in American Indian mounds, and the Smithsonian cover-up*, AP Magazine, Sat, 28 Jun 2014.

87 Richard J. Dewhurst, *The Ancient Giants Who Ruled America*, 2013.

88 Ibid

84 https://grahamhancock.com/vieiranewman1/

85 Dr. Greg Little, *The truth about giant skeletons in American Indian mounds, and the Smithsonian cover-up*, AP Magazine, Sat, 28 Jun 2014.

91 Stone, Elizabeth (1939) "Archaeologists Revisit Iraq", *Science Friday*, (Interview with Ira Flatow), March 2012

88 Chouinard, Patrick – *The Lost Race Of Giants*, 2013.

5   OUT OF TIME AND PLACE

[92] Ley, Willy – article in *Astounding Magazine.*

[93]Blavatsky, H.P. (1877) Isis Unveiled: A Master Key to the Mysteries of Ancient and Modern Science and Theology, New York.

Messiha, Khalil – *Aeronautics: African Experimental Aeronautics – A 2000 Year Old Model Glider,* taken from Ivan van Sertima – *Blacks in Science: Ancient and Modern,* Journal of African Civilizations, vol. 5, no. 1-2, New Brunswick, Transaction Books.

[94] Messiha, Khalil – *Aeronautics: African Experimental Aeronautics – A 2000 Year Old Model Glider,* taken from Ivan van Sertima – *Blacks in Science: Ancient and Modern,* Journal of African Civilizations, vol. 5, no. 1-2, New Brunswick, Transaction Books

[95]Hancock, Graham, *Fingerprints of the Gods,* 1995.

[96] Cremo, Michael A. – *Human Devolution*, Torchlight Publishing, 2003.

[97] Rusch, W.H., Sr. - Footprints in Rocks. *Creation Research Society Quaterly,* 1971.

[98] Steiger, Brad - *World's Before Our Own*, New York, Berkley, 1979.

[99] Jessup, M.K. - The Case for the UFO. Garland, Texas, Uaro Manufacturing Company, 1973.

[100] Charles Berlitz - *Atlantis: The Lost Continent Revealed,* 1984.

[101] Documentary (2012) The 2000 Year-Old Computer - Decoding the Antikythera Mechanism.

[102] De Solla Price, Derek (1974) Gears from the Greeks: The Antikythera Mechanism - A Calendar Computer from CA. 80 B.C. (Transactions of the American Philosophical Society)

[103] Documentary (2012) The 2000 Year-Old Computer - Decoding the Antikythera Mechanism .

[104] http://ancients-bg.com/the-mysterious-sabu-disc/

[105]http://www.earthbeforeflood.com/imprint_of_wheel_in_carboniferous_sandstone_in_coalmine_rostov_region.html

[106]http://www.earthbeforeflood.com/auto_roads_or_cart_ruts_of_neogene_times_in_central_turkey.html

[107] Jochmans, J.R. – *Strange Relics from the Depths of the* Earth, 1979.

[108] Cremo, Michael A. and Thompson, Richard L. - *The Hidden History of The Human Race,* Bhaktivedanta Book Publishing, 1996

6   ADVANCED ANCIENTS

[109] https://sacredsites.com/africa/egypt/luxor_temple.html

[110] Magical Egypt DVD series.

[111] West, John Anthony – *Serpent in the Sky: The High Wisdom of Ancient Egypt,* Quest Books, 1993.

[112] Magical Egypt DVD series.

[113] Graham Hancock, *Magicians of the Gods,* 2015.

[114] https://grahamhancock.com/burleyp1/

[115] Graham Hancock, *Magicians of the Gods*, 2015.

[116] https://grahamhancock.com/burleyp1/

[117] West, John Anthony – *Serpent in the Sky: The High Wisdom of Ancient Egypt*, Quest Books, 1993.

[118] American Association for the Advancement of Science, Chicago, 7 February 1992, debate: 'How Old is the Sphinx?'

[119] Budge, E. A. Wallis – 'Stela of the Sphinx' in *A History of Egypt*, Vol. IV, London, 1902.

[120] Breasted, James Henry – *Ancient Records of Egypt*, Histories and Mysteries of Man Ltd., Vol. II, London, 1988.

[121] Ibid

[122] Maspero, Gaston – *The Passing of Empires*, New York, 1900.

[123] Schwaller de Lubicz, R.A. – *Sacred Science*, 1961.

[124] West, John Anthony – *Serpent in the Sky: The High Wisdom of Ancient Egypt*, Quest Books, 1993.

[125] Interviewed in NBC television documentary *Mystery of the Sphinx*, 1993

[126] Hancock, Graham and Bauval, Robert – *The Message of the Sphinx*, Crown Publishers, 1996.

[127] Quoted in *An Akhbar El Yom*, 8 January 1994.

[128] *Los Angeles Times*, 23 October 1991.

[129] West, John Anthony – *Serpent in the Sky: The High Wisdom of Ancient Egypt*, Quest Books, 1993.

[130] Flem-Ath, Rand and Wilson, Colin – The Atlantis Blueprint, 2000.

[131] John Greaves, Pyramidographia

[132] 'The Emerald Tablet', cited in K.E. Maltwood, *A guide to Glastonbury, Temple of the Stars*, James Clarke and Co., London, 1964.

[133] Graham Hancock, Robert Bauval & John Grigsby, *The Mars Mystery: A Warning from History that Could Save Life on Earth*, 1997.

[134] Graham Hancock and Robert Bauval, *Keepers of Genesis: A Quest for the Hidden Legacy of Mankind*, William Heinemann, 1996.

[135] Hancock, Graham and Bauval, Robert – *The Message of the Sphinx*, Crown Publishers, 1996.

[136] Ibid

[137] Cited in Peter Tompkins, *Mysteries of the Mexican Pyramids*.

[138] Ibid

[139] Flem-Ath, Rand and Wilson, Colin – *The Atlantis Blueprint*, 2000.

[140] Sherry Towers, *Advanced geometrical constructs in a Pueblo ceremonial site, c 1200 CE, Journal of Archaeological Science: Reports* (2016)

[141] Branagan, Mark – *Yorkshire Post*, Friday 22 October 2004.

[142] Brophy, Thomas – *The Origin Map*, 2002.

[143] Ibid

[144] Ibid

[145] Ibid

[146] Magical Egypt DVD series.

[147] Thomas Brophy, The Origin Map

[148] Peter Tompkins, Secrets of the Great Pyramid, 1973

[149] Flinders Petrie - The Pyramids And Temples Of Gizeh, 1883.

[150] Hancock, Graham – *Fingerprints of the Gods*, 1995.

[151] Hancock, Graham and Bauval, Robert – *The Message of the Sphinx*, Crown Publishers, 1996.

[152] *Mystery of the Sphinx*, NBC television documentary, 1993.

[153] www.grahamhancock.com

[154] Ibid

[155] Ibid

[156] Wilson, Colin – *From Atlantis to the Sphinx*, 1996.

[157] Worth Smith, *Miracles of the Ages: The Great Pyramid of Gizeh*, 1934.

[158] Ibid

[159] The Mysterious Origins of Civilization: John Anthony West in conversation with Graham Hancock, Youtube, New York, December 2016.

[160] Brien Foerster, *Were Egypt's Obelisks Ancient Resonance Structures?* Youtube, 2015.

[161] *Mystery of the Sphinx*, NBC television documentary, 1993.

[162] Ibid

[163] Pedro Cieza de Leon – Chronicle of Peru, Hakluyt Society, London, 1864 and 1883

[164] Indians of the Andes: Aymaras and Quechuas

[165] *The Ancient Egyptian Pyramid Texts*, (translated by R.O. Faulkner), Oxford University Press, 1969.

[166] http://www.bibliotecapleyades.net/ciencia/antigravityworldgrid/ciencia_antigravity worldgrid08.htm

[167] http://www.southfloridaonline.com/article_coral_castle.htm

[168] Ibid

[169] Dunn, Christopher – The Giza Power Plant, Bear & Company, 1998.

[170] Chapter 31, *Forbidden History: Prehistoric Technologies, Extraterrestrial Intervention, and the Suppressed Origins of Civilization*, edited by J. Douglas Kenyon, Bear & Company, 2005.

[171] Ibid

[172] Dunn, Christopher – The Giza Power Plant, Bear & Company, 1998.

[173] Chapter 31, *Forbidden History, Prehistoric Technologies, Extraterrestrial Intervention, and the Suppressed Origins of Civilization*, Edited by J. Douglas Kenyon, Bear & Company, 2005.

[174] Ibid

[175] Martin Gray, www.sacredsites.com

[176] Magical Egypt DVD series.

[177] Ibid.

[178] Schwaller R.A. – *The Temple of Man*, 2000.

[179] West, John Anthony – *Serpent in the Sky: The High Wisdom of Ancient Egypt*, Quest Books, 1993.

[180] The Hermetica

[181] John L. Sorenson and Carl L. Johannessen, "Scientific Evidence for Pre-Columbian Transoceanic Voyages" Sino-Platonic Papers, 133 (April 2004)

[182] Ibid

[183] http://www.shee-eire.com/Misc/Articles/EygyptianHemp/hemp1.htm

[184] Hapgood, Charles H. – *Maps of the Ancient Sea Kings*, 1966

[185] Ibid

[186] Ibid

[187] Hancock, Graham – *Fingerprints of the Gods*, 1995.

[188] Ibid

[189] Ibid

[190] Hapgood, Charles H. – *Maps of the Ancient Sea Kings*, 1966

[191] Ibid

[192] Berlitz, Charles – *Atlantis*, MacMillan, 1984

[193] Wingate, Richard – *The Lost Outpost of Atlantis*, Everest House, 1980

[194] Ibid

7 THE LOST CONTINENT

[195] Danny Hilman Natawidjaja, PhD., Senior geologist with the Research Centre for Geotechnology at the Indonesian Institute of Sciences.

[196] Donnelly, Ignatius – *The Antediluvian World*, 1882.

[197] https://www.youtube.com/watch?v=cHSumNdWACc

[198] *Timaeus*, Plato.

[199] Ibid

[200] Marin, Diego, Minella, Ivan and Schievenin, Erik – *The Three Ages of Atlantis*, Bear & Company, 2013.

[201] *Critias*, Plato, translated by George Kimball Plochmann

[202] https://www.thoughtco.com/platos-atlantis-from-the-timaeus-119667

[203] Flem-Ath, Rand and Rose – *When the Sky Fell: In Search of Atlantis*, BCA, 1995.

[204] The Secret Origin of Humanity with Graham Hancock https://www.youtube.com/watch?v=3p9oeTgkW1o

[205] *Timaeus*, Plato.

[206] Richard Wingate, *The Lost Outpost of Atlantis*, Everest House, 1980

[207] Donnelly, Ignatius – *The Antediluvian World*, 1882.

[208] Velikovsky, Immauel – *Mankind in Amnesia*, 1950.

[209] *Critias*, Plato, translated by George Kimball Plochmann

[210] Ibid

[211] Joseph, Frank – *Beyond Atlantis*, Bear and Co., 2013

464

[212][212] Wh[212] Whitmore, Frank C. Jr.; Emery, K. O.; Cooke, H. B. S.; and Swift, Donald J. P., "Elephant Teeth from the Atlantic Continental Shelf" (1967). USGS Staff -- Published Research. 236.

[213] *The Commentaries of Proclus on the Timaeus of Plato* in five books, translated from the Greek by Thomas Taylor, 1820.

[214] Berlitz, Charles – *Atlantis*, MacMillan, 1984.

[215] Kirkpatrick, Sidney – *Edgar Cayce: An American Prophet*, 2000.

[216] Cayce, Edgar – *Edgar Cayce on Atlantis*, 1968.

[217] *New York Herald Tribune*, Oct 4, 1959.

[218] Schoch, Dr. Robert M. – *Ancient Wisdom and the Great Sphinx of Egypt*, 2003

[219] http://robertbauval.co.uk/articles/articles_pe2k/schor.html

[220] http://philipcoppens.com/hawass.html

[221] Zahi Hawass – 'Sandpit of Royalty' by Dorte Quist, *Extra Bladet* (Danish newspaper), January 31, 1999

[222] http://wolf.mind.net/osiris/index.html

[223] Ibid

[224] https://www.youtube.com/watch?v=1Hg-mLcA-GE&feature=youtu.be

[225] http://wolf.mind.net/osiris/index.html

[226] Herodotus ('Histories', Book, II, 148),

[227] Wilson, Colin – *From Atlantis to the Sphinx*, Virgin Books, 1997

[228] https://atlantisrisingmagazine.com/article/exposing-a-skeptical-hoax/

[229] Ibid

[230] Wingate, Richard – *The Lost Outpost of Atlantis*, Everest House, 1980.

[231] https://atlantisrisingmagazine.com/article/lost-civilization-the-bermuda-triangle/

[232] Wingate, Richard – *The Lost Outpost of Atlantis*, Everest House, 1980.

[233] Ibid

[234] https://atlantisrisingmagazine.com/tag/joulters-wall/

[235] Documentary - The Yucatan Hall of Records: The Atlantis Connection

[236] https://news.nationalgeographic.com/news/2008/09/080903-oldest-skeletons.html

[237] Wingate, Richard – *The Lost Outpost of Atlantis*, Everest House, 1980.

[238] Hall, Stan – *Tayos Gold : The Archives of Atlantis*, 2006.

[239] Joseph, Frank – *Archaeological Discoveries of Ancient America*, 2014.

[240] Ibid

[241] Ibid

[242] Beasant and Leadbeater, *Man: Whence, How and Whither*, 1910

[243] Joseph, Frank – *Archaeological Discoveries of Ancient America*, 2014.

[244] Reymond, E. A. E. – *The Mythical Origin of the Egyptian Temple*, Manchester University Press, 1969.

[245] Hancock, Graham – *Heaven's Mirror*, 1998.

[246] Donnelly, Ignatius – *The Antediluvian World*, 1882.

[247] Ibid

[248] Berlitz, Charles – *Atlantis*, MacMillan, 1984.

[249] Ibid

[250] Donnelly, Ignatius – *The Antediluvian World*, 1882.

[251] Berlitz, Charles – *Atlantis*, MacMillan, 1984.

[252] *SANTI PARVA*, SECTION CCCXXXVII

[253] David Hatcher Childress, Atlantis Rising, Issue 9.

[254] Article by Major Kurt Bilau, 1923, cited in *Atlantis* by Charles Berlitz, p.73.

[255] Joseph, Frank – *Atlantis: And Other Worlds*, 1994.

[256] http://www.greekisland.co.uk/santorini/sights/santorini-volcano.html

[257] http://www.in-santorini.com/atlantis_santorini.html

[258] Atlantis Rising, documentary, 2017.

[259] Ibid

[260] Mejías Moreno, M., Benítez de Lugo Enrich, L., Pozo Tejado, J. del y Moraleda Sierra, J. 2014.

[261] http://news.bbc.co.uk/1/hi/sci/tech/3766863.stm

[262] Atlantis Rising Documentary, 2017.

[263] Flem-Ath, Rand and Rose – *When the Sky Fell: In Search of Atlantis*, BCA, 1995.

[264] Flem-Ath, Rand and Rose – '*The Earth Science Revolution and Pre-History*'.

[265] *Critias*, Plato, translated by George Kimball Plochmann.

[266] Whitaker, Joseph – *Almanack of the Year of our Lord*, 1992.

[267] Flem-Ath, Rand and Rose – *When the Sky Fell: In Search of Atlantis*, BCA, 1995.

[268] Ibid

8   THE WORLDWIDE FLOOD

[269] Hooke, S. H. – *Middle Eastern Mythology*, 1963.

[270] Jaye, Michael – *The Worldwide Flood*, 2017.

[271] Ibid

[272] Ibid

[273] Henns, Pete – *Gilgamesh, Atrahasis, and the Flood*, https://biologos.org/blogs/archive/gilgamesh-atrahasis-and-the-flood/, 2010.

[274] http://www.aina.org/books/eog/eog.pdf

[275] Crawford, Harriet – *Sumer and the Sumerians*, Cambridge Univ. Press, 1991), p. 19.

[276] Burstein, Stanley Mayer – *The Babyloniaca of Berossus*, 1978.

[277] https://www.ancient.eu/article/227/the-atrahasis-epic-the-great-flood--the-meaning-of/

[278] Ibid

[279] J. Darmetester and H.L. Mills, Trans, F. Maz Muller, Ed, The Zend Avesta

[280] http://www.collective-evolution.com/2016/10/18/the-zoroastrian-texts-of-ancient-persia-underground-cities-what-they-reveal-about-advanced-ancient-civilizations/#_ednref23

[281] *New Larousse Encyclopaedia of Mythology*

[282] http://www.bigorrin.org/archive33.htm

[283] *Kolig, Erich – Noah's Ark Revisited: On the Myth-Land Connection in Traditional Australian Aboriginal Thought*, 1980.

[284] Hancock, Graham – *Fingerprints of the Gods*, 1995.

[285] Redmond, Eve Anne Elizabeth – *The Island of the Ka*

[286] Hancock, Graham – *Underworld*, 2002.

[287] Jaye, Michael – *The Worldwide Flood*, 2017.

[288] Metivier et al. Journal of Sedimentary Research, 2005.

[289] Jaye, Michael – *The Worldwide Flood*, 2017.

[290] Ibid

[291] Graham Hancock, *Magicians of the Gods*, Coronet, 2015

[292] https://www.youtube.com/watch?v=Vka2ZgzZTvo - Joe Rogan Experience #1124 - Robert Schoch

[293] Charles R. Kinzie et al, 'Nanodiamond-Rich Layer across Three Continents'

[294] https://space-facts.com/oort-cloud/

[295] The Case for the Younger Dryas Extraterrestrial Impact Event: Mammoth, Megafauna, and Clovis Extinction, 12,900 Years Ago. Richard B. Firestone, Ph.D.

[296] Ibid

[297] Joe Rogan Experience #725 - Graham Hancock & Randall Carlson - https://www.youtube.com/watch?v=aDejwCGdUV8

[298] http://www.authortalk.audio/2-hancock-transcript-part-two.html

[299] https://www.youtube.com/watch?v=Vka2ZgzZTvo - Joe Rogan Experience #1124 - Robert Schoch

[300] LaViolette, Paul – *Earth Under Fire*, 183, Starburst Publications, New York, 1997

[301] Hancock, Graham – *Underworld: Flooded Kingdoms of the Ice Age*, 2002.

[302] Hancock, Graham – *Magicians of the Gods*, Coronet, 2015

[303] http://www.telegraph.co.uk/science/2017/04/21/ancient-stone-carvings-confirm-comet-struck-earth-10950bc-wiping/

[304] *Quaternary Extinctions*

[305] J. Tyler Faith and Todd A. Surovell, *'Synchronous extinction of North America's Pleistocene mammals'*, PNAS, vol. 106, no. 49, 8 Dec 2009

[306] http://www.sciencemag.org/news/2014/01/what-killed-great-beasts-north-america What Killed the Great Beasts of North America? By Michael Balter

[307] Ivan T. Sanderson, *Riddle of the Quick-Frozen Giants*, Saturday Evening Post, 16 Jan 1960

[308] Evidence for an extraterrestrial impact 12,900 years ago that contributed to the megafaunal extinctions and the Younger Dryas cooling

[309] Georges Cuvier, *Revolutions and Catastrophes in the History of the Earth*, 1829

[310] Professor Frank C. Hibben, *The Lost Americans*, cited in *The Path of the Pole*

[311] Georges Cuvier, *Revolutions and Catastrophes in the History of the Earth*, in *A Source Book in Geology*, ed. K. Mather, 1939

[312] Flem-Ath, Rand and Rose – *When the Sky Fell*, 1995.

[313] Ibid

[314] Ibid

[315] Brennan, Herbie – *The Atlantis Enigma*, 1999.

[316] Pye, Lloyd – *Everything You Know Is Wrong*, 1997.

[317] Sitchin, Zecharia – *The Wars of Gods and Men*, 1985.

[318] Shepard, Wade – *Göbekli Tepe: the Rise of Agriculture, the Fall of the Nomad*, Published on November 21, 2011.

[319] Ibid

[320] https://www.nationalgeographic.org/maps/doggerland/

[321] Frank C. Whitmore Jr., *Elephant Teeth from the Atlantic Continental Shelf*, 1967

[322] Hancock, Graham – *Underworld: Flooded Kingdoms of the Ice Age*, 2002.

[323] http://www.archaeologyonline.net/artifacts/cambay

[324] *The Study of Submerged Structures Off Yonaguni Island of Japan: The Preliminary Results from Recent Expedition*, 1-12 September 2000, Sundaresh, National Institute of Oceanography

[325] *Underworld – Flooded Kingdoms of the Ice Age*, Channel 4 documentary

[326] http://www.yonaguni.ws/

[327] *Underworld – Flooded Kingdoms of the Ice Age*, Channel 4 documentary

[328] *The Study of Submerged Structures Off Yonaguni Island of Japan: The Preliminary Results from Recent Expedition*, 1-12 September 2000, Sundaresh, National Institute of Oceanography

[329] Ibid

[330] Hancock, Graham – *Underworld: Flooded Kingdoms of the Ice Age*, 2002.

[331] Ibid

[332] *Underworld – Flooded Kingdoms of the Ice Age*, Channel 4 documentary

[333] https://www.elitedaily.com/news/world/has-atlantis-been-discovered-tombs-and-pyramids-allegedly-found-in-bermuda-triangle